Bitter EJB

D0762730

Bitter EJB

BRUCE TATE
MIKE CLARK
BOB LEE
PATRICK LINSKEY

MANNING

Greenwich
(74° w. long.)

For electronic information and ordering of this and other Manning books,
go to www.manning.com. The publisher offers discounts on this book
when ordered in quantity. For more information, please contact:

    Special Sales Department
    Manning Publications Co.
    209 Bruce Park Avenue   Fax: (203) 661-9018
    Greenwich, CT 06830   email: manning@manning.com

©2003 by Manning Publications Co. All rights reserved.

No part of this publication may be reproduced, stored in a retrieval system, or transmitted,
in any form or by means electronic, mechanical, photocopying, or otherwise, without
prior written permission of the publisher.

Many of the designations used by manufacturers and sellers to distinguish their products
are claimed as trademarks. Where those designations appear in the book, and Manning
Publications was aware of a trademark claim, the designations have been printed in initial
caps or all caps.

 Recognizing the importance of preserving what has been written, it is Manning's policy to
have the books they publish printed on acid-free paper, and we exert our best efforts to that
end.

ISBN 1-930110-95-2

 Manning Publications Co.   Copyeditor: Adrianne Harun
209 Bruce Park Avenue   Typesetter: Tony Roberts
Greenwich, CT 06830   Cover designer: Leslie Haimes

Printed in the United States of America
1 2 3 4 5 6 7 8 9 10 – VHG – 06 05 04 03

contents

preface xv

acknowledgments xviii

about this book xxii

PART 1 THE BASICS 1

1 *Bitter choices* 3

1.1 A storm of controversy 5

1.2 A history of EJB antipatterns 6

March 1998: EJB 1.0 7 ▪ November 1999: EJB 1.1 7
August 2001: EJB 2.0 8

1.3 A case study: Benchmarking PetStore 9

1.4 Antipattern: The Golden Hammer 12

Choosing unwisely 13 ▪ Solution: Evaluate carefully 15

1.5 Summary: Looking ahead 19

1.6 Antipatterns in this chapter 20

2   *The bitter cost   21*

2.1   Sparking controversy   *22*

The value of EJB   23 ▪ EJB-appropriate applications   23
Using a litmus test   25 ▪ Passing the test   26
Weighing complexity   27 ▪ Evaluating your talent   28

2.2   Antipattern: A Sledgehammer for a Fly   *30*

Adding complexity   32 ▪ Solution: Simplify   33
Consider the cost of managing many files   36
Grading the finer points   39

2.3   Entity beans are a horse of a different color   *41*

The black sheep of the bean family   42

2.4   Entity beans: Take two   *43*

Local interfaces   44 ▪ Container-managed relationships   45

2.5   Entity beans—a closer look   *45*

Employee management   45

2.6   Summary   *50*

2.7   Antipatterns in this chapter   *51*

3   *Bitter interfaces   52*

3.1   Building a good interface   *53*

Breaking down remote invocation performance   54
Passing by reference vs. value   55

3.2   Designing the application tier   *57*

Looking back on entity beans   59 ▪
Questioning EJB local interfaces   59

3.3   Antipattern: Local & Remote Interfaces
Simultaneously   *60*

Combined interfaces muddle exception management   61
Combined interfaces hurt performance   62 ▪ Mini-antipattern:
Ubiquitous Distribution   63 ▪ Mini-antipattern: Transparent
Distribution   63 ▪ Solution: Achieving equilibrium   64
Knowing when to distribute   65

3.4   Antipattern: Customers in the Kitchen   *66*

Nudging the diners toward the door   68
Solution: Funnel the customers through a waiter   70
Using Data Transfer Objects   71

3.5   Antipattern: Custom DTOs   73

    Solution: Refactor to preserve flexibility   75

3.6   Summary   77

3.7   Antipatterns in this chapter   78

PART 2   SESSIONS AND MESSAGES 81

4   *Bitter sessions   83*

4.1   Threading and synchronization   85

    Antipattern: Tangled Threads   86 ▪ Solution: Standardization to the rescue   87 ▪ Coping with hung threads   88 Searching for a solution   90

4.2   Handling exceptions   92

    Mini-antipattern: Logic in Exception Implementations   92 Solution: Refactor logic out of exceptions   93 ▪ Antipattern: Swallowing Exceptions   94 ▪ Solution: A simple exception handling strategy   95 ▪ Antipattern: Killer System Exceptions   97 Solution: Throw the correct exception type   98

4.3   Iterating large datasets   99

    Antipattern: Database Connection Hog   101 ▪ Solution: Manage connections with surgical precision   103 ▪ Antipattern: Eager Iterator   103 ▪ Solution: Test, test, test   106 ▪ Caching results   107 ▪ Exporting results   108 ▪ Determining the size of a result set   109 ▪ Iterating shuffled data   110

4.4   Interoperating efficiently   111

    Using IIOP   112 ▪ Antipattern: Narrow Servlet Bridges   113 Solution: A generic servlet bridge   113

4.5   Summary   120

4.6   Antipatterns in this chapter   121

5   *Bitter session states   126*

5.1   Making a case for session state   128

5.2   A pivotal antipattern: Conversational Baggage   129

    The burden of state   130 ▪ Lightening the load   131 Solution 1: Strive for statelessness   132 Solution 2: Leverage session state when beneficial   134

5.3 Managing sessions with stateful session beans   *134*

Shopping using a stateful session bean   135
Looking under the hood   136

5.4 Managing sessions with servlets   *140*

Keeping it simple with HttpSession   140 ▪ *Shopping using a servlet   141* ▪ *Scaling up servlet sessions   142*

5.5 Antipattern: Golden Hammers of Session State   *143*

Storing sessions on the client   144 ▪ *Storing sessions on the server using servlets   145* ▪ *Storing sessions on the server using stateful EJB   147* ▪ *Storing sessions in a database   148* ▪ *Revisiting the shopping cart   149*
Overall solution: Pick the right tool for the job   151

5.6 Mini-antipattern: Stateful Session Beans as Shared Data Caches   *151*

5.7 Antipattern: Session Hodgepodge   *152*

Solution: Be explicit and conservative   154

5.8 Mini-antipattern: Session Thrashing   *155*

5.9 Mini-antipattern: Rotting Session Garbage   *155*

5.10 Summary: Taming the beast   *156*

5.11 Antipatterns in this chapter   *157*

6 **Bitter messages   162**

6.1 A brief overview of JMS   *163*

6.2 An early antipattern: Fat Messages   *165*

One size doesn't fit all   167 ▪ *Solution 1: Put messages on a diet   167* ▪ *Solution 2: Use references   168*

6.3 Mini-antipattern: Skinny Messages   *169*

Solution: Use state to allow lazy loading   170

6.4 Seeds of an order processing system   *171*

Defining the system   171 ▪ *Designing messages   172*
Choosing messaging models   173 ▪ *Responding to change   173*
Building the OrderRequest producer   175

6.5 Antipattern: XML as the Silver Bullet   *177*

Solution: Use XML messages judiciously   177

6.6   Antipattern: Packrat   *179*

    *Putting a price on persistence   179 ▪ Paying for durable
subscriptions   181 ▪ Solution: Save only what's important   181*

6.7   Mini-antipattern: Immediate Reply Requested   *182*

6.8   Using message-driven beans (MDBs)   *184*

    *Pooling with MDBs   184
Building the OrderRequest consumer   185*

6.9   Antipattern: Monolithic Consumer   *188*

    *Listening to the test   188
Solution: Delegate to modular components   189*

6.10   Antipattern: Hot Potato   *191*

    Solution: Acknowledge the message, not its result   193

6.11   Antipattern: Slow Eater   *194*

    Solution: Eat faster, if you can   194

6.12   Antipattern: Eavesdropping   *195*

    *Solution: Use message selectors   196 ▪ Declaring message
selectors   197 ▪ Going beyond message selectors   198*

6.13   Antipattern: Performance Afterthoughts   *199*

    Solution: Measure early and often   199

6.14   Summary: Getting the message   *201*

6.15   Antipatterns in this chapter   *202*

PART 3   EJB PERSISTENCE 211

7   *Bitter entities   213*

7.1   Understanding entity bean antipatterns   *214*

    Understanding the entity bean antipattern landscape   214

7.2   Antipattern: Face Off   *215*

    *Network round-tripping chokes applications   216 ▪ Losing
transactional integrity   217 ▪ Solution: A Session Façade   219
Using a façade for transactional integrity   220
Using local interfaces   220*

7.3   Antipattern: Ham Sandwich; Hold the Ham   *222*

    *The choice between BMP and CMP   223
Solution: Choose CMP when possible   225*

7.4   Antipattern: Application Joins   *228*

Solution: Delegate joins to the database   228
Common examples of application joins   229

7.5   Antipattern: Application Filters   *230*

Understanding the types of application filters   230

7.6   Antipattern: Rusty Keys   *233*

Solution: shorten your primary key   234

7.7   Antipattern: Revolving Doors   *235*

Solution 1: Refactor to avoid re-entrancy   237
Solution 2: Disable the container's re-entrancy checking   238
Solution 3: Lobby the EJB specification team   238

7.8   Summary   *239*

7.9   Antipatterns in this chapter   *240*

8   Bitter alternatives   245

8.1   Understanding entity bean alternatives   *246*

8.2   Using EJB persistence   *249*

Implementing CMP   250 ▪ Adding the DTO and facade   253
Including deployment details   257
Rolling your own with BMP entity beans   259

8.3   Simplify with JDBC   *260*

Implementing a simple JDBC model   261 ▪ Implementing the JDBC
Façade   263 ▪ Deploying a Session Façade for JDBC   265

8.4   Using object persistence frameworks   *267*

Surveying the object persistence landscape   267 ▪ Understanding
JDO   269 ▪ Implementing a simple model with JDO   270
Implementing the JDO model's façade   272 ▪ Deploying the
solution   273 ▪ Comparing the options   274

8.5   Antipattern: Persistent Problems   *275*

Generic entity bean weaknesses   276 ▪ Inheritance and
polymorphism   276 ▪ Query language flexibility is often
critical   279 ▪ DTOs require non-EJB solutions for local
entities   281 ▪ Container-bound persistence   282

8.6 Solution: Do not "inherit" a persistence architecture—
choose it *282*

8.7 Summary *283*

8.8 Antipatterns in this chapter *284*

PART 4 BROADER TOPICS...285

9 Bitter tunes 287

9.1 Measures of success *289*

Response time 289 ▪ Throughput 290

9.2 Antipattern: Premature Optimization *291*

Tuning EJB applications blindfolded 292
Solution 1: Plan, but don't act (yet) 293
Solution 2: Write well-factored, modular code 294

9.3 Antipattern: Performance Afterthoughts *296*

Solution: Plan early and often 296

9.4 Grist for the tuning mill *298*

Putting an EJB to the test 299 ▪ Passing the test 300
Specifying response time as a measure of success 301
Seeing light at the end of the tuning tunnel 302

9.5 Antipattern: Thrash-tuning *303*

Solution: Use a performance testing methodology 304

9.6 Mini-antipattern: Manual Performance Testing *305*

Solution: Automate performance testing 306

9.7 Automated performance testing with JUnitPerf *307*

JUnitPerf overview 307 ▪ Testing response time 308
Tweaking code 309 ▪ Specifying scalability as a measure of
success 310 ▪ Testing response time under load 310
Using a connection pool to increase throughput 312
Testing throughput 314

9.8 Modeling performance *315*

9.9 Mini-antipattern: Stage Fright *317*

Solution: Practice on stage 317

9.10   Summary: Tuning with confidence   *318*

9.11   Antipatterns in this chapter   *319*

10 *Bitter builds*   324

10.1   Wrapping big packages without bows   *326*

Understanding an example EJB   326 ▪ *Organizing your
directory structure   328* ▪ *Filling the EJB JAR   329
Loading classes   330*

10.2   Antipattern: System Loaded Application Classes   *332*

Solution: Follow the J2EE guidelines   332

10.3   Antipattern: EJB Code Duplication   *332*

*Solution: Autogenerate the EJB classes   333
Solution: Autogenerate the manifest   334
Solution: Autogenerate the EAR descriptor   336*

10.4   Antipattern: Build Guru   *337*

Solution: Use Ant for heavy lifting   338

10.5   Antipattern: Running with Scissors   *339*

Solution: Test with impunity   339

10.6   Antipattern: Integration Hell   *341*

Solution: Integrate early, often, and automatically   341

10.7   Summary   *342*

10.8   Antipatterns in this chapter   *343*

11 *A bittersweet future*   348

11.1   Marking our place in history   *349*

Early mistakes   349

11.2   Plotting the next moves   *351*

Into the future   351 ▪ *Fix persistence   353
Fix the deployment strategy   354
Putting the economic house in order   354*

11.3   Antipatterns and next moves   *355*

A Bitter tales 356

A.1 A Java development free fall 357

Antipatterns in life 359

A.2 Using design patterns accentuates the positive 360

Design patterns online 361
UML provides a language for patterns 362

A.3 Antipatterns teach from the negative 362

*Some well-known antipatterns 363 ▪ Antipatterns in
practice 364 ▪ Antipattern resources 365*

A.4 Antipattern ideas are not new 366

Learning from the industry 367 ▪ Detective work 368
Refactoring antipatterns 370

A.5 Why Bitter Java? 370

The Bitter Java approach 371 ▪ Bitter Java tools 371
The Bitter Java organization 372
The Bitter Java audience 373

A.6 Looking ahead 374

B Bitter basics 376

B.1 Developing in the EJB architecture 378

Getting acquainted with the cast, the bean triad 378
Know your host, the EJB container 381

B.2 Crafting enterprise beans 384

*Defining the client interfaces 385 ▪ Implementing the business
logic 390 ▪ Playing it safe with transactions 397*
Configuring the bean 397 ▪ Packaging it 399
Invoking your beans from a client 400

bibliography 401
index 403

I told Mike Oehrtman, my best friend for more than ten years now, about the adventure stories in *Bitter Java*. In fact, he was my partner in crime for more than half of the stories in the book. I asked him if he had any stories of his own to contribute, because we were doing another *Bitter* book. He told me he had a few hiking stories. I laughed and informed him that walking around wasn't exactly my idea of high adventure. Mike said, "Indulge me. You'll like this one."

So we're in Alaska for some backpacking. We talk to a park ranger at Denali National Park, and he tells us that our hike has to be planned down to the day. The park has an elaborate grid system in place, so that even though you won't see any other hikers on your route, the rangers still know where you are, give or take a mile or two. I'm an Eagle Scout, so I've got no problem with mapping. I plan the trip, submit the map, and then we catch a bus. Our hike starts in the middle of nowhere.

The bus is full of locals and a driver who truly belongs in Alaska. His beard is longer than Beth, who sits at my side. As we ride, we see tons of wildlife: elk, moose, and even a few rams. You name it; we see it. We round a bend, and there in front of us is a river and a bear—and not one of those little browns that we saw in the Smoky Mountains last year. It's a grizzly bear, and it's huge. Beth taps me on the shoulder and points. On the other side of the bus, massive bears are everywhere. I've seen a few grizzly bears in my lifetime, but never in these numbers. The bus slows as it drives right through the group of bears. Now, I'm getting nervous. I wonder if the bears might get nasty and charge the bus, because we've got a lot of food on board.

Suddenly, the bus driver stops, and I wonder if he's scared too. He just sits there, and I'm really starting to sweat. Have we got engine trouble?

Finally, the bus driver turns around, looks at Beth and me, and says, "Well?" Then, it dawns on me. This is our bus stop. We have to get out of the bus, right there, in the middle of all those bears. I've never felt so scared—or so alive.

People frequently ask me how I can be so passionate about a job in which I regularly spend twelve hours straight in front of a keyboard. They think of writing and see a stained keyboard, a dusty monitor, and a dreary desk.

I see bears and lots of them. If you depend on Java development for your livelihood, you probably have seen your share of bears, too. The economy is probably the biggest of the bunch. I went down with a startup at the beginning of the massive recession that started in 2000. I wrote *Bitter Java* and started my consulting business in the midst of this chaos. Some of the companies that form the foundation of the Java industry are being shaken. Sun is struggling, and WebGain is gone. Power structures are changing. As we were writing this book, Oracle bought TopLink, shifting the balance of power in the object persistence market. And IBM bought Rational, dramatically changing the dynamics at that company.

I also need to guide my clients, readers, and students past another bear—.NET. I know it's a real bear for the client and in Microsoft shops. I need to understand what .NET may do in the enterprise environment. Will it ever be big enough to eat J2EE? Will it take a bite out of my livelihood? I don't see that happening yet, but that bear is still out there, eating and growing. The PetStore benchmark, which we talk about in chapter 1, brought home to me the magnitude of the threat. Things can turn in a hurry, and all of us need to make sure that we don't turn our backs on a dangerous predator like Microsoft.

Which brings us closer to home and another big, fat bear—EJB. The industry has certainly fed it well. IBM, Sun, Oracle, BEA, and many others have let EJB gorge itself. EJB has teeth: We're finally seeing commercial EJB applications that scale to massive proportions. EJB also has stamina: The application server market is still strong.

I've checked out EJB many times from a safe distance and then wandered away, afraid that the bear would turn on me and wind up picking the last of me out of its teeth. And EJB *can* turn on you. EJB projects fail with frightening regularity. That tendency to fail provides the subject for this book. I think that you can be a good developer by studying successful patterns and best practices, but if you want to become a great developer, you've got to know a technology's limits. Push EJB over the edge, and you will be well on your way to the kind of experience that sharpens your skills and opens your mind—and gets you hurt. Fortunately, a better way to learn exists. *Bitter Java* proved to me that learning from the mistakes of others can be appealing and productive, too.

With *Bitter EJB*, my coauthors and I are finally out of the bus. We are not saying that we'll recommend EJB for every project that we encounter—far from it. We are saying that EJB has a place and, in the right circumstances, can be an awesome beast to behold. So, step out of the bus with us. Explore the darkest caves where the biggest bears are sleeping. And embrace the danger and thrill of EJB.

BRUCE TATE

acknowledgments

Bitter EJB was a demanding and enlightening project for each of us. It would never have come to pass without extraordinary support for these ordinary authors. Our friends, family, coworkers, colleagues, and publisher made this book possible. We even received a stunning amount of feedback from people we've never met, many of whom were promised nothing in return.

Thanking all of you individually would be impossible, but your contributions obligate us to try.

Collectively   First, we thank the wonderful people at Manning Publications. You provided truly world-class editing support when we needed it the most, and space to breathe when we didn't. Thanks first to those who toil behind the scenes, who get things rolling and keep things moving. Thanks to Helen Trimes for tireless and effective promotion. *Bitter Java* gave you a tough Amazon record to beat, but we've got every confidence that you will try. Thanks also to Mary Piergies, who always seemed to know what we needed before we asked. Thanks to Chris Hilman for your work on the book's web page, and all of the little things that you do. Thanks in advance to Lee Fitzpatrick for keeping the checks rolling, and Susan Capparelle for doing whatever needed doing, every time we asked. All of you contributed as much as anyone who edited, typeset, reviewed, or illustrated something in the book. As we learn more about the publishing business, we continually come to appreciate more the things that go beyond the printed page.

Next, we want to thank the production team who helped shape and direct the book. Thanks to Marjan Bace. You have simultaneously been a dear friend, mentor, editor, and visionary. Your hand has helped to maintain the Manning quality that all of us so jealously guard. Thanks to the editors: Lori Piquet and Adrianne Harun for your necessarily brutal edits, applied with kindness and a feather's touch. We're in awe of what you do. Thanks too to Tony Roberts and Leslie Haimes, who know how to build beautiful books. We are all human, so reviews were critical. Thanks to Thomas Walkama for an excellent technical review, and to Elizabeth Martin for the proof review. Thanks to Ted Kennedy for leading Manning's review. Thanks to each of you who devoted countless hours reviewing the book for Manning: John Crabtree, Jack Herrington, Adam Maass, Barry Nowak, Dimitri I. Rakitine, and Jon Skeet.

Thanks too to Ed Roman and Floyd Marinescu of TheServerSide.com, for your generous offer to help us review *Bitter EJB* on your portal. As expected, we got some tremendous feedback, so we'd like to thank everyone who participated. Sincere thanks to Jerome Abela, Charles Bear, Peter Bonney, Neelan Choksi, Joanne Christian, David Copeland, Taylor Cowan, Scott Dodson, Pierre Fauvel, Rob Hafernik, Don Hanson, Mike Hogan, Konstantin Ignatyev, Erik Jensen, Shailendra Kadre, Oliver Kamps, Rajesh Koilpillai (thanks for trying, anyway), Eugen Kuleshov, Darrell W. Rials, Seb Rose, Ravi Shankar, Curt Smith, Scott Stanchfield, James Strachan, Bernard Trigaux, Christopher Webster, Matthias Weidmann, Mike Wertheim, Glen Wilcox, Dave Wiltz, David Ziegler, and Dick Zetterberg. Special thanks go to Matt Gibbs and to BORN for sharing him enough to provide some outstanding feedback.

Mike Clark   At first, I was to write a single chapter of this book. Then just two. By the time I was finished, I'd written three chapters and could only wonder where the winter had gone. Thinking back, I realize I have more to show for the work than just the text you see here. Through the writing process I found new friends and colleagues that I hope to keep even when the book has been long out of print.

My sincerest thanks to: Bruce Tate, the tireless architect of this book, for giving me the opportunity to fulfill a lifelong dream; Thomas Walkama for reviewing everything I wrote and making it immeasurably better, and then accepting the mission to be the tech proofer for the whole book; Jason Hunter for being a trusted friend and mentor, gently putting my misguided thoughts on managing session state back on track, and helping me become a better photographer; James Duncan Davidson for teaching me to blog so I could practice writing and for subtly challenging me to expand my horizons; Tyler Jewell for letting me pick his brain about stateful session beasts and graciously sharing material; James Strachan for his outstanding contributions to the messaging chapter after reviewing every draft while commuting to work; Glen Wilcox for listening to my ramblings over countless lunches; and Steve Walker for his honest insights on thrash tuning while crammed in coach somewhere over Nebraska.

And a very special thanks to Mom and Dad for the warmth of their love and for instilling in me a work ethic that made this accomplishment possible. It didn't seem fair at the time, but indeed it has served me well.

This book is for Nicole, my soul mate, for the invaluable gift of time and for always being in my balcony cheering me on. You encouraged me to keep writing and reminded me when it was time to go snowboarding. Thank you for your unconditional love, around-the-clock support, and generous sacrifices throughout this marathon process. You bring me great joy.

Bob Lee   Thanks, Bruce, for this awesome opportunity and for spotting me on my first writing endeavor; you've done way more than your fair share. Thanks to Mike and Patrick for taking some particularly controversial subjects head on and helping to keep the project rolling. It's been a long, trying road, but I'm confident that we've tread a great deal of previously uncovered territory in an incredibly short time. The collective wisdom in these pages has value to enterprise developers that extends far beyond the confines of EJB.

Throughout this project, I dredged up many of the least desirable moments in my career, an admittedly crude but highly effective foundation for this book. In doing so, I also had the pleasure of recalling some of the best aspects, most notably those who helped me along the way (in alphabetical order): Scott Antle, Rick Bayers, Paul Brown, Tim Burns, Dr. Hilton Chen, Bob Cringely, Dan Gluck, Jay Goff, Lori Harvey, Dr. Jim Hayes, Karthik Krishnamoorthy, Pat Niemeyer, Jim Owens, Ed Rich, Tim Saunders, Ken Shealy, Mark Volkmann, Christina Ware, Debbie Wiler, Tim Williams, and Jim Zhou.

I'd like to give special thanks to my family. My dad Rick tricked me into thinking math was a game at an early age and never really minded when I played with (and even broke) his computer. My mother Nan taught me writing and has been an endless source of self-confidence and inspiration. You're my heart, Mom. I'd like to thank my Sigma Chi fraternity brothers and my paternal brother Tim, all of whom made especially sure that I didn't work too hard; no matter where I find myself, I take comfort in the fact that there are strong arms around me. *In hoc signo vinces.*

Patrick Linskey   I would like to thank Steve Kim, Marc Prud'hommeaux, and Abe White for their help and insights. Without their support, my knowledge and understanding of the EJB specification in particular and enterprise development in general would not be nearly as complete. I am also grateful to Bruce Tate for getting me involved in *Bitter EJB* and for all the support, wisdom, and guidance he's provided me throughout the process of writing this book.

I could not have written this book without the support of all the folks at Solar-Metric, who put up with me even during the periods when writing took me away from my regular work.

Greg Campbell, Eric Lindauer, David Karger, and Pat Thomas have all taught me in their own ways that anything worth doing is worth doing well, correctly, and completely.

Finally, I'd like to thank my parents for teaching me that writing can be fun, and my sister for providing the grist of some of the vignettes in this very book.

Bruce Tate   *Bitter Java* was pure joy. *Bitter EJB* wasn't—at least not at first. Thanks to Bob Lee for helping me to slog through the early stuff, and make life bearable amid the carnage as we tried to build the team. You've got promise. Keep writing. *Bitter EJB* became fun when Patrick Linskey and Mike Clark rounded out the team, and gave me some breathing room. Thanks to Patrick, who bravely took on the task of writing three of the most pivotal chapters in the book, without a whole lot of writing experience. You were patient and kind throughout, and your insight was critical to this project. Thanks especially to Mike, who like Frodo Baggins, never quite grasped the enormity of the road ahead: I hope I didn't lead you wrong. But without you, there would be no *Bitter EJB*. I value your time and talent, your incredible work ethic, your sense of humor, and especially your friendship.

Thanks to Marjan, for taking a chance on something different. You've had a tremendous influence on my second career. Here's to a continued, successful partnership. Thanks to Ed Roman and Floyd Marinescu for your friendship, and for access to TheServerSide.com, which turned out to be an invaluable source of feedback, and an outstanding balancing influence on this book. Thanks to Jay Zimmerman for taking me on the road, and giving me the opportunity to evangelize everything *bitter.*

Thanks to Mike Oehrtman for dragging me along throughout your crazy adventures. I know that your mother is still watching, and probably wincing, with each new hydraulic. Thanks for sharing her with me.

Finally, thanks to Maggie, for your tireless support, love, and friendship. It's not always easy to be married to an author, but you've always carried yourself with grace, dignity, and charm. You've also treated my partners in crime far better than they deserve. I delight in your presence, and my love for you grows always.

about this book

Why EJB?

After taking a ten-year break from writing books, Bruce Tate returned to publishing in 2002 with the bestseller, *Bitter Java*. In *Bitter Java*, he introduced the concept of antipatterns, which he defined simply as common programming problems that trap software developers every day. Bruce's goal was to attack basic Java programming problems and establish the concept of antipatterns as a serious topic for Java developers. Considering antipatterns in *Bitter Java* was certainly fruitful, but the scope of the book was limited to beginning Java, and Bruce soon decided he'd like to move the discussion into more challenging territory. Enterprise JavaBeans (EJB) promised a meatier technological context for looking at antipatterns. Consider the following:

- Though strong, the EJB community is in a near constant state of uproar, over one issue or another. Controversial frameworks usually are fertile ground for antipatterns.

- Microsoft's .NET—the primary competitor to Java and, by extension, EJB—is gaining traction, creating the kind of controversy that makes for interesting reading.

- J2EE is experiencing good success in the marketplace but not without some growing pains.

- In particular, J2EE's persistence frameworks, though improved, are under increasing fire and often can't hold up under the weight of commercial implementation. Poor frameworks are suspect to misuse.

- New J2EE frameworks have been released at a frightening pace, often with mixed success. With so many new tools and techniques, developers are bound to misuse some of them.

In short, EJB is experiencing the mixture of practical success and controversy that promises a good *Bitter* book. In *Bitter EJB*, we discuss the antipatterns, or common traps, that developers fall into when working with EJB. We cover many different aspects of EJB, from transactions to persistence to messaging. We also talk about other important topics such as performance and testing.

Together, this team of authors hopes to offer two novel things:

1 Give you a fresh perspective. Most EJB books talk about how easy using EJB can be, if you only adopt this design pattern or that development method. We'd like to acknowledge that EJB can be hard, and you can make big mistakes if you don't know where the difficulties lie.

2 Give you fresh insights. For example, we have yet to see a book that offers a good discussion on choosing a session state management philosophy. We don't claim that one size fits all, or that one philosophy is sufficient for your needs. Instead, we offer a variety of ways to look at messaging, introducing several new messaging antipatterns. We offer insight on persistence alternatives that have not been presented in this way in a pro-EJB book. We also cover performance tuning, which can be difficult for EJB developers without the right approach.

This book is not about bashing EJB. It is about how to get the most out of the EJB frameworks. That doesn't mean that we support and endorse every part of EJB. Indeed, you'll see that we come down hard on entity beans, because we think that better, more practical ways exist for solving your persistence problems. Supporting EJB also does not mean that we recommend you use it in every circumstance just to boost your skills. (Mike calls this practice "design by resume.") You'll see us put EJB into a fairly restricted, but important, box. Our support for EJB means that within the confines of that box, you can learn to apply EJB effectively to build distributed, transactional, scalable systems that solve real problems.

The style

Today, we find two unsettling trends in computer books. The first is the imposing volume of content in many books. While exploring every avenue of a topic and providing a comprehensive reference is sometimes appropriate, fitting every book into this template can be counterproductive. Many authors feel obligated to stretch content too thinly, across too many pages. The result is that you're probably not reading computer books from cover to cover any more. We promise not to fall into that trap. We'll tell you what you need to know, and then we'll shut up.

Most publishers are also stripping everything to do with an author's personality out of a book. That's a good way to keep a book from being offensive, trite, or criticized unfairly. It's also a good way to keep books from being interesting. We did not fill *Bitter EJB* with useless trivia about the lives of the authors, but we tried to keep it interesting. Each chapter begins with a short adventure story. Not only are tales from adventure sports fun, they typically provide great metaphors for antipattern themes. Our true stories are gleaned from the authors' lives or those of our close companions. Many readers of *Bitter Java* reported that the book was fun to read, and that the stories broke up the monotony that plagues some computer books. We kept our vignettes short and placed them in italics so that you can skip them if you want. Tell us what you think.

Although chapters were individually authored, to avoid confusion, we use a collective first person pronoun throughout the book. Think of the voice of the book as belonging to a team with the combined experience of all the authors. We think that this book is far more unified than some other multiauthor creations as a result. When you do come across an "I" in the book, as in the short stories, its identity is the author who wrote the chapter.

The authors of *Bitter EJB* share a common philosophy: We believe our job is to communicate. We're not trying to impress you with jargon. We use plain language, the familiar second person, and shorter sentences, so that you can focus your attention on the subject rather than the words. We communicate with figures or tables when words aren't enough, and we try to have fun along the way. Because EJB examples are long, when we need code we've snipped out the important parts for the book and made the rest available for download at www.manning.com/tate2. There, you can also find the Manning's Author Online forum, where you can communicate with us directly.

The team

To attack EJB, we needed not just programmers, but experts capable of identifying antipatterns and distilling them down to their essence. We also needed to find gifted writers comfortable with the *Bitter Java* style. The *Bitter EJB* team is:

- **Bruce Tate,** author of the successful *Bitter Java*, Manning's first *Bitter* book. Bruce's consulting experience spans fifteen years. His first job was at IBM, where his ten-year career included database and tools development. At IBM, he wrote his first two books and created eight patented inventions. He was recruited from IBM to lead Client Services at Contextual, an Austin startup. He is now an independent consultant in Austin, Texas, where he works with the Middleware Company and other clients to promote and teach effective Java design to his clients.

- **Mike Clark** is president of Clarkware Consulting, Inc. (www.clarkware.com) in Denver, Colorado. He has been crafting software professionally since 1992 and immersed in Java since 1997. He first started stumbling into EJB pitfalls in 1998 while developing a custom EJB container, prior to the emergence of commercial J2EE servers. He has developed several open source tools including JUnitPerf, a collection of JUnit extensions for continuous performance testing. In addition, Mike regularly speaks and writes about his experiences in the trenches helping teams build better software faster.

- **Bob Lee**, an independent consultant and open source developer working out of St. Louis, Missouri, has more than ten years of software development experience. Bob hosts a Java themed web log at www.crazybob.org; feel free to visit and join Bob in his ongoing bitter journey.

- **Patrick Linskey** is the vice president of engineering for a Java persistence company called SolarMetric in Washington, D.C. He's spent the last two years speaking on the problems of Java persistence and building alternatives. A popular speaker and gifted communicator, he has experience that spans EJB application development and product development.

The structure

We build *Bitter EJB* from a simple base, then dive into the core session and messaging APIs, before moving to a lively persistence discussion. We end by offering finer points on building a system and tuning for performance. The book is divided into four parts.

Part 1: The basics

1 **Bitter Choices** We introduce *Bitter EJB* and talk about whether you should use EJB. We also take a look at the EJB controversy and how it has impacted the development of J2EE over time. Author: Bruce Tate

2 **The Bitter Cost** Here we introduce the costs inherent in developing EJB. We also deepen our earlier arguments. Specifically, we look again at why the EJB framework should not be chosen rashly. Finally, we cast the first

critical eye on EJB entity beans and the high cost they incur as a fine-grained service in a coarse-grained wrapper. Authors: Patrick Linskey and Bruce Tate

3 **Bitter Faces**   We talk about traps that get in your way when you try to build an interface. Antipatterns in this chapter serve as a foundation for *Bitter EJB*. Author: Bob Lee

Part 2: Sessions and messages

4 **Bitter Sessions**   We introduce stateless session beans, the workhorse of the EJB architecture. We explore hints for proper use and also look at several antipatterns. Author: Bob Lee

5 **Bitter Session States**   In this chapter, we turn to a discussion of stateful session beans, the most misunderstood of the distributed communication beans. We spend a good deal of time determining exactly when stateful session beans fit your architecture, and look at antipatterns along the way. Author: Mike Clark

6 **Bitter Messages**   In chapter 6, we define antipatterns for message-driven beans. Because this type of EJB is relatively new, some of these antipatterns have not been catalogued before. Author: Mike Clark

Part 3: Persistence

7 **Bitter Entities**   Though we're clearly not fans of EJB entity beans, here we explore antipatterns that may trap you should you decide to use them. We also explore solutions to these problems. Author: Patrick Linskey

8 **Bitter Alternatives**   This chapter is a departure from other chapters in the book. Here we recommend against using EJB entity beans and discuss two major alternatives: object persistence frameworks on relational databases (including OR mapping layers and JDO) and plain old Java objects (POJOs) with a session façade. Authors: Patrick Linskey and Bruce Tate

Part 4: Broader topics

9 **Bitter Tunes**   When you work with EJB, you will have to tune your application for performance. Here we talk about the ways in which tuning techniques can go awry. Finally, we turn to remedies, including automated testing. Author: Mike Clark

10 **Bitter Builds**   In chapter 10 we look at how day-to-day management of a complex framework like EJB can get out of control. We then talk about some remedies, all of which fit into your daily build, including code generation with XDoclet and unit testing with JUnit. Author: Bob Lee

11 **A Bittersweet Future** We reconcile some of the tension we've chronicled throughout the book. We talk about what's right with EJB, and what the future likely holds. Author: Bruce Tate, with feedback from the entire team.

Appendix A: Bitter Basics Since many of you may be new to antipatterns, we decided to include the first chapter of *Bitter Java*, which has a nice introduction to antipatterns.

Appendix B: Bitter Tales Since some readers do not have experience with EJB, we include a brief introduction to EJB to get you started.

Bibliography We include complete bibliographical information for any books or articles mentioned in *Bitter EJB*, along with references to other useful books.

At the end of each chapter, we also present a valuable review of the antipatterns, using the template established in *Antipatterns: Refactoring Software, Architectures, and Projects in Crisis*. Readers who would like more information about this antipattern template may refer to that text.

The reader

Bitter EJB is more advanced than *Bitter Java*. Readers should possess intermediate and advanced Java skills. It's best if you've had experience with EJB, but it is not required. You don't need previous experience with antipatterns. We lay that foundation for you.

The coding conventions

When we use code, if it's in a paragraph, it looks like `this()`, in Courier font, in line. If we need to use a longer code segment, it is also in Courier font, but broken into a different block and annotated, like this:

```
if(we.need(code()) {
  code.show(likeThis);          Code annotation
}
```

Our names use `camelCaseLikeThis`, with the first letter capitalized for class names, and the first word in lowercase for instance variables and method names. We put optional braces around all code blocks. In general, we try to use Sun's conventions for coding where possible.

Bitter EJB wouldn't be the same without bitter code. Therefore, we'd like to show you bad ways to do some things. To do so, we've got to print bad code. However, we want to warn you when we do so. Regular code looks like this:

```
goodCode(looksLikeThis);
```

And bitter code looks like this:

```
bitterCode(looksLikeThis);
```

The black bar alerts you to bad code, highlighting the difference between good code and bad.

We promise to keep things brief. May your cup of *Bitter EJB* be a sweet one.

The cover illustration

The figure on the cover of *Bitter EJB* is a "Turca en trage de ir al Bano," a Turkish woman in her bathing dress. The illustration is taken from a Spanish compendium of regional dress customs first published in Madrid in 1799. The book's title page states:

> *Coleccion general de los Trages que usan actualmente todas las Nacionas del Mundo desubierto, dibujados y grabados con la mayor exactitud por R.M.V.A.R. Obra muy util y en special para los que tienen la del viajero universal*

which we translate, as literally as possible, thus:

> *General collection of costumes currently used in the nations of the known world, designed and printed with great exactitude by R.M.V.A.R. This work is very useful especially for those who hold themselves to be universal travelers*

Although nothing is known of the designers, engravers, and workers who colored this illustration by hand, the "exactitude" of their execution is evident in this drawing. The "Turca en trage de ir al Bano" is just one of many figures in this colorful collection. The diversity of this collection speaks vividly of the uniqueness and individuality of the world's towns and regions just 200 years ago. This was a time when the dress codes of two regions separated by a few dozen miles identified people uniquely as belonging to one or the other. The collection brings to life a sense of isolation and distance of that period—and of every other historic period except our own hyperkinetic present.

Dress codes have changed since then, and the diversity by region, so rich at the time, has faded away. It is now often hard to tell the inhabitant of one continent from another. Perhaps, trying to view it optimistically, we have traded a cultural and visual diversity for a more varied personal life—or a more varied and interesting intellectual and technical life.

In spite of the current downturn, we at Manning celebrate the inventiveness, the initiative, and, yes, the fun of the computer business with book covers based on the rich diversity of regional life of two centuries ago, brought back to life by the pictures from this collection.

Part 1

The basics

Summer 1999: In the Texas hill country, I get my first taste of mountain biking on the difficult rocky terrain of Steiner Ranch. The lessons learned are painful and immediate: Squeezing the front brakes can send you over the handlebars. Going slowly over smaller bumps can cause you to lose your balance. I discover I need to quickly identify what is wrong with my style and how to fix it. My mind is focused: I read about biking and spend time with talented bikers. My ride improves rapidly, and my mistakes gradually become less painful.

On Steiner Ranch I learned to identify antipatterns—wrong solutions to common problems that have negative consequences. I learned to take advantage of other bicyclists' experiences. *Bitter EJB* offers you a similar advantage, helping you to learn from the mistakes of others.

Chapters 1, 2, and 3 lay the foundation for EJB. Chapters 1 and 2 answer an important but often neglected question: Should you use EJB for a given application? We discuss the types of projects that are likely to succeed with EJB and those that are likely to fail. We look at two major antipatterns: The Golden Hammer occurs when you apply a tool or framework, like EJB, to every problem, even inappropriate ones. Swatting a Fly with a Sledgehammer happens when you try to apply a heavyweight tool to a flyweight problem.

In chapter 3, we look at interfaces, a cornerstone of object-oriented design. The antipatterns in this chapter relate to the more difficult interfaces—remote interfaces, data transfer objects, facades, and exception management within interfaces. These topics cover the basic knowledge that you will need to begin to smooth out your ride through this rocky landscape.

Bitter choices

This chapter covers
- The controversy surrounding EJB
- A benchmarking case study
- Guidelines for applying EJB appropriately

July, 2002: the storms line up next to Austin like jets on the Dallas Fort Worth tarmac. The water has no place to go. The ground is soaked, and the lakes are full. The Austin community braces for more flooding. At the Barton Creek put in, vehicles of every size and shape, all with the omnipresent kayak racks, form a line of a different sort, leading right down to the water's edge. The water is higher than normal, and the kayakers are nervous at first. But before long, the fear gives way to paddling bliss. Six-mile class III runs with the accessability and seclusion of Barton Creek are rare for any community, especially for the dry state of Texas. Unfortunately, as the fear dissipates, so does caution. One night, the skies open up with a tremendous storm. Another five inches of rain fall, and the angry creek roars, but still the kayakers come. Each kayaker faces a choice, based on the conditions, his experience, and training. Some choose wisely and walk away. Others persist, betting that their skills will carry them through safely.

As my party of ten puts into Barton Creek, the water is covering the bridge across the creek. The first few rapids show us that this run is much more serious than anyone has anticipated. Throughout the run, we make many decisions. Sometimes, we choose to walk a dangerous rapid, or we pull over and scout a different section. At other times, we choose to plow ahead, confident of our ability to manage the consequences. Our first choice is critical: we divide into three small groups to keep an eye on each other. We see some firefighters lining the banks as we come down the river and wonder what's up. While we're in an eddy contemplating our next move, one of them tells us that hours ago, an expert kayaker, an off-duty firefighter, had gotten trapped in a hydraulic and drowned. Soon after, we notice that our last threesome is no longer behind us.

We think it is fitting to begin this book with a true tale about life-threatening choices, because these are ominous times. The choices that the software industry makes have far reaching implications for the technology economy, the Java programming language, and the careers of many developers reading this book. Our day-to-day choices also have a much greater impact than ever before. Enterprise JavaBeans demand early commitment to sound design principles if you have any hope of achieving adequate performance. In this book, we'll look at the tumultuous backdrop behind EJB, and we'll make the case that such an environment demands a different set of strategies. We need to take a critical look at the technology and understand where the hydraulics are likely to be.

1.1 A storm of controversy

As champions of software antipatterns, we were thrilled that *Bitter Java* achieved such commercial success. The book reached #9 on the Amazon best seller list, an unheard-of ranking for technical books without Amazon advertising. The success of *Bitter Java* prompted a search for other interesting and controversial subjects that might benefit from a similar treatment. The technology should have tremendous value as well as potential for gross misuse. To further validate the *Bitter Java* concept, the topic must also contain great complexity. The next subject was obvious: Enterprise JavaBeans.

Like Austin in July of 2002, the EJB community is currently in the midst of a stormy season. The economic fallout resulting from the technology crash in 2000 has left the software industry reeling, with a staggering list of victims. Gartner warns us that the industry overspent by $1 billion dollars on application server technology between 1998 and 2001. Customers are indeed tightening belts, resulting in a more difficult landscape for Java 2 Platform Enterprise Edition (J2EE) software companies.

Given these economic forces, the shape of the industry is changing with remarkable implications. Consider the following industry shifts and the questions these changes raise:

- IBM scrapped VisualAge, supported the open source Eclipse project, and bought Rational. How will this impact current Rational customers with competing development environments?

- To accelerate the market acceptance of its J2EE application server, Oracle bought the industry's leading relational mapping software just as WebGain was dissolving. Will Oracle continue to support TopLink customers with WebLogic or DB2?

- BEA, once the runaway market leader, now faces growing competition from IBM. Is BEA still the obvious J2EE choice?

- The Open Source community has a rapidly growing footprint that's gaining traction outside of the web server market, with smash hits like Ant for builds, Tomcat as a servlet engine, and JBoss as a viable full-service J2EE server. Do you need to pay for an application server to get value?

Along this journey, J2EE is predictably taking some lumps. Early versions of EJB had significant problems. Compatibility was nowhere near what customers expected. The open standards often evolve much more slowly than their proprietary counterparts. Customers report growing complexity and a high failure rate.

External competition, too, is growing. Behind the marketing muscle of Microsoft, .NET is growing rapidly and is directly attacking J2EE's market share. As we write this, J2EE is under a cloud of controversy and scandal. The community is buzzing over a recent benchmark that showed .NET with a performance lead over J2EE. Critics rightfully claim that the comparison isn't accurate or fair, but gave Microsoft a much-needed infusion of credibility.

Under these storm clouds, we write *Bitter EJB*. It's not our intent to further sow the seeds of dissention. Each *Bitter EJB* author is a strong proponent of J2EE and EJB, who also feels that EJB are complex and prone to misuse. By exploring antipatterns, we'd like to give you the tools to effectively navigate the stormy waters — as a software architect or as a programmer. In the next section, we'll take a brief tour through the evolution of EJB. By doing so, we'll gain some insight into the problems that EJB developers encounter. We'll also have a better appreciation for the tradeoffs made by the fathers of EJB.

1.2 A history of EJB antipatterns

Like many ambitious technologies, EJB started with a bang. If you'd like to amuse yourself, search the Internet to see what people were saying about EJB in 1998 and 1999. We were truly enamored by the possibilities of EJB. The robust infrastructure promised unprecedented security. With a new portable component model, the industry would agree on standards and compete on price. We would soon buy components from a global software EJB component marketplace, and we would choose from a variety of vertical applications that would simply snap into our waiting application servers. With such a head start, we would build enterprise applications in weeks instead of years. Thus simplified, operations personnel would handle menial tasks like enterprise application development, saving Java application developers for important tasks like going to meetings and drinking beer.

In all fairness, we were greatly encouraged in our high hopes. The industry, fearful of Microsoft's toehold on server-side application development, supported EJB with a tremendous amount of muscle and enthusiasm. Oracle, Sun, and IBM formed the front line of support that would eventually drive EJB into the fabric of corporate server-side development. To fully understand the evolution of EJB use, let's look at the history of the EJB specifications.

1.2.1 *March 1998: EJB 1.0*

Behind the scenes EJB has always existed in a near continuous state of controversy. Right out of the chute, Oracle refused to support the EJB persistence model. The other major players compromised with Oracle to make entity bean support optional. Data persistence wasn't the only early problem. The EJB specification left too much room in each implementation, so that the promised portability—not to mention server-to-server compatibility—never materialized.

While the EJB marketing engine was in overdrive, the real world was having mixed results with its product. While a few excited customers began to play with the technology, the technology was much too young to be seriously considered by most customers. The rare early applications ran with significant performance problems and fell short of the promised reality. Some vendors, including IBM, had a hard time releasing critical products on schedule. Others had difficulty getting early customers to adopt EJB. In general, the complexity of the early specifications frustrated all but the most seasoned developers. The best practices and expertise that we now take for granted took time to build. The result of EJB's first release was a hopeful marketplace with limited real-world success.

1.2.2 *November 1999: EJB 1.1*

In November of 1999, Sun released the first minor revision to the EJB specification to an eager community. For the first time, it mandated support for entity beans, the component model that provides EJB persistence. The new specification also added much needed support for XML and moved deployment descriptors from proprietary serialized objects to open XML documents. The security model was strengthened. Industry consultants lauded EJB as ready for the big time.

As EJB 1.1 was being developed, the Java language was making headway into the enterprise. Mainstream enterprise developers, looking for relief from tedious, distributed application development issues like security and transaction management, turned to EJB for solutions. Yet, as the first wave of real customers began to use EJB, they stumbled onto these major problems:

- Objects in a container did not have local interfaces. That meant that components had to use expensive communication alternatives to collaborate, with severe performance penalties.

- Entity beans did not have a way to represent or capture relationships. Because EJB typically were deployed on relational databases, database performance became problematic. Relational databases could process relationships in the form of joins many times faster than an application, but without relationship management, EJB developers were forced to process relationships within the application.

- Stateful session beans provided only a limited implementation that could not be clustered.

- No messaging application programming interface (API) existed, meaning that all communications had to be synchronous.

- The adoption of the entity bean specification further compromised portability.

EJB developers were beginning to get the picture: EJB would allow you to do enterprise applications with distributed objects, but would in no way guarantee good performance. We began to see "best practices" appear in many different places. Ironically, many best practices were simply remedies for problems that existed in the frameworks. Others provided solutions to common performance problems inherent in any distributed system. Readers of *Bitter Java* recognize these programming traps as antipatterns.

The J2EE community was growing so rapidly that many sample applications and early tutorials created in the formative Java years were never updated sufficiently to take advantage of the J2EE best practices. As with any new promising complex technology, many projects failed to take advantage of new optimizations. The seeds were sown for a future EJB backlash.

1.2.3 *August 2001: EJB 2.0*

Under increasing pressure from competition, economic downturns, and customers, Sun released EJB 2.0, with many enhancements that we use today. Currently, local interfaces enable both local and distributed component models, creating huge performance boosts. Relationship management and EJB QL allow relational databases to process entity queries with joins in the database, instead of in the applications. Message-driven beans (MDBs) now permit both synchronous and asynchronous communications. The specification is good enough to provide the following significant advantages:

- You can build enterprise applications with EJB that can scale and perform. Notable enterprises have built and deployed significant applications on EJB with impressive throughput and reliability.

- J2EE, for the most part, supports the critical legacy components. You can access relational database data, integrate with third-party transaction monitors (with a little extra effort), build a unified security policy with a central directory, and integrate with key message-oriented middleware vendors.

- While EJB 2.0 does not have perfect portability, skills do transfer pretty well across J2EE platforms. J2EE skills are available and, at least for the short term, relatively affordable.

- J2EE has a viable economy, outside traditional application server vendors. Consulting companies, like the Middleware Company, can provide effective education and third-party services. Other companies, like Sonic and Precise, produce components, middleware, and tools.

- The Open Source community for J2EE is thriving. A full-fledged EJB server in JBoss has many features that the commercial counterparts don't yet support.

- Industry support for EJB is as strong as ever, with IBM and BEA now carrying the torch from a product perspective and a wide community contributing to the open Java community process (JCP), which forms the standards.

The J2EE community is now large enough to support several highly successful portals such as TheServerSide.com and IBM's developerWorks. Communities like these post and discuss J2EE news and developments. At TheServerSide.com, you can find highly charged political conversation, ask or answer development questions, and check out reviews of the major application servers. At developer-Works, you can find articles from some of the best Java developers in the world, with free downloads.

While EJB has turned the corner in some ways, we're still wandering in the wilderness in others. The specification continues to leave a whole lot of discretion to individual vendors, so we don't yet have a portable standard. Though effective for a set of problems, EJB is undoubtedly highly complex. As we write this in early 2003, we're also seeing a meaningful backlash against all things related to EJB. The trigger, this time, is performance and complexity.

1.3 *A case study: Benchmarking PetStore*

In 2002, the J2EE community found itself in the most tenuous position in its short history. As the founder of Java, Sun was no longer the unassailable giant. The company was under real attack from an increasingly competitive server marketplace, and the software strategy and execution, outside Java, had met with mixed results. Microsoft was also eager to cut into the J2EE marketplace, and in late 2002, that company managed a marketing coup.

PetStore is a sample application written to show people how to use EJB. Designed to promote reuse over performance, PetStore offers none of the performance optimizations required for a typical benchmark. It's been updated several times, but still lacks fundamental techniques for achieving high performance, like a uniform caching strategy. And, as a sample available for most commercial and Open Source J2EE servers, PetStore is probably the most visible J2EE application. These factors made it an ideal target for a Microsoft benchmarking effort.

Just as a hunting lion will separate the weakest and youngest antelope from the herd, Microsoft identified PetStore as a perfect candidate for a benchmarking contest. Microsoft asked the Middleware Company to step forward as the J2EE champion and to manage the J2EE implementation. The Middleware Company started with the original PetStore design, with JSP user interfaces accessing BMP entity beans through a session façade, and tuned the design to achieve a 17-fold increase in performance (figure 1.1). Still the Microsoft benchmark was nearly twice as fast. This benchmark was stacked in Microsoft's favor from the beginning for many reasons:

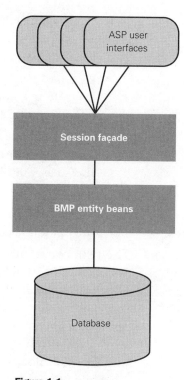

Figure 1.1
The original PetStore design adopted by the Middleware Company uses an ASP user interface to access Bean Managed Persistence entity beans through a session façade. Accessing the database directly from the façade would have been faster, but tougher to maintain.

- The benchmark pitted old J2EE technology against recent Microsoft technology. At the time Microsoft performed its benchmark, one of the industry's leading J2EE engines did not support the latest J2EE performance and design enhancements. (The vendor names were never released, but many assume the non-supporting vendor was IBM.) Though the most popular application server used a much more recent version of J2EE, the benchmark used two-year-old technology, with few of the performance optimizations supported by EJB 2.0.

- The Microsoft design optimized performance, but the PetStore design was modular and loosely coupled, optimizing ease of maintenance over performance. In particular, it used a full-service persistence layer. This decision was questionable, because the persistence was hand-coded as bean-managed persistence. Therefore, the benefits of using a persistence layer at all are unclear.

- PetStore's original code base does not take advantage of many best practices that EJB developers have come to understand. As such, it may have been better to design the application from scratch, instead of starting from such a loose foundation.

While the Middleware Company was tuning the original poor PetStore application, Microsoft wrote a version of PetStore from scratch, without consideration of a multitiered approach. Microsoft did little to separate the data access layer from its business logic. It even cached full tables in memory! The code was tightly coupled and difficult to maintain, but brutally simple and effective. Without the overhead of a full-service persistence layer and with unrealistically aggressive caching, Microsoft's version of Pet-Store outperformed J2EE's PetStore by a factor of two (figure 1.2). It should have—it was doing less than half of the work.

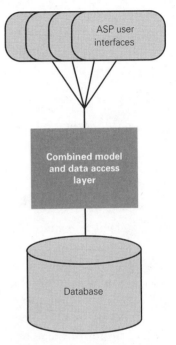

Figure 1.2
By contrast, the Microsoft design accessed the database directly from the model logic. This design effectively tightly couples the business logic to the database. Removing one layer improves the performance significantly, but would make the application maintenance more difficult.

The incendiary responses from both Microsoft and J2EE camps made immediate claims and counter claims. Microsoft shouted "Victory" and immediately equipped their sales staff with a PowerPoint presentation and report to take maximum advantage of the benchmark results. On the other side, more than 30 critiques from major J2EE news services and independent consultants published scathing reviews of the Middleware Company's PetStore application. Microsoft representatives continued to use the report to full advantage while confusion reigned.

So what should we make of the PetStore fiasco? Obviously, the preponderance of evidence strongly suggests that the comparison between the original PetStore and Microsoft's redesign was not an equitable one. The Middleware Company has accepted some responsibility for the failings of the initial benchmark. Don't be satisfied with assigning the blame, though. We, the J2EE community, need to do some things to put our own house in order. If we're willing to listen, the PetStore example can teach us much. Consider the following:

- Even seasoned developers are susceptible to antipatterns. Many of the problems inherited in the original PetStore design went against accepted best practices. Perhaps we need a catalog of basic J2EE antipatterns.

- We should take as much care designing sample applications as we do in the code base. Samples are far more than "gee whiz" demonstrations; they form templates for countless enterprise applications. We need to take notice when a consulting company with a highly touted reputation is unable to execute on a benchmark of a reasonably simple application. In several ways, EJB examples need revision.

- EJB 1.0 persistence continues to need revision. EJB 2.0 entity beans did not go far enough to plug the holes in the EJB persistence strategy.

This case study brings us to the crux of the matter. It's tough for even seasoned consultants to keep a firm grasp on all of the pitfalls of EJB development. While the J2EE community has been diligent about capturing design patterns and best practices, proponents of EJB must stand back and take an inventory of a different sort. We need to make an honest assessment of where the EJB land mines are likely to be. Throughout *Bitter EJB* we will catalog basic EJB antipatterns and prompt frank discussion about EJB problems and pitfalls. We believe that this discussion is healthy for EJB and for application developers.

1.4 Antipattern: The Golden Hammer

The surreal day on Barton Creek continues. We hope that the missing group has taken some time to scout one of the rapids, or has taken out, uncomfortable with the danger. We head down the river and find the empty boat of the drowned kayaker, a poignant reminder of the danger all around us. We wait in an eddy until the approaching night makes further delay dangerous. When we finally reach the bottom safely, we are relieved to meet our missing friends. They tell us a hair-raising story about a thirty-minute battle with a hydraulic, a losing struggle followed by a helicopter rescue. We are shaken. After losing its first expert kayaker, the paddling community in Austin will never be the same.

Often, techniques that serve a kayaker well in one situation will prove disastrous in another. Nonetheless, kayakers—like application designers—often remain loyal to approaches that may not fit every situation. Unfortunately, when you have a golden hammer, such as EJB, every problem looks like a nail. In *Bitter EJB*, the golden hammer will be a recurring theme. Many EJB problems stem from misuse of individual EJB components. With this technology, you need to consider a problem at two levels. Throughout this book, we'll explore one of those levels—understanding each piece of a problem and determining how individual EJB services and components might create a solution. Another level demands that you step back and view your problem from a broader perspective, deciding whether EJB is the correct match for your problem *at all*, or whether EJB has become your golden hammer. In this first chapter, we've begun to take a look at the historic turmoil surrounding EJB. Customers who have opted to enter the EJB waters so far have demonstrated some successes as well as more than their share of spectacular failures.

1.4.1 *Choosing unwisely*

Every five years or so, a massive new technology, like DCE or CORBA, comes along. Some early adopters apply the technology well, with clear understanding and often with good results. Vendors, having read the latest marketing strategy books like *Crossing the Chasm*, understand the value of early references, and they take advantage of early success, selling others with references. Then come the lemmings. Eager to reap over-hyped benefits, these developers follow the leaders into all kinds of peril, long before the technology is ready. J2EE and EJB are merely the latest iterations of this phenomenon. We saw the hype of early expectation. We saw disillusionment as the early masses tried to adopt EJB and failed. Now, we've got better technology—and an opportunity. EJB will thrive only to the extent that the community understands how to apply the technology correctly.

Enterprise application programming is difficult even with the right tools. EJB development is also tough in the best of circumstances. When the marriage between the tool and the problem is a good one, the benefits can be astounding. When they aren't, success is nearly impossible to achieve. Let's look at some of the reasons *not* to use EJB:

- **You've already paid for the server** Most Java servers include EJB, so you may as well get the benefit, right? And while you're going in for open-heart surgery, you may as well have your appendix out, too. After all, there's no need in healing twice, and you may need it out one day.

Regardless of who sold you a set of tools, you should be using the right tool for the job. If you need to supplement your tool set to do a job, do so. If you don't need all the features of brand X's super-charged web application server, don't use them. Additional costs of using poorly fitting tools will dwarf the small savings gained by skimping on software or saving a few lines of code by using a complex component architecture.

- **You're doing Java enterprise development**   EJB is the best way to do enterprise development in Java, right? And you should trade in that six-cup coffee maker for your tiny department for an industrial-strength, 50-cup Starbucks job. It's industrial strength, and you're a business.

  Many forms of enterprise development do not need all the services of EJB. A prevalent architecture (and need) is to put a simplistic user interface around a basic database table or small collection of tables. Such applications, along with those that create reports, are inherently relational in nature. These types of problems do not require the sophistication of EJB. In fact, a persistence framework gets in the way.

- **You want to use a sexy technology on this project to improve your resume or attract better talent**   And we'd like to add brain surgery to our resumes. Are there any volunteers?

  You'd be amazed at how often we see "design by resume." To build your skills in a meaningful way, you've got to attack the right problems with the right technologies in the right context.

- **You want a fully portable architecture**   And we want a Ferrari for Christmas.

  EJB is not a fully portable architecture. In fact, you'll probably find yourself using vendor-specific enhancements for things like integration, caching, and even object-relational mapping. You will find that EJB skills commute reasonably well.

Not all misguided projects choose EJB for such superficial reasons. Many problems appear to be perfect fits for EJB on the surface. You can successfully implement simple applications with EJB, but you'll write more code, with more complexity, than you would with simpler alternatives. You may decide to implement a reporting application with EJB entity beans, but you'll wind up translating from relational database tables to entities and back to relational tables again. In many instances, EJB just don't add enough *value*. Most of this stuff is probably not new to you, but with the number of projects that misapply EJB, it bears repeating.

1.4.2 Solution: Evaluate carefully

More and more, knowledgeable architects are looking at EJB with a critical eye—and walking away. Though this team of authors firmly supports EJB, we believe that this attitude is healthy. More than anything else, this technology needs success that comes from confident application to the right set of problems. In table 1.1, and in the following discussion, you'll see some factors that should influence your decision.

EJB and high complexity

The best reason to use EJB is that it simplifies your life. With EJB, you begin with high complexity. Your potential solution then must be highly complex without EJB for you to break even. Most developers underestimate the break-even point. Figure 1.3 shows the break-even threshold—the point at which your project complexity without EJB surpasses your project complexity with EJB. Our experience tells us that EJB makes the most sense for large enterprises, for the compilation of a variety of applications and application services, for the creation of a monolithic architecture, and for web-based deployment. You'll see more about what complexity means to an EJB application in chapter 2.

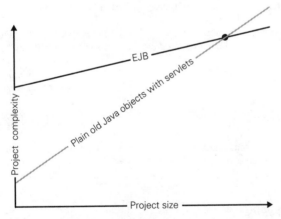

Figure 1.3   The EJB complexity graph shows that EJB starts complex, but ramps up more slowly with project size. Other simpler technologies tend to start simple, but break down as project complexity grows. The break-even point with EJB tends to be with larger, more complex projects. This chart does not reflect a formal study.

Table 1.1 EJB projects are more successful when you apply EJB appropriately. In this table, you can see a few factors surrounding an EJB decision. On the technical side, you should consider specialized needs, your application design, and the value you're likely to generate. Your choice is dependent on technical issues and the skills of your development staff.

Decision criteria	EJB fit better when:	EJB fit worse when:
Complexity	• Higher complexity • Large projects • Massive integration concerns	• Lower complexity • Small projects • Minor integration concerns
Skills	• Staff has EJB skills • Budget allows for mentors • Developers are well compensated, making it easier to retain key personnel • Enterprise understands EJB deployment and tuning issues, and staffs accordingly • Staff understands distributed object development	• Staff has little EJB skill • Budget does not allow for mentors • Developers are not compensated well • Enterprise has little EJB deployment experience • Staff experience is limited to development centered on one tier

Value	• Application needs to be
	  ○ Distributed
	  ○ Transactional
	  ○ Secure
	  ○ Scalable
	  ○ Persistent
		• Application does not require many major EJB services or components

Application design	• Application has classic J2EE tiered structure • Classic EJB clustering works • Required third-party components integrate with EJB well	• Clustering is problematic with this design • Third-party components require massive integration or duplicate many services • Legacy components require different transactional or security model
Specialized needs	• Single-threaded transactions • Traditional resources like relational databases and legacy transactions • EJB servers available on required hardware	• Highly specialized needs don't match EJB • Multithreaded transactions • Rigid hardware requirements make EJB unfavorable

EJB and J2EE development skills

In our experience, the top reason for J2EE project failure is the lack of sufficient skills. EJB can insulate you from a few technical complexities, but will introduce many others. You'll still need specialized skills to develop and tune complex, distributed applications. Experience with the J2EE tool set is preferred; experience with EJB is a must. A good understanding of design patterns, best practices, and antipatterns will help you choose designs that work and avoid those that don't.

This understanding is not a substitute for experience. You'll want a team that understands how to

- set up and administer an automated J2EE build environment with effective source control
- build automated tests for EJB applications
- design multitier applications with low communications overhead
- work efficiently in your development environment, whether with an IDE or a collection of OpenSource tools like EMACS, Ant, and XDoclet
- avoid J2EE services that are problematic or poor matches for your application
- deploy J2EE applications

True, your team can learn some of this stuff on the fly, but if you try to force a staff which is not ready into this environment, you'll be courting disaster. Luckily, EJB is mature enough that you should not have any problems finding good skills in the work force. In fact, as we write this in early 2003, the technology economy remains soft, and the market favors the employer.

EJB services and components and value

Perhaps the key to choosing the right platform is to make your decisions based on the value that you'll get from employing EJB, and offset that value with EJB's added costs, including the complexity of the platform. At each step, you'll want to justify the value—and the fit—of each EJB service you plan to use. If the service doesn't provide enough value, don't use it. In chapters 7 and 8, we'll see that the EJB entity model is frequently not the best choice for EJB persistence. Don't be afraid to walk away from parts or all of EJB if it's not meeting your needs. Usually, to be a good fit for EJB, applications should be one or more of the following:

- **Distributed** If your application is not distributed, it will rarely be a good fit for EJB. The core problems for many EJB services revolve around distributed name lookup, distributed transaction management, messaging, and connection services. Conversely, with highly distributed applications, EJB can easily make sense.
- **Transactional** Integration of a single global transaction context can significantly simplify enterprise development.
- **Secure** Not all EJB applications have a strong security requirement, and some applications have needs that don't fit the structure of the EJB security

model. Nevertheless, if you're able to use the built-in security model, you can save yourself significant time and effort.

- **Persistent** Of course, EJB entity beans can provide persistence, and improvements to EJB 2.0 make the solution much more viable than it has been in the past. Considering the position we take on persistence management later in this book, you may be surprised to see persistence listed here. But even though EJB entity beans are rarely the best option for persistence, using EJB may make it easier to wrap your persistence model with services that you need, like transactional awareness, distribution, and security.

- **Scalable** One of the unforeseen benefits of web-based development has been the relative ease of building scalable solutions. Because EJB are designed with clustering and scalability in mind, scalable solutions are often much easier to build with this architecture.

EJB and your application design

Good recognition is another consideration to keep in mind when deciding whether to use EJB. If your application has a tiered structure similar to those described in Sun's recommended application blueprint (http://java.sun.com/blueprints/patterns/catalog.html), then you'll probably find that your application has a better chance for a good fit with EJB. If you intend to fully separate your data access tier from your model and user interface, EJB will allow you to do so. If your application needs third-party components, you must evaluate whether you can buy or integrate components easily into your expected design.

Specialized requirements and EJB development

Your application may have special development needs that eliminate EJB from consideration. If you're integrating certain types of legacy software, EJB integration may be difficult or impossible without significant effort. For example, if you need a high degree of control over your own threads, EJB development can be much more difficult. The current paradigm is that the EJB container balances and manages single-threaded transactions. Adding your own can be problematic.

Keep in mind that politics will nearly always cloud your decision. The expense of an application server, the "resume potential," and the vendor relationship can easily influence major decisions. The key to good decisions is to recognize those factors and compensate. Ultimately, your call is simple: Will EJB make your life better or worse?

1.5 *Summary: Looking ahead*

Like *Bitter Java*, *Bitter EJB* is about war stories. We want to change the way that you think about patterns. This book will help you identify new EJB traps and use your experience to create solutions. We also want to cast light on the beneficial aspects of EJB as well as those that potentially should be avoided. We hope to provide this information in an entertaining and thought-provoking manner. If you've come to *Bitter EJB* by way of *Bitter Java*, you're familiar with the concept and importance of antipatterns. If you're new to the subject—or you need a refresher—please read appendix A, which contains the first chapter of *Bitter Java*. This chapter contains the basic ideas behind the use of antipatterns. If you'd like to be sure that your EJB skills are what you need to follow this book, you can check out our EJB 101 chapter in appendix B. Once you're ready to roll up your sleeves and get busy, you'll want to start with chapter 2. We'll discuss a few core antipatterns for all EJB applications. We'll talk about the basic pitfalls that occur when designing an over-all EJB application interface, and then we'll work through the foundational design patterns that solve those problems, like session façades and value objects. In the chapters that follow, we'll then consider each major EJB component, from sessions to entities to messages. Finally, we'll look at important issues related to a sound EJB development process, including strategies for performance tuning and builds.

1.6 Antipatterns in this chapter

This section covers the Golden Hammer antipattern.

GOLDEN HAMMER

DESCRIPTION
When you have a golden hammer, everything looks like a nail. A development team or architect can become infatuated with a particular solution, and apply it inappropriately.

MOST FREQUENT SCALE
Application, enterprise

REFACTORED SOLUTION NAME
Litmus test

REFACTORED SOLUTION TYPE
Software

REFACTORED SOLUTION DESCRIPTION
You should first decide whether a technology is appropriate for a given project. A litmus test can help you decide.

ANECDOTAL EVIDENCE
"I didn't know that you could use a spreadsheet as a word processor." "EJB is perfect for our department calendar."

SYMPTOMS, CONSEQUENCES
When you use the wrong tool for a job, you wind up with solutions that don't work, perform badly, or are difficult to maintain.

The bitter cost

2

This chapter covers

- A litmus test for deciding whether to use EJB
- The inappropriate use of EJB for flyweight problems
- An introduction to problems inherent in EJB entity beans

When the days get shorter and the nights longer, Austin high-tech mountain bikers turn to night riding. Night riding is significantly more dangerous than day riding, but we bear these risks gladly for the opportunity to scream through the Texas hill country after a full day of work. As we approach each ledge or rock, the flat light hides the variations in terrain that can deflect a wheel or send a rider over the bars. Our tiny two-foot circle of visibility gives us little time to respond to the many turns of the terrain.

One danger lies heavily on our minds. In the central Texas hill country, the rumor is that the big cats—large black panthers—are back. We paid only passing attention to the tiny newspaper article that reported a sighting but one night as we hear an intense, guttural, blood-curdling growl from a backyard near our favorite trails, the risk we are taking snaps into focus.

The EJB framework can provide substantial value, but most EJB books pay little attention to an important question: Does the cost of using EJB ever outweigh its value? As you might expect, "cost" stands for not just the measurable dollar value of the application server software, but also the unquantifiable effects of schedule delays and added workloads that come from building solutions with a complex framework. If you want to have success with EJB, it's critical that you apply it to the right problem. In this chapter, we'll take a hard look at the question of EJB's value versus its cost. And we'll consider the fundamental question, "Should you even use EJB?"

2.1 Sparking controversy

At the turn of the century, customers—with increasing frequency—signed massive contracts with software and services firms for EJB projects. Everyone was eager to usher in the new emperor. Giga Information Group estimates that the J2EE application server market was at $2.25 billion in 2002. Undoubtedly, some of this money was well spent. EJB can hide much of the complexity from our applications. Component-oriented designs allow you to reuse major services from the container. Deployment descriptors let you delay major decisions until deploy time. But Nirvana has not been achieved.

Gartner (www.gartner.com) estimates that customers overspent $1 billion on EJB technologies in 2001. Today, the outcry against EJB is, at times, deafening: "Entity beans are too bloated and slow." "Deployment descriptors are too complex." "Technologies and frameworks swirling around J2EE move so fast that we can't keep up."

Only the rare EJB project succeeds when measured against the expectations raised by all the marketing hype surrounding the capabilities of EJB. In this chapter, we will attempt to deflate the hyperbole of each polarized perspective, shifting the balance back toward the center. We'll address the services that make EJB useful, and we'll discuss the cost of services. We'll work through the criteria for using EJB and address situations when an alternative might be a better choice. For the most part, we'll let other books address specific alternatives to EJB. In the second part of the chapter, we'll take a focused look at entity beans. For reasons that will become clear, entity beans are different beasts—that demand particular treatment.

2.1.1 *The value of EJB*

Many early antipattern studies were based on software engineering principles. Books like the *Mythical Man Month* and *Death March* have made the case that our software complexity has outpaced our ability to organize and manage the development process. One could make the same case for software architecture. As complexity goes up, productivity plummets. The role of EJB, then, is to abstract out necessary core services for enterprise software development. Doing so allows the developers on a project to focus solely on their application logic, rather than on reimplementing infrastructure code.

2.1.2 *EJB-appropriate applications*

The EJB specification marked the entrance of Java into the enterprise space. The goal of the EJB team was to put together a standard, portable mechanism for creating, assembling, deploying, and managing distributed components in Java. EJB was designed to integrate seamlessly with CORBA, a pre-existing distributed component standard. In this standard, multiple components deployed on multiple Java Virtual Machines (JVMs) can all participate in a single logical transaction, and the system administrators can control access to sensitive component methods.

The resulting specification, EJB, was the enterprise equivalent of Java's original WORA (Write Once, Run Anywhere™) badge of honor—Write Once, *Deploy* Anywhere. The EJB specification now makes it theoretically possible to write a set of distributable components, deploy them to a variety of application servers, and build applications with these and other third-party components. Such a process is even relatively painless, provided you carefully follow the rules. Take that, CORBA!

EJB applications are scalable. They also provide failover services more easily, and communicate with a variety of client technologies. Think about it. A Java client can be

- a swing client
- a servlet
- a J2ME device
- a JMS-based message producer
- anything with a CORBA binding

The benefits don't stop there. You can execute transactions involving a number of components on disparate systems, using only a little declarative transaction coding. System administrators, rather than developers, manage security policy at deploy time or even dynamically at runtime. You can see that the EJB specification provides features that truly help you build enterprise-strength applications.

So, when would you actually use these features in the real world? The EJB specification provides services that make it easier to build complex distributed components. For that reason, EJB has become tightly associated with enterprise applications. You could claim, then, that you should use the EJB specification when working on enterprise applications. That would be fine, except that the term "enterprise application" conveys two vastly different types:

1 **Large-scale, complex, distributed applications**   On the one hand, enterprise applications are applications that glue together many different IT services used by a large company or set of companies. In this sense, the enterprise application must integrate large pre-existing systems that were never designed to work together. These systems typically have a set of rigid, documented APIs used to perform business operations; for example, a warehouse inventory application communicating with a parts procurement system.

    These types of systems also usually have complex business requirements defined by disparate, but equally important, projects. Additionally, the subsystems glued together by the enterprise application are often under the control of different departments, or even different organizations altogether. So, it is essential that the different subsystems be broken down into sets of well-defined APIs. The EJB specification was defined for this type of enterprise application.

2 **All applications built in an enterprise**   On the other hand, the term enterprise application is often applied to anything written by enterprise application developers. Of course, this definition is circular, and that's the point— the IT industry has essentially redefined the term enterprise application to

include merely those applications written by people working at a company, especially if that application has any HTTP-based or client/server capabilities. In this sense, corporate websites, discussion forum software, and front-office sales tools are all enterprise applications. These types of enterprise applications generally don't mesh well with the EJB specification.

2.1.3 Using a litmus test

Sometimes, you may want to simplify the choice of a technology. You'd like a litmus test of sorts. Dip the test paper into your application. If it comes out red, choose EJB. If it comes out blue, look for something else. To make your determination, take a look at properties that enterprise applications—both those defined by the EJB specification and those written within a company—tend to exhibit. Enterprise applications may possess any of the following:

- **Loosely coupled components** Enterprise applications often contain several independent components, potentially developed by different companies. These components generally do not share the same life cycle or release schedules.

- **Massive scalability requirements** A fundamental aim of an application server is to provide a transaction monitor that serves as a "throttle." Without this kind of service, every client in an enterprise could dive head first for the same database resource, creating a hot spot. With a transaction monitor in front of a resource, it's possible to gate the number of concurrent users that can use the resource. In EJB, stateless session beans serve that role well.

- **Distributed business transactions** Heterogeneous back-ends and loosely coupled components may all need to participate in the same logical business transaction. In other words, if one component or back-end fails to commit its part of a unit of work, it may be essential that the other components and back-ends involved in the transaction be able to roll back, allowing all the components to participate in a single atomic unit of work.

- **Asynchronous APIs** Clients will communicate with your application via a message queuing service or via web service APIs such as SOAP.

Each of these four needs should serve as a piece of a decent litmus test for EJB. The more criteria that an application passes, the better the fit for EJB. Of the four, the two most critical are massive scalability and distributed business transactions. Many applications could use these services, but consider how strong their actual need might be. The additional costs of EJB may not warrant the burden of EJB for just a passing need.

Be careful, though. No litmus test is perfect. Many applications make excellent use of stateless session beans, without using EJB persistence or messaging at all. With complex business transactions and the need for the scalability, the security, and the clustering that EJB provides, its use is perfectly justified. By contrast, some applications demand these requirements in spades, but specialized requirements like the support for certain threading models in legacy Java applications make EJB completely impractical. Although not foolproof, this test nonetheless offers one quick method for narrowing the criteria and determining whether EJB are appropriate for an application (figure 2.1).

2.1.4 Passing the test

Before we look at a poor fit for EJB, let's take a look at a few applications that meet the requirements well:

- An **online order processing system** might need to integrate with a bank's automated account access services. This integration might not be achievable through a few simple APIs that provide enough functionality for the business needs without EJB.

- A **rail yard management system** may need to manage the trains in the yard. The application may need to integrate with several back-end databases, including Informix and DB2. Since tracks are shared across multiple enterprises, a transactionally aware messaging layer using message driven beans and XML would fit well.

- The **OSS Java Initiative** (http://java.sun.com/products/oss) is a set of standards designed to address the needs of telecommunications operations support systems (OSS). As an industry standard, different telecommunications companies implement a variety of loosely coupled distributed components for their individual systems. These systems may use different technologies for storing application data and may interact with different proprietary components to perform the new standards-based business operations using distributed transactions.

You can see that EJB can work well for massive and complex enterprise applications. In fact, we've seen enterprise Java applications work in each of these situations. The people working on these types of problems can muster the considerable resources necessary to make an EJB application fly.

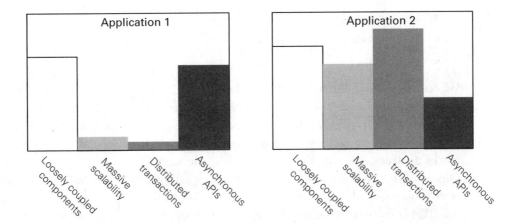

Figure 2.1 When considering EJB for an application, you want to balance the application's complexity against the capabilities of EJB. Application 1 has a number of loosely coupled components and relatively high scalability requirements, but is not transactional and does not have many asynchronous API needs. It would probably not be a good fit. Though application 2 has few asynchronous transactions, it''s a much better fit for EJB, in terms of complexity.

2.1.5 *Weighing complexity*

When scoring your application's requirements against the four pieces of our litmus test, consider how important each is to your application and make a decision based on all considerations. Do not choose to go with EJB solely because of a need for a single EJB service. For example, if you find yourself in need of just distributed transaction support, consider a stand-alone transaction manager instead of a full-blown EJB container.

Once you've analyzed how much your application can use the services provided by the EJB specification, you will be able to determine where it falls in the continuum between the two types of enterprise application. If your application will take advantage of several EJB services, then your project will likely benefit from the power of the EJB specification. If, on the other hand, your application is not likely to use much of the EJB specification, then deciding to go with EJB might cause more problems than it solves.

Applications appropriate for EJB will generally score well against a good litmus test, which simply represents common sense. In contrast, any application will possess one or more of the following design goals:

- simple data persistence
- transactional integrity requirements

- three-tiered design
- scalability or future scalability
- performance

When you evaluate an application, take a close look at the goals and the implied requirements. For each requirement, you need to ask yourself if that rumored cat is real, and if it has the teeth that you're imagining. These design goals are not the only determining factors for choosing the EJB specification. Many good frameworks address each of these problems quite well. For example, the Java Data Objects (JDO) and the Java Database Connectivity (JDBC) standards are excellent persistence frameworks for many applications, and newer tools, like Hibernate, will likely evolve into competitive persistence solutions as well. In addition, other aspects of the J2EE specification, without EJB, can achieve perfectly acceptable scalability and performance metrics for many uses. So, unless your application already meets a few of the more complex requirements for EJB use outlined earlier, you should *favor* non-EJB solutions to these problems.

A common EJB misconception is that an EJB container is necessary to guarantee transactional integrity. This is not correct. The EJB specification provides semantics for defining transactional boundaries in a declarative manner, but does nothing else with transactions. This declarative transaction behavior is useful, but not required for configuring multiple data sources to participate in a distributed transaction. So, if your transactional requirements only require that you interact with a single data store (a relational database, for example), then a non-EJB solution such as pure JDBC will be just as transactionally correct as an EJB solution.

2.1.6 *Evaluating your talent*

The perfect architecture will result in the perfect application only if the team executing the design has the necessary skills. This is especially true of EJB applications because many requirements of the EJB specification involve seemingly arbitrary rules that place limitations on the availability of certain Java language features, such as threading. Some may even change the semantics of certain parts of the Java language. So, in addition to learning EJB APIs and file formats, an EJB developer must also unlearn a few familiar Java concepts and replace them with the EJB equivalents.

An old maxim says that you should never use a tool until you understand fully what it does. You can—and should—debate the meaning of "fully" in the EJB domain. Tool vendors (BEA, Borland, IBM and Sun, for starters) continue to push their particular solutions as silver bullets that will make EJB development easy. The top market research consulting firms, including Gartner, Giga, and Forrester, all agree that the tools' battle will play a crucial role in the future of J2EE—both in terms of J2EE's relationship to .NET and in terms of the relative positions of the players within the J2EE space. However, for the most part, these tools merely automate a portion of EJB's tedious development. With few exceptions, they do not address the more fundamental differences between EJB development and J2EE development without EJB.

For example, the use of threads is not allowed in the EJB specification. You can't get around that fact, no matter what tool you choose. For all practical purposes, the EJB specification does not have a concept of component inheritance—an EmployeeEJB entity bean cannot extend the PersonEJB entity bean (except in a language convenience manner). Nor can you change the fact that remote interfaces to EJB use pass-by-value semantics.[1] These and other fundamental restrictions in the EJB specification make it important that a team working on EJB development knows the specification very well. In general, a team should understand the following:

- *All* high-level EJB concepts, so that they can effectively apply the appropriate parts of the specification to the project at hand
- General EJB concepts such as implications of re-entrancy, the relationship between transactions and threads, and restrictions on resource loading and threading
- More specific EJB concepts for the areas being used, such as session, entity or message-driven beans
- Higher-level concepts of client/server programming with EJB

Teams short on such expertise should either invest in training—mentoring and cross training on other internal EJB projects works well—or consider alternatives to EJB. Note: The team members who write the client code that use the EJB

---

1 In this book, we will use the terms pass-by-value and pass-by-reference a little loosely. When we say that a technology uses pass-by-value semantics, we mean that non-primitive method arguments and return values are copied (via cloning or serialization) before invoking the method. When we say that a technology uses pass-by-reference semantics, we mean that non-primitive method arguments and return values are not copied, but that object references are passed around instead. This differs from the compiler definitions of pass-by-value and pass-by-reference. Technically, Java bytecode is always pass-by-value—what we think of as pass-by-reference in Java is actually implemented by passing a copy of an object reference to a method.

components can have a less complete understanding of EJB, but they're not completely excused.

Now that we've discussed EJB-relevant needs, let's consider a few ineffective EJB applications.

2.2 Antipattern: A Sledgehammer for a Fly

The mere thought of swatting a fly with a sledgehammer evokes a certain cartoon-like impossibility. Super-human ninjas or ultra-lucky uber-geeks may be able to pull it off. Though you might get lucky, the results are usually going to be predictable. You'll have lots of damage without meaningful results.

In our J2EE world, EJB is like a sledgehammer. It provides considerable power and durability to applications that need it, but is heavy and unwieldy. Look at one uncontroversial example of a service that should not be implemented using EJBs—logging. Full-featured logging frameworks already exist and are sufficiently mature. One is even bundled into the J2SE APIs as of the J2SE version 1.4. However, bear with me. I chose this problem because it's well understood, because many people choose to build from scratch, regardless of alternatives, and because a logging framework may have enterprise characteristics that might seduce an unwary team into choosing EJB.

System event logging is a common component of any application of medium-to-large scale. Developers typically expect a logging framework to be easily configurable and deployable. They also expect high availability and reliability from a logging framework. Multiple machines often are able to log to a central location and, usually, you want to analyze the resulting logs as a whole. Consider the following points and note how each might indicate EJB as a good approach:

- Logging is a *component*, often written by a third party and never tightly coupled to the application domain. Well, EJB is a component architecture. It is designed with loosely coupled, independent components in mind.

- EJB is a *distributed* component architecture. So, assuming the common case of the application in question running on multiple machines, it will need a distributed logging framework, right?

- Most EJB containers provide *failover*, so high availability is no problem with EJB. For a system event logger, failover is a useful, but not a central issue.

- Application servers often include features targeted at simple component configuration and deployment. A simple configuration for our logging component would be a nice extra.

- Loggers must manage resources efficiently. Because deployments typically have fewer application servers than clients, memory-intensive resources such as database connections can sometimes be pooled more effectively in systems that access the resources exclusively from the application server tier.

As we said, if you looked at only these criteria, EJB would seem the obvious choice. This EJB application is a potential solution. EJB best practices indicate that you should perform all client access through session beans, not entity beans, and that you should use EJB 2 container-managed persistence (CMP) entity beans to store data in a database. So, we will define a session bean façade with a single method: `logMessage (int severity, String message)`. This façade will then create a CMP entity bean through that bean's local interface and set the log severity and message. That's it.

As we examine the implementation in table 2.1, we quickly see we are holding a sledgehammer. This simple task requires that we author as many as ten (yes, ten) files, including two configuration files and a simple test class. The existence of the configuration files and the complexity is dependent on your application server; our test class represents what the application code in a servlet, a Swing GUI, or another client environment would have to incorporate to interact with this logging component if no extra levels of abstraction were put in place. We chose to use WebLogic as our application server, but most other application servers have similar configuration requirements.

You could simplify this test application by putting a generic interface in front of our session bean, but the purpose of this discussion is to analyze the complexity involved in an inappropriate use of EJB, not to demonstrate ways to hide that complexity. Additionally, bear in mind that adding such an interface would add at least one file to our picture, making the EJB solution even larger. With these goals in mind, take a look at the breakdown of the example Logging EJB in table 2.1.

Table 2.1 This file listing for session bean façade logging implementation shows the complexity of a simple logging component. The line count provides a pretty good handle of the potential complexity and drudgery that we're dealing with in the EJB arena.

Classification	File name	File line count
Entity bean	LogEntry.java	8
	LogEntryBean.java	48
	LogEntryHome.java	13
Session bean	Logger.java	10
	LoggerBean.java	54
	LoggerHome.java	9
Sample client code	TestLogger.java	58
Deployment descriptor	ejb-jar.xml	55
Vendor-specific deployment configuration	weblogic-cmp-rdbms-jar.xml	26
	weblogic-ejb-jar.xml	28

2.2.1 Adding complexity

It seems as if you've authored a lot of code for what should have been a pretty simple problem and solution. Maybe using EJB for our logging framework is not such a good idea after all. Let's look at what the EJB specification gives us:

- **Declarative transactions** Typically, transactional integrity is not a big concern when it comes to a logging framework. An application developer generally does not care if some messages are recorded and others are not. In fact, the opposite is usually true. An application developer expects each log attempt to succeed independently of any other log invocations. So, the EJB semantics for declarative control of transactions is not of much value. It is often desirable for a single log message to be logged in an atomic fashion, but this is a different concern than the transactional behavior of multiple logging statements.

- **Distributed transactions** Because transactions are not typically important in logging frameworks, distributed transactions (transactions involving multiple transactional resources) are even less important. For example, you don't want to roll back log messages when a database insert fails. If you're not going to use transactional features in the first place, then you are certainly not going to integrate with another transactional resource.

- **Security** Logging is not typically a big security risk. So, it is unlikely that anyone would care to implement strict security policies for our logging framework.

- **Distributed component architecture** This logging tool is a reusable component, so you do receive advantages from the component architecture that EJB provides. However, log entries are predominantly write-only, so while you need to be able to log messages in a distributed fashion, you rarely (if ever) need to mutate or read those messages. Thus, most of the life cycle management parts of the EJB specification are wasted on our example.

- **Component-level caching** An application server's ability to cache instances of particular components can result in considerable performance improvements. However, since you do no reads, typical forms of caching won't help much. Write-behind caches in some application servers might help, but the major application servers do not offer write-behind caches as part of a standard product offering.

Because the EJB specification tends to bundle all these services together, you will pay a price in coding complexity and runtime performance for unused features. If you were to choose not to use an EJB container, you would lose a couple of the services provided by EJB: simple, unified, standardized configuration interfaces and high availability support. So, you need to decide whether or not these two needs merit the complexity and likely performance implications of using an EJB-based architecture for our logging framework.

2.2.2 Solution: Simplify

Ten files and 300 lines of code seems like rather a lot for a task as simple as storing a string and an integer. So, how could we rewrite this application to be simpler? First, let's consider the simplest solution—go with a product like the Apache Jakarta Commons Logging component. The Commons Logging component (available at http://jakarta.apache.org/commons/logging.html) provides a powerful, full-featured logging API that can delegate to a number of standard logging tools, such as Log4J (http://jakarta.apache.org/log4j/index.html) or the java.util.logging package available in Java 2 Platform Standard Edition Version1.4 (http://java.sun.com). It is simple to write your own custom logging back-ends for the Commons Logging component to use, so we could conceivably use either our JDBC or EJB example with Apache's tool:

```
import org.apache.commons.logging.*;

...

Log log = LogFactory.getFactory ().getLog ("log-channel");
log.info ("log-message");
```

Assume for now that Commons is not appropriate for your application, for whatever reason. The logging problem is representative of flyweight problems often erroneously implemented using EJB. For the sake of argument, let's see how you could simplify things if excellent third-party solutions to our problem did not exist already. For the purpose of this discussion, assume that you need your own logging framework because you must put log information into a table in a relational database, so that entries may be mined by your enterprise-reporting tool. This table is named LogEntry and has the following:

```
+-----------------+-----------------+
| Field           | Type            |
+-----------------+-----------------+
| log_entry_id    | numeric(10)     |
| severity        | numeric(10)     |
| message         | varchar(255)    |
+-----------------+-----------------+
```

This is the same basic schema definition we used earlier.[2] However, you've implemented this system in just two files. As before, one file is a test harness, so in reality, your non-EJB implementation is just a single class. The file breakdown in this situation looks like that in table 2.2.

Table 2.2 This table shows the files for a JDBC logging implementation, including line count. We've reduced the total lines of code by two-thirds and expect a similar reduction in complexity.

Classification	File name	File line count
JDBC logging component	JDBCLogger.java	51
Sample client code	TestJDBCLogger.java	42

Now, let's compare the client code in these two examples. Listing 2.1 shows the important excerpts from the EJB and the JDBC test client applications.

---

2 We used container-managed persistence for our LogEntry entity bean, so the details of this mapping are stored in the vendor-specific configuration files.

Listing 2.1 Partial code from TestLogger.java, the test client for the EJB logging
                implementation

Listing 2.1 Partial code from TestLogger.java, the test client for the EJB logging implementation

```java
public class TestLogger
{
    private Context ctx;

    public void test ()
        throws Exception
    {
        Object loggerOb = getContext ().lookup (LoggerBean.class.getName (
        LoggerHome loggerHome = (LoggerHome)
            PortableRemoteObject.narrow (loggerOb, LoggerHome.class);

        Logger logger = loggerHome.create ();
        String msg;
        for (int i = 0; i < 5; i++)
        {
            msg = "Test Message: step " + i + " of 5";
            logger.logMessage (i, msg);
            System.out.println ("Logged:" + msg);
        }
    }

    private Context getContext ()
        throws Exception
    {
        if (ctx == null)
            ctx = new InitialContext (System.getProperties ());

        return ctx;
    }
}
```

Look up the session bean in JNDI

Create a new home interface for our test

Set provider and naming environment variables

Listing 2.2 Relevant excerpt from TestJDBCLogger.java

```java
public class TestJDBCLogger
{
    public void test (String url, String username, String password)
        throws Exception
    {
        JDBCLogger logger = null;
        try
        {
            logger = new JDBCLogger (url, username, password);

            String msg;
            for (int i = 0; i < 5; i++)
            {
                msg = "Test Message: step " + i + " of 5";
                logger.logMessage (i, msg);
                System.out.println ("Logged:" + msg);
```

Create a new JDBCLogger object

```
            }
        }
        finally                  Manually manage the JDBC logger object
        {
            if (logger != null)
                logger.close ();
        }
    }
}
```

Listings 2.1 and 2.2 are roughly comparable. Obtaining the logger home interface is a bit more difficult in listing 2.1, the EJB example, than the comparable process of creating a new JDBCLogger object in listing 2.2, the JDBC example. However, in listing 2.1, you do not need to do any resource cleanup as we do in listing 2.2. So JDBC has a marginal advantage so far.

2.2.3 *Consider the cost of managing many files*

Next, compare the EJB session bean (listing 2.4) to the JDBCLogger class (listing 2.3). The JDBCLogger class is defined in a single file. On the other hand, the Logger session bean definition consists of three Java files and entries in one deployment descriptor and two WebLogic-specific metadata files (assuming we're not using XDoclet or another tool to generate part of this). So, before even looking at the business logic, EJB is already losing the battle; maintaining four or more files will inevitably cause problems.

Listing 2.3   Excerpts from JDBCLogger.java

```
public class JDBCLogger
{
    private long                id = System.currentTimeMillis ();
    private Connection          conn;
    private PreparedStatement   ps;
    private boolean             closed = false;

    public JDBCLogger (String url, String username, String password)
        throws SQLException
        {                        Obtain a connection and set up a prepared statement
        conn = DriverManager.getConnection (url, username, password);
        ps = conn.prepareStatement
            ("INSERT INTO LogEntry (log_entry_id, severity, message) "
                + "VALUES (?, ?, ?)");
    }

    public void logMessage (int severity, String message)
        throws SQLException
```

```
{
    if (isClosed ())
        throw new IllegalStateException ("This JDBCLogger is closed");

    ps.setLong (1, ++id);   Do the database insert
    ps.setInt (2, severity);
    ps.setString (3, message);
    ps.executeUpdate ();
}

/**
 * Closes any resources maintained by this logger. After this is
 * invoked, {@link #logMessage} should no longer be invoked.
 */
public void close ()
    throws SQLException
{
    closed = true;   Free up resources
    ps.close ();

    if (conn != null)
        conn.close ();
}

public boolean isClosed ()
{
    return closed;
}
}
```

Listing 2.4   Session bean version of LoggerBean.java

```
public class LoggerBean implements SessionBean
{
    public void logMessage (int severity, String message)
        throws RemoteException, EJBException
    {
        try
        {                                                 Find the bean's
            Context ctx = new InitialContext ();          home interface
            Object candidate = ctx.lookup (LogEntryBean.class.getName ());
            LogEntryHome entryHome = (LogEntryHome) candidate;

            String id = System.currentTimeMillis () + "";
            entryHome.create (id, severity, message);     Create a new
        }                                                 bean with the
        catch (Exception e)                               appropriate
        {                                                 values
            throw new EJBException (e);
        }
    }
}
```

We've left out the CMP entity bean definition, because it has no business logic at all. We also excluded standard implementations of the methods in the Session-Bean interface. However, do not forget that, in the session façade plus CMP entity bean solution presented here, you must create three more EJB files and make modifications to the deployment descriptors.

The session bean snippet shown in listing 2.4 is considerably simpler than that shown in listing 2.3, the JDBC version. Our JDBC code must know how to obtain a connection to a database and how to create and execute prepared statements. Additionally, the JDBC code must handle closing resources. On the other hand, the session bean just looks up an entity bean home and creates a new bean. Because the EJB specification takes care of life cycle management issues, the client code need not deal with any resource management issues. The decision points are shown in table 2.3.

Table 2.3 The decision between EJB and the JDBC alternative is often easier when you take a critical look at what the EJB framework is actually doing for you. One look at this table shows that EJB will probably not be the best solution for our logging framework.

	JDBC	EJB
Amount of code	Win	Lose
Complexity of implementation APIs	Win	Lose
Client API allows for potential pitfall (resource closing)	Lose	Win
Performance	Win (probably)	Lose
Migration to non-relational back-end	Tie—would require rewrite of one class	Tie—would require a CMP implementation for the back-end
Standard configuration and administration interface	Lose	Win
Dollar cost	Probably win	Lose

If you assign +1 to each win, the score is 4 to 2 in favor of the simpler JDBC approach to your logging scenario, with the gray-zone issue of performance. Performance tradeoffs are discussed in more detail in section 2.2.4. To summarize thus far, you can see at least two principal costs of using EJB exist: the complexity, which impacts the total lines of code, and a possible performance dip due to added overhead. These costs translate directly and indirectly to dollar costs, due to added development time and maintenance. You do have the benefits of EJB, including improved deployment and management of resources, but you've got to conclude that, in many cases, the added benefits do not offset the additional cost. Let's now address the finer points in greater detail.

2.2.4 *Grading the finer points*

The complexity of implementation APIs bears further discussion. JDBC wins over EJB in this category because the JDBC implementation uses standard Java and SQL syntax. So, any developer familiar with basic Java and basic SQL can easily develop and maintain this code. On the other hand, the EJB implementation requires that the initial developer and any maintainers obey the numerous contracts specified in the EJB specification that are not enforceable by a compiler. The developer must ensure that threads are not used, remember pass-by-value vs. pass-by-reference semantics, and guarantee that EJB-related method names (finders, CMP field accessors, ejbCreate methods) all obey the correct syntax and have the correct parameter types and count.

A number of tools—like XDoclet and integrated development environments—that use EJB can help reduce the complexity of some issues. However, none of these tools can address the basic fact that the EJB specification imposes constraints upon a developer whose violation cannot be effectively detected by a compiler—the developer must remember them on his own. A post-compilation verifier can detect some constraints, but others cannot be validated.

Performance deserves a few words as well. As we listed no performance numbers, our claim that the JDBC solution probably wins requires a little more justification. Our conclusion is based on the assumption that write-behind caching is not common in application servers. Because of this, and because this CMP example stores data in a relational database, it will take the application server at least as many cycles to write to the data store as it took our JDBC example. The application server could get a slight edge by doing better connection pooling, but the JDBC 3 example could replicate that easily by using a JDBC 3-compatible pooling data source, though it would further complicate the example.

Additionally, the application server interposes itself between the client code and the EJBs in order to do transaction management and perform security checks. Even though our example does not make use of these services, that no-op interposed code is still there, so a certain amount of overhead will be added.

Further, the application server might be on a separate physical machine than the client code, putting an extra network step between the client and the database. This will significantly increase the time needed to execute each logging operation. Based on these factors, it would be quite surprising if the EJB implementation outperformed a straight-JDBC solution.

Finally, the claim that the JDBC solution will be cheaper also requires some justification. Let's assume that the size and makeup of the development team is constant and everyone already has the enterprise development tools they plan to use. Let's also ignore any other potential development-time costs (such as training). That leaves us with deployment considerations. If this logging framework is the only EJB component in our system, then it will be responsible for 100% of the cost of license and hardware fees for an application server. If there are already other EJB components in the architecture, then the cost will be proportional to the amount of extra load the logging framework puts on the application server. This deployment cost could be directly manifested as a need for more hardware and licenses in a cluster or could more indirectly affect hardware or software costs by increasing the load on the server, slowing down business transactions, and limiting the number of simultaneous users of the system.

On the other hand, depending on system configuration, the JDBC solution could incur heavy costs. We mentioned that systems that use an application server can reduce the costs (from either a computational or price standpoint) incurred by expensive resources such as database connections. This cost reduction can occur because the resources in question can be pooled by the application server more effectively than by each client. Imagine a system with 100 clients that all communicate with a database. In the best-case scenario, that means 100 connections to the database. If the clients begin any connection pooling, this number could easily jump to 500 or even 1,000 open connections. If all the clients communicated with the database through the application server, then a single connection pool of, say, 10 connections could serve all 100 clients. This last scenario could produce considerable savings in costs for both pay-per-connection database licensing and database hardware necessary to keep up with the extra connection management overhead.

Sledgehammers are not for swatting flies, and the EJB framework is not for flyweight applications. Given our analysis, we must conclude that, to justify EJB, an application needs to have significant size and complexity. So far, we've discussed general needs used to justify EJB for any given application. In the next section, we'll switch gears and take a more detailed look at EJB persistence, uncovering a few inherent problems.

2.3 *Entity beans are a horse of a different color*

> *The night after we hear the big cat, we're on the trail again. Everyone knows that cats hunt nocturnally. His shadow stalks us on every trail. Though we never encounter him, the big cat still creates mischief, distracting us from the trail long enough to cause us to crash or lose our way. Three years go by, and although no one has yet seen the big cat, he continues to plague many riders in the Texas hill country.*

Like night rides in the Texas hill country, it's not always clear where the danger lies. The trail, the night, and the fear of both intangible and concrete danger all contribute to the overall risk. Likewise, the EJB landscape hides peril. It's important to discriminate between real and imagined danger. Let's cast some more light on the trail itself: the EJB framework. In the earlier sections, we've seen that the EJB architecture forces the developer to conform to certain design restrictions to realize the benefits provided by an application server. These are relatively small problems, like tree roots on a mountain bike trail. In this section, we'll encounter a more serious obstacle—entity beans.

Many people who approached the EJB specification a couple years ago didn't quite understand what session beans did. Entity beans, on the other hand, seemed simple. Entity beans provide a mechanism for dealing with data stored in a database as Java objects, so the entity beans can be used to implement a persistent domain object model. If you implement persistent classes such as Employee, Invoice, and PurchaseOrder as entity beans, everything will be great. Right?

Wrong. Entity beans are not merely classes whose instances may be stored to a database; they are full-fledged EJB components, capable of being deployed to an EJB container. Entity beans differ from session beans in that they support a more durable persistent state than that supported by session beans. (Keep in mind that stateful session beans can lose state in the event of a crash.) However, the persistent state supported by entity beans does not really map to the needs of a persistent domain object model. The additional services contained within the entity bean specification may be useful in isolation, but they present complexities and constraints that get in the way when you need to use entity beans to implement a persistent domain object model.

In this section, we'll talk about the origins of entity beans and what they were designed to accomplish. We'll look at how the industry has used them in the past, and we'll consider the changes made in EJB2 to accommodate the industry's desires. We'll determine when it's appropriate to use entity beans and when to avoid them. By the end of this chapter, you will understand why using entity beans seems a bit clumsy, and you'll see that the entity bean and EJB specifications require this awkwardness. We will not discuss *how* to use entity beans—or how *not* to use them, for that matter. That topic will be covered in greater depth in chapter 7. Here we'll simply focus on the cost of the service.

2.3.1 *The black sheep of the bean family*

Entity beans are one of three types of beans defined in the EJB specification. Like session beans and message-driven beans, you can access entity beans from remote JVMs. Entity bean methods can also participate in global transactions governed by a transaction manager. Further, you can control access to entity bean methods via the security services provided by an EJB container. In addition to these common services available to all Enterprise JavaBeans, entity beans provide a mechanism for persisting data into a database.

Because of this persistence mechanism, J2EE users primarily use entity beans to implement persistent domain object models. To do so, you define an entity bean for each class that must be persisted into a database. This approach has problems because it means that the domain classes must adhere to all EJB specification rules. Often all we want is a way to make application-defined objects persistent. As table 2.4 illustrates, we don't need all the services built into EJB. As you can see, we need only the persistence services and not the declarative transaction, security, or distributed object services

Table 2.4 Many EJB services typically go to waste. The problem is that the EJB container provides coarse-grained services, but persistence needs to be a fine-grained service. Persistence, security, and distributed declarative transactions do not belong at the fine-grained level.

Service	Granularity
Declarative, distributed transactions	Coarse
Security and authentication	Coarse
Distributed object access • failover • scalability	Coarse
Persistence	Fine

At first glance, the existence of these extra services may not seem problematic. But on closer examination, a key difference becomes apparent. The transactional, security, and distribution services are typically applied at a *coarse-grained* level, whereas persistence services are typically used in a much *fine-grained* manner

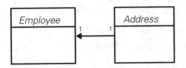

Figure 2.2 This design with a 1-1 relationship between Employee and Address is not recommended in EJB 1.1 because Address is dependent on Employee. But with container-managed relationships, this design is fine for EJB 2. The design is not inherently wrong, but we'll see problems as we dive deeper.

(see figure 2.1). That is, typical applications perform many persistence operations in a given transaction or in a given remote method invocation.

From a design standpoint, we can see that the EJB specification team never intended entity beans to represent a complex domain object model. Data persistence is mentioned only in passing in the EJB 1.0 specification. Instead, the specification focuses on the distributed object issues mentioned earlier. The best that the original specification does is to say that an entity bean "represents data in the database." (EJB 1.0, section 4.3.2) However, object persistence remains one of the biggest everyday infrastructure challenges for EJB developers. This need is more pervasive than the need for true distributed components. As a result, when EJB hit the streets, everybody used entity beans—preferably container-managed persistence entity beans—in the hopes that they would provide a solution for the object persistence problem.

Unfortunately, EJB was not designed with this problem in mind, and entity beans were not quite up to the challenge. Entity beans were an optional part of the original EJB standard, yet all major EJB containers were quick to implement them. Entity bean methods were exclusively remote-capable, meaning that method arguments and return values were copied even if the entity bean was in the same JVM as its client. The role of the entity bean in a domain object model was not clearly defined. The 1.1 specification clarified that entity beans should be used only to represent independent objects. The specification went on to define dependent objects as those wholly managed by independent objects (EJB 1.1, section 9.1.2). This definition includes common object model situations such as an `Employee` class that contains one or more `Address` instances. An instance of `Employee` owned each `Address` object, so `Address` objects are dependent objects and therefore not appropriate candidates for entity beans, according to the 1.1 specification.

2.4 *Entity beans: Take two*

The EJB 2.0 specification acknowledged the unexpected use of patterns and made changes to the EJB standard to accommodate them. The members of the spec team embellished CMP greatly. (EJB 2.0 CMP is essentially a complete rewrite of the CMP specification.) They added local interfaces to bypass most of the significant overhead involved in a local call between beans. Then they added container-managed relationships (CMR) to the CMP spec, allowing CMP entity beans to establish relations to the local interfaces of other entity beans. The spec team also added a standardized query syntax for CMP entity beans. Nonetheless, the EJB specification remains fundamentally concerned with distributed components, not data model persistence.

2.4.1 Local interfaces

The most immediately visible problem with EJB 1.x entity beans was remote interfaces. Entity beans coupled distributed method invocation with object model persistence. The utopian goals of the specification team were ambitious—to create a persistent model with complete location transparency. A model could be deployed in one container or within many containers across distributed servers. That model completely ignored the overhead of distributed models and local interfaces. So, as we've said, conventional wisdom dictated that you wrap your entity beans in a session bean façade and deploy your entity beans to the same machine as their façades, to reduce network overhead.

Given that the entity beans were in the same JVM as their façade, and that client code was forbidden to access the beans, entity bean performance became manageable. However, EJB 1.x left yet another hole. A significant amount of overhead remained in the entity bean method invocation process. The container had to guarantee that the method semantics were the same even if the invocation happened to be in the same JVM. At a bare minimum, method parameters and return values had to be serialized and deserialized to ensure that the pass-by-value method invocation semantics were maintained within the container. Amazingly, some containers simply used the same expensive Remote Method Invocation (RMI) pathways that two remote JVMs would use, even when method calls were made in the same JVM! (We'll talk more about this problem in chapter 3.)

The EJB 2 team solved this problem by adding the concept of a local interface to the EJB specification. Local interfaces differ from remote interfaces in calling semantics; parameter values in local interface method invocations are passed by reference, rather than by value as with remote interfaces. For that reason, local interfaces can be invoked only from within the same JVM, allowing a bean developer to design a system that bypasses the method invocation overhead of remote interfaces. Local interfaces are not unique to entity beans, but they are most useful with fine-grained entity beans such as those you would see when implementing a domain object model with entity beans.

We've gone into great detail to make an important point. As you've seen, EJB 1.x supported only remote interfaces, leading to unacceptable performance. The EJB 2.x specification solves this problem by adding local interfaces. You'll soon see that local interfaces are a necessary addition, even though they remain a compromise. First, let's consider the additional improvements in the EJB 2.x specification.

2.4.2 Container-managed relationships

Local interfaces were a key prerequisite for another new entity bean—CMR. CMR make it possible for an entity bean to have complex relationships with other entity beans. To guarantee that CMR perform well, the EJB 2.0 team required that all CMR always relate to a local interface. For example, if an `Invoice` entity bean has a relation to a `LineItem` entity bean, the `LineItem` bean must have a defined local interface.

The introduction of CMR lets you implement more fine-grained object models with entity beans. With EJB 2.0, the `Invoice-LineItem` relationship that was not recommended in the EJB 1.1 specification is now efficient. You have local interfaces, a session façade, and CMR, so your EJB problems are solved, right? Take a deeper look, then decide for yourself.

2.5 Entity beans—a closer look

Let's look at what happens inside a container when an entity bean method is invoked. First, we'll see what happens when we implement an example using EJB 2 CMP entity beans. Then, we'll compare it to what we actually need.

2.5.1 Employee management

Imagine that we are developing an employee management system. One requirement of the system is that it be capable of changing an employee's home address. Additionally, the system must be designed with high fault-tolerance limits in mind, so this operation must be idempotent.[3] If we were to implement this algorithm as a session bean that employs EJB2 CMP entity beans for representing the `Employee` and `Address` domain objects, our code might look like that in listing 2.5.

---

3 An idempotent operation is one that can be repeated without altering the final state of the system. That is, if an idempotent method is invoked twice, the final state of the system will be the same as if it had been invoked only once. `i = i+1` is not idempotent, but `i = 9` is. Idempotent EJB methods can be transparently re-executed in the event of container failover.

Listing 2.5   Session façade for Employee bean

```
public class EmployeeManager implements SessionBean {

  /**
   * Finds the employee referenced by <code>employeeId</code> and
   * Changes the home address to reflect the new information.
   */
public void resetHomeAddress (long employeeId, String addr1, String addr2,
  String city, String state, String zip) {

  EmployeeEJB employee =
    employeeHome.findByPrimaryKey (new Long (employeeId));

  AddressEJB address = employee.getHomeAddress ()
  address.setAddress1 (addr1);
  address.setAddress2 (addr2);
  address.setCity (city);
  address.setState (state);
  address.setZip (zip);
  }
}
```

Let's assume that the session bean method in listing 2.5 is invoked from a remote client, and that the client allows the application server to perform transaction management. Additionally, assume that EmployeeEJB and AddressEJB are local interfaces for CMP 2 entity beans, and that the methods invoked on these entity beans represent CMP and CMR fields. The interaction between our application objects and the EJB container demonstrates that the EJB 2 specification is relatively efficient compared to what we would have seen with EJB 1, but is still component-oriented. The EmployeeEJB get method and each AddressEJB set method in the example code will be interposed with container code to check the state of the current transaction and ensure that the current security principal has access to the AddressEJB methods invoked.

While this overhead is small compared to the cost of method parameter serializing or RMI communications overhead, it does increase significantly the amount of work that the JVM must do each time a persistence operation is performed. If entity beans were accessed through local interfaces only, this overhead would be hard to justify because the security and transactional EJB services would have already been performed at the session bean invocation level.

Now what if our session bean looped over an arbitrarily long list of addresses? You can see that the number of interactions between the session bean code and the application server would be proportional to the number of operations that the session bean performs on the address list. So the extra time consumed by the transactional and security code would grow with the number of operations performed, making each access to the entity beans slower (figure 2.3).

In a distributed component system, this extra overhead is negligible since invocations of the remote public component APIs are typically coarse-grained in nature. However, if an object model is represented via entity beans, this overhead can quickly add up. Because each field access is part of the entity bean API, it is therefore subject to this additional overhead. So if your data model includes

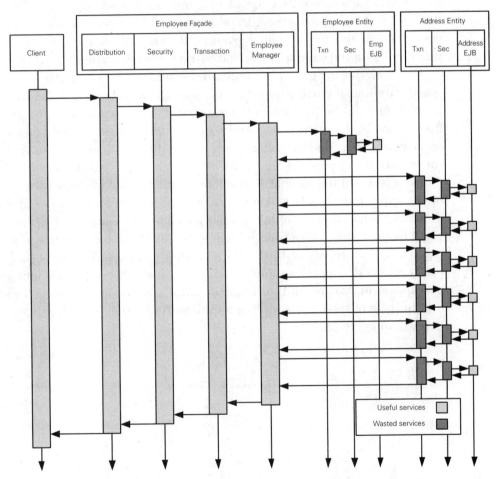

Figure 2.3   This simplified object interaction diagram shows the inherent overhead for EJB persistence. The problem is that EJB uses a coarse-grained framework for a fine-grained problem—persistence. You can see the wasted services in dark gray.

objects with—or many objects with an average number of fields—you can see that merely accessing all the data necessary to perform a business operation would be a heavyweight task.

Now, let's imagine that the EJB container did not couple the coarse-grained services mentioned in figure 2.2 with the persistence service we are using in this example. Then, the object interactions would be more along the lines of what we would expect, as in figure 2.4. The extra overhead and complexity of checking and re-checking transactional status and security parameters would be eliminated, and the necessary execution time for a single operation would decrease. This means that the overhead of using the EJB specification would be less, and our application would be able to run faster on a given hardware configuration or process more user requests at the same speed in that hardware configuration.

However, this imaginary EJB container would not be compliant with the EJB specification as it currently stands, because the Employee and Address entity beans would not be performing many services required of an Enterprise Java-Bean, namely, the orthogonal services mentioned earlier: transaction control, security, and distribution. As we've seen, the EJB specification team revised the specification to permit using beans without the distribution service. Perhaps future versions of the specification will decouple the rest of the services provided by the application server, making transactional and security services optional. A developer would then be able then to pick and choose among the services provided by the EJB specification, incurring the performance and design penalties implied by each service only when that service is needed. That the EJB specification team has decoupled remote access from the other services indicates progress may appear in this area in future specification updates. In fact, JBoss 4 will allow just this type of service decoupling and, hopefully, other application server vendors will follow its lead.

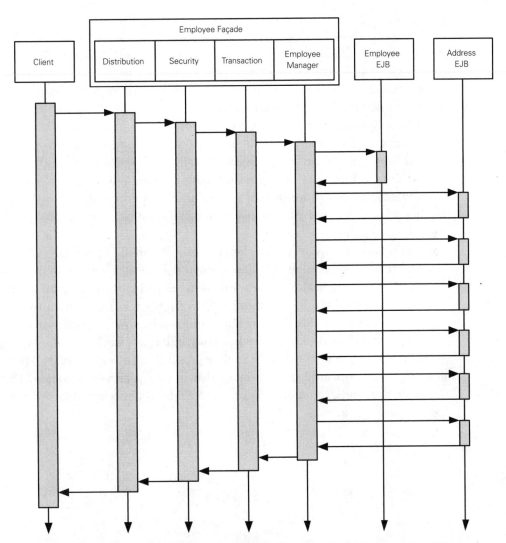

Figure 2.4 This simplified object interaction diagram shows a hypothetical modified EJB implementation of the EmployeeManager.resetHomeAddress() session bean method. The entity beans need not use the transactional or security services of the EJB specification, saving significant overhead and making a much cleaner design.

2.6 *Summary*

We began *Bitter EJB* with a premise: you may not want to use EJB at all. In fact, you should carefully justify EJB each time you choose to use it. We have seen that the EJB specification has a number of costs—some related to performance, others to developer productivity. We weighed the constant tension between cost and value considering factors for choosing EJB and determining which projects are truly "enterprise applications" from the standpoint of the EJB specification. We concluded that you should not dive into EJB as if it were a lifeboat. Instead, you should thoughtfully weigh the pros and cons of using EJB. Plenty of both exist. In other words, carefully consider your application requirements and make sure that the benefits you'll see from EJB will offset the additional complexity that you're bound to encounter.

In addition to considering application requirements, we considered the entity a possible hidden cost of EJB. Shoehorned into a role for which it was not designed, the entity bean specification contains services that may be unnecessary baggage for certain implementations and, consequently, may cause problems that certainly would add to the cost of using EJB. In subsequent chapters, we'll assume that you've concluded that EJB *is* a framework that will work for you. We'll look at global EJB issues in chapter 3. From there we'll drill into each major EJB component, including session beans, message-driven beans, and entity beans. Throughout our discussions, remember to keep the tradeoff between value and cost in the back of your mind.

2.7 Antipatterns in this chapter

This section covers the A Sledgehammer for a Fly antipattern.

A SLEDGEHAMMER FOR A FLY

DESCRIPTION

Using the wrong tool can often result in disaster. EJB is often applied to situations when much simpler technologies would be better choices.

MOST FREQUENT SCALE

Project

REFACTORED SOLUTION NAME

Well-chosen technologies

REFACTORED SOLUTION TYPE

Technology

REFACTORED SOLUTION DESCRIPTION

Choose a technology appropriate for the needs of your project. Choosing an overly complex solution could cause a simple project to fail.

ANECDOTAL EVIDENCE

"We're using EJB CMP entity beans on one part of our project, so we should just use it for all database access."

SYMPTOMS, CONSEQUENCES

Overly complicated implementations of simple projects, inadequate scalability, and/or performance

Bitter interfaces 3

This chapter covers

- Rules for good interfaces
- Local and remote interfaces
- Rules for distributing an application
- Data transfer objects

I want to be one of the few people who learns to surf on a long board in the mighty Hawaiian waves. I am an avid skateboarder and a strong swimmer, so I'm sure that I can handle the surf. I rent a long board that's waxed to provide good traction and feel. It's huge. I lather up with SPF 40 to protect my mainland skin, and get fifteen minutes of pointers from a pro. Then, I paddle out to the big breakers over the reef. There the waves look bigger and more powerful than they did near the shore. As I paddle out, the sunscreen on my chest rubs off on the board and makes it as slippery as an eel in grease. After every third wave, I slip off and must chase down the board and paddle through the ocean toward the swells. Finally, I'm ready to go. I turn, look over my shoulder, and see a monster seven-foot wave. Against my better judgment, I go for it, frantically plunging my hands into the surf, to catch the tiger by the tail.

3.1 Building a good interface

Well-designed interfaces are crucial to success in the EJB architecture. EJB components break down into three fundamental parts:

- The interface
- The implementation
- The deployment

Although implementation and deployment descriptions may change, once someone starts using your component, you are stuck supporting the interface. The interface embodies the essence of a component's contract. We often see developers dive into the EJB architecture, abandoning everything they know (or don't know) about Java programming and object-oriented design. Making the right interface design decisions up front can determine whether or not you can easily plug, reuse, and maintain an interface. In the simplest terms, good design will ensure the success or failure of your component.

The EJB container implicitly provides many services that seem like magic, and until we understood the details, breadth, and depth of these services, we had a difficult time deciphering where exactly this magic begins and ends. EJB does not supplant objects. Quite the contrary, EJB complements plain Java by abstracting some domain-specific, system-level concerns and facilitating modular reuse in a standard fashion. When it comes to designing bean interfaces, no substitute exists for strong Java skills and traditional object-oriented (OO) design practices. Throughout this chapter, we'll explore the decisions that go into making the best possible interface. We'll pay close attention to the decisions that can and should be made early on in the development life cycle and to the factors that influence these decisions.

3.1.1 *Breaking down remote invocation performance*

The EJB architecture features transparent object distribution. As an EJB developer, you can invoke an Enterprise JavaBean, regardless of whether you're invoking a bean running in the same process, in a different process running in the same machine, or in a process running in an entirely different machine across a network. Though EJB puts remote concerns out of sight, they are certainly not out of mind. Even though EJB doesn't expose you directly to the mechanics of remote invocations, you must remain mindful of the performance and reliability concerns surrounding remote distribution. Though local and remote method invocations appear similar on the surface, under the hood they are very different. Effective interface design makes the difference between an application that responds like a finely tuned European sports car and one that behaves more like my brother's vintage VW bus (0 to 60 in four-and-a-half days).

Local method invocations—method calls within the same process or virtual machine—are lightweight, so much so that the HotSpot compiler can often optimize them away. An in-process method invocation primarily consists of the following:

1 Creating a new stack frame
2 Redirecting execution to the method's instructions

The Java language passes the method arguments and returns value by reference, using their pointer, with the exception of primitive types. Rather than copy the argument objects in their entirety, the virtual machine passes a reference or pointer to the target method. In a 32-bit virtual machine, whether the size of a method argument is 10 or 10,000 bytes, the invocation time will be relatively constant. The machine passes a 4-byte reference on the method stack in either case. The same applies to the return value. (Note that Java uses strictly pass-by-value semantics, but we'll play a little loosely with the language in this chapter to keep the concepts readable.)

Remote invocations have considerably more overhead. The caller must marshal the method invocation, serializing the method arguments and passing them in their entirety to the remote virtual machine. Then, the target machine invokes the desired method and marshals the result back to the caller. J2EE passes the arguments and result by value. Consequently, the method invocation time increases proportionally with the sizes of the method arguments and return value.

A 10,000-byte argument may take three orders of magnitude (1,000 times) longer to transmit than a 10-byte argument.

Additionally, *round tripping* also affects remote invocation performance. An invocation takes a finite amount of time to get to the remote process. And, depending on network conditions and the size of the values, the return value takes a comparable amount of time to get back to the calling process. Depending on the network speed, the number of switches, and the distance between the source and target machines, the length of time these trips take may vary, but remote call times will *always* dwarf local invocation times by many orders of magnitude. EJB client code typically invokes methods in sequence. Consequently, even invocations between processes on the same machine take far longer than in-process invocations. EJB invocations also entail passing the security and transaction context. Throw in Web services, which brings along XML creation and parsing for each method invocation, and you can quickly drive performance down to unacceptable levels.

That brings us to our first set of design compromises. If method invocations are too small and frequent (we'll call these fine-grained invocations), the cost of these round trips can add up quickly. However, finer grained interfaces are more flexible. You need to balance interface flexibility and performance. We'll dive into this compromise in more detail through the course of this chapter.

3.1.2 *Passing by reference vs. value*

Whether an EJB method passes arguments and return values by their object reference or their serialized value bears heavily on performance and the bean's contract with the client. In pass-by-value semantics, the virtual machine passes the object in its entirety; the caller and callee work with completely separate copies of the object. In pass-by-reference semantics, the virtual machine passes the object's reference; the caller and callee work with the same copy of the object. Conventional Java code passes objects (anything that inherits from `java.lang.Object`) by reference, and primitives (`int`, `long`, `double`, `boolean`, etc.) by value. This approach amounts to, at most, copying a few bytes per parameter, per method invocation, regardless of the argument's size. For example, when code passes a `String` object into a local, vanilla Java method, whether the passed `String` contains someone's name or the complete text of *Romeo and Juliet*, the machine copies only a 4-byte reference (table 3.1). In other words, the two invocations should take about the same amount of time.

Let's look at a few finer points of Java's parameter passing. When you're calling across JVMs or using EJB, you're passing-by-value. That means that you must make a copy of your argument before you use it. When your argument is an object, you must serialize it. When your value is a primitive, the serialization is no big deal, but when you're dealing with a Shakespearian play, then you have real performance implications. Both the following list and table 3.1 detail the intricacies of pass-by-reference.

- **Java uses pass-by-reference by default** Pass-by-reference, in absence of other concerns, is much faster than pass-by-value.

- **Changes are visible to both method and caller** When using pass-by-reference semantics, changes to objects passed or referenced from method arguments will reflect in the client's view of the objects. Likewise, client changes to a return value object reflect in the service's view, because both reference the same object in memory.

- **The EJB specification requires pass-by-value semantics** Because pass-by-value semantics are required, the client method and the service method work on completely independent copies of the method arguments and the return value.

- **Calls between JVMs are by-value and automatic** When the client and service run in two different virtual machines, this copying happens implicitly as the client stub serializes the method arguments and transports them to the target virtual machine. There, the service's container deserializes the arguments, creating new objects, and passes them to the service method. The same holds true for the return path and the method result.

Table 3.1 When you pass objects by reference, the entire text of *Romeo and Juliet* is passed in the same amount of time as the name "Mercutio." EJB mandates pass-by-value, which is much slower, but EJB2 allows local interfaces, which pass by reference.

Object type	Passed by	Notes
Plain Java objects, same JVM	Reference	The size of arguments is irrelevant to performance.
Plain Java across JVM	Value	The Java objects are copied transparently by Java.
EJB	Value	EJB mandates pass-by-value, since EJB can be remote.
EJB local interfaces	Reference	Pass-by-reference for local interfaces is a performance optimization. Local interfaces pass-by-reference in the same JVM.

With these tidbits in mind, consider what we can accomplish with local interfaces. When the EJB client and the target service run in the same virtual machine, the container can optimize the invocation. Technically, the container should clone the arguments and return value to maintain the pass-by-value semantics, but in our experience this is not often the case. Many application servers implement the local optimizations with pass-by-reference semantics by default. As long as a bean client and implementation don't depend on having exclusive access to an object and its state, passing-by-reference doesn't hurt anything. However, application developers should anticipate an extra degree of added performance overhead when moving an EJB client outside the container's virtual machine.

Given many containers' optimizations, the EJB implementation of our name vs. Shakespearean play example may perform comparably to the local implementation. In other words, invocations with one argument may take nearly the same amount of time as with the other. When the client moves to a separate container from the deployed EJB and pass-by-value semantics becomes inevitable, invoking a method with the full text of *Romeo and Juliet* will take far longer than passing a 20-character name. The invocation time may depend on numerous factors: the protocol, the network bandwidth, the network speed, the distance, or the status— open/closed—of the network cable in the door.

3.2 Designing the application tier

When we model the application tier or design an application's business logic implementation, our design approaches tend to fall into one of two categories. One approach starts with the use cases and works backward (figure 3.1). We'll call this "service-driven." The other centers heavily on the domain objects. We'll refer to this approach as "domain-driven" (figure 3.2).

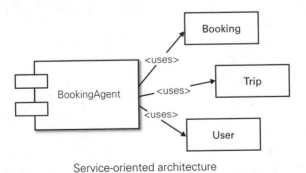

Service-oriented architecture

Figure 3.1 **Service-oriented interfaces start from a use case and work back. The majority of the business logic resides in the service classes. The domain objects are lightweight mere data place holders.**

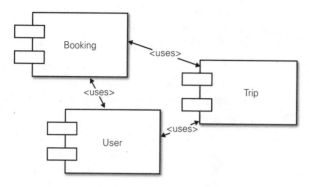

Domain-oriented architecture

Figure 3.2   Domain-oriented architecture uses the objects of a business domain as the building blocks of the system. Entity beans embrace a domain-oriented design, but fine-grained access to the model usually harms performance. Modern designs hide the fine-grained objects of a domain behind a facade.

In a purely service-driven design, most business logic resides in the service classes. The domain objects—objects that model entities in the application's domain— are relatively lightweight, limited mostly to simple data holders. The service methods correspond closely to the use cases, each method manipulating the domain objects and performing a specific task. When a new use case requirement comes along, you simply implement another method in the service. For example, in a trip-booking application, you might have a Booking domain object to represent a trip booking and a BookingAgent service to manage the actual business logic.

A purely domain-driven approach lays more responsibility on the domain objects, coupling function with data. The domain-oriented approach moves function to objects in the know. For example, a Trip object, representing one of many possible trips that can be booked, most likely knows best what to charge. Rather than hard coding the pricing logic for each trip type into a BookingAgent, the Booking object simply asks its Trip object how much to charge the client.

Though the service-oriented approach seems more straightforward in the context of simple domain models, the object-oriented nature of the domain-driven approach scales in a maintainable manner when applied to more complicated domains (figure 3.2). The key here is that, as in object-oriented programming in general, the domain-driven approach factors logical complexity into the object model. Rather than confusing the business logic with a single dimensional nest of if-then-else blocks, the domain-driven approach relies on the objects to delegate responsibility to the most natural locations.

3.2.1 *Looking back on entity beans*

The original entity bean conception (EJB 1.0-1.1) wholly embraced a purely domain-oriented design. At the time of those earlier specifications, the EJB community advocated entity beans as an indispensable member of the architecture.

What could be better? Imagine a design consisting purely of your domain objects, modeled using heavyweight, distributed, pluggable components, and likely tied to the underlying persistent store. Continuing our example, Trip beans talk to Booking beans, which talk to User beans, none of which cares whether the sibling component lives in the same virtual machine, in a separate process, or in a separate machine all together. If the Booking bean starts running low on resources, we can deploy Booking to more machines. The client meanwhile orchestrates this ubiquitously distributed domain layer with the flexibility you'd expect from an object-oriented system.

Unfortunately, reality sets in. We see past the vendor brochures' glossy veneers. Yes, the application server hides the mechanical differences between local and remote invocations quite well, but abstracting the performance and stability issues associated with remote communication is another story altogether.

In addition, early entity bean developers following the distributed domain model fell subject to another pitfall. With the fine-grained flexibility of the methods in the domain model often came numerous, fine-grained queries to the persistent store. These queries were flat and expensive for the most part, making more round trips and pulling back more data than needed, neglecting such simple tools as database joins. Many entity bean early adopters learned these interface lessons as we did—the hard way.

3.2.2 *Questioning EJB local interfaces*

The EJB 2.0 specification introduced the concept of separate local and remote interfaces. The performance issues associated with entity beans' fine-grained nature contributed primarily to this addition. The EJB API already contained EJBHome and EJBObject, representing the base home and client interfaces for EJB, respectively. The extension added local versions of the two interfaces, EJBLocalHome and EJBLocalObject, solidifying the legacy interfaces as implicitly remote.

The decision to add separate local interfaces did not come easily, and rightfully so. For example, during the specification's development, the specification team solved problems with entity beans by using dependent objects, the idea being that lighter, dependent objects for which the container could maintain cardinality relationships would back the heavyweight entity bean components. However, once the team took into account the complications and reusage roadblocks, they abandoned dependent objects and solved the entity bean problem in a more general sense with local interfaces.

Local interfaces empower developers to create fine-grained EJB components—entity beans, in particular—and prevent clients from misusing these same components by trying to access them remotely. At the same time, explicitly limiting component access to a single VM allows container implementers more flexibility, specifically enabling the EJB container to manage entity bean relationships and improve query performance.

This would be fine except that we've traded in our utopian distributed domain model in favor of a local model, negating many of the features provided by entity beans. Now we must tuck our entity bean domain model away behind a coarse-grained, service-oriented remote interface, such as a session bean. In that case, features such as the component model, transactions and security become redundant, as we discussed in chapter 2, section 2.5. If our domain model must be locally restricted, we might as well go with a lighter-weight, easier-to-use persistence framework and dodge the restrictions imposed on entity beans by their legacy obligations—that is, by their obligations to their original design—and their heavyweight component-oriented nature. (See chapter 9 for alternative persistence frameworks.)

3.3 *Antipattern: Local & Remote Interfaces Simultaneously*

Every once in a while, we'll see a miracle pattern solution posted to a J2EE patterns list, claiming to have solved the *problem* with separate remote and local interfaces. The posting designer usually outlines an elaborate interface hack that enables EJB developers to swap local and remote EJB interfaces without affecting the bean's implementation or the client code.

Figure 3.3 shows the implementation of the pattern, which usually goes something like this: The developer creates a non-EJB business interface. The bean's local and remote EJB interfaces extend both the generic business interface as well as their respective interface from the EJB API. The developer codes the EJB client to the generic interface. After swapping out the local and remote versions of the EJB interfaces, the only task that remains is a simple tweaking of the deployment descriptor.

Sounds good in theory but in practice, myriad semantic and design-related issues rear their ugly heads. You can read about many of these issues in the timeless paper from Sun Research called *A Note on Distributed Computing* (http://research.sun.com/techrep/1994/abstract-29.html). The specification designers

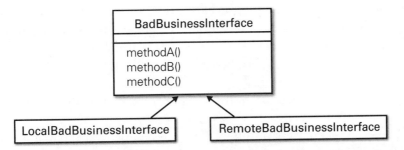

Figure 3.3 This attempt to gain the flexibility of both local and remote interfaces falls flat. This design has tactical problems, including increased overhead for all objects. The bigger trap lies here: To handle the performance implications, you need to stay aware of how an object is deployed. You should treat remote objects differently than local ones.

chose to separate local and remote interfaces, not because they had to do so, but because they wanted to do so. In the next two sections, we'll talk about some of the reasons why the specification designers made that decision.

3.3.1 *Combined interfaces muddle exception management*

The exceptions thrown by the EJB methods present both semantic and design issues. With Java inheritance (actually object-oriented inheritance in general), a subclass can only weaken the contract imposed by the superclass. For example, if a superclass method throws RemoteException, the subclass implementation of that method may choose to not throw RemoteException, such as in listing 3.1. However it cannot throw another type of checked exception—that is, a checked exception that does not inherit from RemoteException.

Listing 3.1 BadBusinessInterface exposes remote and local versions of the same interface

```
public interface BadBusinessInterface {
    public void methodA() throws java.rmi.RemoteException;
    public void methodB() throws java.rmi.RemoteException;
    public void methodC() throws java.rmi.RemoteException;
}

public interface LocalBadBusinessInterface
    extends BadBusinessInterface, javax.ejb.EJBLocalObject {
}

public interface RemoteBadBusinessInterface
    extends BadBusinessInterface, javax.ejb.EJBObject {
}
```

Since all methods in remote EJB interfaces are required to throw `RemoteException`, to get our antipattern code to compile, the generic business interface methods must throw at minimum `RemoteException` as well, even though the local implementation will never use it as shown in listing 3.1. Likewise, the client bound to the generic interface must deal with the complications of handling and recovering from `RemoteExceptions`–whether or not it needs to—simply because the potential exists.

The client's implementation suffers from these same issues. When it comes to exceptional conditions, local and remote invocations are two different animals. In the local context, identifying and recovering from failures comes easily. In a distributed setting, determining when and what failures have occurred and how to get the system back to a consistent state is a mixed bag. Did the remote system fail? Did the network go down? Did the method execute on the remote system and fail on the way back, or did the request not make it there at all? Should the client throw its hands up and croak, or should it sit around until the remote system comes back up? Will it even help to reattempt the request? The problems with exceptions only scratch the surface. Next, we discuss performance—a much more serious concern.

3.3.2 *Combined interfaces hurt performance*

Worse, when combining local and remote interfaces, you have performance implications. Though not explicitly declared in the interface, clients of local and remote interfaces have certain expectations. Local clients depend on consistent performance and immediate responses. Remote clients, on the other hand, are more complicated and must anticipate such issues as latency and network congestion. An invocation taking longer than expected should not drag the system to its knees. Also, if performance drives the decision to support both local and remote interfaces, explicitly implementing the local EJB interfaces is not necessary. Even though the bean supports a remote interface, many containers detect that a client and bean live in the same virtual machine, and they optimize accordingly. (Of course, if you're developing an EJB that's intended to be truly portable, you can't make this assumption.)

On a similar note, the local-interface performance optimization creates other problems. Memory issues directly affect the implementation of the enterprise beans. Local invocations share the same memory space. The bean's implementation creates defensive copies for variables. On the other hand, since different copies of the objects exist on the local and remote machines, remote invocations implicitly defend. If a bean implementation supported both local and remote interfaces, the implementation would have to err on the side of caution, always creating defensive copies of shared objects. When accessed through the remote interface, redundant copies would be made. Let's take a look at a few variations of this antipattern.

3.3.3 *Mini-antipattern: Ubiquitous Distribution*

When faced with the decision between local and remote interfaces, leaving the door open by designing every interface to be accessed remotely may seem a logical conclusion. Then, you can run the entire system locally, breaking it out across multiple boxes at arbitrary points as needed. You can rely on the container to recognize interactions within the same machine and optimize accordingly.

In doing so, you severely limit the flexibility of your interfaces, overcomplicate the implementation of the client code and, all in all, take on monster responsibilities and headaches to match. Given that any interface may be or may not be accessed remotely, you must always program to the distributed case.

Your interfaces must guarantee a degree of consistency after a failure. Is the method idempotent—in other words, will the result be the same no matter how many times you invoke the method? Is it okay to retry a request after a failure? If not, should the client throw up and die? Is there any state that needs to be cleaned up? In a remote context, a designer must anticipate all these issues in the interface design and developers must code for them in the client. On the other hand, while local interfaces still need to manage exceptions, they need not shoulder any of these complications, so exception management can be simplified.

Next, you must face the issue of performance and method granularity. Given the cost of remote invocations, remote interface methods must be combined and their frequency limited as much as possible. This combination leads to a lack of flexibility in the interface and duplication across the method implementations as requirements for slightly different functionalities arise. By forcing an interface to handle distribution, the application designer inevitably sacrifices both robustness and ease of maintenance for the sake of performance.

3.3.4 *Mini-antipattern: Transparent Distribution*

While we're building all components of our application for possible distribution, designing our system with the coarse-grained, service-driven approach, we might as well see how the other half lives. If method granularity weren't an issue in distributed performance, would our purely distributed domain model be viable? Unfortunately, the answer is, "No."

A recurring theme in distributed system design is that state is evil. Our distributed domain model is an object-oriented design. By definition, objects have state and identity. If we modify the state of a domain component on another box, we've essentially signed on with that instance for the duration of our transaction. We can't go to another box, because the component deployed there will not necessarily reflect the state change we just made. If the box hosting my component goes down, we can't just fail over to another deployment. One alternative is to replicate the component's state to a backup deployment. In the event that one component fails, our client fails over to the duplicate on another box. Replication, however, comes with its own myriad issues including, but not limited to, bad performance—we must effectively duplicate the component's state in its entirety, possibly over the wire or to a database. Another issue concerns synchronization. In the event of a fail-over, how can we as a client definitively determine where the failed component's state left off, or even that of the backup deployment?

These are just a taste of the issues associated with distributed state. Like other distributed computing concerns, the application server can abstract away and hide some of these issues, but, like the distributed performance concerns, there are limits to this abstraction.

3.3.5 Solution: Achieving equilibrium

As the massive wave approaches, my speed builds. Just like my instructor told me, I press the front of my board to accelerate it down the concave surface of the front of the wave. I keep my balance as I get up to my knees, but the sunscreen that's all over the board mixes with the wax to make a slippery interface between me and the board. I slip off and the waves rake me across the reef.

Like the body and surfboard in Hawaii, you need to think about how the parts will fit together before you implement your system. In Hawaii, sunscreen and board wax protect bodies and boards from the elements; they just don't work together. In your system, you want a seamless bridge that meets the needs of both sides of an interface. Often, when you're defining an interface between client and server, the crucial points are that, for the purposes of designing the remote interactions, state should be avoided where possible and remote interfaces should be sufficiently coarse-grained. In designing an EJB-based architecture, the safest approach is to find a balance and draw a clear line between an object-oriented local domain model and a procedural remote service layer. Essentially, we work hard to get the best of both worlds. Our preferred approach includes implementing as much of the functionality as possible in the domain model. How we map the domain layer to the persistent store (entity beans, plain Java objects, or another persistence framework) is less important than the purity of the interface: you should be able to easily and independently understand, extend, and test the layer's functionality. To enable remote access, we then wrap our domain layer with a thin service layer. In the EJB context, the service layer may be implemented as a Session Façade, a common EJB design pattern we'll discuss momentarily. The service layer provides a coarse-grained, stateless view of the underlying domain model. Where the service methods may correspond closely to the required use cases, the functionality in the model is fine grained by comparison and reusable across multiple use cases.

The most robust, flexible (however slowly performing) design enables the client to access the domain model directly. A thin service layer, the next best thing when it comes to flexibility, essentially serves as an isolated extension of the client and reduces the frequency of network traffic. As code duplication in the service layer starts to crop up, simply refactor the redundant logic into the domain model where the service methods can build off of it.

3.3.6 *Knowing when to distribute*

Spreading your application heterogeneously across multiple nodes hurts performance and complicates your application, not to mention its deployment and management. To some, the moral of this story is: avoid distribution at all costs, trading your left thumb if you have to. After all, if the network is the computer, it's a wonky, crashy computer that takes forever to get anything done. Dodging distribution increases performance and simplifies development, letting the developer concentrate on the real problems at hand, meeting the customer's requirements.

Antidistribution zealotry aside, sometimes having a remote boundary makes sense. For example, distributing between the client and server is definitely acceptable, as figure 3.4 illustrates. In a typical client/server environment, where the client and server applications execute on physically different machines, separating the two with a Session Façade makes sense. The separation between a web server and application server falls into this category.

Putting a clean separation between the web interface and the business logic can also enable a team to easily plug in new clients including thick, stand-alone applications or even other middleware applications, which brings us to a second reason to distribute: integration. Remotely communicating with pre-existing third-party components makes sense, whether it's an off-the-shelf component or one that you developed in-house. Databases fit into this category, SQL being the coarse-grained remote interface, as do message-oriented middleware systems.

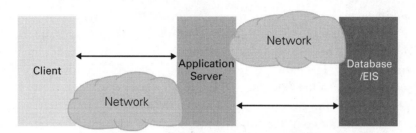

Figure 3.4   Distribution is expensive, so you've got to make sure that each distribution step has value. In this classic three-tier scenario, distributing the client separates the view and simplifies deployment, and separating the application and resource tiers makes it easier to manage the logistics of integrating legacy applications.

Figure 3.4 shows a reasonable architecture. We've got strong reasons for each of these distribution decisions. Sun provides some guidelines for classic J2EE deployment tiers at java.sun.com, but this good advice may be overkill in some cases.

We've talked about some general issues that help you define interfaces between components. In the next part of the chapter, we begin to talk about how interfaces within a logical tier fit together.

3.4 *Antipattern: Customers in the Kitchen*

You'd rarely, if ever, see a restaurant that lets its customers into the kitchen. They would distract the cooks, interfere with the cooking process, and clog all of the hallways and doors throughout the kitchen. But even with the warnings against it, clients frequently access entity beans directly. In this antipattern, I'll discuss the interface issues related to this practice. In chapter 7 we'll look at more of the performance implications.

Remote performance and stability issues aside, other reasons exist for clients to not access entity beans directly. We once joined a hastily constructed JSP/EJB project. To save time, the application designer skipped the Session Façade and coded direct access to the entity beans in the Java Server Pages (JSP). The EJB and web containers ran together, alleviating remote performance concerns.

The application ran more than acceptably despite minor shortcomings in its maintainability, until the team upgraded to a later version of the application server. Suddenly, the system testing team started complaining of excessive performance problems (beyond that of JSP compilations). Upon examination, the heavier the page that accessed the database, the slower it ran. Many page response times ran in minutes.

Contrary to our initial hypothesis, remote calls did not degrade the performance (not those between the JSPs and entity beans anyway). The vendor had not started separating the web and EJB containers into different class loaders or virtual machines. The culprit here was transactions. The EJB specification requires containers to always invoke `ejbLoad()` on entity beans at the beginning of transactions and `ejbStore()` at the end of transactions. This requirement ensures that the database and container's views of the data state are synchronized.

In the application's current design, the JSP invoked the entity bean accessors and mutators directly. The transaction attribute for these entity bean methods was set to `Required`. This transaction attribute is defined as follows: "If a client invokes a method in the context of a running transaction, the EJB method inherits that transaction. If the client is not running a transaction, the container starts and commits a new transaction for the duration of the method invocation." This means that, for each call on a getter method, the container started a new transaction, loaded the data for that field from the database, and committed the transaction. For each call to a setter, the container at a minimum started a new transaction, updated the field in the database, and committed the transaction.

It got worse. Additionally, the database transaction's atomicity had field granularity. Because rows were modified one field at a time, independent requests could query or update the same row concurrently, resulting in collisions and poor performance. Why the sudden performance degradation? Between the old and new versions of the application server, the vendor modified the default caching strategy.

In the old version, the vendor configured the server to have exclusive access to the database by default. The container knew it was the only application capable of modifying the database. In effect, there were no cluster and no external applications that wrote to the database. What this means is that the container could perform caching that would not otherwise be possible. The container did not have to make a trip back to the database (by calling `ejbLoad()`) if the application did not modify the data. Additionally, the container could batch updates, resulting in fewer calls.

In the new version, the vendor's default changed to what it called database synchronization, undoubtedly to make cluster setups smoother. The new strategy relied on the underlying data store to handle concurrent access to data, the side effect being that the container called `ejbLoad()` and `ejbStore()` for each and every transaction.

3.4.1 *Nudging the diners toward the door*

As a temporary fix, we simply reconfigured the beans so that the container knew it had exclusive access to the database. The current architecture had one application server (it was a big box) with manual failover to a completely different location with a separate database. Our fix, however, simply put functional testing back on track, yet did not solve the underlying problems, even in the short term. The following difficulties remain:

1   The transaction granularity was still too fine. The transactions started and committed each time the application read or wrote a single field; there may as well have been no transactions at all. Independent requests within the database modified the same rows concurrently and one operation could see another's partial updates. The implications of this issue are dependent on the nature of the application, the operations, and the data model.

2   More importantly, the fix only worked for the current architecture. If the client added another application that modified the same data or clusters the current application, the exclusive caching strategy would no longer be an option. Each transaction would need to synchronize at the database each time to prevent stale data and update collisions, resulting in nasty performance.

The simple solution to this second problem would be to manually start and commit JTA (Java Transaction API) transactions that surround the entity bean access code; however, given that the client application is implemented using JSP, this would be easier said then done. The JSP developer needs to take care that a transaction starts and commits or rolls back for each logic flow through the page, accounting for redirects, includes, and exceptions. Otherwise transactions may not get started or may be left hanging, in which case the results will be unpredictable at best. A hanging transaction may even throw an exception when the current thread services the next client. In a nutshell, embedding transaction logic into JSP plasters on a new level of complexity and potential fragility that a web developer typically doesn't have to deal with. We'll discuss a more robust approach in a moment, the Session Façade pattern.

Last, business logic directly accessing entity beans embedded in JSP scriptlets is a unit testing nightmare and a surefire recipe for disaster. It's simply too tough to automate. The only testing possible in this scenario is system testing, in which case the developer must manually click through and test each page or use a tool capable of testing web applications. Developers tire quickly of monotonous, repetitive tests and tend to neglect them. Tools that test the web application automatically must be modified themselves each time the interface changes, whether or not the change is pertinent to the test's goal. Additionally, GUI design changes run the risk of breaking working code. Before you know it, the quick solution turns into an intertwined nest of if-then-else statements and JSP includes, and you have a maintenance nightmare on your hands.

A cleaner design is the Model-View-Controller (MVC) pattern shown in JSP and the controller logic uses servlets and plainer Java. The view JSPs contain the minimal logic necessary to query the model classes and generate HTML pages that present the information and—as required—post requests to the controllers. In this design, you can easily unit test the model and controller business logic automatically. Discussion of MVC falls out of the scope of EJB; however, the Jakarta Struts project is a popular open source framework based around the pattern.

The designer can further abstract the entity bean persistence layer in such a way that the business logic code can run against stubbed test classes rather than actual entity beans. In this case, unit tests can run without an EJB container and consequently without the overhead of running an application server.

In the past, we've passed over this design suggestion. Instead, we've favored lighter weight persistence mechanisms such as JDO or even a custom persistence framework instead of entity beans. The benefits here are that the code is easy to test outside an application server and, perhaps even more importantly, reusable outside a J2EE environment. This can be a real boon for productivity as it reduces testing times and makes your code available for use in stand-alone J2SE applications. See chapter 8 for details on implementing alternative persistence layers.

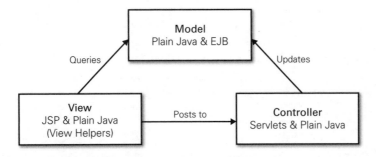

Figure 3.5 Model-view-controller simplifies interfaces by delegating the responsibility for business logic, user interface, and data marshaling to different components. Each view queries the model independently, and all updates to the model go through the controller, yielding an application that's easier to build and maintain.

3.4.2 *Solution: Funnel the customers through a waiter*

Of course, modern restaurants funnel orders and complaints to the kitchen through a waiter. A Session Façade fills that role for us, providing a thin (hence façade), coarse-grained layer over your fine-grained, in-process classes. You use Session Façades primarily for remote invocations; they are a kind of gateway or adaptor from remote clients to the fine-grained local methods.

Going back to our trip booking service example, take the client in figure 3.6 that accesses trip booking information. It's not practical for a remote client to request each field of a Booking instance individually, making multiple round trips to the server. Alternatively, the client accesses a method in the Session Façade and completes its work in a single trip. Such methods are typically referred to as bulk accessors. Likewise, methods that group data modifications are referred to as bulk mutators.

Session Façade interfaces should be grouped to reflect use cases that are similar to one another. As the implementation for the façade method is typically simple, catering to many use cases in a single façade implementation is not usually a maintainability issue. However, having too many Session Façades does create questions about maintenance. If you have too many façades, the client will spend too much time and effort dealing with lookups and home interfaces. In general, your application should have few façades. One is often sufficient. Don't treat this rule as an absolute. Your façades are simply stateless libraries, and you (the library developer) and your customers (the library clients) need to be able to navigate and organize them efficiently. Just understand that each façade has associated overhead, and plan them wisely.

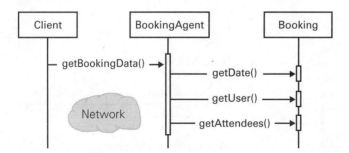

Figure 3.6   This customer gets booking data through the booking agent. The booking agent serves as a Session Façade. The façade tends to implement individual use cases, and serves as the point of access to the objects in the model. From an interface standpoint, it simplifies our implementation, and isolates the client from the business model.

The methods in a Session Façade should not contain domain logic. This includes data validation. Such logic should be incorporated into the domain layer where it can be reused. As with all object-oriented development, you should try to separate and encapsulate concerns. Separation of concerns is one of the philosophies that drove development of JSP. A designer can create JSP in a scripting language with little support from a dedicated programmer. In our case, we want to separate and encapsulate all logic pertaining to remote access in the Session Façade implementation and no more.

I typically implement the Session Façade using a stateless session bean. If we find ourselves needing to maintain some client-specific state, we usually try our damnedest to refactor some logic to the client side and simply pass the state back to the server each time. As it can get monotonous passing the same data to the server over and over with each method call, we like to abstract out these state arguments as part of a Business Delegate, a design pattern we'll discuss shortly.

Choosing a stateless over a stateful implementation is more about scalability than performance. Passing the state back and forth may have overhead, but storing state in the server has substantially finite limitations. First, you have memory. For thousands of concurrent users, the server must maintain thousands of instances of the state information until the user explicitly leaves or their session times out in which case the server automatically destroys the state (in our case a stateful session bean instance).

Second, you have failover. If you want to support failover with stateful session beans, the server has to replicate the state to a backup server. In this case the stateful session bean instance must be serialized and transferred to another server at the end of each invocation. The client might as well provide the state itself each time, especially if the client is on the same network as the cluster. With a stateless session bean, the client holds on to the state information and can simply fail over to any other machine in the cluster.

3.4.3 Using Data Transfer Objects

The Data Transfer Object (DTO) pattern often comes in handy in the development of Session Façades. Actually, in our trip booking service example, the `BookingAgent.getBookingData()` method returns a booking data transfer object (listing 3.2).

A DTO is nothing more than a plain JavaBean or lightweight data holder. The implementation consists of a Java object, the required fields, and getters and setters (if the object is mutable) to access the fields.

Listing 3.2   BookingData.java is a data transfer object, not a domain object

```java
package bitterejb;

import java.util.*;

/**
 * Booking data transfer object. Immutable.
 */
public class BookingData implements java.io.Serializable {

        private final long date; // truly immutable
        private final String user;
        private int attendees;

        /**
         * Constructs a new Booking data transfer object.
         */
        public BookingData(Date date, String user,
                int attendees) {
           this.date = date.getTime();
           this.user = user;
           this.attendees = attendees;
        }

        /**
         * Gets the date of the booking.
         * @return A Date instance.
         */
        public Date getDate() {
           return new Date(this.date);
        }

        /**
         * Gets the user that booked the trip.
         * @return The user's ID.
         */
        public String getUser() {
           return this.user;
        }

        /**
         * Gets the number of attendees for this trip
         * booking.
         */
        public int getAttendees() {
           return this.attendees;
        }

}
```

Though they may present the same data, DTOs are typically separate from domain objects. This mostly has to do with the object relationships. It may not be desirable or possible from a performance standpoint to return your entire domain object map. Also, your domain implementation may contain logic only pertinent to the server environment such as code for accessing external services such as databases or other applications. These services may not even be physically visible to the client. Also, the client may only be interested in a subset of the data, in which case having a separate DTO implementation comes in handy.

3.5 *Antipattern: Custom DTOs*

In large applications with many clients and/or use cases, the clients often require varying subsets of the application data. Continuing our example of a trip-booking agency, figure 3.7 shows applications A and B accessing our middleware. As illustrated by the class diagram, client A queries user information and accesses the user's trip bookings. Client B looks up trip types and their corresponding bookings.

The DTOs for client A consist of a user DTO and a booking DTO. The user DTO has a getter for a collection of booking DTOs while the booking DTO has the inverted getter for the user DTO. The DTOs for client B follow a similar pattern supplanting the user with a trip.

Note that the two use cases require two variations on the booking DTO. This exemplifies the Custom DTO pattern. In the Custom DTO pattern, the designer implements custom DTOs to fit the requirements of the use case. In the case of client A, the booking DTO contains a reference to the DTO for the user that booked the trip. To fill client B's requirements, the booking DTO for client B contains a

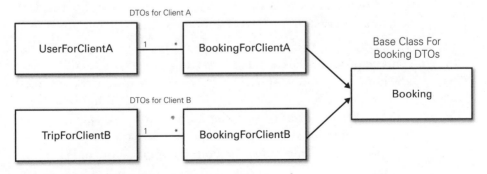

Figure 3.7   Client A and Client B use different DTOs. This approach severely inhibits the reuse of code between client applications, even within the same application. Second, it requires dual maintenance as a single change in the interface can hit all DTOs.

reference to a trip type DTO containing trip information. A single booking DTO base class contains the methods common to the booking DTO implementations, and the client-specific DTOs contains the client-specific references that make up the custom DTO map. This approach has many problems.

- **This approach inhibits code reuse** between client applications (or even within the same application if multiple use cases use custom maps). Client A must take care to code as much logic as possible to the booking DTO base class, otherwise the logic will be incompatible with client B's own version of the booking DTO and thus unusable.

- **The approach requires duplicated relationship logic**   What happens when client A's requirements change such that it needs to look up the trip information for a particular booking? Client A can't reuse client B's booking DTO implementation because client A needs the reverse reference back to the DTO for the user that booked the trip. The developer has to duplicate B's trip relationship logic for client A. Additionally, this change requires a change and redeployment for both the server and the client application. In the event the clients A and B could share DTO implementations, the developer creates fragile dependences and runs the risk that changes in client A or B's requirements could require duplication or heavy refactoring of the blocks of code dependent on the common DTO.

   One alternative is for client A to take the trip's unique identifier (if it's even available) from the booking DTO and make another query to the server for the trip DTO. This strikes me as messy and inconsistent, especially considering that the server knows how to create trip DTOs and provides the implementation of the booking DTO to the client. Having the client call a getter to follow an object relationship in one case and perform an entirely separate query to the server in another similar operation seems counterintuitive from a client perspective.

- **This approach takes a lot of up-front guesswork**   The developer must decide at design time how the clients will typically use the provided services. For example client A realizes that it only needs user information 90% of the time and that the added booking information hurts performance. Modifying the code so that client A re-queries the server for booking information can prove to be a big ordeal for both the application and client developers.

3.5.1 *Solution: Refactor to preserve flexibility*

The solution is simple. Refactor the logic that requeries the server and fulfills the DTO relationships into the DTO itself and implement a lazy-loading scheme. For example, when client A now queries user information, client A only gets user DTOs. When A needs booking information, client A simply calls `user.get-Bookings()` and gets back a collection of booking DTOs. Behind the scenes, the user DTO implementation checks to see if it already has the booking information. If not, the user DTO implementation queries the server for the booking DTOs and returns them to the client (listing 3.3).

Clients A and B can use the same generic booking DTO implementation. Should client B ever need access to user information from a booking instance, client B simply calls the getter. In the meantime, client B need not incur the overhead of downloading the unnecessary information.

Listing 3.3 UserData.java is refactored to add flexibility and preserve reuse

```java
public class UserData implements java.io.    Serializable {

    . . .

    // bookings for this user.
    private Collection bookings = null;

    /**
     * Gets bookings for this user.
     * @return Collection of BookingDatas.
     */
    public synchronized Collection getBookings()
            throws RemoteException {
        if (bookings == null) {
            // 'server' is the remote stub with the
            // query methods.
            bookings = server.getBookings(this.getId());

            // we must set the inverse relationship.
            Iterator i = bookings.iterator();
            while (i.hasNext())
                ((BookingData) i.next()).setUser(this);
        }
        return bookings;
    }

}
```

The real beauty of this implementation shines through its three-tiers of performance configuration options:

1 **Lazy loading**   The server can simply return the user DTO to the client. In the event the client needs booking information for a user, it simply calls the accessor and the user DTO transparently queries the server.

2 **Preloading**   If client A always needs the booking information, the service method that returns the user DTOs can call the `user.getBookings()` method before it returns the user DTO. This effectively causes the user DTO to query for the booking DTOs and cache them while still in the application server. As the call runs in the server, the container can optimize it as if it's a local invocation saving the client the cost of the round trip. This can also be useful if there's a chance the data can become stale and the relationship should be fulfilled within a single transaction.

3 **The old-fashioned way**   If preloading results in too many queries and hurts performance, the server implementation can resort to executing a single query with a join and building the DTO map manually. This modification does not affect the client as the DTO implementation stays the same.

You may choose to implement your lazy loading as we did in the code example, having a different method for each type of query you will run. We took a different approach on a recent project. Using a JDO-like persistence tool, we implemented a single remote data access service that took an arbitrary query and returned a collection of DTOs. The client passes in an identifier for a particular query along with the query arguments and the service returns the results in a collection. The application manages security per query and thus has a comparable model to that of the EJB architecture, which manages access at method granularity.

In implementing this solution there are a couple of traps to watch out for, one of which we account for in the previous code example. Take care to set the inverse of many-to-one relationships. When you don't do this, tools that recursively traverse the object hierarchy will overflow the stack, as each call to the relationship method will requery the server, returning a new and different (reference-wise) instance.

Second, if there's a chance your relationship can be `null`, avoid hitting the server each and every time, by differentiating between not-yet-loaded and `null`. In our personal implementation, the data access service always returns a collection of objects. In the case of a one-to-many relationship, you will always get an empty collection rather than `null`. In the case of a reference to a single object, we always store the collection (which will be empty when you should return `null` and contain a single object otherwise). In the getter method for that relationship, we return either the single object or `null` if the collection is empty.

Lastly, we've never personally run into a many-to-many relationship when implementing this pattern. Should you find one, we'd advise implementing it the old-fashioned way (option #3), since the alternative lazy-loading approach would be highly involved, bug prone, and most likely inefficient.

3.6 Summary

In this chapter, we identified the importance of interface design and discussed the effect of interface design on an application's performance, scalability, and reliability. We also considered patterns for maximizing your application's maintainability and robustness in the face of distribution fallacies. We looked at both the antipatterns related to local and distributed interfaces and the perils of DTO maps. And we refactored solutions that balanced the concerns of local and remote interfaces, and we developed a flexible solution.

In the next chapters, we'll dive into session beans. We'll look at the best times to use session beans, and we'll consider the types of issues that should be considered when designing an effective session bean. You'll see how to manage a transaction effectively and how to avoid common mistakes.

3.7 *Antipatterns in this chapter*

This section covers the Local and Remote Interfaces Simultaneously, Customers in the Kitchen, and Custom DTOs antipatterns.

LOCAL AND REMOTE INTERFACES SIMULTANEOUSLY

DESCRIPTION
> Many developers try to implement an interface that supports both local and remote interfaces.

MOST FREQUENT SCALE
> Application

REFACTORED SOLUTION NAME
> Local *or* remote interfaces, but not both

REFACTORED SOLUTION TYPE
> Software

REFACTORED SOLUTION DESCRIPTION
> Local and remote interfaces have dramatically different requirements, in terms of performance and exceptions.

ANECDOTAL EVIDENCE
> "That's cute, but I don't know if it will work." "What do I do if a local framework throws a distributed exception?"

SYMPTOMS, CONSEQUENCES
> Exception management becomes muddied, and performance is weak.

CUSTOMERS IN THE KITCHEN

DESCRIPTION
Accessing fine-grained objects directly can complicate the model.

MOST FREQUENT SCALE
Application

REFACTORED SOLUTION NAME
Session Façade

REFACTORED SOLUTION TYPE
Software

REFACTORED SOLUTION DESCRIPTION
Use a Session Façade to build a coarse-grained interface.

ANECDOTAL EVIDENCE
"Does my business logic really have to worry about that?"

SYMPTOMS, CONSEQUENCES
Changes in one layer have rippling effects on the model.

CUSTOM DTOS

DESCRIPTION
Building custom DTOs for every menial task leads to additional coding and maintenance.

MOST FREQUENT SCALE
Application

REFACTORED SOLUTION NAME
Refactor

REFACTORED SOLUTION TYPE
Software

REFACTORED SOLUTION DESCRIPTION
Build an architecture that will accept more general DTOs. Reduce coupling by building additional responsibilities into the DTO itself, using the techniques described in section 3.5.1.

ANECDOTAL EVIDENCE
"Does my business logic really have to worry about that?"

SYMPTOMS, CONSEQUENCES
Changes in one layer have rippling effects on the model.

Part 2

Sessions and messages

I*n the Royal Gorge, one of our kayakers spills out of his boat and is swimming. Half of the remaining kayaks go after the swimmer, and the rest go after the boat and paddle. After twenty minutes, the empty boat is pinned against a rock on the north bank, and the swimmer is in an eddy, hanging onto a piece of iron rebar against a cliff on the south bank. With no way to communicate, we set up an elaborate rope system that allows two kayaks to ferry the empty boat to the other side. Unaware, the other kayakers are ferrying the swimmer back to our side of the river. The teams succeed in exacting and demanding tasks, but do not communicate. In the end, we're left no better than when we started: We're still on opposite banks. It takes us another hour and a half to get the boat and kayaker back together, so that we can continue the run.*

This story shows the importance of maintaining effective communication and handling transactions. You can't simply finish an atomic task, however effectively you perform. Each portion of a transaction must succeed or fail based on the rest of the system's state. In these chapters, we address sessions and messages, which manage both transactions and distributed communications.

Chapter 4 deals with the workhorse of EJB, the stateless session bean. Antipatterns in this chapter cover managing large data sets within a session, threading issues, and other session bean concerns. Chapter 5 deals with the often misunderstood stateful session bean. We discuss the best way to manage session state. In chapter 6, we focus on messaging, including message content, the deliverer, and the receiver of JMS messages. The common thread is the management of transactions across a distributed boundary.

Bitter sessions

4

This chapter covers
- An overview for session beans
- Rules for threading session beans
- Traps related to exceptions with sessions
- Problems with large data sets within sessions

I fly down the hill, feeling the wind through the vents in my helmet. The two- and three-foot ledges are rattling my spine to the core. The loose rocks and curves only add to the danger. I am going as fast as I possibly can in these conditions. I don't like to be last but, today, the bikers ahead of me are simply better, with superior conditioning and skill. I surrender to prudence and slow down. I concentrate on biking within my abilities and keeping myself in one piece. Finally, I turn the corner toward the last hill that will take me back to the safety of my car. The backs of my peers are barely visible thousands of yards below.

As I round the corner, one that I've ridden dozens of times, I anticipate the bumpy terrain and loose rocks. I loosen my shoulders and knees, absorbing the bumps made by the landscape timbers that control erosion. I see a tangle of bikers below me, a massive pileup. Even with my reduced speed, the hill proves too steep. I am about to crash.

Session beans, the first of the three major bean types in the EJB architecture, model services and contain the meat and potatoes of business logic. Session beans effectively extend a client's functionality to the server. Entity beans persist across server restarts, but session beans have a more transient nature. While message-driven beans respond to asynchronous messages, clients invoke session beans synchronously, much as they would a normal Java object. Unlike plain Java objects, however, session beans expose hooks enabling the EJB container to provide implicit, declarative security authentication and authorization, distributed transactions, error handling, scalability and failover, interoperability via web service and CORBA Internet Inter ORB Protocol (IIOP) interfaces, and more.

Session beans come in two flavors: stateful and stateless. A stateful session bean maintains client-specific state across method invocations. When a client invokes a stateless session bean, the EJB container may route the invocation to any available stateless session bean instance. If a client invokes the same method on a stateful session bean twice in a row, the invocation will make it to the same bean instance on the server side. When a client invokes the same method on a stateless session bean twice in a row, the two invocations may not even go to the same physical server, let alone the same bean instance.

When we first started developing with EJBs, given our sincere affection for object-oriented programming, we definitely found the stateful variety to be more intuitive. By the object-oriented definition, objects have state, identity, and behavior. Stateful session beans share these same three characteristics:

- **Stateful session beans have state**   A bean's state stays consistent across multiple method invocations from the same client.

- **Stateful session beans have identity**   A client can compare two stateful session bean stubs for identity equality. In other words, a client can see if the stubs reference the same bean instance on the server side. A client does so by using the `EJBObject.isIdentical()` method. Methods obviously fulfill the third behavioral aspect.

- **Stateful session beans have behavior**   Of course, the primary job of a session bean is to have behavior.

Stateless session beans, on the other hand, share only behavior in common with plain Java objects or stateful session beans. Each time a client invokes a stateless session bean, the bean reverts to its original state. If a client compares two stateless session bean stubs for identity equality, the result will always return true for beans of the same type. These characteristics represent a severe departure from the OOP concepts you've grown to love. Statelessness, however, is both a necessary evil and an unlikely comrade when battling the latency and unpredictability of distributed enterprise systems. Luckily, you have strong shoulders on which to stand. Proven design strategies enable us to factor these concerns into shallow façades whose sole purpose is to make the transformation from service to object-oriented and back again.

4.1 *Threading and synchronization*

The EJB specification imposes a number of restrictions on bean implementations, such as using the threading or core I/O APIs, using AWT, and accessing statics. Some restrictions are hard and fast, and others are just suggested best practices, but reasoning exists for backing them all. Nonetheless, the need to question the validity of each restriction, combined with the behind the curtain nature of EJB architecture, leaves many new EJB developers confused. As a result, posts such as, "My utility class uses a static variable—Is this okay?" are common on EJB interest lists.

Many limitations, the use of synchronization primitives included, stem from the fact that EJB applications must run in a cluster, even when the application server spreads the application across multiple virtual machines. Because the scope of static variables and synchronization primitives ends at the virtual machine, you can't expect a static variable to be unique for the entire application (as you could with plain Jane, single virtual machine Java applications). Nor can you expect the `synchronized` keyword to apply to the whole cluster.

Take the GoF Singleton pattern, for example. The goal of the traditional Java implementation of the pattern is to have only one instance of a given object for the entire application. The implementation accomplishes this by storing the Singleton instance in a static field. Obviously, this implementation breaks down in a distributed environment because, in actuality, you have one instance per class loader and, potentially, multiple instances per virtual machine.

By disallowing static fields, the EJB specification protects developers who may not know better, who may, in fact, use a Java GoF Singleton implementation for an object that really must be a Singleton for the scope of the entire application. A globally unique ID generator is one example. If you rely on a static instance to dole out unique IDs within the scope of the application, you'll find yourself in trouble. Two instances running in different virtual machines may pass out the same ID. On the other hand, where you can tolerate duplication, in a local cache for example, you can safely use static variables and synchronization.

4.1.1 *Antipattern: Tangled Threads*

Many restrictions imposed on EJB implementations revolve around threading—spawning new threads or synchronizing multithreaded access, for example. The EJB container alleviates many concurrency concerns by guaranteeing single-threaded access to beans. Two clients will never share the same bean instance at the same time. If you're using a stateless session bean, you can be sure that, for the duration of the method invocation, you will have sole access to your own dedicated bean instance.

One limitation listed in the specification prohibits spawning new threads. Talk about a bag of traps. Threads spawned by application code compete with the application server's threads for resources. Most application servers finely tune thread counts and priorities to optimize performance and response times. Spawning new threads undermines this effort, limiting your ability to monitor resource usage.

We've witnessed situations where new threads competed so strongly for resources that some of the application server's threads received virtually no CPU time. A bean implementation's custom threads can prevent critical tasks such as updating leases on remote resources and cleaning up expired data. Allocating new threads is an expensive and fragile operation.

Application servers pool and manage threads well, balancing workloads, preventing leaks, and so on. Many application servers depend on thread contexts to implement such services as transactions and security. However, new threads may not inherit these contexts correctly and can lead to undefined results, depending on how the vendor implements them.

Next, the EJB specification restricts use of thread synchronization primitives. Java handles concurrent access by multiple threads to shared resources using mutually exclusively (mutex) locks. Every Java object has an implicitly associated monitor that threads can use as mutex lock. When multiple threads synchronize on an object, each thread must obtain the object's monitor before entering the synchronized code block. The virtual machine ensures that only one thread can hold a lock at time.

J2EE throws a wrench into this thread synchronization model by allowing for multiple virtual machines. An application server may have multiple VM instances in a cluster or even within the same deployment. Each virtual machine will have its own copies of the object and its monitor, meaning that, within the scope of the entire application, multiple threads that should be synchronized will indeed process concurrently.

As an added drawback, a lengthy synchronized block of code can seriously bottleneck an application's scalability if all client threads line up, waiting for synchronous access to a shared resource. Session beans solve this problem for some situations through pooling. If each client can operate on its own instance of a non thread-safe resource, the session bean can create and reuse multiple instances. With stateless session beans, a developer stores an instance of the shared resource in an instance field and gets both pooling (the container will reuse bean instances) and synchronization for free. Examples include synchronizing access to socket connections, pooling socket connections, or generating unique IDs.

The specification also lists read/write static fields as prohibited. This restriction falls under the same umbrella of issues as the prohibition against using the synchronized keyword. Rather than having a single copy of your static field as you would in a classic Java application, you now have one copy per class loader and no clear way to synchronize access to it.

4.1.2 Solution: Standardization to the rescue

Thankfully, you can use the standard APIs provided by the J2EE framework to solve the majority of concurrency-related problems. JMS and message-driven beans simplify asynchronous invocations and executing concurrent processes. You have both the Java Management Extensions (JMX) and EJB 2.1 timer services, which you can use to schedule system- and business logic-related tasks, respectively.

Vendor-specific APIs usually fill in the remaining holes, enabling developers to utilize the application server's thread management infrastructure. In this case, the application designer must weigh the risks of disrupting the server's runtime environment with foreign threads against those of binding the code to a proprietary

API. You can hope that future versions of the J2EE specification standardize on this service but, in the meantime, the aforementioned timer services are certainly a step in the right direction.

In situations where we side with the vendor's framework, we decouple the code as much as possible, minimizing future porting efforts. In the handful of situations where we've introduced new threads into the virtual machine, we've always gone the conservative route, using minimally sized thread pools and documenting and testing exhaustively.

When it comes to keeping data consistent across clusters and multiple virtual machines, transactions are your friends. Among other things, transactions can act as distributed synchronization. Rather than synchronizing access to data stored in a static field, you can offload this responsibility to a database instead. The database will ensure that only one client modifies the data at a time, in effect using transactions as a sort of distributed synchronization block.

As another alternative, some developers host a single instance of an object for the entire cluster and access it through JNDI. I usually avoid this practice, because every instance in the cluster synchronizes on this single instance. Consequently, the machine hosting the instance stands as a single point of failure for the entire application.

4.1.3 *Coping with hung threads*

Time and time again, frozen threads wreak the most havoc and pose the greatest threat to an application's stability. As with almost all thread-related code, tracking down bugs can be a daunting task. Java threads hang for a number of reasons.

First, you have deadlocks. For example, when thread A holds a lock to resource A and waits for resource B, and thread B holds onto resource B and waits for resource A, both threads will wait in an infinite, deadly embrace. As another example, consider an object pool with four objects, where threads A and B each need three objects to complete their task. If thread A holds two objects and thread B holds two objects, the threads will deadlock waiting for a third. When resource pools have set size limits such as this, they should take care to implement timeouts for waiting clients to prevent deadlocks. Most application server database connection pools do exactly this.

A second and more complicated situation occurs during blocked I/O—for example, while creating a connection, opening a stream, or reading from an input stream. Solving these situations is a little less straightforward as some I/O framework implementations ignore timeouts. These situations can take down an application server easily as clients place multiple requests, eventually hanging every thread in the server's thread pool until the application can service no more requests.

In either case, your best comrade in tracking down the cause or causes of a deadlock is the thread dump. You can trigger a thread dump on a running application by hitting Ctrl+Break in a Windows environment or by invoking a "kill -3" against the process in a Unix environment. In both situations, the virtual machine prints a thread dump to standard out (listing 4.1):

Listing 4.1 A sample thread dump

```
"Thread-2" prio=5 tid=0x119570 nid=0x11 waiting for monitor entry
   [f1681000..f168199c]
        at MyClass.run(Hang.java:54)
        - waiting to lock  (a java.lang.Object)
        - locked  (a java.lang.String)

"Thread-3" prio=5 tid=0x118a18 nid=0x10 waiting for monitor entry
   [f1781000..f178199c]
        at MyClass.run(Hang.java:54)
        - waiting to lock  (a java.lang.String)
        - locked  (a java.lang.Object)

"Thread-1" prio=5 tid=0x117660 nid=0xf waiting on condition
   [f1881000..f188199c]
        at java.lang.Thread.sleep(Native Method)
        at Deadlock$3.run(Hang.java:35)
        - locked  (a java.lang.Object)
      at java.lang.Thread.run(Thread.java:536)
```

As you can see in listing 4.1, a thread dump looks a lot like an exception stack trace. The dump shows the call stack for every thread in the VM in addition to what locks the thread holds, where it's holding them, what locks the thread waits for and where it waits for them.

Many times, when a thread hangs due to blocked I/O, you can do little to recover. You can, however, do your best to isolate temperamental operations from other operations and the client. We once worked on an application that accessed a highly secure database. The database required user-based authentication for each request, coupled with other implementation limitations, which forced a new connection for almost every request. (Users ran one or two queries at a time, negating any benefits that might be derived from pooling.)

One day we came in to find that the entire application had inexplicably crashed, with no sign of a pending return, and our team was listed at the top of the company vice president's daily report (not a good place to be—questions are asked, bonuses lost; you get the picture).

When the database in question went down, threads attempting to open the database connection simply hung. Even worse, thanks to thread dumps, we discovered that the crashing code used `java.sql.DriverManager.getConnection(String url)` to open connections. The `DriverManager` implementation synchronizes all access to the class. Once the first thread hung waiting for a connection, any other thread accessing the `DriverManager` class hung as well. This occurred whether or not a second thread accessed the inoperable database, because the original thread still held a lock on the class's synchronization monitor. As the clients tried apparently failed requests again, more and more threads locked up, until no more threads existed to service client requests (figure 4.1).

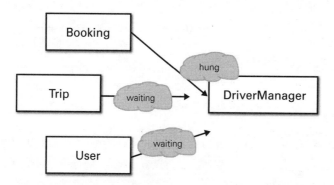

Figure 4.1   Threads hung while connecting to database through DriverManager

4.1.4 Searching for a solution

As a first step toward a solution, we modified the code to use `DriverManager.get-Driver(String url)` to look up the correct driver implementation, then call `Driver.connect(String url)` to open a connection directly. This approach still used the `DriverManager` to choose driver implementations. However, threads that hung while opening a connection would not have the `DriverManager` class's monitor.

The application still collapsed because the bad code eventually monopolized the entire thread pool. These threads continued to hang on opening connections. And those connections just would not time out, no matter what we did. One developer suggested using transaction timeouts. No help. Most transaction timeout implementations simply roll back the transaction and throw an exception if the transaction exceeds the timeout duration. For reasons we'll discuss shortly, they do not attempt to stop the thread midexecution when the timeout expires.

A second developer suggested stopping the thread explicitly using the `Thread.stop()` method. Sun deprecated the use of this method for a reason. First and most importantly, doing so leaves the application in an inconsistent state, whose results will be unpredictable at best. Sun's FAQ *"Why are* `Thread.stop`, `Thread.suspend`, `Thread.resume`, *and* `Runtime.runFinalizersOnExit` *Deprecated?"* (http://java.sun.com/j2se/1.3/docs/guide/misc/threadPrimitiveDepreca- tion.html) details the reasons why these methods will probably never provide such functionality. Additionally, the success of stopping depends heavily on the hung code's implementation. The best we could hope for was to fail quickly, providing the end user with a meaningful error as soon as possible. Users of web applications almost always favor seeing a descriptive error message after two seconds, rather than waiting the full minute it might take for their browser to time out, during which they're left wandering who's at fault and how they should proceed.

To accomplish a swift failure, we decoupled the questionable code as much as possible, in which case a JMS server was our friend. Using JMS, we simulated a syn- chronous request by sending a request to one queue and receiving the response on a temporary queue, using the `javax.jms.MessageConsumer.receive(long tim- eout)` method. The method returned null if the timeout expired before receiving a response message, causing us to throw an error to the client. (To simplify things, we could have hidden these details behind a synchronous interface that looked exactly like the original implementation.) Next, we implemented a message con- sumer that took those requests, delegated to our original hang-prone code, and then sent the response back on the temporary queue.

Now, so long as we configured our application server to use separate thread pools to service client requests and messages on our JMS queue, only the con- sumer that delegated to the questionable code hung, and the client code ran freely. We could have even moved the consumer into a separate virtual machine that we bounced independently of the remaining application elements to clean up the hung threads. The reliability and robustness of the JMS architecture made this a snap.

Now, we come to the moral of the story. In the absence of a JMS implementa- tion, or when the client and questionable code absolutely must run in the same virtual machine, you may alternately implement this model using application server-specific threading facilities and the `Object.wait(long timeout)` method to implement the timeout functionality. In doing so, you execute the troublesome code in a separate thread to prevent hanging the client thread. In addition, you pause the client thread up to a given timeout duration by waiting on an object monitor. When and if the code returns successfully, it notifies and wakes the client thread so that the thread can immediately pick back up the execution. Using the vendor's API to implement the threading—or, at least, using a well-implemented thread pool—is key. A pool not only allows you to reuse threads; it also limits the number of threads that will spawn. If you spawn a new thread each time without limit, the application server may stay up a little longer. Eventually, however, the application server will come down. Still, if you have the choice between failing early and gracefully or slowly grinding to a halt and taking the rest of the application down with it, you want to opt for the former.

4.2 *Handling exceptions*

Based on countless interactions with other EJB developers, we've concluded that exception handling easily stands as one of the fuzziest, oft-misinterpreted aspects of EJB development. Handling exceptions well can mean the difference between an API that works intuitively and instructively and an API that seems to bust at the seams. You've all fallen victim to the latter at one time or another. Either you've shuffled countless checked exceptions that have little relevance to the task at hand, or you've given in and thrown up the `java.lang.Exception` superclass, thus defeating the original intentions of exceptions altogether.

In normal, localized Java applications, you can easily handle exceptions by following simple rules: First, use clearly named application exceptions that fit with the semantic nature of the API to denote conditions clients can handle. Secondly, throw `RuntimeExceptions` for programming errors or other unexpected conditions.

Moving to an EJB environment complicates the situation. You now have a new class of system exceptions. These new system exceptions identify system-level errors, not pertinent to an application's business logic. These errors are classified as `RuntimeExceptions` as well. The EJB specification provides a degree of guidance. In fact, the specification dedicates an entire chapter to the subject However, because `RuntimeExceptions` now shoulders dual responsibilities, the developer will find the tasks of keeping things straight and determining client reactions touch and go to say the least.

4.2.1 *Mini-antipattern: Logic in Exception Implementations*

Coding logic into exception class constructors often leads to obfuscation of the call path, unnecessary coupling, and inconsistent implementations. Exceptions are not meant to hold business logic, hence `Throwable` is a class rather than an interface. We've had the pleasure of debugging/deciphering in two specific cases—rolling back transactions and logging.

Rolling back transactions upon exception instantiation confuses program flow. In the first place, looking up a transaction manager and rolling back a container-managed transaction (CMT) is not a straightforward task. EJB developers should really use the `EJBContext.setRollbackOnly()` method instead. Secondly, rolling back a transaction in response to an exception is not always appropriate. Once you have factored this logic into your exception implementation, you're stuck. You either have to always roll back, or you have to track down every point where the code instantiates a rolling back transaction and refactor out the rollback logic. Thirdly, rolling back falls apart outside transactions. What if the application throws an exception from an EJB method running with the `NotSupported` transaction attribute? Should the surrounding, suspended transaction roll back? It won't—unless you catch the exception on the way through and explicitly roll back. You're left with a rift in your application's consistency. That is, sometimes transactions roll back automatically; sometimes you have to roll them back explicitly; and sometimes they roll back unexpectedly. Unfortunately, the applicable situation is not always immediately evident from the application code. In contrast, consistently rolling back explicitly leads to clear, straightforward code.

Embedding logging logic into exception implementations creates multiple issues as well. If you do so, you'll find that messages either won't log, will log multiple times, or will fail to record pertinent state surrounding the exception. If all exceptions log upon creation, error messages will log each time an application nests an exception. Missing exceptions and exceptions logged at random points in the application flow (sometimes multiple times) can make tracking down bugs difficult.

4.2.2 Solution: Refactor logic out of exceptions

You have two options for refactoring your exception logic. The first and most straightforward solution would be to move the code to the exception `catch` block. This code admittedly has a slight odor, which is most likely the reason the crafty developer moved it into the exception implementation in the first place. Unfortunately, traditional object-oriented development doesn't handle this sort of duplicated logic very well. Another programming paradigm, Aspect-Oriented Programming (AOP), helps organize these types of crosscutting concerns. Visit http://aosd.net/ for information on tools supporting this relatively new approach. For a more in-depth discussion, take a look at Manning Publications' *AspectJ in Action*.

4.2.3 Antipattern: Swallowing Exceptions

The most common and detrimental mistake we've come across regarding exception handling—simply logging the exception message and continuing execution—results in debugging difficulty, uncertainty of outcomes, inconsistent application state, and security holes:

```
try {
    ...
}
catch (Exception e) {
    System.err.println(e);
}
```

This code simply prints the error message to the log, which is not much help when we have to track down the cause. We once worked on a fairly complicated web-based application for a credit card company. The application mysteriously failed, and upon investigation of the server logs, we found this (and only this):

```
java.lang.NullPointerException
```

What could we do? Nothing. When faced with poor exception reporting, the best you can do is to roll up your sleeves, start looking for the erroneous code, and fix it as soon as you find it—a task easily on par with searching for a needle in a haystack.

Instead of simply logging the exception message, you can print the location of your logged message—that is, the class and method name. In the end, however, you really care more about where the exception was thrown and how it originated—all information provided by the stack trace. Go Java.

So you don't know where the exception occurred, and simply continuing execution leads to unexpected results at best. Most developers program to the best-case scenario. After all, fulfilling the requirements leaves you with plenty on your plate. If you ignore exceptions in a complex application, predicting every possible outcome will be next to impossible. We once witnessed one extreme case. A financial institution's web-based application ignored `TransactionRolledBack-Exceptions`. The exception ignorance facilitated a separate SQL injection security hole, enabling an attacker to pull back arbitrary records until the transaction timed out.

Exceptions enable you to handle situations just like this by allowing you to fail early and cleanly. When you fail early, you'll find that you spend less time tracking down the causes of bugs. If the method parameter should not be null, you can throw a `NullPointerException` rather than waste time trying to handle the invalid value. This will save time down the road when debugging other pieces of functionality that could break as a result of the null value.

Exceptions also enable you to separate code (for exceptional conditions) and error handling from your application logic. With exceptions, you can break execution midstream, preventing further damage. Catching and rethrowing exceptions awards you the perfect opportunity to react and restore your system to a consistent state.

4.2.4 Solution: A simple exception handling strategy

We've settled on a simple process for exception handling. First and foremost, you should maintain the stack trace. The exception stack trace tells a developer exactly what has happened, exactly where it happened (possibly even the line number in the source code), and exactly what path led to it. If you don't know how to handle a checked exception pertinent to the task at hand, you can throw it up until someone knows how to handle it. If the current process can't recover from a checked exception, you can simply wrap it in a runtime exception (maintaining the stack trace) and throw it to the top. Listing 4.2, inspired by a friend and mentor, Tim Williams, does exactly that.

> **Listing 4.2   A class for wrapping checked exceptions in runtime exceptions while maintaining the stack trace**

```
import java.io.*;

/**
 * Turns a nested exception into a runtime exception.
 * Shields client from vendor-specific implementations.
 * Use for exceptions that you don't
 * know how to or shouldn't handle in your code.
 * Maintains original exception's message and stack trace.
 *
 * @author Bob Lee (crazybob@crazybob.org)
 */
public class NestedException extends RuntimeException {

    /** Wrap another exception in a RuntimeException. */
    public static RuntimeException wrap(Throwable t) {
        if (t instanceof RuntimeException)
            return (RuntimeException) t;
        return new NestedException(t);
    }

    private String message;
    private String stackTrace;
```

```
/** Wraps another exeception. */
private NestedException(Throwable t) {
    super();
    this.message = t.getMessage();
    StringWriter out = new StringWriter();
    t.printStackTrace(new PrintWriter(out));
    this.stackTrace = out.toString();
}

public String toString() {
    return this.getMessage();
}

public String getMessage() {
    return this.message;
}

public void printStackTrace() {
    System.err.print(this.stackTrace);
}

public void printStackTrace(PrintStream out) {
    printStackTrace(new PrintWriter(out));
}

public void printStackTrace(PrintWriter out) {
    out.print(this.stackTrace);
}
}
```

Let's consider the preceding implementation. First, you can implement the nesting in a number of ways. In fact, JDK 1.4+ adds support for nesting causal exceptions to the Throwable base class. Because we use this approach most often to debug unexpected conditions, we're more interested in preserving the information than the exception instance itself. Additionally, as is often the case with third-party persistence frameworks, the class for the wrapped exception may be present in the server application, but not in the client application. With this in mind, you can see that the implementation captures and outputs the information, rather than the nested exception instance itself. This enables the nested exception instance to safely propagate to the client, free of ClassNotFoundExceptions.

Secondly, we built the logic for wrapping exceptions into a factory method in the NestedException class itself, greatly simplifying the effort required by client developers. The factory method only wraps checked exceptions, returning RuntimeExceptions without modification. Client code simply catches, wraps, and throws unexpected exceptions as we can see in listing 4.3:

Listing 4.3 Wrapping a checked exception in a runtime exception

```
try {
    ...
}
catch (CheckedException e) {
    throw e;
}
catch (Exception e) {
    throw NestedException.wrap(e);
}
```

4.2.5 Antipattern: Killer System Exceptions

The EJB specification breaks up exceptions into two categories: system and application. System exceptions denote truly unexpected, system-level events. Application exceptions, on the other hand, signify exceptional events at the application level. They are also part of the API.

Application exceptions are checked exceptions and are part of the application's interface. If a bean implementation throws an application exception, the container must propagate the exception to the client as is. Examples of application exceptions include input validation errors and exceptions concerning the business logic. In a trip-booking application, trying to book a trip naming an unacceptable number of travelers or an invalid date would result in application exceptions being thrown.

System exceptions denote errors not related to the application's business logic. The EJB specification classifies `RuntimeExceptions` as system exceptions. `EJB-Exception` extends `RuntimeException` making it a system exception. System-level events such as network outages, running out of memory, or I/O errors also result in system exceptions.

If a system exception results from a bean implementation, the container must log the exception, mark the current transaction for rollback, and throw away the bean instance. The container then throws remote clients a `RemoteException` and local clients an `EJBException`.

We often see bean developers throw unchecked exceptions as an easy way to roll back a transaction in response to an application-level event. Doing so creates subtle side effects. First, you have the logging aspect. Standard compliant containers log system exceptions when thrown by the bean implementation. When you encounter truly unexpected exceptions in your application logic (possibly due to a system failure, a misconfiguration, or a low resource), you can simply wrap the

cause in a runtime exception and throw it to the top. You can count on the EJB
container to log the event, wrap the exception, and throw it to the client. The
same pattern applies to servlet containers. There, the servlet container displays
the default error page to the user and logs the exception. Expected or application-level exceptions thrown as system exceptions pollute the logs, which
increases the noise level and makes tracking down bugs and their causes difficult.

You must also face the issue of state. A bean that catches and rethrows an application exception has ample opportunity to restore the bean instance's state.
Throwing a system exception lays this responsibility on the container—kludgy at
best. The container automatically rolls back the current transaction in an attempt
to leave the application data in a consistent state. Next, the specification requires
the EJB container to dispose of the bean instance. The container may not invoke
any more business or even container `callback` methods on the bean instance.
This fact can disrupt the container's ability to cache and pool instances. If a system exception occurs, the container will *not* invoke `ejbRemove()`.

Lastly, you must consider the semantic differences between a system and application exception. A system exception insinuates that a problem exists with the system itself and that another application instance or even another invocation on
the same instance may not fall victim to the same issue. With an application
exception, the container knows that the outcome is expected and will be the same
in any setting. Some containers implement automatic retry logic. If a bean developer marks a method as idempotent, the container can catch system exceptions
and automatically retry the invocation on another instance. This approach would
obviously not be desirable for application logic since the invocation would have
the same outcome from instance to instance. Throwing an application exception
as a system exception cripples your ability to utilize system exceptions to handle
genuine system failures.

Clients have a vested interest in semantic issues as well. If the application throws
an application-level exception as a system exception, the container will throw the
client a `RemoteException` or an `EJBException`. The client won't be able to tell from
the API that the exception may be thrown, as system exceptions are unchecked.
Any client that knows about and wants to handle the exception in question must
also develop fragile logic that unwraps the `RemoteException` or `EJBException`.

4.2.6 *Solution: Throw the correct exception type*

You should consider system exceptions' automatic rollback of transactions as a
side effect rather than a means to an end. Application code should catch an
application exception explicitly and roll back the transaction using either

`setRollbackOnly()` on the bean's context for CMTs or the `UserTransaction` for bean-managed transactions (BMTs). When you choose the correct exception type, the container logs the correct exceptions, keeps the system logs clean, reuses resources properly, and awards beans the opportunity to clean up their state, when appropriate. When developers throw application exceptions and system exceptions appropriately, you know exactly the EJB-thrown exceptions you can handle and those that are beyond your ability to control. Consequently, you can implement robust retry logic for idempotent methods, in addition to any support the container already provides. If the application frequently throws application exceptions as system exceptions, retrying the method will always throw the same exception, and you can't sacrifice these superfluous invocations. On the other hand, when you only have to consider true system exceptions and programming errors, you can hope that the programming errors are rare enough that any resulting retries would have little impact on system performance and stability. Table 4.1 shows the causes and results of both applications and system exceptions to help you apply them appropriately.

Table 4.1 Exception type matrix

Exception category	Exception types	Causes	Result
Application	Checked Exceptions	Application-level events—for example, trying to book a trip on an invalid date	The container throws the exception to the client.
System	RuntimeExceptions (including EJBException)	System-level exceptions, such as network and memory errors, and programming errors, such as unexpected NullPointerExceptions.	The container logs the exception, throws away the bean instance, rolls back the transaction, and throws remote clients a RemoteException and local clients an EJBException.

4.3 *Iterating large datasets*

Remote clients often work with subsets of larger result sets. One such example is a web-based search engine. A client's query may return thousands of results. Yet, the web application will transfer only a few results at a time, since the client often works with only the first couple of pages of results before altering and rerunning the query. We have encountered such a requirement at least once in every project on which we've worked. Without fail, the implementation of a solution pattern has been a subject of great debate.

The variations in the requirements will greatly influence your implementation choice. We've designed applications that paged threaded message lists on a bulletin board where the backing data is globally shared. We've also faced situations, such as credit card transactions, where the data is largely user-dependent and security is of the utmost concern. And then we've encountered gray areas, like doctor listings, where the data pertains to clients subscribed to a given insurance plan. Each requirement and environment calls for a differently tuned implementation.

A high-level pattern extends the GoF Iterator pattern, providing a clear interface for clients iterating these datasets. This pattern appears under many different names. Some developers refer to these as Page-by-Page Iterators. The Sun Core J2EE Patterns use the name Value List Handler, as the pattern describes the iteration of what was once called Value Objects. Actually, the name Value List Iterator more appropriately describes the pattern since Sun's detailed description refers to the interface as `ValueListIterator` and the interface implementation as `ValueListHandler`. Further complicating things, the Core J2EE Patterns have stopped using the name Value Object to describe objects meant to transfer data between tiers. Instead, the Core J2EE Patterns use a more common name: DTO. So what should you call this high-level pattern—Data Transfer Object List Iterator? That's a mouthful. Herein, we'll stick with our personal preference: Page-by-Page Iterator.

Superfluous naming debates aside, you must make several decisions when implementing your Page-by-Page Iterator. We'll talk more about those decisions in the paragraphs that follow. For now, we want to emphasize that these decisions dramatically impact your application's scalability and performance. A wrong decision can result in an implementation that simply does not work. In other words, you might end up with an implementation that hogs memory or other resources for extended periods of time, or one that takes an unreasonable amount of time to deliver a response to the user, effectively defeating the pattern's original purpose.

In any case, whether the client is a web browser or stand-alone Swing application, when an application server hides the details of the data model, session beans can suit Page-by-Page Iterator implementations well. One iterator interface variation defines a single method, enabling users to pull collections of DTOs from a larger data set:

```
public interface MyIterator implements javax.ejb.EJBObject {
   java.util.Collection retrieve(int startIndex, int count);
throws RemoteException;

}
```

Clients simply provide the service with the start index and the number of records desired, and the service returns the corresponding `Collection` of DTOs. You can see (in figure 4.2) that the service does not require a fixed page size. Consequently, one or more clients can easily query the service for pages of arbitrary sizes.

4.3.1 *Antipattern: Database Connection Hog*

Early versions of the JDBC API, —that is, those before version 2.0—defined a synchronous `ResultSet`. An application ran a query, then iterated over the result from beginning to end—no going back, no jumping ahead. The introduction of JDBC 2.0 with the J2SE 1.2 brought a scrollable `ResultSet` interface, enabling applications to access result sets randomly. Specifically, using the new API,

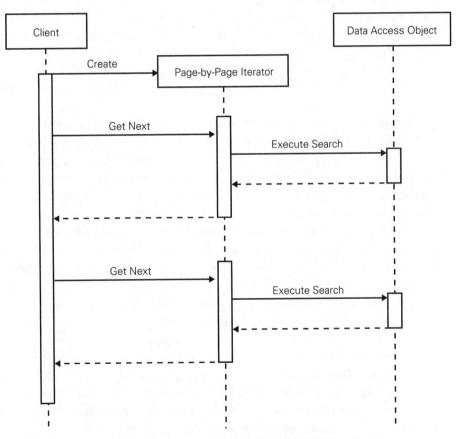

Figure 4.2 Sequence diagram illustrating client invoking a Page-by-Page Iterator.

developers could jump to the result set's beginning or end, to an absolute position within the result set, or even to a position relative to the current position.

With this new tool in our belts, our first thought was how incredibly instrumental this new API could be in implementing patterns such as the Page-by-Page Iterator. For example, an active `ResultSet` could back an iterator instance, pulling records randomly and constructing the corresponding data transfer objects on demand.

Our euphoria was short-lived, however. An open database connection backs the open `ResultSet`. So, monopolizing a database connection for the duration of a user's session simply does not scale. For example, consider a web application that keeps a pool of 20 database connections. You implement your Page-by-Page Iterator using a stateful session bean (or a plain Java object stored in the HTTP session) with a `ResultSet` instance field. The stateful session bean executes the query upon creation and holds onto the `ResultSet`. Effectively, the bean retains a cursor containing the database's query results, along with the corresponding connection. Each time the user moves to a different web page, you hit the stateful session bean, which in turn uses the JDBC 2.0 `ResultSet` to scroll to the desired location and returns the requested records.

To implement this procedure properly, you must address a few difficulties. The first problem is how to maintain the stateful session bean and result set for the user session duration. You could limit the user to one instance at a time, but if you do, you also prevent the user from opening multiple browser windows and running and paging multiple queries concurrently—not a good practice.

Maintaining the bean instance for the user session duration means you must hold onto the bean instance until the user explicitly logs out (which, in the best of circumstances, users won't always do) or until the user's session expires. Session timeouts typically run somewhere between 20 minutes and an hour. Let's say you have 20 database connections in your pool. If you dedicate a database connection to each user, your application can only handle 20 unique users over a given 20-minute period, or more if the session timeout is longer. Keep in mind that 20 minutes is the best case scenario, because an active user will not time out at first. Compounding the problem, a user will often accidentally or intentionally close their browser, then reopen it and relog in. You can't definitively differentiate this situation from one in which two people are logged into the same account from different computers. Therefore, in this case, the user effectively counts as two unique users and monopolizes two database connections. As you can see, it doesn't take many concurrent users under this model to drag the system to its knees.

4.3.2 *Solution: Manage connections with surgical precision*

The real problem in our database connection hog antipattern is idle time. In expectation of the user's return (and thus the next request), you greedily hold onto resources, memory, and database connections. In reality, the user may never return or, conversely, a user may make another request 10 seconds later. If you wait around for the length of the session timeout or for 10 seconds, you'll have monopolized resources for too long. And you can't afford to waste scarce resources in this manner.

Let's look at that second possible scenario—a 10-second wait. The user browses several records and clicks through to the next page fairly quickly. You've made use of your database connection only twice over that 10-second span. However, your application could handle hundreds of requests per second. If you could instead return this user connection to the pool at the end of each request, you could use this connection to service hundreds of requests in the time it takes for your user to click through one page. Making resource usage dependent on user behavior will not scale. By keeping as little state as possible and using resources with surgical precision—that is, by holding onto resources for the smallest amount of time possible—your application can handle thousands of unique users concurrently, rather than a double-digit number smaller than or equal to the number of connections in your connection pool.

Bean implementations should retrieve a connection, use it quickly, and return it to the pool. Holding onto database connections between requests is hardly ever a good idea. First, look into optimizing the query time at the database level. When all else fails, look into caching in the application server, preferably using an off-the-shelf solution.

4.3.3 *Antipattern: Eager Iterator*

Most Page-by-Page Iterator pattern descriptions primarily address a remote interface's location between the client and application tier, which makes transferring the entire result set impractical. However, the descriptions fail to consider the most common mistake we see in the pattern's actual implementation. Developers tend to forget that another remote interface sits between the application and data tiers. Though the throughput may be much higher than that of the client interface, it's a remote interface nonetheless, and you must limit the amount of data that passes across it as much as possible.

How you design your Page-by-Page Iterator implementation depends heavily on your application and your environment's unique characteristics. Does the database sit on the same machine or across a network? How big is a typical result set? To whom are the results applicable? Developers often incorrectly assume that executing the query consumes most application effort. If queries have an optimal configuration and a properly worded SQL command (combined with indexing, partitioning, caching, and other optimizations in the data tier), they typically run surprisingly efficiently.

Developers often fail to realize the possible efficiency of query execution, nor do they keep in mind that they can't keep the database connection open across requests. Consequently, developers often implement a Page-by-Page Iterator that executes the query and pulls back all results up front. The implementation stores the entire DTO collection in the user's session, either globally or in a stateful session. In any case, the results consume nontrivial amounts of memory, even past the duration of a user's request.

Storing large amount of nonglobally applicable data for extended time periods may severely cripple an application's scalability. For example, if the results of a query take up 5 MB of memory and you've allocated 128 MB to your application, you can support a maximum of 25 unique users before you use up all your memory. On the other hand, if you maintain no state across requests, you can scale to serve as many clients as the server can throw. Doing so would incur a reasonably low amount of memory.

Another option would be to rerun the query each time the user makes a request, then pull back only the necessary data. Those who have implemented these types of applications in the past know that queries don't always lend themselves to pulling out randomly located pages, especially when the SQL WHERE clause gets complicated. Two options for pulling out given pages remain. First, you can use a vendor-specific SQL extension. For example, with Oracle, you'd use the ROWNUM keyword:

```
SELECT * FROM (SELECT e.*, rownum rn FROM employee e WHERE id=?)
   t WHERE t.rn >= [startIndex] AND t.rn < [startIndex+_count];
```

Another possibility would be to use PostgreSQL, which accomplishes the same using the LIMIT and OFFSET keywords:

```
SELECT * FROM employee WHERE id=? LIMIT [count] OFFSET [startIndex]
```

The approach you choose will depend primarily on performance and platform-independence considerations. When marshaling objects from a ResultSet to Java objects by hand, we've found the PostgreSQL keywords perform more efficiently. In other cases—that is, when we're not sure which database the application will run against or we don't have access to the generated SQL—we'll chose the Oracle keyword, ROWNUM, sacrificing performance for vendor independence. For example, we chose the scrolling ResultSet implementation when using Castor (http://castor.exolab.org/) as a persistence framework. Castor did not enable us to use the vendor-specific result set limiters. Castor did, however, provide a scrolling result set of its own, undoubtedly implemented behind the scenes by the JDBC 2.0 ResultSet.

Using a test setup, we implemented a small suite of performance test cases to exercise and further explore these conjectures. In our test setup, the application server and database sit on different boxes across a LAN, as is often the case with n-tier enterprise applications.

Our test cases include running the query itself without pulling back any results; running the query and pulling back all results (as blindly implemented Page-by-Page Iterator implementations often do); and pulling back 20 records from the middle of the result set using the two aforementioned implementations. We ran these tests multiple times, excluded the outliers, and used the mean of the results. We executed the suite for small row counts in excess of 200,000 records.

As you can see from the graphed results in figure 4.3, the time necessary to pull back all records from the database grew much more quickly than the time needed to execute the query alone (not to mention the time required to pull back a single page (20 records) using either of your implementations).

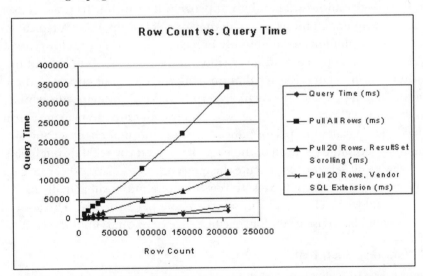

Figure 4.3   These test case performance results show the performance implications of strategies for iteration. As you can see, rerunning the query and pulling a page using the vendor's SQL extension yields the best performance for this configuration.

You can also see that pulling back a single page of data using the vendor-specific SQL extension performed many times faster than sticking to the scrollable `ResultSet`. In fact, note that pulling back a page of data using the vendor's extension barely took longer than running the query itself.

Pitting one approach—pulling back a single page using the vendor's SQL—against another—pulling back the entire result set upon the first request—the user will have to view more than 13 pages of data to make up for the performance cost incurred on the first request. We know from usage statistics from our applications that users typically stop at one or two pages before executing a new query or moving on.

In this scenario, if you decide to go with the implementation that pulls back all data up front, you will risk memory-based scalability issues. In addition, the user will have to wait an inordinate amount of time to receive a response to their first request, quite possibly the only one they really care to see.

Mini-antipattern: Paging with a Scrollable ResultSet

The JDBC 2.0 API supports the notion of a scrollable result set. In earlier implementations, developers were forced to synchronously iterate a `ResultSet` from beginning to end. Now they can jump to random, absolute positions. Using a scrollable result set to implement a page-by-page iterator may seem like a tempting, database vendor-independent approach. Be careful. In practice, scrollable `ResultSet` implementations aren't all they're cracked up to be. A typical scrollable `ResultSet` implementation actually behaves more like a caching result set. A developer can jump to a random position in the result set but, behind the scenes, another action occurs. Rather than moving the database cursor to the absolute position, the implementation actually scrolls to the absolute position, pulling back and caching each row along the way. When using a page-by-page iterator, this behavior is equivalent in performance to using a normal result set and simply iterating to the absolute position of the page. If we need rows 890 through 900 out of a 1,000 row result set, and we execute the query and use `ResultSet.absolute(int)` to scroll to row 890, then pull back 10 rows, the operation will actually result in pulling back 900 rows. This results in unacceptable performance. The alternative, of course, would be to use a vendor-specific SQL extension to limit the result set size.

4.3.4 Solution: Test, test, test

The only way to truly know which implementation strategy works best for you is to test in the target environment. Network speed on the client and database ends of the application server, database vendors' implementations, memory restrictions, database indexing, and result set sizes are just a few factors that affect the performance of the Page-by-Page Iterator implementations. If you begin by running a simple test suite, you'll most likely save yourself a lot of heartache down the road—not to mention the time gained and team spirit enhanced by avoiding subjective arguments between team members over which implementation will perform fastest.

When performance issues do arise, you'll want to measure and find out exactly where your problem lies. They may be in the data tier. If so, you'll determine the problem, and repair it, possibly by tweaking an SQL query or the database configuration; pulling back excess data from the database to the application tier is a foul practice. You should leave this data in the database, if possible, to avoid incurring the overhead of remotely transferring.

4.3.5 *Caching results*

When the time arrives for you to cache in the application tier, you must ask yourself the following questions:

- How expensive is the query?
- How big is the result set?
- How fast is the network between the application server and the database?
- How applicable is the data? Does it apply to one user, ten percent of users, all users?
- How long until the data expires?

If the query doesn't change often, is executed repeatedly, and produces globally applicable results, you should attempt to cache the results. If the results apply to a single user or expire quickly, caching isn't much of an option.

To make an educated decision, you should consider performance tests in the target environment as your best option. Again, you can speculate all you want as to how the query time compares to the time it takes to pull results back from the database, but from our experience you'll be wrong as often as you are right. You really can't know for sure until you execute at least rudimentary tests in your target environment.

In deciding on a caching strategy, we've found that we can rarely—if ever—get by without caching. However, we've found a reasonably safe alternative: limiting caching to already-requested data, rather than trying to predict future data requests. The latter leads down a slippery and often wasteful slope.

When caching data, developers often like to roll their own custom frameworks using hash tables and soft references and expiration algorithms. Caching implementations can complicate quickly, especially in concurrent, distributed environments. Creating a `String` instance when memory is tight easily results in `OutOfMemoryErrors`. When creating caching implementations, you should take care to account for all possibilities. Inadvertently strongly referencing cached objects can prevent the collection of those objects. Expiring and synchronizing cached data across a cluster (or across different applications) can require a bag of tricks.

In a nutshell, you should consider the benefits of using an off-the-shelf caching framework before implementing your own. Implementing custom, robust caching can be rocky, at best. Worse, this approach can be detrimental to an application's scalability—and even its functionality. Like application server vendors, caching tool vendors have the time and resources to dedicate to testing, performance, and quality. Additionally, such tools are varied enough to fit any application's needs, from explicit custom APIs to JDBC proxies that operate completely transparently.

4.3.6 Exporting results

In some Page-by-Page Iterator clients, users may browse a couple pages, then export the entire result set to a different format, one viewable outside a web browser. We've used applications that exported results to spreadsheets, comma-delimited flat files, Adobe PDFs, and more.

Just because users might possibly utilize the export functionality frequently doesn't mean you should cache all results in memory on the first request. Once again, the performance increase you'd observe in the export functionality wouldn't outweigh either the performance degradation incurred on the first request or the scalability risks associated with holding the result set in memory between the initial request and the export request.

In most configurations, the connection between the client and the application tier uses more overhead than that of the connection between the application tier and the data tier. Therefore, the client connection is the limiting factor. Of course, the client might be many things, including a Java applet, a JSP, or a servlet talking directly to EJBs. The export implementation should execute the query on demand, streaming the results to the client. Specifically, to reduce the amount of memory necessary to fulfill the export request, the application should read records from the result set collection in a streaming fashion. The application can then transform and output the data to the client, if possible. This use enables the application to perform exports that wouldn't fit on the heap otherwise, to scale and serve more clients concurrently, and to increase its responsiveness. In other words, the application will start sending data to the client almost immediately instead of pulling all data into memory first.

4.3.7 *Determining the size of a result set*

Developers new to JDBC often ask how they can determine the number of records a query returned. For example, in your Page-by-Page Iterator implementation, you may want to tell the user exactly how many pages of data were returned.

The ResultSet interface has no notion of a size() method. Consequently, you must derive the size indirectly. We follow one of two patterns to determine the size of a ResultSet. The pattern we choose depends on the environment's characteristics such as the time needed for query execution, the JDBC version supported by the driver, and the nature of the query. For example, does the query run relatively quickly? How well does the database cache? Am I already using a scrollable result set?

The first implementation consists of a simple variation on your SQL query. For example, if I'm executing

```
SELECT * FROM employee WHERE id=?
```

I execute a separate query with the COUNT() function ahead of time:

```
SELECT COUNT(*) FROM employee WHERE id=?
```

The SQL-based implementation applies when the query time is low or when the database can execute the two queries efficiently. This implementation also applies if you don't have a JDBC 2.0 driver or you're not using a scrollable result set.

If you're already using a scrollable result set, you may determine the row count size by scrolling to the end of the ResultSet and obtaining the row number:

```
ResultSet rs = ...;
int size = (rs.last()) ? rs.getRow() : 0;
```

If ResultSet.last() returns false—that is, if the current row is not valid—you know that you have zero results. Otherwise, the current row number is the size.

In the absence of a JDBC 2.0 driver or a scrollable result set, some developers erroneously suggest calling ResultSet.next() over and over again and incrementing a counter-variable until you reach the end of the ResultSet. We avoid this practice, choosing instead the SQL COUNT() approach. Depending on the JDBC driver implementation, rerunning the query and iterating over all results will almost always result in lower performance.

4.3.8 *Iterating shuffled data*

Every once in a while, a truly unique requirement comes down the pipe. A few years ago, shortly after the release of EJB 1.0, we signed onto a team developing medical decision management software. Roughly halfway through the project life cycle, the team fell victim to a few minor scalability issues. One application function, displaying a paged list of medical care providers, came under immediate scrutiny.

In practice, when utilizing a Page-by-Page Iterator pattern, users typically execute a query, view the first couple pages of data, then either tweak and rerun the query or leave. This case was no different. But because the users were selecting from an alphabetical list of doctors' names, the application inadvertently gave doctors whose last name came earlier in the alphabet an unfair advantage. To remedy the situation, the business analysts required that the list be shuffled or randomized to ensure that the application awarded consistent exposure to each doctor.

The initial implementation generated a randomized list copy for each user and stored it in the session. Each time the user requested another page, the application simply queried against the user's in-memory list copy. Though simple, this approach fell flat on its face when it came time to scale. With multiple lists of hundreds or thousands of doctors, giving each user his own randomized copy sitting in memory quickly took its toll. Additionally, having so much stateful data severely limited our options for failover because the application server had to replicate all data to another server in the cluster.

Thanks to the elegance of the J2SE APIs, our vision of complete statelessness came to fruition. The random number generator used by the collections API, `java.util.Random`, allows developers to specify the random seed, or starting value, for the generator. Two random number generators, each seeded with the same value, generate identical sequences of pseudorandom numbers. So, given the original list and a seed value, we could regenerate the randomized list upon each request (listing 4.4):

Listing 4.4 Statelessly creating the shuffled list

```
List doctors = ...;

// create a defensive copy.
List copy = new ArrayList(doctors.size());
copy.addAll(doctors);

// shuffle the list.
long seed = ...;
Collections.shuffle(copy, new Random(seed));
```

By deriving the seed value from user information—that is, the hash of the user ID—you can ensure that the user will see the identically ordered list across login sessions, assuming the data and the random number generator implementation stay the same. In our case, clients added new doctors sparingly. And, because the `java.util.Random` class publicly and clearly documents its internal implementation details (based on well-proven algorithms), the chances of the generator implementation changing were now slim to none.

4.4 *Interoperating efficiently*

> *While sizing up my options on the steep hill, I realize that all that I can do is buy time. Slamming on the brakes will send me over the handlebars. I delicately feather the brakes and begin a sideways slide. That slows my momentum just enough, and I spot a gap between two trees beside the trail. I manage to slip through and am able to bring the bike slowly to a stop. As I reach the pileup below, I learn that the biker at the bottom of the pile is one of my companions. His shoulder is broken. Too much confidence is as dangerous as too little.*

EJB applications frequently integrate with other EJB applications as well as with plain Java applications. The best path toward integrating two different applications is not always clear. Firewalls, security restrictions, and implementation differences often obstruct the path. The problems are intricate, requiring patience and thought. Like the hill in Austin, overconfidence and imprudence can prove fatal.

The safe path may run between two enterprise applications sitting behind the firewall. If so, you must still worry about the underlying protocols used in remote calls. Sometimes your clients sit on the other side of HTTP firewalls. When they do, you must often tunnel invocations and cope with all the associated tradeoffs.

Mini-antipattern: Passing DOM Objects

Java applications may pass around XML as document object model (DOM) object trees rather than parsing and marshaling the same data over and over. Though many consider this practice acceptable in certain situations, developers should never pass DOM objects across a remote interface. A problem occurs in the serialization step. Depending on the DOM implementation, the DOM objects may not be serializable at all. When DOM objects are serializable, the client or server may have a different, incompatible DOM implementation or the client or server may not have DOM implementation at all. Applications planning on passing XML remotely—or even just serializing it—should work with the XML in its text form.

4.4.1 Using IIOP

The Object Management Group (OMG) provides a standard for distributed systems, the Common Object Request Broker Architecture, or CORBA for short. CORBA uses a wire protocol called IIOP to communicate remotely in a platform-independent manner. As long as you have a CORBA binding in place, applications implemented in C can communicate with applications written in Java and with applications running on completely different platforms.

Java introduced CORBA support in version 1.2. Java 1.3 went one step further, adding support for RMI-IIOP, an RMI implementation that uses IIOP as the underlying wire protocol. Java applications running in servers implemented by different vendors (or even different versions from the same vendor) may use incompatible RMI wire protocols. In these situations, the applications can communicate compatibly using RMI-IIOP instead.

The EJB 2.0 specification mandates support of RMI-IIOP in addition to optional vendor-specific wire protocols for EJB containers. In other words, EJB 2.0-compliant containers from different vendors theoretically should be able to communicate. As an added bonus, non-Java applications using IIOP can invoke EJBs with no extra development effort.

Understanding narrowing

Because your application may be using IIOP for the underlying communications, the EJB specification requires clients to perform the added step of narrowing the stub:

```
InitialContext context = new InitialContext();
MyHome myHome = (MyHome) PortableRemoteObject.narrow(
  context.lookup(...), MyHome.class);
```

Why can't you just down cast the stub as you would with normal Java objects and as you have in the past? Because you transferred the object using IIOP, you lost any notion of the object's Java type. The returned object does not implement your bean's Java interface. The returned object, a generic CORBA stub, actually implements `org.omg.CORBA.Object`. This interface provides generic mechanisms for invoking the remote methods.

The `javax.rmi.PortableRemoteObject.narrow()` method instantiates a new stub that implements your Java interface, wraps the generic CORBA stub, and delegates method invocations to it. If your application uses another protocol and the returned stub already implements your Java interface, the `narrow()` method will return the object unmodified.

4.4.2 Antipattern: Narrow Servlet Bridges

CORBA and even Web services fall short in some interoperability endeavors. Simply routing IIOP through firewalls can be like opening a can of worms, not to mention that the clients must run J2SE 1.3 or later. Web services potentially bloat method invocations, reduce performance, limit functionality, and require an even later version of Java, making them at times impractical to use for Java-to-Java communications. You can tunnel RMI over HTTP, but vendor incompatibilities and stub class sizes may anchor you here. Stub class sizes are especially important in situations, such as within an applet, where the client may be communicating over a low bandwidth connection. Transferring megs of stub support classes in such cases is not acceptable.

In these types of situations, servlet bridges come to the rescue. Servlet bridges use plain HTTP, requiring no vendor-specific classes or web service frameworks. With a servlet bridge, the client makes an HTTP request to a servlet, which in turn delegates to a service (a stateless session bean, in your case), and returns the result to the client.

Most servlet bridge implementations that we've encountered are not problem-free. They are servlet-specific and convert all types to strings, shoehorning us into some of the same limitations you find with web services. They also don't hide the implementation details of the servlet bridge. Additionally, while implementing custom servlet bridges, we often run into issues with type-checking that can be horribly difficult to debug.

4.4.3 Solution: A generic servlet bridge

You can avoid these faults by implementing a generic servlet bridge. You can easily implement the mapping of a servlet to a stateless session bean and generate the stubs that delegate to that mapping generically, completely eliminating duplicate coding and type-checking concerns.

Listing 4.5 illustrates how a bridge instance maps to a stateless session bean. You map the bridge to a given URL in the web.xml file, specifying the JNDI binding for your session bean in an initialization parameter (listing 4.5).

Listing 4.5 Bridge servlet mappings

```
<servlet>
<servlet-name>MyBeanBridge</servlet-name>
<servlet-class>Bridge</servlet-class>
<init-param>
<param-name>jndi</param-name>
<param-value>ejb/MyBean</param-value>
</init-param>
</servlet>

<servlet-mapping>
<servlet-name>MyBeanBridge</servlet-name>
<url-pattern>/MyBeanBridge</url-pattern>
</servlet-mapping>
```

The bridge servlet implementation looks up and narrows the session bean stub upon initialization. The bridge receives the method and arguments from an HTTP POST, then reflectively delegates the implementation to the configured service. Afterwards, the bridge marshals the result back to the client in the HTTP response (listing 4.6).

Listing 4.6 Example bridge servlet implementation

```
/**
 * Servlet bridge for stateless session beans.
 */
public class Bridge extends HttpServlet {

  /** EJBObject instance for stateless session bean. */
  private Object homeObject = null;

  /** Home interface's create() method. */
  private Method createMethod = null;

  public void init(ServletConfig config)
        throws ServletException {
    try {
      // get home interface jndi binding parameter.
      String jndiBinding = config.getInitParameter("jndi");    // Get the JNDI binding in web.xml
      if (jndiBinding == null)
        throw new ServletException(
          "JNDI binding init. parameter required.");

      // look up home object.
      InitialContext context = new InitialContext();    // Look up the home stub using JNDI
      Object homeObject = context.lookup(jndiBinding);
      if (homeObject == null)
        throw new ServletException(
```

```
        "Home object not found in JNDI tree.");
    EJBHome ejbHome =                                  ◁──┐  You must
      (EJBHome) PortableRemoteObject.narrow(                 narrow the
        homeObject, EJBHome.class);                          stub twice
    Class homeClass =
      ejbHome.getEJBMetaData().getHomeInterfaceClass();
    this.homeObject = PortableRemoteObject.narrow(
      homeObject, homeClass);

    // find create() method on home interface.
    this.createMethod =                                ◁──┐  Look up the
      homeClass.getMethod("create", null);                   create()
  }                                                          method
  catch (ServletException e) {
    throw e;
  }
  catch (Exception e) {
    throw new ServletException(
      "Error creating EJBObject instance.", e);
  }
}
public void doPost(HttpServletRequest request,
    HttpServletResponse response)
    throws ServletException, IOException {
  try {                                                     Read the client's
    // read invocation from request.                        Invocation data
    ObjectInputStream in =                           ◁──┘   transfer object
      new ObjectInputStream(request.getInputStream());

    BridgeInvocation invocation =
      (BridgeInvocation) in.readObject();
    in.close();

    Object result;
    try {                                                   Create an object
      // create EJBObject instance.                          with create()
      Object ejbObject =                             ◁──    method
        createMethod.invoke(homeObject, null);

      // invoke bean method on EJBObject instance.
      result = invocation.invoke(ejbObject);         ◁──┐  Invoke business
    }                                                       method on
    catch (BridgeException e) {                             EJBObject
      result = e;
    }
    // output result.
  ObjectOutputStream out = new ObjectOutputStream(   ◁──┐  Output the
response.getOutputStream());                               results to the
    out.writeObject(result);                               client
    out.close();
  }
```

```
      catch (InvocationTargetException e) {
        throw new ServletException(
          e.getTargetException());
      }
      catch (IllegalAccessException e) {
        throw new ServletException(e);
      }
      catch (ClassNotFoundException e) {
        throw new ServletException(e);
      }
      } catch(IOException e) {
...
      } catch(IllegalArgumentException e) {
...
      }
    }
}
```

You implement the example client using dynamic proxies. J2SE introduced
`java.lang.reflect.Proxy`, a class that dynamically generates new classes that
implement a specified set of interfaces and delegate to an instance of the
`java.lang.reflect.InvocationHandler` interface. This framework enables us to
dynamically implement arbitrary interfaces at runtime.

Client code simply creates a stub and invokes it as it would the normal service:

```
MyBean myBean = (MyBean) BridgeClient.create(
  new URL("http://myhost/MyBeanBridge"), MyBean.class);
myBean.doSomething();
```

You can generate stubs using dynamic proxies that implement your service interface as we do in the client stub factory example in listing 4.7. The underlying
`InvocationHandler` implementation posts the method invocations to the specified
bridge URL and extracts and returns the result.

Listing 4.7 Example client stub factory

```
/**
 * Bridge stub factory. Manufactures session bridge stubs.
 * The default implementation uses dynamic proxies.
 */
public class BridgeClient {

  private static BridgeClient instance = new BridgeClient();

  /** Prevent public instantiation. */
  private BridgeClient() {}

  /** Gets factory instance. */
```

```java
public static BridgeClient getInstance() {
  return instance;
}
/** Marshals invocations to session bridge. */
private static class ClientInvocationHandler
    implements InvocationHandler {

  private URL bridgeUrl;

  /**
   * Constructs new invocation handler for a session
   * bean type.
   */
  private ClientInvocationHandler(URL bridgeUrl) {
    this.bridgeUrl = bridgeUrl;
  }

  public Object invoke(Object proxy, Method method,
      Object[] args) throws Throwable {
    // create invocation value object.
    BridgeInvocation invocation =
      new BridgeInvocation(method, args);

    // post invocation object to bridge Servlet.
    URLConnection connection = bridgeUrl.openConnection();
    connection.setDoOutput(true);
    connection.setDoInput(true);
    connection.setUseCaches(false);

    // output session invocation object.
    ObjectOutputStream out = new ObjectOutputStream(
      connection.getOutputStream());
    out.writeObject(invocation);
    out.flush();
    out.close();

    // input result.
    ObjectInputStream in = new ObjectInputStream(
      connection.getInputStream());
    Object result = in.readObject();

    // if the result is an exception, throw it.
    if (result instanceof BridgeException) throw
      ((BridgeException) result).getCause();

    // return the result.
    return result;
  }
}

/**
 * Gets a session object client stub.
 * Stub uses session bridge to marshal invocations.
```

InvocationHandler for the dynamic proxy

Construct a BridgeInvocation value object

Open a connection to the bridge

Output the BridgeInvocation instance

Input the result

If the result is a BridgeException, unwrap the cause and throw it

```
    * @param bridgeUrl URL of bridge Servlet.
    */
   public Object create(URL bridgeUrl,
       Class remoteInterface) {
     return Proxy.newProxyInstance(
       remoteInterface.getClassLoader(),
       new Class[] { remoteInterface },
       new ClientInvocationHandler(bridgeUrl)
     );
   }
}
```

◁─┐ **Create new stub using dynamic proxy**

The bridge and client stubs communicate using a `BridgeInvocation` object. The `BridgeInvocation` (listing 4.8) simply encapsulates the method and arguments in a serializable form so that you can pass them via HTTP:

Listing 4.8   BridgeInvocation.java

```
/**
 * Bridge invocation.
 * @author Bob Lee
 */
class BridgeInvocation implements java.io.Serializable {

  static final long serialVersionUID = -1;

  private Class remoteClass;
  private String methodName;
  private Class[] parameterTypes;
  private Object[] parameters;

  /**
   * Constructs a session bean invocation to be invoked
   * at a later time. Used by the client.
   * @param jndiBinding Location of home object in JNDI tree.
   * @param method Method to invoke.
   * @param parameters Parameters to pass the method.
   */
  BridgeInvocation(Method method, Object[] parameters) {
    this.remoteClass = method.getDeclaringClass();
    this.methodName = method.getName();
    this.parameterTypes = method.getParameterTypes();
    this.parameters = parameters;
  }

  /**
   * Invokes method on EJBObject instance.
   * @param ejbObject Object to invoke on.
   */
  Object invoke(Object ejbObject) throws BridgeException {
```

◁─┐ **Convert method invocation into a Serializable form**

```
    try {
      Method method = remoteClass.getMethod(this.methodName,    ◁──────────┐
        this.parameterTypes);                                  Invoke method
      return method.invoke(ejbObject, this.parameters);        invocation on
    }                                                          passed object
    catch (NoSuchMethodException e) {
      // never happens for a valid request.
      throw new IllegalArgumentException(
        "Method not found. Invocation: " + this);
    }
    catch (InvocationTargetException e) {
      // target method threw an exception.
      throw new BridgeException(e.getTargetException());
    }
    catch (Exception e) {
      // covers other exceptions (i.e. RuntimeException).
      throw new BridgeException(e);
    }
  }

}
```

This basic example bridge implementation allows us to do almost anything you could do with a normal, stateless RMI-based invocation. However, extensions could make your implementation more robust and production-worthy. Consider these possible extensions:

- Support for stateful beans using an HTTP session
- Support for plain Java objects. You could run your application in a Servlet container to begin with and easily migrate to a full-blown application server down the road.
- Declarative XML configuration for client lookups
- Support for generating the source for the clients stubs at build time rather than using dynamic proxies to support clients using older virtual machines and to reduce the overhead of reflection
- Support for pooling HTTP connections using the HTTP 1.1 keep alive header

We've used a similar implementation, without Dynamic Proxies, to invoke EJBs between different incompatible versions of the same vendor's application server. The vendor's interoperability track depended on support for RMI-IIOP requiring J2SE 1.3 or later. As is often the case, many invoking clients ran older virtual machine versions.

Using a generic servlet bridge reduced the workload considerably since configuring a new stateless session bean only required adding an entry to the web.xml file, and invoking the service from the client took a single line lookup. As an added bonus, the error potential was greatly reduced because we regained compile time type-checking.

4.5 Summary

In this chapter, we explored half the session bean story: the stateless session bean. We identified the implications of handling threads and using thread primitives in an EJB container. We discussed how the EJB architecture impacts your existing exception handling strategies; we examined the performance and scalability of Page-by-Page Iterator implementations; and we outlined options for interoperating safely and efficiently in heterogeneous environments.

In the next chapter, we'll dive into a traditional problem child of the EJB specification—the stateful session bean. In addition, we'll cover many state management techniques at your disposal, considering when each should be applied.

4.6 *Antipatterns in this chapter*

This section covers the Tangled Thread, Swallowing Exceptions, Killer System Exceptions, Database Connection Hog, Eager Iterator, and Narrow Servlet Bridge antipatterns.

TANGLED THREADS

DESCRIPTION

The EJB specification restricts the multithreading of applications. Still, some break the rules.

MOST FREQUENT SCALE

Application

REFACTORED SOLUTION NAME

Refactor

REFACTORED SOLUTION TYPE

Software

REFACTORED SOLUTION DESCRIPTION

The EJB specification has strict rules on threading applications. Though you can break the rules by understanding the intent of the restrictions, it is not recommended.

ANECDOTAL EVIDENCE

"It seems to work OK in the debugger."

SYMPTOMS, CONSEQUENCES

Applications behave unpredictably, because libraries and code are not adequately protected.

SWALLOWING EXCEPTIONS

DESCRIPTION

It's easy to ignore exceptions by just logging them and continuing processing as if nothing happened.

MOST FREQUENT SCALE

Application

REFACTORED SOLUTION NAME

Exceptions

REFACTORED SOLUTION TYPE

Software

REFACTORED SOLUTION DESCRIPTION

When possible, be deliberate about your handling of exceptions. Test adequate exception management.

ANECDOTAL EVIDENCE

"This bug happened from a method called long ago."

SYMPTOMS, CONSEQUENCES

Exceptions do not get processed correctly, resulting in unpredictable crashes and other problems. Bugs are difficult to find.

KILLER SYSTEM EXCEPTIONS

DESCRIPTION

Often, the easiest way to roll back a transaction is to throw a system exception, but it's a problematic solution.

MOST FREQUENT SCALE

Application

REFACTORED SOLUTION NAME

Application exceptions

REFACTORED SOLUTION TYPE

Software

REFACTORED SOLUTION DESCRIPTION

Use application exceptions for application errors. Use system exceptions only for system type errors.

ANECDOTAL EVIDENCE

"Don't write all of that code to roll it back. System exception will do it all for you automatically."

SYMPTOMS, CONSEQUENCES

The consequences are not always clear at first. Code is difficult to maintain. Logs become muddied with application errors, making it difficult to find the cause of true system exceptions. The heavy-handed approach often leads to poor performance if the application logs many exceptions.

DATABASE CONNECTION HOG

DESCRIPTION
Some database extensions can cause a long-term database connection, limiting connection pooling and scalability.

MOST FREQUENT SCALE
Application

REFACTORED SOLUTION NAME
Refactor

REFACTORED SOLUTION TYPE
Software, technology

REFACTORED SOLUTION DESCRIPTION
Refactor your database code to use database extensions that release the connection after each logical operation.

ANECDOTAL EVIDENCE
"Our connection pooling doesn't make any difference."

SYMPTOMS, CONSEQUENCES
Poor scalability and poor performance.

EAGER ITERATOR

DESCRIPTION
Sometimes, developers neglect the performance between the database and application tier, hurting performance.

MOST FREQUENT SCALE
Application

REFACTORED SOLUTION NAME
Test and refactor

REFACTORED SOLUTION TYPE
Software

REFACTORED SOLUTION DESCRIPTION
The best solution is to automate performance tests (see chapter 9) and refactor based on the results.

ANECDOTAL EVIDENCE
"I thought page-by-page iterators were supposed to help performance."

SYMPTOMS, CONSEQUENCES
Changes in one layer have rippling effects on the model.

NARROW SERVLET BRIDGES

DESCRIPTION

Building servlet bridges can solve some problems, but implementing a separate servlet bridge per interface is cumbersome and expensive.

MOST FREQUENT SCALE

Application

REFACTORED SOLUTION NAME

Generic server bridge

REFACTORED SOLUTION TYPE

Software

REFACTORED SOLUTION DESCRIPTION

Generalize the servlet bridge. Map a bridge onto a servlet and session bean combination. The bridge looks up the bean and narrows it upon invocation.

SYMPTOMS, CONSEQUENCES

Each interface requires a new servlet bridge, adding layers, complexity, and maintenance burdens to the code.

Bitter session states

5

This chapter covers

- A definition of session state
- A discussion of stateless vs. stateful services
- An example of storing session state in a stateful session bean
- An example of storing session state in a servlet
- A guidebook for choosing where best to store session state
- Antipatterns when stateful session beans are misused

Snowboarding in the Colorado backcountry offers breathtaking views and bountiful untracked powder. Anxious to take it all in, we've organized a multiday outdoor adventure. Each night we'll relax in a different hut, one of a series of huts connecting segments of premium terrain.

After arriving at the trailhead late in the day, we gear up in snowshoes for the short hike to our first hut. As I lift my backpack from the vehicle, I'm reminded of all that it contains. In preparing for the trip, I had thought obsessively about each item I would bring, knowing it would be strapped on my back for the duration of the trip. Yet as we approach the end of the hike, I'm once again having second thoughts about what I've packed. My back and shoulders are already protesting under the heavy load.

With the benefit of a good night's sleep, we're ready to go in the morning. We notice that a fresh blanket of snow has fallen overnight, adding to an already spectacular base. A snowboarder's dream—sick powder!

Donning my heavy pack, I start getting hooked into my board. I have to rock back and forth a little longer than usual before I finally break free of the board's depression in the snow, deepened by the weight of my pack. I look back over my shoulder as last night's shelter fades into the distance. The safety of our next hut is miles away, miles over the remote backcountry. As we start into our first turns of the day, I feel a twinge of fear that before long this pack will prove to be my millstone.

Stateful session beans have been around since the earliest version of the EJB specification. Indeed, stateful session beans were intended to be the rule; stateless session beans the exception. Over time, however, stateful session beans have fallen out of favor. As with most technologies, after a few years of actual use, significant chinks appeared in the stateful session bean armor. Unfortunately, in many cases, stateful session beans have been dismissed outright by misguided strokes of the broad scalability brush. Mention stateful session beans now, and you'll frequently evoke the gag reflex. Stateless session beans, on the other hand, have arguably become EJB's crown jewel. In this chapter we'll put stateful session beans under the microscope in an effort to uncover their advantages and disadvantages. We'll start by defining session state, and we'll discover why it's handy in certain situations. Then we'll polish up that rusty stateful session bean tool to review its true purpose in managing session state, just in case we need it.

We'll also review how session state can be stored in servlets, giving us a different perspective on the session landscape. Then we'll distill all this information into a guidebook of sorts, one that can tell us when to reach for stateful session beans as the best tool for the job. Finally, we'll identify common ways in which stateful session beans are misused. In the end, we'll have gained a better sense of how to pack our gear to ensure a safe and swift journey to our next project.

5.1 Making a case for session state

Before we dive headlong into choosing tools for storing session state, we need to fully understand what we're trying to achieve with these tools. Specifically, what is session state and when is it valuable?

Session state is simply a working set of information that spans a given conversation. In fact, it's often referred to as *conversational state*. We'll use both terms interchangeably throughout this chapter. We rely on conversational state anytime we engage in any meaningful conversation. As we're chatting with someone, we build up a history that gives context to our conversation. That is, the words we hear and speak have meaning insofar as they are relevant to something we've already said. Using this conversational state as a backdrop, we can communicate much more efficiently. We don't need to qualify every statement by reiterating the sum of the conversation to date.

Conversations between software clients and servers are no different. For example, if you've purchased anything over the Internet recently, then you're probably familiar with the virtual shopping cart. When you show up at an online store to shop, you get your own personal shopping cart. You push your virtual cart around the e-commerce site, filling it with goodies from the vendor's shelves. If you happen to wander off for a moment, leaving the cart in the middle of an aisle, you'll find it right where you left it when you return. Moreover, your cart will still contain all the items you've already added. Once you're done shopping, you wheel the cart to the checkout line and surrender your wallet.

From the time you take control of the shopping cart until the checkout process is complete, you are holding a stateful conversation with the e-commerce server. As you navigate through pages of the web site and pluck merchandise from the shelves, the server at all times remembers who you are and what is in your cart. The contents of your shopping cart represent the session state—a history of you and your shopping spree. Figure 5.1 depicts your private conversation with the e-commerce server.

Imagine what the same conversation might be like if, every time you added something to your shopping cart, the server conveniently forgot what it already contained. The exchange would probably sound more like "The Twelve Days of Christmas" in which adding a new item in turn causes all prior items to be named.

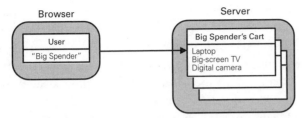

Figure 5.1 Session state is simply a working set of information relevant to any given conversation. HTTP, the communication protocol used by web applications, is stateless. When a dialogue between the web browser and the server is dependent on conversational state, the server must have a strategy to manage session state.

In other words, you'd be responsible for repeating all the conversational history each time a new piece of information was introduced.

As another experiment, imagine the chaos that would ensue if the server failed to keep your conversation private. That is, suppose the server forgets which shopping cart belongs to you. As you're rummaging through the shelves with your back turned, another eager shopper fills your cart with 1970s love song albums. You're in for an unwelcome surprise at the checkout line!

In summary, session state is a private workspace of information that's retained throughout a conversation. Keeping this information intact is valuable because it reduces the amount of data that must be exchanged back and forth to carry on a meaningful dialogue. Alas, there's no such thing as a free lunch, especially here. The convenience of session state comes at a price that must be carefully considered. This is the subject of our first antipattern.

5.2 A pivotal antipattern: Conversational Baggage

Using state simplifies a conversational exchange. Only new information needs to be offered, and once relayed, information does not need to be repeated. That sounds efficient, but there's a rub—someone has to remember the history of the conversation.

Take, for example, the e-commerce server that greets each customer with a personal shopping cart. Throughout a customer's shopping experience, which could vary from a few minutes to several days, the server is burdened with the responsibility of remembering the cart's contents. And no matter how much floor space the store might have, at some point all the aisles become crowded. In other words, the server has a finite amount of memory in which to juggle all the assigned shopping carts.

In addition to the memory overhead of session state, customers expect their shopping carts to be reliable. If the server were to suddenly develop a case of amnesia, a customer would be faced with starting her shopping adventure all over again. To minimize the risk of a memory lapse, the server could record the contents of shopping carts in a backup location, such as a database. While this approach is more convenient and robust for online shopping, it nevertheless requires double-entry bookkeeping. Each time the contents of a cart are changed, the server must take the time to update the backup cart.

Therefore, the convenience afforded by session state often comes at a steep price in memory resources and performance. At the end of the day, someone must be responsible for hauling around the conversational baggage. This overhead can be especially problematic in distributed systems such as those developed using EJB components. On the surface, the use of session state simplifies the interfaces through which distributed components communicate. However, that simplicity masks a more complex need—the session state must be stored and managed efficiently. So, before we tap into the potential benefits of session state, it's important we understand its cost.

5.2.1 The burden of state

Let's dig a bit deeper into the burden of state by taking a sneak peek at the type of EJB intended to manage session state—the stateful session bean. Later in this chapter, we'll look at an example of a stateful session bean in detail. First, we can draw important conclusions by looking at how stateful session beans manage state.

A *stateful session bean* stores conversational state on behalf of its client over the course of a business process, such as online shopping. A stateful session bean that models a shopping cart, for example, retains the contents of a particular cart associated with a particular shopper across multiple requests to the e-commerce server. In other words, a stateful session bean always has a one-to-one relationship with its client. As such, a representative amount of exclusive memory is needed to store each bean's state. Figure 5.2 illustrates the relationship between stateful session beans and their clients.

As the number of simultaneous stateful conversations increases, the overhead in juggling the necessary memory resources while delivering tolerable performance takes a toll on the server. Consider, for example, a case in which 1,000 shopping carts are active at the same time. The EJB server is burdened with managing the memory resources required by 1,000 shopping carts, many of which may be piled high with items. Fortunately the EJB server has tricks up its sleeve to make the most out of limited memory. For example, it can use secondary storage like

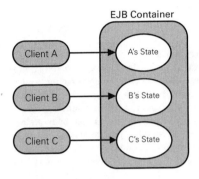

Figure 5.2
Stateful session beans are dedicated to one client throughout their life. As with other state management alternatives, every client's unique state incurs a memory and management overhead.

virtual memory to store idle shopping carts. These techniques may yield accept-able results under certain conditions but, eventually, shoppers will begin to notice sluggish performance.

When a tool such as stateful session beans shows up in our toolbox, we usually start noticing all kinds of wonderful opportunities for storing session state to sim-plify conversations. This zeal has a deceptive way of blinding us to the potential drawbacks. Consequently, we can accumulate conversational baggage quickly throughout our application. Before we take on that additional weight, let's con-sider an alternative.

5.2.2 *Lightening the load*

Now, imagine a slightly different shopping experience. Rather than pushing around a shopping cart and intermittently adding items over time, let's say we keep a shopping list offline instead. When we're ready to purchase the items on our list, we submit it to the e-commerce server, which performs the checkout pro-cess. We've made a subtle, but important, change to the way we communicate with the server. From the server's perspective, the conversation is now stateless. This alleviates the need for the server to keep track of our shopping cart contents. Consequently, the server can make do with much less memory.

Designing the checkout process as a stateless service offers another advantage. Since the process holds no state, nothing can be lost. If the service fails, the shop-ping list can be submitted to another identical service. Again, there's no free lunch; something must store the shopping list. In this case, the shopping list could be stored in the client itself. A number of advantages to shifting this responsibility may exist, including the distribution of memory requirements across a wider range of resources.

EJB Container

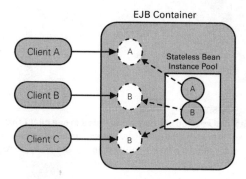

Figure 5.3
Stateless session beans are pooled and swapped between clients to achieve higher levels of scalability. In this example, bean instance A is busy servicing Client A. When Client B invokes a method on a stateless session bean, bean instance B is plucked from the pool to service the request. Once the request is complete, bean instance B is returned to the pool and later reused by Client C.

Stateless conversations are best handled by the other type of session bean—the *stateless session bean*. Unlike stateful session beans, stateless session beans don't hold onto conversational state between client requests. The client is responsible for passing any relevant state each time it communicates with the bean. For example, a stateless session bean modeling a checkout process could provide a `check-out()` method that takes a shopping list as a parameter.

The upshot is that stateless session beans have no allegiance to any given client and can therefore be shared among many clients. The EJB container simply creates a pool of identical stateless session beans and meters them out to handle client requests. As soon as the `checkout()` method returns from processing one client's shopping list, it can be reused immediately to service a different client. Figure 5.3 illustrates how a stateless session bean can be reused by multiple clients. By reusing stateless session beans in a pool, a small number of beans can handle a large number of concurrent clients. Consequently, stateless session beans generally scale better than stateful session beans. That's not to say that one type of bean is always better than the other, but it should nudge us toward making services stateless where possible.

5.2.3 Solution 1: Strive for statelessness

Although certain situations do justify creating stateful services (e.g., e-commerce), you should avoid creating stateful services without close consideration of your situation's particular needs. Shopping cart applications specifically rely on a relatively large amount of conversational state to ensure a robust shopping experience. Indeed, we're willing to pay the price of managing shopping cart resources in return for lots of satisfied customers in the checkout line. However, if you do begin by building stateful services, you may add unnecessary complexity to other services added later. And, if you begin by creating stateless services, you can avoid overburdening future services. When no real benefit to managing session state exists, using stateful session beans should be avoided. In other words, stateful services should be the exception, not the rule—not because they don't scale, but because, in the absence of session state, they're the wrong tools for the job. Just as you wouldn't go to the trouble of pushing around a shopping cart just to buy one item, you shouldn't use stateful session beans for stateless conversations. If the conversation is stateless, then stateless session beans are a better choice. Indeed, stateless session beans scale better because they're *not* burdened by state.

For this reason, you should strive to design business methods that take client-specific information as parameters when convenient. An example might be a credit card processing service that takes a DTO representing the card number, expiration date, and transaction amount as a parameter. It could then return the results in a separate DTO. Figure 5.4 illustrates a stateless credit card processing service.

By all means, use stateless session beans to the maximum extent possible. Then use stateful services when necessary.

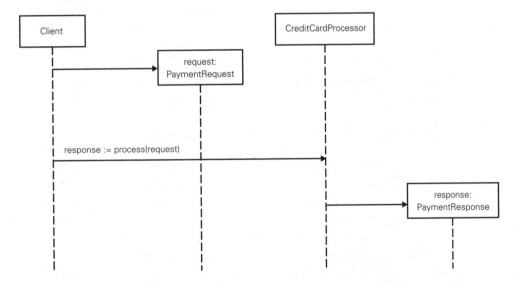

Figure 5.4 **Stateless services, such as this credit card processor, take client-specific information as method parameters. Consequently, these services aren't burdened with remembering session state across multiple method requests. As a result, stateless services are generally less complex and more scalable. Packaging information in data transfer objects helps to keep the interface to a stateless service clean and efficient.**

5.2.4 Solution 2: Leverage session state when beneficial

So because stateless session beans scale better, stateful session beans should be banished from our toolbox, right? Not so fast! Remember, stateful session beans are a tool for storing session state. If we don't need session state, then stateful session beans aren't the right tool. Therefore, the fundamental question we must answer is not, "Should we use stateless or stateful session beans?" Instead, we should step back and contemplate the question "Do we *really* need session state?"

Often, making the choice to use session state is a no-brainer. The online shopping cart illustrates a common situation where the benefits of session state definitely outweigh its burdens. We can offer a friendlier shopping experience by keeping track of shopping cart contents for users. Moreover, managing session state in this way helps ensure the maximum selling opportunity. When an item goes into the cart, it should stay in there until the customer completes the checkout process. Using a tool designed to manage session state on the server makes this job easier.

If after considering the needs of a service, you decide that, yes, you really do need session state, the next question that arises is, "How should we manage session state?" In the next two sections we'll get our hands dirty using two tools for managing session state—stateful session beans and servlets. Keep in mind that stateful services can be more complex and less scalable than stateless services. Nevertheless, these tools are invaluable when we can't live without session state.

5.3 Managing sessions with stateful session beans

Stateful session beans are server-side components that model a business process while encapsulating session, or conversational, state. The conversation is nothing more than a sequence of business methods invoked by a client on the bean. The client may be a servlet, a fat-client application, or any other component with access to the stateful session bean.

Once a client initiates a conversation with a stateful session bean, the bean's sole purpose in life is to do work at the request of that client. Their conversation is kept private. As the client invokes methods, the bean stores conversational state in its instance variables. Any changes made to the state during the conversation can affect the results of subsequent method invocations. In this sense, a stateful session bean is nothing less than we'd expect from any self-respecting object. It encapsulates state as well as the logic that operates on that state.

Despite their relative simplicity, over time stateful session beans may have become rusty tools in your toolbox. You've no doubt heard that they don't scale as well as stateless session beans. Indeed, they generally don't. (There, that's out of the way!) In all fairness, stateful services of any variety generally can't be scaled as efficiently as stateless services. Memory resources are limiting factors to scalability and stateful services require exclusive memory. Nevertheless, when session state is beneficial, we need to use a tool best suited for the job, and stateful session beans are one obvious choice. With this in mind, let's look at how a stateful session bean can be used to model a shopping cart.

5.3.1 *Shopping using a stateful session bean*

Shopping carts are a staple of any e-commerce site. Building a stateful session bean to hold a shopping cart's contents is relatively easy. For brevity's sake, we'll assume you've probably already crafted a few stateful session beans, so we won't get mired down with drawn-out examples. We'll forego creating the required EJB remote and home interfaces. The stateful session bean class is worth looking at in detail, however, before we move on to bitter things. (And trust us, we will!)

The canonical shopping cart, reinvented by nearly every e-commerce shop in the universe, is simply a wrapper enclosing a collection of items. Clients can add items, delete items, and query for all the current items in the cart. Okay, some shopping carts do have a bit more gold plating, but if you've seen one shopping cart, you've seen them all. Listing 5.1 shows the implementation of a simple shopping cart as a stateful session bean.

Listing 5.1 Managing a shopping cart using a stateful session bean

```
public class ShoppingCartEJB implements javax.ejb.SessionBean {

  private Map cart;
  private javax.ejb.SessionContext context;

  public void ejbCreate() {
    cart = new HashMap();
  }

  public void addItem(String item, int quantity) {
   cart.put(item, new Integer(quantity));
  }

  public void removeItem(String item) {
   cart.remove(item);
  }

  public Map getItems() {
    return cart;
  }

  public void ejbActivate() {
```

```
    // Called after bean has been activated
    }

  public void ejbPassivate() {
   // Called before bean is passivated
   }

  public void ejbRemove() {
   // May be called before bean is destroyed
   }

  public void setSessionContext(javax.ejb.SessionContext context) {
    this.context = context;
   }
  }
```

Aside from the EJB life cycle methods that we must implement (which we'll discuss in section 5.3.2), there's not much to constructing the shopping cart. When the client creates a cart, the ejbCreate() method is called indirectly to initialize an empty collection of items. As the client looks through a vendor's catalog of products, it invokes the addItem() method for any items of interest. Invoking this method incurs a side effect: the bean commits the item to memory by updating the cart instance variable. The same holds true whenever the client removes an item by invoking the removeItem() method. Because the bean retains the contents of the shopping cart across method invocations, at any time the client can invoke the getItems() method to obtain all the items added since the shopping cart was created.

It's important to note that session state is temporary. It exists for the duration of the conversation. As long as the client continues to use the same shopping cart reference, the server will recognize it as the owner of the cart. Once the client has broken off communication with the cart, its contents are lost forever. In other words, this example shopping cart is not saved to any long-term storage, such as a database.

Now that we've laid down the code for a stateful session bean, let's peek inside the EJB container—the environment that sustains the life of a stateful session bean.

5.3.2 *Looking under the hood*

Developing stateful session beans is relatively easy, thanks in no small part to the EJB container. It does all the heavy lifting; all we have to do is supply the business logic. That sounds like a pretty sweet deal and, indeed, relying on the EJB container often pays off. Nevertheless, before we commit to using stateful session beans, we need to understand the role of the EJB container.

The EJB container's first responsibility is to maintain the one-to-one relationship between a client and its stateful session bean. When a client invokes a business method on a bean's remote or local interface, the container must ensure that the right stateful session bean instance receives that request. If the container fails to correctly match up the request with its bean instance, then conversations quickly will become scrambled with irrelevant state.

In addition, the EJB container has the unenviable job of maximizing memory resources for the best possible performance. Every stateful session bean managed in memory takes up prime real estate that could be used to store other things. If resources were infinite, we'd want to put everything in memory for fast access. Realistically, memory is a limited resource, so the EJB container must strike a tolerable balance between memory and performance.

Looking under the hood of the container reveals the tricks the container uses to service multiple concurrent clients with maximum responsiveness. It's a relatively straightforward series of life cycle events, focused on using a finite amount of memory efficiently. Figure 5.5 illustrates the life cycle of a stateful session bean instance.

Let's consider each stage in the life cycle of a stateful session bean instance more closely:

- **Creation event** When a client wishes to strike up a conversation with a stateful session bean, it invokes the `create()` method (or an overloaded variant) on the bean's home interface. This causes a new instance of the bean to be created and brought to life in the EJB container's cache. Before the bean instance is assigned to the client, the bean's `ejbCreate()` method is invoked to initialize any session state. Once initialized, the bean instance is assigned to the client that created it and enters the method ready state.

- **Method ready state** In this state, the bean instance dutifully goes about the work requested by its client. To fulfill the needs of its client, the bean

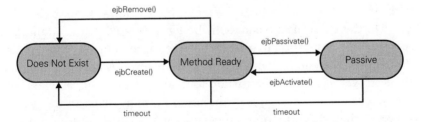

Figure 5.5 Once created, a stateful session bean stands ready to do its client's work. It's either immediately ready in the EJB container's cache or activated into the cache from its passive state. To conserve cache space, the container may passivate the bean if it goes idle. If the client lets the bean go idle for too long, or explicitly removes it, the bean is destroyed.

instance may employ the services of other resources, such as entity beans or a database.

- **Passivation event** If the bean instance remains idle for a relatively long time between client requests, the EJB container may choose to evict it from the cache to conserve memory. The criteria used by the container to make this decision are vendor-specific, though usually influenced by the bean's deployment configuration. In general, to maximize limited memory the container will favor active bean instances. Before a bean instance is passivated, the container invokes its `ejbPassivate()` method to give it an opportunity to close any open resources and prepare its state to be written to secondary storage.

- **Passive state** In this state the bean instance's nontransient instance variables are written to secondary storage, usually the file system. The EJB container stores the bean's state relative to the client that created it. If the client calls on the bean to do subsequent work, the container knows where to find it. Meanwhile, by using secondary storage such as virtual memory the container's cache can be used for popular bean instances.

- **Activation event** While a bean instance is in the passivated state, its client may once again pick up the conversation by invoking one of the bean's business methods. At this point the container restores the passivated bean instance into the cache. When the bean has been successfully revived in the cache, the container invokes its `ejbActivate()` method. This gives the bean instance an opportunity to refresh any transient instance variables or reopen resources closed prior to passivation. Once this callback method has returned, the bean goes back into the method-ready state.

- **Remove event** At any time, a client may choose to end the conversation with its stateful session bean instance by invoking its `remove()` method. Prior to the bean instance actually being destroyed, the container invokes its `ejbRemove()` method to give it a chance to clean up any loose ends. Once destroyed, the bean instance's state is lost forever. A bean instance may also be destroyed if it's left idle for too long and its timeout value expires. This may occur while the bean is in the method ready or passivated state. Note, however, that when the timeout occurs on a passivated bean, the container is not required to invoke the bean instance's `ejbRemove()` method.

Wow! There's a lot going on under the hood of the EJB container. But because the client always accesses its bean instance indirectly through the container, it's oblivious to the gyrations the container must go through to make sure the bean instance is always ready to service requests. Indeed, when a client invokes a method on a passivated bean instance, it appears as if the bean has always been active in the cache. In truth, the bean may be passivated and activated multiple times over the course of the conversation. If the container is doing its job well, its resource management duties are hidden from the client.

That's all well and good, but when the container is under a lot of stress, cracks begin to show. Remember, only so much memory is available for the cache. When there's not enough memory to hold all active bean instances in the cache, clients can become painfully aware of the passivation/activation shell game. It's similar to the thrashing of multiple applications on your desktop, all competing for space in physical memory. To bring an idle application into physical memory, another application must be swapped out to virtual memory on disk. The familiar grinding sound usually indicates a lot of disk reads and writes going on. Figure 5.6 illustrates the sacrifice of one stateful session bean instance to make room for another in the cache.

Alas, often we create unnecessary work for the container. This needless work is the subject of many antipatterns explored throughout the remainder of this chapter. Before we take a look at those antipatterns, let's detour briefly to explore another tool for storing session state—the HttpSession class offered by Java servlets. (Note that, although we'll discuss the use the Servlet API in this section as a comparison to stateful session beans, a comprehensive discussion of servlets is beyond the scope of this chapter.)

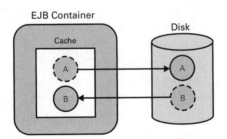

Figure 5.6
The stateful session bean cache has limited headroom. To make space for instance B to be activated in the cache, instance A is passivated to disk. The shell game of passivating beans to allow others to be activated can lead to excessive thrashing if the cache size and the number of concurrent clients are unbalanced.

5.4 *Managing sessions with servlets*

When users visit our web site, we'd like to store information for them as they move from page to page. This ability to identify users and manage their private session state is often referred to as *session tracking*. Although HTTP is stateless, and does not include built-in support for session tracking, several techniques are commonly used to track a session across multiple page requests. As a default strategy, servlets can store a cookie on the browser machine. The browser then automatically sends the cookie to the server every time the user requests a page. In this way, the server is able to identify the client. Alternatively, the client can be identified by rewriting all requested page URLs to include the client's unique session identifier. By inspecting each requested URL, the server is then able to recognize the client.

Fortunately, the Java Servlet API defines an `HttpSession` class that offers a convenient façade to session tracking. The beauty of this API is that the session-tracking details are hidden from the servlet programmer. If the user's browser won't take a cookie, for example, then the server can resort to URL rewriting.

5.4.1 *Keeping it simple with HttpSession*

So where does a web client keep its private stash of session state? Well, it's stored in the Web server, but the client must present its golden key before getting its hands on the goods. The first time a client makes a request of the server, the server generates a unique session identifier. This session ID may then be set in a cookie on the browser's machine or used to rewrite subsequently requested URLs. Regardless of where it is stored, the session ID must be presented to the server on each request for the server to recognize the client.

Once the session ID has been generated, the servlet can create an `HttpSession` object on behalf of the client. The `HttpSession` object is simply a collection of key-value pairs used to hold a client's session state. The server stores the `HttpSession` object in memory mapped to the client's session ID. That way, every time the client makes a request and presents its session ID, the server can look up the client's corresponding `HttpSession` object. Figure 5.7 shows the relationship between session IDs and their associated `HttpSession` objects.

Note that a servlet may also store a handle to a stateful session bean in the `HttpSession` object. This is especially useful when a web application is designed to delegate session management to a stateful session bean.

Now, let's put a servlet to work storing the items in a shopping cart.

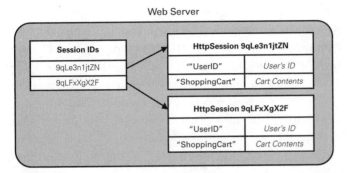

Figure 5.7 Each session ID relates to one `HttpSession` object that may contain zero or more key-value pairs representing a user's session state.

5.4.2 *Shopping using a servlet*

Using the Servlet API to track the contents of a shopper's cart is remarkably easy and convenient. Listing 5.2 shows an abbreviated version of our shopping cart as managed by a servlet.

Listing 5.2 Managing a shopping cart using a servlet

```
public class ShoppingCartServlet extends HttpServlet {

 public void doGet(HttpServletRequest request,
                   HttpServletResponse response)
   throws ServletException, IOException {

   HttpSession session = request.getSession(true);

   Map cart = (Map)session.getAttribute("ShoppingCart");

   if (cart == null) {
    cart = new HashMap();
    session.setAttribute("ShoppingCart", cart);
   }

   String item = request.getParameter("item");
   String quantity = request.getParameter("quantity");
   if (quantity == null) {
      quantity = "1";
   }

   if (item != null) {
     cart.put(item, new Integer(quantity));
   }
  }
 }
}
```

Obtain the client's HttpSession object

Bind the client's shopping cart into the HttpSession object

Identify the item and quantity to add

Add the item to the cart

When the client first accesses the servlet, invoking the `request.getSession(true)` method creates a new `HttpSession` object. If a session had already been created for this user, this method simply returns the existing `HttpSession` object. The servlet then queries the user's `HttpSession` object, using its `getAttribute()` method to see if a shopping cart already exists. If this is the first time the client has accessed the servlet, then a new `HashMap` object representing the shopping cart must be created. Once created, the new object is bound into the `HttpSession` object under the "ShoppingCart" key using the `setAttribute()` method. If a shopping cart already exists for this client, the same cart continues to be used throughout the shopping spree.

With the shopping cart now in position, the servlet identifies the item and quantity to be added by parsing the URL request parameters. After a bit of validation, the new item is added to the shopping cart.

That's it! The coding was relatively painless. We just dumped data in the session and let the server figure out which data goes with which client. If we always had web clients and we could afford to lose their session state, that would be the end of the story. However, we can't always live with these limitations.

5.4.3 *Scaling up servlet sessions*

Invariably, every time a discussion about stateful session beans comes up, scalability is the focal point. After a round of teeth gnashing, the discussion usually gravitates toward the use of `HttpSession` as a superior way to store state. While we may wish servlet sessions were a panacea for poor scalability, they're not. As we've already learned, there's no free lunch when session state is involved, regardless of the tool used.

A servlet container will attempt to manage resources to yield optimal scalability. Not unlike an EJB container, it may passivate and activate `HttpSession` objects to conserve memory resources. This feature is a vendor value-add, however, and not standardized like the life cycle of stateful session beans. Depending on how the servlet container chooses to juggle resources, it may scale equally well as or better than an EJB container. On the other hand, it might not scale as well. In any event, remember that the degree to which a servlet or EJB container is able to scale is vendor-specific. Unfortunately, we can't make any generalizations without tying ourselves to a particular vendor's implementation.

More to the point, the scalability argument can be a red herring. The argument draws attention away from the critical decision—where best to store necessary session state. Deciding whether to use a stateful session bean or the `HttpSession` isn't based solely on scalability. In the next section, we'll drive some stakes in the ground as guideposts. Using these guideposts and our objectives as guides, we can navigate through the possible session state storage choices.

5.5 *Antipattern: Golden Hammers of Session State*

> *By midafternoon I'm miserable. I've been fighting my heavy-laden pack all morning. When I'm pointed downhill, it's pushing me too far forward on the board. When I lay into each turn, my body must absorb the G-force of the extra weight. And when I stop to rest, it tries to drown me in the powder.*
>
> *A couple times when riding through deep drifts, I'm sucked down into heavy powder and lose my balance. What would normally be soft spills end up being painful falls as the torque of the flailing pack jerks me around. Digging out of the crash site with the heavy tug on my back is exhausting. Worse yet, all that thrashing about in the snow has made my gear wet: I cannot look forward to the comfort of a warm bed at the end of this day.*
>
> *As we finally approach the second hut, I couldn't be more relieved. A snowmobiler with a grin from ear to ear reads our tired faces. For a small fee, he'll make sure our gear is cached at each hut along our route. We can ride with freedom all day and be greeted by warm clothes and dry food each night. This is money well spent!*

Reflecting on that trying day, we can see now that we could have avoided a lot of frustration by considering some options while planning the trip. Unfortunately, our experience as backpackers blinded us to the possibility of having our gear stored for us rather than hauling it around all day. Indeed, hiking on dry ground with a heavy pack is a lot less dangerous than carrying the same load while barreling through the backcountry on a snowboard. Applying the same approach universally to every situation usually sets us up for a painful fall.

Once we've decided that session state is a must-have, we stand at a crossroads. We're faced with the decision of where best to store it. Down each possible road lies a solution crafted with a distinct tool set. Some roads appear well traveled. Depending on prior experience, we may have become more comfortable following a particular path and wielding a certain trusty tool. Other roads may appear overgrown or littered with debris. The solutions they offer may require unfamiliar tools or approaches that have let us down in the past.

In general, session state can be stored in one of three locations: the client, the server's memory using a stateful session bean or a servlet session, or a database. As we'll find out, the solution we choose will depend heavily on the type of data we plan to store in a session. At first glance, we might be tempted to use a familiar tool that has served us well over time. We know the tool can get the job done, though the solution might get ugly and take a little more time. On the other hand, when we continually reach for the same tool for every job, it can become a golden hammer that may negatively influence the quality of the work. Once we start swinging that golden hammer, everything around us starts looking like a nail. At best, we might miss an opportunity to learn how to use a tool better suited for the job. At worst, we might end up botching the job completely.

We'll break form slightly in this section to compare and contrast different tools used to store session state. Try as we might, we won't succeed in coming up with a grand unifying principle (and that's the point—a unifying principle doesn't exist). Rather than taking a shortcut by suggesting that one size fits all, we'll just take a short stroll down each road. Along the way we'll point out advantages and disadvantages to each approach, then describe scenarios in which each approach really shines. At the end of our walking tour, we'll offer quick rules of thumb for picking the right tool for the job.

5.5.1 *Storing sessions on the client*

For the purposes of this discussion, a client can be a web browser or any fat-client application. Regardless of the approach, the chosen client will need to store an unambiguous identifier for the user. This identifier may be a cookie containing a unique session ID or a reference to a stateful session bean. When the client presents the cookie or uses the reference, the server is able to match a user with her corresponding session.

At the other end of the spectrum, a client can be designed to store all the session state, not just references to it. That's exactly the kind of client we're referring to in this section. For example, a web browser can store all session values in cookies, URL parameters, or hidden HTML form fields. In fat-client applications, the state can be represented as first-class objects held in the client's memory or persisted to disk. Table 5.1 summarizes the advantages and disadvantages of storing all the session state on the client.

Table 5.1 Storing session state locally on the client allows for fast access and the potential for high scalability at the expense of session volatility.

Advantages	Disadvantages	Best used when:
Allows the client to use state-less server-side components that offer optimal scalability	When users move to a different client machine or change/restart their browsers, their session state is lost.	The loss of session state is tolerable.
Distributes the memory requirements of session state across clients.	If the client crashes, all session state may be lost.	Only small amounts of data are exchanged with the server to avoid the cost of network round-trips.
Improves performance of clients that manage UI workflow using local session state	Some data must be transferred across the network to the server with every request.	Session state can be used locally to efficiently control a client-specific workflow.
	Session state must be transformed from client's format to server's format.	
	If session state contains sensitive information, it must be encrypted before being transmitted to ensure security.	

An important benefit of this approach is the opportunity to design the server to be stateless. This of course requires that the client send an amount of session state with each request. The server may then send back updated session state with each response. Being stateless puts the server in a good position to deliver the best possible scalability. Pooling stateless session beans to be reused between client requests is one way to maximize resources. However, this advantage may be offset by the overhead of frequently transferring state over the network. Another downside is that the life of the session state is at the mercy of its hosting client. If the user moves to another client machine, their session state is no longer available.

5.5.2 *Storing sessions on the server using servlets*

As we've seen, using an `HttpSession` object to store session state is easy and convenient. Doing so does, however, require that clients communicate with the server using HTTP. With each request they must also send a unique session ID. Table 5.2 summarizes the advantages and disadvantages of storing session state on the server using servlets.

Table 5.2 For web clients, the simplicity of a servlet has appeal insofar as session state is kept in a local cache.

Advantages	Disadvantages	Best used when:
Easy and convenient to use for servlet programmers Minimizes the amount of data passed between the client and server over the network Quick access to local session state without incurring network round-trips to back-end resources	When users move to a different client machine or change/restart their browsers, their session state is lost. When users log out, their session state is lost. If the Web server crashes, all session state may be lost. When a user's session timeout expires, their session state is lost. Not accessible by non-web clients Web server's memory resources are a limiting factor to scalability.	The loss of session state is tolerable. All clients are web browsers or use HTTP to communicate with the server. No existing investment in an EJB server

This approach makes sense when web clients need to store temporary information relevant to a user's current location. Pay careful attention to the number of conditions that result in a user's session being lost. It's evident that a session is intended to live for a limited time at any given location. As such, only temporal information should be added to a session. When a user moves locations, the session should be able to be destroyed without adverse side effects.

Take, for example, the case where a session tracks whether a user is currently logged in. When the user logs out using a form in the browser, a well-designed servlet invokes the `session.invalidate()` method. This, in turn, destroys all session state. That's a good thing since you don't want someone maliciously using your session when you're gone. It's a bad thing if you want to log the user out without losing the session state. That is, if the `HttpSession` object is storing shopping cart contents, they'll vanish when the user logs out. A servlet session is best when you need to store information that can be recreated easily when the user logs in from any location. For example, the existence of information in the session can be used to indicate a user's login status.

5.5.3 *Storing sessions on the server using stateful EJB*

As we've discussed, the EJB container manages the life cycle of stateful session beans. The most active bean instances are held in memory for maximum performance. Beans that have not been used recently may be passivated to disk to conserve memory resources. When a client invokes a method on a stateful session bean's remote interface, the container dispatches the request to the bean instance originally created by the client. Table 5.3 summarizes the advantages and disadvantages of storing session state on the server using stateful session beans.

Table 5.3 Stateful session beans encapsulate reusable business logic with session state for use by disparate types of clients.

Advantages	Disadvantages	Best used when:
All the benefits of an EJB component, including concurrency, declarative transactions, and security management	When users move to a different client machine, their session state is lost.	The loss of session state is tolerable.
Accessible by web and non-web clients alike	If the EJB server crashes, all session state may be lost.	Web and non-web clients can benefit from sharing the same business process or workflow.
Encapsulates business logic with session state	When a bean's timeout expires, the user's session state is lost.	An investment in an EJB server has already been made.
Minimizes the amount of data passed between the client and server over the network	EJB server's memory resources are a limiting factor to scalability.	Your Web server doesn't sufficiently manage a cache of `HttpSession` objects to meet your scalability needs.
Wide support for clustering and failover to prevent a single point of failure.		

This approach really shines when applications need to retain session state across a multirequest sequence, but they don't have a servlet front-end. In these cases, a stateful session bean is the logical equivalent of a servlet's `HttpSession` object. This approach is also advantageous when web and non-web clients can benefit from reusing the business logic offered by a stateful session bean. Remember, however, that if a bean isn't used frequently by its client, its timeout may expire and the bean may be destroyed. Therefore, only temporary information should be stored between service requests.

It's also possible to use a hybrid approach in cases where your Web server doesn't scale as well as you'd like with large numbers of `HttpSession` objects. For example, if your web server doesn't support the passivation and activation of HttpSession objects to control memory consumption, a servlet can instead delegate cache management duties to the EJB server by simply storing a reference to a stateful session bean in the HttpSession object for each user. This keeps the memory requirements of the Web server at a minimum so that cache management isn't warranted. The EJB server can then manage the cache of stateful session beans in a standardized fashion. If the servlet and stateful session bean aren't colocated in the same server, the benefits of this hybrid approach may be offset by network round-trips.

Stateful session beans are not intended to survive in the event of an EJB server crash. Don't let the advanced clustering and failover support offered by some EJB server vendors lull you into thinking otherwise. Even if a stateful session bean has been replicated to a backup server in a cluster, a possibility still exists that the servers hosting the bean could crash. If data is important, don't store it in something as fragile as a stateful session bean.

5.5.4 *Storing sessions in a database*

Every approach we've touch on so far has at least one thing in common—it's best used when users can afford to lose their session forever. When state in a session must be permanent, transcending the length of a conversation, a database is the best tool for the job. This may involve directly accessing a database, using an EJB component that fronts a database, or applying any other persistence mechanism. The session ID is typically used as a key for locating a user's session-oriented data. Table 5.4 summarizes the advantages and disadvantages of storing session state in a database.

Using a database creates confusion, however, when it comes to defining session state. A session may have both temporary and permanent values. For example, login information would exist only as long as the current session is valid, while the contents of the user's shopping cart may be stored over the long term. A stateful session bean or HttpSession object can be used to cache the stored information to avoid hitting the database for read-only operations. Updating important information in the session will require a write operation on the database. This overhead is generally outweighed by the need to permanently store state critical to your business or the happiness of your customers.

Unlike the other approaches, state stored in a database doesn't automatically expire. You'll need to develop a strategy for reaping old session data, such as periodically searching the database for session data that falls outside a set time limit.

Table 5.4 Databases offer the most reliable storage of permanent session state, though sometimes at the expense of network round trips and development time.

Advantages	Disadvantages	Best used when:
All or part of the session state can be made durable to outlive a conversation. Reliable and recoverable storage of critical information Authenticated users can access data from any client platform at any time.	State must be marshaled between the database and the Web/EJB server. If state is also cached in the Web/EJB server for fast access, it must be kept consistent with the database. Session state must be transformed from server's format into database tables. Not as easy to develop as in-memory alternatives	Information contained in a session should never be lost. Users frequently move to different client platforms but don't want to lose important information. An opportunity exists to cache user-specific information for better performance.

This process is easy if a database table associates user IDs with the last modification time of their session.

5.5.5 *Revisiting the shopping cart*

So, which approach is best suited for our shopping cart application? Let's use the guideposts we set up in previous sections to help steer our decision.

Most shopping cart applications are web-based, so we can easily rule out storing all the session state on a fat client. We could elect to store all the session state in the browser, but if our Web server already supports servlets then we won't gain much by taking that route. What about using stateful session beans or the HttpSession object in a servlet? From an accessibility standpoint, not much difference actually exists between the two in this instance. Even though we're building a web-based application, a servlet could store a handle to a stateful session bean in the HttpSession object. And, if our Web server has difficulty balancing the memory requirements of many sessions, that would certainly be an option. However, both approaches share a common disadvantage. Our choice is made easier if we consider the implications of losing session state.

When a shopper puts things in a cart, we'd rather those items stay there until checkout is completed. Yet myriad possibilities exists for disaster. For starters, if either the Web server or the EJB server crashes, all session state could be lost. This risk might be minimized in a clustered environment with good support for failover, but barring any failures, the end result will be the same if a shopper puts a few items in his cart using the browser at work, logs out, then goes home later to finish shopping. Once logged in at home, he'll be staring slack-jawed at an empty cart. In other words, to avoid losing their shopping carts, shoppers must add all their items and check out using the same browser, on the same client machine before the session expires or lose their previous shopping. If the session is lost, chances are shoppers won't take the time to readd everything. Therefore, if we put the shopping cart contents in a stateful session bean or an `HttpSession` object, we can affect our bottom line directly—and in a bad way.

Sessions are just too transient and unreliable to be held responsible for managing a shopping cart full of goods. That leaves us with the choice of storing the cart's contents in a database. Figure 5.8 illustrates our shopping cart architecture.

In figure 5.8, we use an `HttpSession` object both to store the user's unique ID and to serve as a local cache of the cart's contents. Each time a new item is added to the cart, the item is also pushed back into the database relative to the user's ID. If a shopper logs out and switches browsers, the session is invalidated to keep the cart secure without losing its contents. When the shopper successfully logs in at the new location, the user ID is once again stored in an `HttpSession` object. At that time, the database is queried to populate the local cache represented by the `HttpSession` object with the current cart items.

Users that don't log in are considered guests. As such, the contents of their carts are only stored in the `HttpSession` object. That is, their cart is volatile; its lifetime is tied to the length of their session. In contrast, when a user logs in, the state of the cart in the session is replicated to the database. The session is then just a local cache. In other words, guests don't enjoy the benefits offered by a database-backed session. With this solution in place, shoppers can shop 'til they drop! Now, let's sum up what we've discovered by looking at the session management tools available to us.

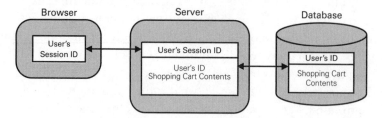

Figure 5.8 Shopping cart applications are best designed using a combination of temporary session state for user information and local caching, and a database for reliable, location-independent shopping.

5.5.6 *Overall solution: Pick the right tool for the job*

Throughout this chapter, we have surveyed the session landscape and sifted methodically through a lot of information. If you remember just one thing, let it be that all the approaches we've looked at have distinct advantages and disadvantages. You must pick the one that best meets your application's needs. To do so, you may have to learn how to use a new tool. So be it. The alternative may be like using a hammer as a pipe wrench. Before you know it, water will be running down your arms and dripping off your elbows, and you'll be swearing like a sailor.

Keep in mind the limitations of stateful session beans and HTTP sessions. Here's the bottom line: If the data exchanged in a conversation is vitally important and can't be easily reconstructed, don't store it in a stateful session bean or an `HttpSession` object. If losing conversational state would be considered a disaster, store it someplace safe. Databases are particularly good at that kind of thing. Sessions in any form are best used in the following situations:

- **Storing temporary user information** Examples include a login status, preferences, and anything else that's dependent on the user's location.

- **Storing user-specific cached data** Local caches of this sort can reduce the number of round-trips to back-end data sources. Cached data—for example, search results—can be easily recreated if lost.

- **Managing a repeatable business process** Some business processes that span multiple client requests can benefit from session state. Just make sure the potential loss of that state isn't damaging to your business.

- **Storing UI-specific state** A history of user gestures or workflow steps is expected to remain intact only for the duration of a user's interaction with a user interface. Resetting this state on a failure or location change is usually tolerable.

If you've decided to use stateful session beans for any of these situations, then you won't want to miss the antipatterns that round off this chapter.

5.6 *Mini-antipattern: Stateful Session Beans as Shared Data Caches*

Because of their ability to manage data in memory, stateful session beans can tempt you into misusing them as shared data caches. EJB server vendors have added fuel to the fire by permitting concurrent client access to a single stateful session bean. The temptation is stronger once you discover that a stateful session bean can optionally implement the `javax.ejb.SessionSynchronization` interface to make it a transactionally aware object.

The `SessionSynchronization` interface provides callback methods to notify the bean at three junctures: when the container-managed transaction in which the bean participates has begun; when the transaction is nearly finished; and when the transaction is fully completed. The intent of the `SessionSynchronization` interface is to allow stateful session beans to use transactional notifications to manage and store persistent data across client requests. For example, after a transaction has begun, the bean's state can be initialized by reading the database. Before the transaction completes, the bean can update the database to reflect the bean's state. With every client request, the bean's state can be kept in sync with the database.

From a distance, a stateful session bean might walk and talk like a shared data cache, but up close it certainly is not one! Stateful session beans shouldn't be used as shared data caches for the following reasons:

- The data managed by stateful session beans is not transactional. A true data cache must provide concurrency control to ensure data integrity.

- Stateful session beans may be passivated at the whim of the container to make room for active objects in memory. The activation/passivation scheme may be slow for a cache of shared data. Moreover, passivation is an all-or-nothing proposition, so passivating an entire cache of data may slow down the system unnecessarily.

- Stateful session beans may be destroyed, either explicitly or as a result of the timeout value expiring. The cost of creating a new stateful session bean instance and reloading its cache is relatively high.

Using stateful session beans as shared data caches is a specific instance of the golden hammer antipattern. Stateful session beans are best used as local caches of client-specific data that could be lost without consequence. If multiple clients can benefit from a shared cache of persistent data, then you should use an entity bean or any other truly transactional object.

5.7 *Antipattern: Session Hodgepodge*

Storing conversational state in memory between client requests can be a slippery slope. It's all too easy to fall into a habit of using the session as a dumping ground for data. Most sessions start off innocently, as a flat structure holding a handful of simple types. However, before long, the session is bloated with a hodgepodge of information, perhaps even strung out across a deep and wide object graph. The poor sod maintaining this tangled mess can't always tell what data is actually used, where exactly to find it, or even what it represents.

Session Hodgepodge tends to germinate quickly when conversational state is stored in a hash table (or map) structure, such as that used by an HttpSession object. The convenience this structure offers—easily storing an assortment of data types—is offset by its crude key-value pair interface. To understand what's in a session, we're faced with turning each key to see what data it unlocks. To do so requires that we not only know the names of all keys, but also that we can properly cast their corresponding value to the correct type. In other words, the session isn't explicit. We can't look at it and easily understand the data it contains, nor can we easily to access that data. Consider the code used to coerce the data out of an HttpSession object in listing 5.3.

Listing 5.3   Storing a hodgepodge of data in an HttpSession object

```
String item = (String)httpSession.getAttribute("Item");
int quantity =
    ((Integer)httpSession.getAttribute("Quantity")).intValue()
double price =
    ((Double)httpSession.getAttribute("Price")).doubleValue();
```

What other data might be available in the session? We can't discern the answer from the example code. Unfortunately, the compiler can't help us out much with the data types. If we fail to properly cast a data type contained in the session, an onerous ClassCastException will be raised at runtime.

Equally troubling is the cost of session hodgepodge from the server's perspective. Bloated HttpSession objects work against the server's cache management strategy. For starters, when an HttpSession object is cached, the transitive closure of all its bound objects must be held in memory. That means all instance variables of objects in a session, and any objects they in turn reference recursively, occupy limited cache space. So, if the HttpSession object is passivated, all nontransient instance variables and any objects reached from those variables must be serialized to disk. Finally, if the HttpSession object is activated once again, the same bulk of information must be deserialized from disk into the cache. Session hodgepodge is the unwanted gift that keeps on giving.

Keep in mind that the overhead of adding new information to a session is incurred on a per-session basis. Adding a new attribute to each user's HttpSession object, for example, will have a multiplying effect on resources. If that attribute references a node in an object graph, the resulting overhead may be exponential.

Another unwanted side effect of session hodgepodge is the potential for naming collisions. Without knowing the keys already being used in a session, it's easy to end up using the same session key for two completely different purposes. Take, for example, the case where two developers unknowingly use the same key, such as "id." One developer expects the key to map to a unique customer while the other expects it to map to a unique bank account. If this "unique" key maps to a `String` value, then tracking down the collision will be difficult. Keeping the session well organized prevents a hodgepodge of information.

5.7.1 *Solution: Be explicit and conservative*

Sessions can be made more explicit—and therefore easier to understand—by organizing data in simple JavaBeans. Such classes offer a clean, object-oriented interface to session state. If we look at their methods, we can know right away what type of data these classes contain. Contrast the code in listing 5.3 with the use of an explicit `Session` object stored in the `HttpSession` object in listing 5.4.

> **Listing 5.4   Storing an explicit Session object in an HttpSession object**

```
Session session = (Session)httpSession.getAttribute("Session");
String item = session.getItem();
int quantity = session.getQuantity();
double price = session.getPrice();
```

The second code sample is both type-safe and easier to read. Better yet, we can look at the methods of the `Session` class to see what other data might be available. Stateful session beans generally define explicit methods like this for managing session state. To get the same effect using an `HttpSession` object, you'll need to bind exactly one object value by a well-known key. This single object should then provide access to all other objects containing session state, either directly or through the composition of other explicit objects.

For maximum performance and scalability, it's imperative that only essential information be stored in a session. Superfluous information consumes memory and taxes the server with expensive passivation and activation. Before adding a new piece of information to the session, see if the same information can be derived from data already in the session. If new information must be added, make sure to get your arms around the transitive closure of other objects it references. Use the `transient` keyword with impunity on instance variables to pare down the session as much as possible. Being conservative also helps avoid session thrashing, the focus of our next antipattern.

5.8 *Mini-antipattern: Session Thrashing*

The use of virtual memory as an extension to physical memory is a wonderful thing, but it's not without limitations. Though idle applications can be put on the back burner, active applications must use some physical memory. Therefore, the available amount of physical memory is a limiting factor to the number of active applications that can peacefully coexist. You can have all the virtual memory space in the world on disk, but trying to run too many applications with a machine with only 64 MB of RAM will be painful.

Conceptually, stateful session beans are managed in the same way virtual memory is used. The EJB container has only a finite amount of physical memory. Adjusting the size of the stateful session bean cache size allows you to throttle the cache's memory footprint as a subset of the total amount of physical memory. When the cache fills up, the container attempts to passivate inactive bean instances to disk. If a passivated bean is called to action once again, it is activated back into physical memory, possibly by replacing a less active bean.

The number of bean instances that can live in the cache at any given time typically is configurable in a vendor-specific deployment descriptor. Unfortunately, the folks who set the default cache values before putting the EJB container in the box didn't know much about your application. Once you've unwrapped the box, it's up to you to set the size of the cache, based on your in-depth knowledge of the application.

Failure to tune the cache size for an application's expected load may have an adverse affect on performance and scalability. The goal of tuning the cache size is to minimize the number of expensive passivation/activation cycles. As a general rule, the best performance is realized when the cache size is equal to the maximum number of concurrent clients. This ideal is realistically bound by the amount of physical memory and threads available to the EJB container.

But wait! Before you start turning performance knobs willy-nilly, you should set up some performance tests to establish a benchmark. Once you've made an adjustment, rerun the tests to see if adjusting the cache size actually improved performance. Measure, don't guess!

5.9 *Mini-antipattern: Rotting Session Garbage*

It's only fitting to talk about the final moments of a stateful session bean's life at the end of this chapter. Up until its last moments, a bean faithfully serves at the pleasure of its client. Barring any exceptional conditions, a bean will live as long as its client continues to use it. It may be passivated and activated at the whim of the EJB container many times throughout the conversation.

A stateful session bean's life is also running on a clock. If a bean instance is inactive for a configurable amount of time, the EJB container may destroy it to conserve memory. The timeout may expire when the bean instance is in the cache or passivated on disk. While this is a convenient housecleaning feature of the container, it's no excuse for the client to get sloppy with its trash.

If you put the garbage out a couple days early in the sweltering heat of summer, you're likely to get a visit from your neighbors as soon as the foul smell wafts down the block. Stateful session beans have neighbors, too—the other beans in the cache. Once a client is done using a stateful session bean, it should let the container know so that it can pick up the session garbage before it starts to rot. Explicitly invoking the `remove()` method of the bean's home or remote interface not only gives the bean an opportunity to perform any necessary cleanup of resources it uses, but also allows the EJB container to pick up the trash as soon as possible.

If a bean is not explicitly removed by its client, the orphaned bean will continue to live until it times out. In the meantime, the EJB container may be burdened with the relatively expensive job of passivating the doomed bean to make room for other active beans. This same advice applies to servlet sessions as Web servers must continuously keep memory in check. Explicitly invoking the `HttpSession.invalidate()` method when the session is no longer needed will keep the streets of the Web server clean.

5.10 *Summary: Taming the beast*

In this chapter, we went head-to-head with the stateful session beast. We waged a rather long and methodical battle, but we hope it made you hurt in the good kind of way. Stateful session beans are generally misunderstood, and rightfully so. Throughout their history, they have earned an undeserved reputation for having a nasty bite. In some cases, blind ambition has cornered them into situations where they have no choice but to show their teeth, such as shared data caches. In other cases, irrational fears have convinced us to lock stateful session beans away in a cage and throw away the key. Alas, situations they were designed specifically to handle often end up being bent nails under another golden hammer.

Keeping the beast on a leash requires that we start by casting a skeptical eye on session state. When it benefits our design—and often times it does—then we have several tools at our disposal. Choosing the best tool involves carefully considering a tool's respective advantages and disadvantages in light of your application.

When tamed, stateful session beans are a viable solution to managing temporary data on behalf of their master. Let loose to roam, they can mercilessly bring your application to its knees. Above all, remember to put important session data in a safe location, and then add any necessary layers for local caching.

In the next chapter, we'll shift gears to look at the newest type of EJB—the message-driven bean.

5.11 *Antipatterns in this chapter*

This chapter covers the Conversational Baggage, Golden Hammers of Session State, Stateful Session Beans as Shared Data Caches, Session Hodgepodge, Session Thrashing, and Rotting Session Garbage antipatterns.

CONVERSATIONAL BAGGAGE

DESCRIPTION
Stateful conversations are inherently more complex and resource-intensive than stateless conversations. For every stateful conversation, something has to remember the history of the conversation.

MOST FREQUENT SCALE
Application

REFACTORED SOLUTION NAME
Strive for statelessness

REFACTORED SOLUTION TYPE
Software

REFACTORED SOLUTION DESCRIPTION
When it's possible, design services to be stateless to increase their potential to scale under load. Stateful services should be the exception rather than the rule.

ANECDOTAL EVIDENCE
"The server is spending most of its time passivating and activating session state."

SYMPTOMS, CONSEQUENCES
Memory is a limiting factor to scalability.

GOLDEN HAMMERS OF SESSION STATE

DESCRIPTION

Using the same tool universally to store session state

MOST FREQUENT SCALE

Application

REFACTORED SOLUTION NAME

Pick the right tool for the job.

REFACTORED SOLUTION TYPE

Software

REFACTORED SOLUTION DESCRIPTION

The tool for storing session state is dependent on the application requirements rather than experience with a specific tool. One size doesn't fit all. Consider all the options for managing session state before making a decision.

ANECDOTAL EVIDENCE

"Stateful session beans are evil." "We always use servlets to store session state because it's the easiest approach."

SYMPTOMS, CONSEQUENCES

The tool, rather than the requirements, drives the solution. The system may become more complex than necessary when an inappropriate tool is used.

STATEFUL SESSION BEANS AS SHARED DATA CACHES

DESCRIPTION

Caching data in stateful sessions beans for use by multiple concurrent clients

MOST FREQUENT SCALE

Application

REFACTORED SOLUTION NAME

Use entity beans.

REFACTORED SOLUTION TYPE

Software

REFACTORED SOLUTION DESCRIPTION

If multiple clients can benefit from a shared cache of persistent data, then use an entity bean or any other truly transactional object.

ANECDOTAL EVIDENCE

"We spent a lot of time designing an intelligent stateful session bean that serves as a transaction-aware data cache."

SYMPTOMS, CONSEQUENCES

Cache suffers from dirty reads; passivation cost is high; and the cached data is frequently lost.

SESSION HODGEPODGE

DESCRIPTION

Using the `HttpSession` object as a dumping ground for session state

MOST FREQUENT SCALE

Application

REFACTORED SOLUTION NAME

Be explicit and conservative.

REFACTORED SOLUTION TYPE

Software

REFACTORED SOLUTION DESCRIPTION

Organize data in the `HttpSession` in simple JavaBeans. Understand what's already in a session before adding something new.

ANECDOTAL EVIDENCE

"I don't know what's available in the session." "This session key maps to a different type of value than I expected."

SYMPTOMS, CONSEQUENCES

The session state is not explicit or understood; the servlet container must manage extra memory; and naming collisions frequently occur when new session state is added.

SESSION THRASHING

DESCRIPTION
Failure to size session state caches based on the system's intended use and user load

MOST FREQUENT SCALE
Application

REFACTORED SOLUTION NAME
Tune caches for best performance.

REFACTORED SOLUTION TYPE
Process

REFACTORED SOLUTION DESCRIPTION
Write performance tests to validate that caches are sized appropriately for the system's operating environment and user load.

ANECDOTAL EVIDENCE
"I'm sure the default cache sizes are fine." "What's that thrashing sound coming from the disk?"

SYMPTOMS, CONSEQUENCES
Inability to scale and increased hardware costs with minimal gain

ROTTING SESSION GARBAGE

DESCRIPTION
Not explicitly removing session state when it's no longer needed

MOST FREQUENT SCALE
Application

REFACTORED SOLUTION NAME
Take out the garbage.

REFACTORED SOLUTION TYPE
Software

REFACTORED SOLUTION DESCRIPTION
Explicitly remove session state rather than let the server clean it up when it finally times out.

ANECDOTAL EVIDENCE
"Just let the container handle collecting all the garbage."

SYMPTOMS, CONSEQUENCES
Increased memory utilization and inability to scale

Bitter messages

6

This chapter covers
- An overview of JMS and message-driven beans
- An example messaging application using JMS and MDBs
- Message-level design antipatterns
- Application-level design antipatterns
- Asynchronous communication antipatterns
- Performance antipatterns

We have been shredding the powdery slopes relentlessly since catching the first lift of the day. As we ascend one of Colorado's epic mountains to take yet another adrenaline ride, a storm rolls in and quickly begins blowing in a fresh layer of powder. Once off the lift, we take a seat, snowboarder style, at the top of the run to plot our line of descent. The density of snowflakes swirling in the low light conditions has decreased our visibility. Donning goggles, we push off and immediately fall into a rhythm of parallel S-turns that kick up wispy snow fans. Halfway down the mountain the slope suddenly forks, but I fail to see it through the blowing snow. After a few more turns, it hits me—I don't hear the familiar sound of another board carving across the snow. I wait at the edge of the silent slope for a while, but it's soon evident that my buddy zigged when I zagged. We're out of synch on an enormous mountain enveloped by a storm.

In *Bitter Java*, our fellow author, Bruce Tate, accurately predicted that message-driven beans (MDB) would provide fertile ground for antipatterns. Unveiled in EJB 2.0, MDB are still relatively new, yet unfortunate antipatterns have already begun to rear their ugly heads. The painful lessons these antipatterns teach aren't new. Indeed, message-based systems have been around for a relatively long time. Many seasoned developers wear the battle scars of messaging gone bad, but fueled by the need to quickly integrate applications with other internal and external applications, messaging has become increasingly pervasive. With the advent of MDBs, which promote asynchronous messaging as a first-class distributed computing model in the J2EE platform, the stakes have been raised. Yet another tool has found a home in our already brimming toolbox. And, as always, the wisdom of a craftsman will lie in knowing how and when (or when not) to use it.

In this chapter, we'll review the Java Message Service (JMS) and its recent introduction into the J2EE platform in the form of MDBs. Working through a simple example, we'll encounter potential pitfalls in designing message-based applications. Some antipatterns we'll uncover are related to application performance, while others fester at the application design level. As we look at each bitter scenario, we'll explore practical alternatives to ensure that our applications don't end up stranded.

6.1 A brief overview of JMS

JMS is an API that allows applications to communicate asynchronously by exchanging messages. JMS is to messaging systems what JDBC is to database systems. JMS is best used to glue together applications through interapplication messaging.

These applications, referred to as *JMS clients*, engage in asynchronous conversations by using a common set of interfaces to create, send, receive, and read messages. That's not to say you also couldn't use JMS for intra-application messaging to send messages between multiple threads, for example.

JMS itself is an industry-standard specification, not an implementation. Vendors of messaging products—commonly referred to as message-oriented middleware (MOM)—support JMS by providing implementations of the interfaces defined in the JMS specification. By relying only on vendor-neutral interfaces, applications are decoupled from any specific vendor. That is, the underlying vendor's implementation can be changed or substituted with another without breaking the JMS clients.

A vendor's JMS implementation is known as a *JMS provider*. A JMS provider includes the software that composes the *JMS server*, or message broker, and the software running within each JMS client. A *JMS application* therefore comprises multiple JMS clients exchanging messages indirectly through a JMS server. Figure 6.1 illustrates a common JMS application.

Notice that the JMS server acts as a middleman between JMS clients. This enables loosely coupled communication; neither client knows about the other. This loosely coupled communication improves reliability, since one client will not be dependent on the location, availability, or identity of another. Indeed, clients are free to come and go without adversely affecting reliability. This situation is in stark contrast to the remote procedure call (RPC) computing model used by CORBA and Java RMI. Applications using RPC communicate directly with each other. As such, they tend to be tightly coupled.

That's enough theory. We'll learn far more about JMS by getting our hands dirty building an example application.

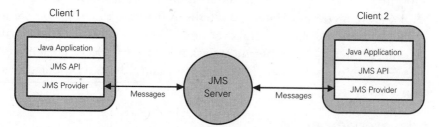

Figure 6.1 In a JMS application, applications use the interfaces of the JMS API to communicate indirectly through the JMS server. Under the hood of each JMS client and within the JMS server, a vendor's JMS implementation does all the heavy lifting.

6.2 An early antipattern: Fat Messages

Messages are the lingua franca of messaging systems. Any application that can speak in messages is welcome to join in conversations. *Message producers* are JMS clients that send messages. *Message consumers* are JMS clients that receive messages.

The message language is defined by the JMS specification, which specifies six different message types that vary with the type of payload they transport. Think of these message types as dialects of the message language. They all sound similar, but each has a slightly different accent. Their similarity lies in a common structure: headers, properties, and a payload. The headers and properties define routing and other information about the message. The payload, or message body, is the meat of the message. It contains data of specific interest to message consumers. The structure of the payload is unique to each message type. Table 6.1 breaks down each message type by its respective payload.

Table 6.1   JMS message types vary by the structure of their payload. Each can carry light or heavy loads. Fat messages clog up the messaging pipes and invariably impact the performance of a messaging application.

Message type	Payload
Message	No payload, just headers and properties
TextMessage	Java string (text or serialized XML document)
MapMessage	Set of name-value pairs
ObjectMessage	Serialized Java object
BytesMessage	Stream of uninterpreted bytes
StreamMessage	Stream of primitive Java types

Each message type is useful in different scenarios. Picking the best message for the situation is a critical design decision that affects not only the semantics of the message exchange, but also the performance of the system. Table 6.2 presents each message type that contains a payload, along with a few considerations to keep in mind when choosing a message type.

Table 6.2 Before picking a message type, carefully consider if the data being exchanged fits neatly into the payload the message type was designed to carry.

Message type	Key considerations
TextMessage	Because the JMS specification does not define a standard XML message type, the TextMessage commonly is used to transport a serialized XML document. However, any time the payload contains formatted text, such as XML, it must be parsed by consumers before it can be used intelligently.
MapMessage	Messages of this type are the most versatile. Predefined keys are used to read specific values of the payload. This allows the payload to grow dynamically over time without affecting consumers. Consumers that aren't aware of new keys will be ignorant of their existence. If consumers always read the entire payload in a well-defined order, carrying the keys around may become a dead weight. In these cases, StreamMessage may yield better performance.
ObjectMessage	Producers and consumers of this type of message must be Java programs. When a producer sends a message of this type, the object in the payload and the transitive closure of all objects it may reference must be serialized. That is, if the object in the payload references other objects, then consumers will receive the graph of objects reachable from the object in the payload. Deep object graphs bloat the message and restrict message throughput. Additionally, all consumers must be able to successfully deserialize the object(s) in the payload using a class loader within their respective JVMs. This means that all consumers must have access to the class definitions of the objects in the payload.
BytesMessage	Because this message type's payload is raw uninterpreted bytes, all consumers must understand how to interpret the payload. No automatic data conversions are applied to the payload as it's transported between consumers. This message type is rarely used, and, when it is, only to transport data of a well-known format, such as a MIME type, supported by all consumers. In most other cases, a StreamMessage or a MapMessage is more convenient.
StreamMessage	Unlike the BytesMessage, the StreamMessage retains the order and type of the primitives in the payload. Moreover, data conversion rules are automatically applied to the primitive types as they are read by consumers. A StreamMessage is a more rigid variation of a MapMessage in that keys do not index its data. However, because it doesn't carry around keys, this message type is generally more lightweight than a MapMessage. Nevertheless, unlike the MapMessage, a StreamMessage requires that consumers have explicit knowledge of the message format.

It's not always clear which message type is best to use. Some message types are used more commonly than others, based simply on the type of data being exchanged. The TextMessage, for example, is the natural choice for exchanging structured text. Without carefully considering the flavor of payload consumers will require, you may easily fall into the comfortable habit of using the same message type for all situations. Often, the result will be awkward, like fitting square data in a round message.

6.2.1 One size doesn't fit all

Designing messages in a vacuum is like designing a software component in the absence of clients. Speculation often leads to messages that are neither useful nor efficient. Take, for example, a message representing a purchase order. How much information must the message carry to be useful? The answer depends on the consumer of the message.

If the consumer is a sales automation system using the message to spot cross-selling opportunities, then including a wealth of information about the customer may be important. If the message is too brief, this type of consumer may have insufficient information to efficiently process the message. Attempting to gather more information may lead to a two-way dialogue between the producer and the consumer. Chattiness of this sort negates the benefits of loose coupling and asynchronous communication offered by JMS.

On the other hand, if the consumer is an inventory system using the message to fulfill an order, then the customer information may be unnecessary. Making the message unnecessarily verbose will fatten it up, thus requiring additional network bandwidth and CPU resources. Moreover, if the fat message is persisted to nonvolatile storage to ensure guaranteed delivery, it will require additional storage space. That being said, if the frequency at which a fat message is produced is low, then the respective overhead may be tolerable. However, as the message frequency increases, the overhead will compound until it adversely affects message throughput.

So, fat messages end up being a common problem because assumptions about consumer needs are easily made. A message that tries to be everything to everybody inevitably carries a high delivery price; it clogs up the messaging pipes and wastes space.

6.2.2 Solution 1: Put messages on a diet

Ideally, a message should contain just enough information to enable its consumers to handle it on their own. Designing such a message is akin to designing a programmatic interface to a distributed service. To decrease coupling and chattiness, thin interfaces generally are used to encapsulate business logic behind coarse-grained methods. Given just the right amount of information, these methods go about their business without exposing any implementation details. In contrast, fat interfaces usually are guilty of hiding monolithic business processes that are tightly interdependent. Getting anything useful to happen often requires calling multiple methods and supplying superfluous information.

Therefore, when designing loosely coupled messaging applications, it's best to follow the lessons taught by good interface-based design:

- Start by designing the interfaces—the shape and size of the messages.
- Choose a message type capable of carrying the simplest payload that meets the needs of known consumers.
- Avoid fattening up the message by speculating about the kinds of data needed by future consumers.
- Eliminate duplication by omitting data that a consumer could derive from the information already in the message.
- Take into account how often the message will be delivered and whether the delivery of the message must be guaranteed.

Knowing when to put a message on a diet isn't an exact science. No scale exists that can accurately weigh a particular message. In addition to including the size of the static payload and any application-specific headers and properties, the JMS provider may pile on additional properties at the time of delivery that contribute to the overall size of the message. If you know the approximate size of the payload, you'll find that is usually sufficient as a rough estimate when planning for performance. Remember, too, to factor in the frequency of the message delivery. Little messages can add up quickly to big performance headaches.

6.2.3 *Solution 2: Use references*

Sending references to information otherwise contained in a message can help reduce the size of the message. Rather than sending a fat message stuffed with raw data, it's often possible to send a lightweight message instead, one that simply contains a reference to that data. Think of it as a particular type of weight loss program where a message is encouraged to eat references. References are especially powerful in situations where large amounts of data need to be exchanged without incurring excessive performance overhead. A reference could be a URL, a primary key, or any other token pointing to the data.

For example, consider a workflow application that uses messages to route electronic documents to multiple departments. As the document transitions through its life cycle, from draft to approval, it travels from one department's message queue to the next. At each stopping point, more information may be added to the message. This workflow could be implemented using the BytesMessage message type to route the document in its native format. However, a downside to that approach exists: as its size increases, the document will become unwieldy. Each

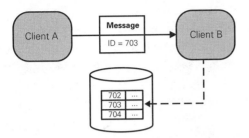

Figure 6.2
References can be used to point to the actual information otherwise contained in the message. This approach has the potential to significantly decrease the size of fat messages. In this example, the message contains a primary key for a row in a shared database table. When the consumer receives this message, it can load and interpret the data at its leisure.

department's queue will be burdened with managing the document in memory until it's been processed. The situation turns particularly sour if a copy of this fat message is broadcast to multiple consumers. Every network path from the producer to each consumer will have to swallow the fat message like an egg-eating snake. In the end, not all consumers may want the message after it's delivered. References can come in handy in these situations because they significantly decrease the size of the message.

If all message consumers have access to a shared resource, such as a database or a file system, consider trimming down messages to contain references to shared data. As an alternative to transporting an entire document, for example, the message representing the document could simply contain the name of a shared file. When a consumer receives the message, it can process the referenced document at its leisure by reading the document from the file system. Figure 6.2 illustrates the use of references to reduce the size of messages.

It's never too early to start putting messages on a weight loss program, but don't go overboard. MOM products have matured significantly over the years. Some vendors have had time to optimize their products for sending large messages over different networks. Before making any assumptions, write a few tests to measure performance. A message that may be perceived as being too large actually might transmit much faster than you think. And, if a fat message is sent infrequently, it may not be a problem. Prematurely hacking away at the message size can lead to another common problem—skinny messages.

6.3 *Mini-antipattern: Skinny Messages*

Despite warnings about fat messages, skinny messages are equally problematic. Striking a balance between too much and not enough information is the essence of good message design.

In general, it's always better to send a bit too much information. A couple of extra bytes on a message will generally have little overall effect on performance. On the flip side, a skinny message with too few bytes may create more work for a consumer. To successfully handle the message, the consumer may have to make extra remote calls to get more information.

Using references isn't always the right answer either. First, each consumer is burdened with resolving the references on his own. In other words, the producer can't package up all the information once and then share it with all the consumers. Worse yet, consider the case where several consumers attempt to resolve a reference to a document as soon as the message arrives. Consumers may end up competing for access to the shared file system in a flurry of network activity, causing them to block. Consequently, message throughput suffers as the consumer can't process new messages until the current message is handled. In the end, this may be far more CPU- and network-intensive than just sending the entire document in the first place.

To reiterate, not sending enough information in a message can weigh down an otherwise efficient messaging application. The virtues of asynchronous communication may be taken over by a much slower, synchronous conversation induced by contention and blocking.

6.3.1 *Solution: Use state to allow lazy loading*

One performance-boosting variation of references is to include some state information in the message, along with the reference. For example, in addition to the document reference, the message could also include the current state of the document. For instance, states might include: NEW, REVISED, or APPROVED. The presence of the state in the message allows consumers to make a decision about whether loading the document is necessary. Consequently, only consumers that actually need the document will access the shared file system, reducing the potential for delayed blocking. State can be added to a message in a variety of ways. Putting state in the payload is one way, although the consumer will bear the burden of filtering. In section 6.12, we'll discuss how to use message selectors. Message selectors tell the JMS server how to filter messages before delivering them to consumers. The filtering is based on the contents of each message's headers and properties.

6.4 Seeds of an order processing system

We ran into two pitfalls before starting our journey: fat messages and skinny messages. We would do well to keep these potential troublespots in mind before messages start swirling around. Now, we're ready to dive into a working example. We want an example we can sink our teeth into, so we'll develop the underpinnings of an asynchronous order processing system using JMS. Although we'll write gratuitous amounts of code, as an example of JMS, ours will fall well short of providing a comprehensive tour of JMS. Albeit easy to learn and use, JMS can be applied in a range of enterprise application integration (EAI) and business-to-business (B2B) scenarios. Our example will illustrate merely one isolated application of JMS—with a few pitfalls sprinkled in along the way to keep us on our toes. Throughout the rest of the chapter, we'll continue to refactor the application example, each time eliminating a weakness in its design.

6.4.1 Defining the system

Let's assume that we have a legacy order fulfillment application that we'd like to tie in with a J2EE online order processing system. Rather than modifying the legacy system to interface directly with the new system, we'd prefer to integrate the two worlds using a loosely coupled design. When an online order is initiated through the order processing system, it should trigger the following business logic sequentially:

1. Store the order information in an order database.
2. Deliver the order to the legacy order fulfillment application.
3. Broadcast a notification indicating the order's status.

These tasks must be completed in lock-step as an atomic business process. If any step fails, the entire process will also fail and would have to be repeated anew. However, we don't want our online customers to be blocked, waiting for the completion of this relatively lengthy business process. Customers don't need to wait; they are happy to place an order request and receive later notification—an email, for example—to confirm that the order has been fulfilled.

Reliability is paramount because we can't afford to lose any customer orders. When an order request is issued, we should be able to guarantee its disposition. In light of these requirements, we decide to use JMS as the integration glue. Using it correctly is the challenge.

6.4.2 Designing messages

As we learned in the previous section, designing the messages that form the interface between our applications will help us determine how those applications interact. Based on our admittedly simple use case, we need two messages: an `OrderRequest` message and an `OrderStatus` message.

The OrderRequest message

An `OrderRequest` message is used to initiate the order fulfillment process. Messages of this type are sent to exactly one consumer—the legacy order fulfillment application. Table 6.3 dissects the payload of an `OrderRequest` message.

Table 6.3 An `OrderRequest` message requests fulfillment of an online order.

Name	Description	Type	Example value
Order ID	The order's unique identifier	String	104-549-736
Product ID	The product's unique identifier	String	Ride Timeless 158
Quantity	The number of units to buy	int	1
Price	The product's unit price in dollars	double	479.00

At this point, we can't be certain that we've considered all possible attributes of an `OrderRequest` message. We'll keep the message simple for now.

The OrderStatus message

The second message we need, an `OrderStatus` message, is just an indication of an order's disposition. This type of message is broadcast to any application that has registered interest in the life cycle of orders. For example, the sales automation system might monitor the status of an order as it progresses through the system. This message is broadcast only after the legacy order fulfillment application has had an opportunity to process the order represented by an `OrderRequest` message.

Imagine that a message of this type contains a unique identifier for an order, an order status code, and an optional text describing the order's status. Notice that the unique order identifier is actually a reference to the original order. We don't need to include all the details of the original order in an `OrderStatus` message because subscribers of this message type are generally only interested in the order's disposition. However, if a particular subscriber wants the details of the original order, the identifier can be used to query the shared order database. In other words, the `OrderStatus` message is designed for a specific type of consumer. A reference is used to accommodate the few subscribers that may have special interests.

Having considered the message design, we're ready to decide now how these messages should be delivered.

6.4.3 *Choosing messaging models*

We have a couple of choices when deciding how our messages should be delivered to consumers. In general, the JMS server receives messages from producers and delivers the messages to consumers. Specifically, JMS provides two different messaging models: *publish/subscribe* and *point-to-point*.

The two messaging models use a slightly different vernacular. The publish/subscribe messaging model allows a message publisher (producer) to broadcast a message to one or more message subscribers (consumers) through a virtual channel called a *topic*. The point-to-point messaging model allows a message sender (producer) to send a message to exactly one message receiver (consumer) through a virtual channel called a *queue*. Figure 6.3 illustrates the two messaging models.

By communicating indirectly through virtual channels managed by the JMS server, producers and consumers are decoupled from one another. That is to say that a consumer's location, availability, and identity are unknown to the producer.

In our example application, an OrderRequest message should be processed by only one consumer—the order fulfillment application. Therefore, we'll use the point-to-point messaging model to deliver these types of messages. In contrast, an OrderStatus message must be delivered to all clients that have registered interest in the disposition of orders. Therefore, we'll use the publish/subscribe messaging model to broadcast these types of messages. Figure 6.4 shows an architectural diagram of the JMS components collaborating to fulfill an order.

Notice in the architectural diagram that the client that receives the Order-Request message is also a publisher of OrderStatus messages. A JMS client can serve both roles—producer and consumer—to bridge between messaging models. Also, keep in mind that each client could be running in its own virtual machine and perhaps even on separate machines in the network.

6.4.4 *Responding to change*

Fortunately, the JMS API for the publish/subscribe and point-to-point messaging models are remarkably symmetrical. In general, only the names change when switching from one messaging model to the other. Every method and class name containing the substring Topic can be changed to Queue, and vice versa. A few other minor details and model-specific features exist, but by and large, the APIs

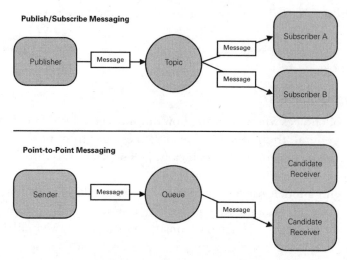

Publish/Subscribe Messaging

Point-to-Point Messaging

Figure 6.3 The publish/subscribe message model publishes a copy of a message to each subscriber through a topic. The point-to-point messaging model sends any given message to exactly one of possibly many receivers through a queue. The topic or queue decouples all participants to allow their location, availability, and identity to vary independently.

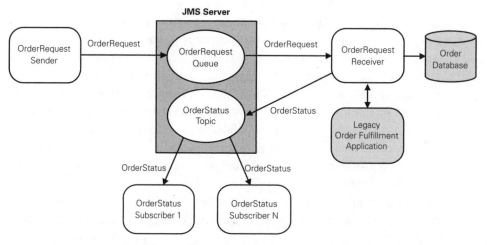

Figure 6.4 Messaging applications can be a hybrid of publish/subscribe and point-to-point messaging, depending on the number of message consumers interested in each message.

mirror each other. The upshot is that the skills you learn using one messaging model are portable to the other. It's worth mentioning that the open source Messenger (http://jakarta.apache.org/commons/sandbox/messenger/) library makes using JMS a bit easier. It effectively hides the differences between messaging models and their delivery options.

In the future, more than one consumer may want to know when an order is placed. For example, a sales automation system might also track OrderRequest messages to identify potential cross-selling opportunities. For now, we'll use the point-to-point messaging model, keeping in mind that the JMS APIs are on our side if needs change down the road.

We've yet to delve into how the consumer of OrderRequest messages is developed and packaged. We'll get there in good time, but first, let's look at the system from the perspective of the order producer. It's here that we'll gain valuable insight into the design of our application.

6.4.5 *Building the OrderRequest producer*

In the architectural diagram, the client that produces the OrderRequest messages appears to be stand-alone. However, we can safely assume that this client has more responsibilities. Indeed, if we were to zoom out a few thousand feet, we'd see that the OrderRequestSender is actually just a single component in a larger J2EE application. Orders are placed over the Internet through a web application that, among other things, uses this component to integrate with the order fulfillment application through messaging.

Using a flexible message format will allow us to add new attributes easily to OrderRequest messages later, if necessary. Several JMS message types will work, but we might be tempted to use serialized XML in the payload of a TextMessage. After all, the message could be easily represented as structured text, and XML offers the ultimate in flexibility and portability. Indeed, XML is a wonderful technology and a million ways exist for using it well, but this isn't one of them. To see why, let's look at listing 6.1 to see how we might send an OrderRequest message containing XML.

Listing 6.1 A JMS client that sends OrderRequest messages to a message queue

```
public class OrderRequestSender {

  private QueueConnection connection;
  private QueueSession session;                    Creates a QueueSender
  private QueueSender sender;                          connected to the
                                                     OrderRequestQueue
  public void connect() throws NamingException, JMSException {  ◁

    Context ctx = new InitialContext();

    QueueConnectionFactory connectionFactory =
      (QueueConnectionFactory)
      ctx.lookup("OrderRequestConnectionFactory");

    connection = connectionFactory.createQueueConnection();

    session = connection.
      createQueueSession(false, Session.AUTO_ACKNOWLEDGE);

    Queue queue = (Queue)ctx.lookup("OrderRequestQueue");

    sender = session.createSender(queue);
  }

  public void sendOrder(OrderRequest order) throws JMSException {

    TextMessage message = session.createTextMessage();   Fills the
                                                          OrderRequest
    message.setText(order.toXML());  ◁                   message payload
                                 Sends the OrderRequest   with XML
    sender.send(message);  ◁     message to the Order-
  }                              RequestQueue
  public void disconnect() throws JMSException {  ◁   Disconnects from the
    connection.close();                               OrderRequestQueue
  }
}
```

Notice that we create a TextMessage containing a serialized string of XML by invoking the toXML() method of an OrderRequest business object. In other words, the OrderRequest message is simply an XML representation of the OrderRequest business object. Unfortunately, the contents of the message aren't explicit. That is, without parsing the XML, we can't tell what types of data it contains.

Now that we see the world through the eyes of the OrderRequestSender and in the context of our architecture, we can tell all is not exactly as we imagined. Indeed, there's a bitter taste in our mouth. Using XML as the payload of the OrderRequest message seemed like a good idea since XML is both flexible and portable. However, data portability isn't really an issue because we'll be building the consumer of OrderRequest messages. Furthermore, we can achieve flexibility with other message types. So, given that both the producer and the consumer are within our control, no clear advantages exist to using XML in this scenario. Before going much further then, let's reconsider the decision to use XML.

6.5 *Antipattern: XML as the Silver Bullet*

At first blush JMS and XML appear to be a match made in heaven. To some extent they are kindred spirits that can team up to solve historically vexing problems. One beauty of JMS is that it allows messages to be exchanged throughout a heterogeneous environment in a platform-neutral fashion—a noble challenge of EAI. In practice, although Java applications themselves are platform-neutral for the most part, not all systems glued together with JMS are Java applications. To further extend the reach of messaging, some JMS vendors provide support for messaging between Java and non-Java clients.

JMS is aimed at enabling the ubiquitous transfer of messages, and XML stands tall when it comes to expressing data in a portable and flexible format. Indeed, because XML distills down to a stream of text, it can be interpreted by any platform. It's also flexible in the sense that, despite conforming to a well-defined structure, an XML document can easily be extended to include new data elements without affecting current applications using it.

Sounds great, right? Not so fast. It comes as no surprise that XML has the potential to be overused. It's a fate shared by many new technologies that come on the scene with great fanfare. While some may contend that putting XML in the drinking water will make everyone's teeth whiter, XML is best used in moderation. We'll go out on a limb here and predict that a book on bitter XML wouldn't be known for its brevity. Swinging the XML hammer for the sake of XML is not without its price. When a JMS consumer receives an XML message, that message must be parsed before it can be used for anything meaningful. The overhead of parsing XML will elongate the time required for the consumer to process the message. This extra processing may in turn limit the overall message throughput of the application. As such, XML loses many of its advantages when you control all the producers and consumers. Regardless of the performance implications—which certainly must be measured before forming any conclusions—the burden of parsing should be hoisted on consumers only when a definitive advantage exists in using XML.

6.5.1 *Solution: Use XML messages judiciously*

XML is no panacea. In many cases, the `MapMessage` has all the same virtues as a message containing XML, without the performance hit of parsing. With respect to portability, most JMS vendors will automatically convert a `MapMessage` produced by a Java application to an equivalent message in a non-Java environment. Native conversions of this sort are generally less expensive performance-wise than parsing XML. The format of a `MapMessage` is also flexible in that new name-value pairs can be added easily without breaking existing consumers. Moreover, messages containing XML have the disadvantage of not supporting runtime validation afforded by the explicit, strongly typed methods of a `MapMessage`.

That's not to say a powerful synergy doesn't exist sometimes between XML and JMS. For example, messages that must be represented in a hierarchical structure can certainly benefit from the flexibility of an XML message. As well, messages that travel beyond the edges of your intranet to communicate with other systems can reap the rewards of portable XML. In the future we're likely to see an even tighter coupling between these two technologies in a wide range of applications from EAI to B2B.

In any event, the best approach is to start with the simplest message type and benchmark its performance. Then, if an XML message becomes necessary, you'll have something to compare that message against. Is parsing XML messages a performance bottleneck? Wait! Don't answer that just yet. First, gather hard evidence with a performance test for the actual situation in question. Then, use that information to make an informed decision. You might be pleasantly surprised.

To reiterate, serializing XML into an `OrderRequest` message doesn't buy us much over a `MapMessage` in our application. We're designing all the producers and consumers and, at this point, the message has a flat structure. With a `MapMessage`, we're also free to add new data without affecting current clients, should that become necessary. Listing 6.2 shows the refactored method that uses a `MapMessage` type when sending an `OrderRequest` message.

Listing 6.2 Refactoring from an XML message to a MapMessage

```java
public void sendOrder(OrderRequest order) throws JMSException {

    MapMessage message = session.createMapMessage();

    message.setString("Order ID", order.getOrderId());
    message.setString("Product ID", order.getProductId());
    message.setInt("Quantity", order.getQuantity());
    message.setDouble("Price", order.getPrice());

    sender.send(message);
}
```

Notice that the message is now more explicit. And we get the advantage of strong type checking. When the consumer reads the message, each attribute's type is unambiguous. For example, a consumer can now read an `OrderRequest` message as shown in listing 6.3.

Listing 6.3   Reading an OrderRequest message

```
String orderId = mapMessage.getString("Order ID");
String productId = mapMessage.getString("Product ID");
int quantity = mapMessage.getInt("Quantity");
double price = mapMessage.getDouble("Price");
```

We finally have our messages nailed down! Next, we must decide if guaranteeing their delivery brings anything to the party.

6.6   *Antipattern: Packrat*

Guaranteed message delivery, one of the cornerstones of messaging systems, always comes at a price in terms of resources and performance. Anything advertised as guaranteed seems to bear that caveat. Alas, no free lunch exists here.

The JMS specification contains provisions for configuring a messaging system to achieve different Quality of Service (QoS) levels. Building on that foundation, JMS vendors compete by including value-added reliability features to their product offerings. The QoS level we choose is dependent largely on our specific application's requirements. After all, we want to get something for the price we pay.

Reliability is measured on a sliding scale. It's not just a single toggle switch we flip on or off, but rather a panel of control knobs. If we turn them all to their highest setting, we'll get maximum reliability and, possibly, horrible performance. Turn them down to their lowest setting, and we'll get minimum reliability with improved performance. It's a trade-off; the right setting usually lies somewhere in the middle. Two mechanisms for guaranteeing message delivery with the highest potential for misuse are persistent messages and durable subscriptions. Failure to understand their potential cost can set us up for a big fall.

6.6.1   *Putting a price on persistence*

JMS defines two message delivery modes: *persistent* and *nonpersistent*. When a message marked as persistent is sent to the JMS server, it's immediately squirreled away in nonvolatile storage. Only after the message is stored safely does the message producer receive an acknowledgment that the JMS server has agreed to deliver the message. By taking this responsibility, the JMS server guarantees that the message will never be lost. As the server metes out each persistent message to consumers, it keeps track of consumers that have actually received the message. The consumers help by acknowledging the receipt of each message. If the JMS server fails (or is restarted) while delivering messages, then upon recovery, the server will attempt to deliver all persistent messages that have yet to be acknowledged.

Non-persistent messages, on the other hand, aren't stored on disk. Therefore, they aren't guaranteed to survive a JMS server failure or restart. As such, non-persistent messages generally require fewer resources and can be delivered in less time than persistent messages. Higher levels of message throughput usually can be realized by using non-persistent messages at the expense of reliability.

By default, a message producer marks all messages as being persistent. Each message sent will be stored on disk before it's delivered. With our `OrderRequest-Sender`, that step works to our advantage because we can't afford to lose `Order-Request` messages if the JMS server fails or is restarted. Figure 6.5 illustrates the sequence of events in delivering a persistent `OrderRequest` message.

Every `OrderRequest` message is guaranteed to be delivered once—and only once—to the `OrderRequestReceiver`. In contrast, ensuring that every `OrderStatus` message is received by its consumers may not be a requirement of our business. Instead, we may be able to deliver these messages once at most and avoid the overhead of guaranteed delivery. That is, it won't be the end of the world if one of these

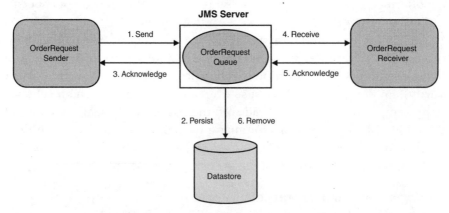

Figure 6.5 Persistent messages must be stored in nonvolatile storage by the JMS server before acknowledging the message producer. These messages are then removed from storage upon successful delivery. Not all messages require this degree of reliability. For messages that need to be delivered once at most, better throughput can be realized.

messages falls on the floor. Unless we explicitly mark `OrderStatus` messages as non-persistent, our application will suffer the burden of guaranteeing their delivery.

It's important to note that messages sent using the point-to-point messaging model must be placed on a queue in the JMS server prior to delivery, regardless of whether or not they are marked persistent. A point-to-point message not marked as persistent lives on the queue until it's consumed or the JMS server fails or restarts. Therefore, messages not consumed at a rate equal to or greater than their rate of arrival may cause the queue to grow unchecked, putting additional strain on the JMS server. Publish-subscribe messages, in contrast, don't necessarily have to be stored internally before delivery.

6.6.2 *Paying for durable subscriptions*

Durable subscriptions, another mechanism for guaranteeing message delivery, are a feature specific to the publish/subscribe messaging model. A durable subscription outlives a subscriber's connection to the JMS server. That is, when a message arrives at a topic for which a durable subscriber has registered interest, and the subscriber is disconnected, the JMS server will save the message in nonvolatile storage. In essence, the undelivered message is treated as a persistent message. The JMS server will continue to store any outstanding messages until the durable subscriber has reconnected. Once the subscriber has reconnected, all outstanding messages are forwarded to it. If a message expires before the subscriber reconnects, the message will be removed.

Here's the rub: If a durable subscriber is disconnected for relatively long periods of time, and messages have a long life span, the JMS server is burdened with having to manage all outstanding messages. The resulting strain on resources is similar to that of persistent messages. For each durable subscription, the message server must internally keep track of the messages each durable subscriber has missed for a given topic.

6.6.3 *Solution: Save only what's important*

Certain types of messages are so critical to your business that you can't afford to lose one. By all means, use the power of JMS to guarantee their delivery to the extent necessary. If, however, certain types of messages can be missed when things go bad, then you should avoid incurring the unnecessary overhead to guarantee their delivery.

In our order processing system, for example, losing an order request if the JMS server fails will adversely affect our bottom line. We must guarantee that every `OrderRequest` message ultimately arrives at our legacy order fulfillment application. Therefore, the `OrderRequest` message is persistent. Additionally, if the legacy order fulfillment application itself fails, or is taken offline for maintenance, we must guarantee that any messages it misses will be delivered once it has recovered. Therefore, its subscription must be durable. We don't have to do anything special for durability in this case. Messages sent to a queue are implicitly durable; they'll be waiting when the consumer comes back online. At the end of the day, we're willing to incur the overhead of persistence and durable subscriptions in exchange for peace of mind.

Conversely, we may be willing to tolerate the loss of an `OrderStatus` message, a temporal message reflecting an order's state at a given instant. If a subscriber misses an `OrderStatus` message, the worst-case scenario is that the subscriber must check the order status in the order database. The inconvenience of missing a message just doesn't warrant the cost of burdening the JMS server with the tasks of storing each message, then deleting the message later once all interested subscribers have successfully acknowledged it. And remember, because we can easily bolt on more reliability later, if necessary, we'll do best by starting simple.

6.7 *Mini-antipattern: Immediate Reply Requested*

When I reach the base of the slope, there's no sign of my snowboarding buddy. He may have waited for me patiently somewhere, or already started back up. I could wait at the base to see if he shows up, but if he's already on the lift, I'll miss the opportunity of another ride. All slopes on this side of the mountain converge in this spot, and at the head of the lift line, there's a small whiteboard. I decide to scribble a message for him. The next time he gets on the lift, he will be sure to see it, and we'll hook back up. In the meantime, the powder is getting deeper, and I'm ready for the next ride.

If you're blocked waiting for a reply, you're stuck. You can't move on or coordinate new activities. As a result, you may miss out on opportunities. In other words, waiting creates an opportunity cost. To work (and play) efficiently, you'd like to rendezvous when it's most convenient. Asynchronous messaging frees you from waiting and lets you get in a few more runs.

Excessive coupling is the enemy of asynchronous messaging. Indeed, it flies in the face of a powerful aspect of asynchronous messaging—loose coupling. If message producers have intimate knowledge of the consumers with which they communicate, then assumptions are inevitably made. In particular, a producer may rely on a particular consumer's identity, location on the network, and possible connection times. Consequently, the system can't grow and shrink dynamically. In other words, producers are susceptible to the changes of the consumers on which they rely. If, for example, a consumer on which a producer relies disconnects or moves to a new host on the network, then the producer may end up waiting indefinitely for the consumer to reconnect.

That said, JMS does support a synchronous request/reply style of communication. Message producers can send a request in the form of a message to an outbound destination (topic or queue). When a message consumer receives the message—either synchronously or asynchronously—it can then reply by sending a message to a predetermined inbound destination. The two participants may agree on well-known destinations ahead of time. Alternatively, the producer can dynamically create a temporary inbound topic and assign it to the request message's `JMS-ReplyTo` property. Figure 6.6 illustrates a synchronous request/reply conversation.

It's true that the producer and consumer are decoupled in the sense that they are unaware of each other's identity or location, but an implied association exists. Indeed, their life cycles are coupled. After publishing the request message, the `TopicSubscriber.receive()` method invoked by the producer blocks until a consumer sends a reply message. The producer must wait on the line until a consumer is connected. Even then, the producer is at the mercy of the consumer's duty cycle. If the consumer is never able to connect and send a reply, the producer will continue to block, forever waiting for a reply. To avoid freezing the producer indefinitely, use the `receive(long timeout)` or `receiveNoWait()` method. These methods will break the producer free of the synchronous bonds before it's too late.

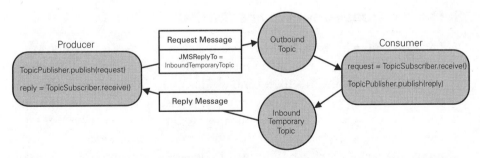

Figure 6.6 Although JMS does support synchronous request/reply messaging, if used extensively this messaging tends to create undesirable coupling between the message producer and consumer. From the producer's perspective, the round trip is synchronous; it blocks waiting for a consumer to reply. If a consumer isn't able to reply, the producer may block indefinitely.

The sequence of steps required by a message producer to engage in a request/reply conversation can be executed in one fell swoop using the `javax.jms.Topic-Requestor` or `javax.jms.QueueRequestor` utility classes. These classes define a `request()` method that encapsulates the lock-step process of sending a request message and blocking until a reply message is received. If not executed in a separate thread, invoking the blocking `request()` method from a message producer will block the calling thread until a reply has been received. This risk alone may warrant a move from convenience to safety by using a variant of the `receive()` method directly.

In general, asynchronous messaging is utilized best for a fire-and-forget style of communication. When a request/reply conversation is needed, the power of asynchronous communication is diminished, and the scales start to tip back in favor of RPC communication. Therefore, before using JMS, carefully consider if your system has the potential to benefit from asynchronous messaging. Indeed, asynchronous communication should sometimes be eschewed in favor of synchronous communication. If specific use cases require an immediate reply in response to a request, consider using synchronous protocols such as Java RMI or SOAP. Although JMS may afford better reliability through guaranteed message delivery, it may also be overkill for the task at hand. Remember that it's just another tool whose value is derived from the circumstances in which you use it.

Speaking of new tools, we've now learned enough about JMS to start cracking message-driven beans. It's been a long journey to this point, but you won't want to miss what's around the next corner.

6.8 *Using message-driven beans (MDBs)*

Let's pick up where we left off on our order processing system. We built the `OrderRequestSender`, picked the best message type, and then dialed in the right amount of reliability. It's high time we designed the consumer of `OrderRequest` messages. We could choose to create the consumer as a stand-alone JMS client. However, we want to scale our application to handle many `OrderRequest` messages concurrently. So, in the spirit of this book, and because we already have an investment in an EJB server, we'll design the message consumer as a message-driven bean (MDB).

6.8.1 *Pooling with MDBs*

MDBs were introduced in EJB 2.0 as server-side components capable of concurrently processing asynchronous messages. In contrast, while session and entity beans can produce asynchronous messages, they can only consume messages synchronously. An MDB's life cycle is similar to that of a stateless session bean. Instances of a particular MDB are identical. They hold no state that makes them distinguishable. Therefore, MDB instances can be pooled. Message producers unknowingly interact with an MDB instance by sending a message to a topic or queue subscribed to by the MDB. Figure 6.7 illustrates the advantage of pooling MDB instances.

An MDB is equipped to handle JMS messages by implementing the `javax.jms.MessageListener` interface. This interface defines a single `onMessage()` method. When a message is delivered to the topic or queue, an MDB instance is plucked from the pool and its `onMessage()` callback method is invoked with the message. If more messages are delivered to the topic or queue before the instance's `onMessage()` method returns, then other instances are called into action to handle the messages. When an instance's `onMessage()` method returns, the instance is returned to the pool to await the next message.

To summarize, the use of MDBs offers a distinct advantage over managing multiple JMS clients. Instead of trying to load balance messages between stand-alone JMS clients for optimal throughput, the container effectively distributes the load using a pool of available MDB instances. So, let's take advantage of an MDB to handle requests for orders.

6.8.2 *Building the OrderRequest consumer*

Unlike a session or entity bean, an MDB does not have a home or remote interface. In other words, an MDB does not define business methods accessible directly from remote clients. Instead, it simply defines the `onMessage()` method that

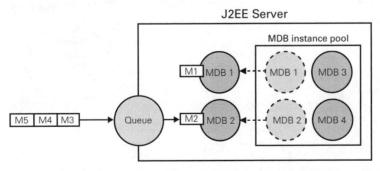

Figure 6.7   MDB instances are pooled in preparation for handling incoming messages. In this example, two MDB instances have been enlisted from the pool and are now busily handling messages. When the next message arrives (M3), if MDB1 and MDB2 are still busy, then an idle MDB instance (MDB3 or MDB4) will be plucked from the pool to handle the message. In this way, multiple messages can be consumed concurrently for better performance.

contains the business logic for handling a message. The business logic encapsulated in the `onMessage()` method is executed in response to asynchronously receiving a message. Listing 6.4 shows how an `OrderRequest` is consumed by our MDB.

Listing 6.4   A message-driven bean that handles OrderRequest messages

```java
public class OrderRequestReceiverMDB
  implements javax.ejb.MessageDrivenBean,
             javax.jms.MessageListener {

  private MessageDrivenContext ctx;

  public void setMessageDrivenContext(MessageDrivenContext ctx) {
    this.ctx = ctx;
  }

  public void ejbCreate() {}

  public void onMessage(Message message) {

    if (message instanceof MapMessage) {

      MapMessage mapMessage = (MapMessage)message;

      try {

        String orderId = mapMessage.getString("Order ID");       ← Crack the
        String productId = mapMessage.getString("Product ID");      message
        int quantity = mapMessage.getInt("Quantity");
        double price = mapMessage.getDouble("Price");

        OrderRequest orderRequest =          Create an order value object
          new OrderRequest(orderId, productId, quantity, price);

        recordOrder(orderRequest);       Store order in order database

        OrderStatus status = fulfillOrder(orderRequest);  ← Send order to
                                                             fulfillment system
        notifyOrderStatusSubscribers(status);  ←  Broadcast
      } catch (JMSException jmse) {             notification to
        jmse.printStackTrace();                 OrderStatus
      }                                         subscribers
    } else {
      System.err.println("OrderRequest must be a MapMessage type!");
    }
  }

  public void ejbRemove() {}
}
```

In addition to the performance benefits gained by MDB pooling, this type of bean is much easier to develop than a stand-alone JMS consumer. Notice that we didn't have to write all the boilerplate setup code needed to connect to the JMS server through JNDI and subscribe to a queue as we did in building the `OrderRequest-Sender`. The EJB container takes care of all that plumbing, based on the contents of deployment descriptors. Listing 6.5 shows the standard XML deployment descriptor (`ejb-jar.xml`) relevant to our MDB example.

Listing 6.5   XML deployment descriptor for the OrderRequestReceiverMDB

```
<message-driven>
  <ejb-name>orderRequestReceiverMDB</ejb-name>
  <ejb-class>com.bitterejb.order.ejb.OrderRequestReceiverMDB</ejb-class>
  <transaction-type>Container</transaction-type>
  <message-driven-destination>
    <destination-type>javax.jms.Queue</destination-type>
  </message-driven-destination>
</message-driven>
```

By declaring the message destination as a queue using the `<destination-type>` tag in the deployment descriptor, the code in the MDB itself becomes oblivious to a message's point of origin (topic or queue). That is, this same MDB could be configured to subscribe to a topic without changing any code. This means that the business logic this MDB encapsulates easily can be reused across messaging models. That's a markedly easier solution than developing a new JMS consumer client.

The actual JNDI name of the queue to which our `OrderRequestSender` is sending `OrderRequest` messages is declared in a vendor-specific XML deployment descriptor. The EJB container automatically subscribes MDB instances to this message queue when the instances are created. This same vendor-specific deployment descriptor may also declare the initial and maximum size of the MDB instance pool. Sizing the pool allows us to easily throttle the message throughput, based on expected message volumes.

We haven't yet discussed the actual business logic involved in handling a message. Once a message arrives, the business logic can do whatever is necessary to fulfill the order. That process isn't all that relevant to the antipatterns in this chapter. We could imagine the business logic using the J2EE Connector Architecture (JCA) to communicate with the legacy order fulfillment application, for example. The logic might even collaborate with other EJB components—session and entity beans—in a more complex workflow. For example, to create an easily supported order status notification, a subscriber of `OrderStatus` messages could use JavaMail to send an email to the person who placed the order. The email could contain an indication of the order's status. In any event, this arbitrary business logic should be decoupled from JMS as we'll see in our next antipattern.

6.9 Antipattern: Monolithic Consumer

At this point, we might be tempted to walk away from the MDB that consumes `OrderRequest` messages, satisfied that it dutifully handles messages. If we did, we'd miss a golden opportunity to improve the design. Before wandering off, let's take a minute to reflect on ways to keep the code clean and the design pristine. A small investment to pay off design debt now will help prevent interest payments from accumulating down the road.

As it stands, our MDB's `onMessage()` method creates the unfortunate side effect of undesirable coupling. It's not a particularly long method, but after cracking the message, it inlines a sequence of method calls. As a result, the business logic `onMessage()` encapsulates—the real meat of the order fulfillment process—is intimately tied to an asynchronous messaging infrastructure. No clean separation of concerns exists between the communication mechanism used to interact with the business logic and the logic itself. Left untouched, this tightly wrapped ball of code is, and forever will be, a JMS consumer. This coupling has a severe consequence. The only way to execute the business logic is by publishing a JMS message for consumption by the MDB. However, we'd like to reuse this business logic in the absence of JMS. Without overengineering the design, what's the simplest thing we can do now to head off potentially painting ourselves in a corner later? It might surprise you to hear that a test is in order.

6.9.1 Listening to the test

If we had attempted to write a test for the business logic before digging into the implementation of the MDB, the pain that would be caused by undesirable coupling would have been evident. By paying attention to the test, we would have uncovered a better design opportunity much sooner. Indeed, when writing a test is painful, we can usually assume that something's wrong.

Consider how difficult it is to write a test for the business logic through the MDB's `onMessage()` method. To do so, we would have to follow this procedure:

1   Write a full-blown JMS message producer similar to the `OrderRequest-Sender`.

2   Register the message producer as a subscriber of `OrderStatus` messages.

3   Create and publish an `OrderRequest` message.

4 Wait for the asynchronous `OrderStatus` message.

5 Validate that the resulting `OrderStatus` message contains the expected status.

6 Query the order database to ensure the order was properly recorded.

That's a lot of work! And most of our effort is geared toward appeasing the JMS infrastructure. While this approach might create a good integration test, we're once again forced to use JMS. We really just want to know if the business logic works. However, given the current design, testing the business logic independent of JMS proves difficult because the test doesn't distinguish between the two. The test forces us to separate JMS from the business logic by refactoring the MDB to delegate its work to a testable component.

6.9.2 Solution: Delegate to modular components

Modular designs that use cohesive and loosely coupled components are generally easier to test. Imagine how the design improves if we look at it first in light of a test. Without worrying about how a JMS message arrives, the test is simply concerned with validating the business logic. After all, the test really only cares about the guts of the `onMessage()` method. This tells us that inside the `onMessage()` method is a unique component just waiting to be let free. So, let's refactor the logic contained in the `onMessage()` method into a separate component, called the `OrderRequestHandler` class. Listing 6.6 shows the updated `onMessage()` method.

Listing 6.6 Refactoring onMessage() to delegate to an order request handler

```
public void onMessage(Message message) {

  if (message instanceof MapMessage) {

    MapMessage mapMessage = (MapMessage)message;

    try {                                             ⟵──┐  Crack the
      String orderId = mapMessage.getString("Order ID");  ⟵─┘  message
      String productId = mapMessage.getString("Product ID");
      int quantity = mapMessage.getInt("Quantity");
      double price = mapMessage.getDouble("Price");

      OrderRequest orderRequest =      Create an order value object
        new OrderRequest(orderId, productId, quantity, price);

      OrderRequestHandler handler = new OrderRequestHandler();
      handler.handle(orderRequest);  ⟵──┐ Delegate to encapsulated
    } catch (JMSException jmse) {         business logic
      jmse.printStackTrace();
    }
```

```
    } else {
      System.err.println("OrderRequest must be a MapMessage type!");
    }
  }
```

If we extract the inlined code into the `OrderRequestHandler` class, then the code's business logic is decoupled from asynchronous messages. The `OrderRequestHandler` class is solely responsible for the order fulfillment process: recording an order, submitting the order to the legacy order fulfillment application, and notifying order status subscribers. In addition, the business logic easily can be tested outside the MDB container, completely separate from JMS technology. Once we've gained confidence that the handler works as expected, it can be used by many clients. Local clients within the same JVM, for example, can submit an order request simply by invoking a method directly on an instance of the class. We've successfully put JMS in its rightful place—as a glue technology.

Now, imagine we want to expose the logic of the `OrderRequestHandler` to remote clients. Using the Session Façade design pattern, a session bean can service remote synchronous clients by delegating directly to an `OrderRequestHandler` instance. Moving a step further, we can expose the same business logic to remote asynchronous clients by creating an MDB that either delegates directly to an `OrderRequestHandler` instance or indirectly through the Session Façade. Figure 6.8 illustrates the multiple communication paths used to access the business logic that processes an order request.

Notice that by decorating a modular component in a layered fashion, we've effectively created two communication paths: one synchronous and the other asynchronous. Moreover, no code duplication exists. We need only to change the business logic in one place to affect the synchronous and asynchronous clients uniformly. That is, the business logic can be varied, independent of the client types that may chose to use it.

The moral of the story is to remember that an MDB is simply a conduit between JMS clients and business logic. As such, it should be kept as thin as possible. After receiving a message, and possibly converting it into a lightweight business object, the MDB should delegate to other components that act on the contents of the message. And we discovered all that by starting from a testing perspective. Go figure!

Now for a little fun with a familiar, albeit tiresome, game: hot potato.

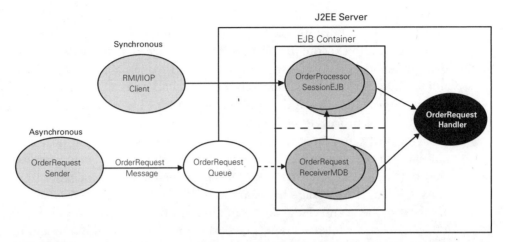

Figure 6.8 Layering is a design technique used to build loosely coupled systems capable of servicing disparate clients. By decorating a simple component that encapsulates business logic, enabling technologies can serve as thin communication adapters. This maintains a clean separation of concerns, improves testability, and allows the business logic to be changed in one location to affect all clients.

6.10 *Antipattern: Hot Potato*

When a JMS server doesn't receive an acknowledgment for a message sent to a consumer, the server's only recourse is to attempt to redeliver the message. This sets the stage for a potentially wicked game of hot potato. The game goes something like this:

- The JMS server sends a message to a message-driven bean.
- The MDB raises an exception or rolls back its transaction.
- As a result, the MDB container doesn't acknowledge the message.
- So the server attempts to redeliver the message.
- The message again causes the MDB to raise an exception or roll back its transaction.
- Once again, the server does not receive an acknowledgment.
- Rinse and repeat.

The JMS server and the MDB container continue to toss the message back and forth, neither one wanting to get caught with the message when its timeout expires (if ever). Round and round they go; where they stop, nobody knows.

This begs a question: what might cause a message to go unacknowledged by an MDB. As first-class EJB components, MDBs are transaction-aware in their own right. Often we want to execute the business logic, triggered by the arrival of a message, as an atomic business process. Let's look at our example again. The arrival of an `OrderRequest` message kicks off a sequence of actions: updating a database, accessing an external system, and sending notification. If any step fails, we want the entire business process to be rolled back.

Using MDBs greatly simplifies handling messages within a transaction. MDBs can manage their own transactions or let the container manage transactions on their behalf. If CMT are used, then message consumption is included in the same transaction as the message handling logic. Only if the transaction succeeds will the message be acknowledged. It's an all-or-nothing proposition. If either of the following occurs while executing the `onMessage()` method, the transaction will be rolled back and the JMS server will attempt to redeliver the message:

- A system exception (e.g., `EJBException`) is thrown from the `onMessage()` method.

- The `MessageDrivenContext.setRollbackOnly()` method is invoked.

Because the message acknowledgment is tied directly to the success of a transaction, MDBs that use CMTs are easy candidates for a game of hot potato. Rolling back the transaction because business logic fails causes the message to never be acknowledged. Figure 6.9 depicts the hot potato game played between the JMS server and an MDB instance (note that the steps are presented in clockwise sequence).

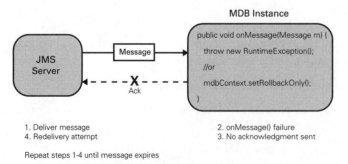

1. Deliver message
4. Redelivery attempt

2. onMessage() failure
3. No acknowledgment sent

Repeat steps 1-4 until message expires

Figure 6.9 **If an MDB instance continuously throws a system exception from its `onMessage()` method, or rolls back the transaction, then the MDB container doesn't acknowledge receipt of the message. Consequently, the JMS server assumes the message wasn't successfully delivered. In an effort to set things straight, the server will attempt to redeliver the message. The message becomes like a hot potato tossed back and forth between the JMS server and MDB instances.**

MDBs that choose to manage their own transactions are slightly less likely to get into a game of hot potato, though they are not immune to it. When BMT are used, the consumption of a message is not included in the same transaction as the message handling logic. Messages are acknowledged, regardless of whether the transaction is committed or rolled back. To force the JMS server to redeliver a message if the transaction is rolled back, a system exception can be thrown from the onMessage() method.

Although hot potato appears to be good, clean fun, it's not a game with many prizes. The JMS server on one side is frazzled, juggling all outstanding messages. On the other side, the MDB instances are thrashed, trying to deal with recurring messages they can't handle. Until an acknowledgment is made, the games will continue.

6.10.1 *Solution: Acknowledge the message, not its result*

The easiest way to avoid a game of hot potato is to acknowledge the successful receipt of the message, not whether the resulting business logic was successful. The JMS server can't do anything about the latter, so don't put the server in a position to let you down.

Toward this end, you don't want to throw system exceptions in response to business logic errors. System exceptions should be raised only in response to genuine system (or container) failures. Because application exceptions cannot be thrown from the onMessage() method, it's best to log any business logic errors and return gracefully from the onMessage() method. This lets the JMS server know that the consumer got the message, which is all the server really cares about anyway. A variation on this theme is to send an error-related message to a special error queue. To handle unexpected error conditions intelligently, exception-handling consumers can subscribe to this queue.

Be mindful of the repercussions of rolling back an MDB transaction by invoking the MessageDrivenContext.setRollbackOnly() method. It, too, will force the JMS server to attempt redelivery. Ask yourself whether the next MDB instance chosen to handle the message will be able to execute the business logic successfully, or if it will suffer the same fate. If the problem that triggers the rollback is unrecoverable, then the next MDB instance to receive the redelivered message will likely encounter the same problem. Incoming hot potato! If it's possible that the next MDB instance to receive the redelivered message will be able to recover from the error, then rolling back the transaction may be appropriate.

Some JMS providers automatically support the use of a Dead Message Queue (DMQ). If, for example, an attempt to deliver a message is unsuccessful after a preconfigured number of redelivery tries, the message is automatically redirected to the DMQ. Our application is then responsible for monitoring this queue and taking appropriate action when a doomed message arrives. JMS providers may also support a configurable redelivery delay whereby the JMS server waits a predefined amount of time before attempting redelivery. Understanding the conditions under which a message will be redelivered helps minimize the chance of creating a berserk message. Equally troublesome is the subject of our next antipattern: a message that takes a while to chew on.

6.11 Antipattern: Slow Eater

An MDB can chew on only one message at a time. Until its onMessage() method returns (swallows what's in its mouth), an MDB cannot be used to handle other messages. That is, an MDB instance is not re-entrant. If another message is delivered to the MDB container before a busy instance's onMessage() method returns, then the container will pluck another MDB instance from the instance pool to handle the new message. This is true for both publish/subscribe and point-to-point messaging. Messages published to a topic are delivered to one MDB instance in every MDB container registering interest in the topic. Messages sent to a queue are delivered to one MDB instance in exactly one MDB container registering interest in the queue. In either case, an MDB instance can only handle messages serially.

When the onMessage() method takes a relatively long time to handle a message, more and more instances in an MDB instance pool will be needed to handle high message volumes. Messages will start to back up any time the average arrival time of messages is greater than the average time to consume each message, thereby creating a bottleneck that restricts message throughput. In general, anytime the ratio of message production to consumption is high, message throughput will suffer.

6.11.1 Solution: Eat faster, if you can

If high message volumes are expected, it's wise to keep the onMessage() method as fast as possible. An MDB with a short and sweet onMessage() method can achieve higher levels of message throughput with a smaller number of MDB instances in the pool. Because every MDB instance in the pool is stateless and identical, any idle instance can handle an incoming message. As soon as the onMessage() method returns, it can immediately handle another message. That's all well and good, except for one minor detail: MDBs are usually tasked with time-consuming work on which message producers can't afford to block waiting.

Indeed, if faced with a quick and dirty job, we might just use a synchronous method call.

We should strive to keep the code paths invoked by the `onMessage()` method optimized as necessary to support a tolerable message throughput. Delegating to modular components that perform the actual message handling makes it much easier to write isolated performance tests that continually measure the response time of the logic encapsulated in `onMessage()`.

When we dig a bit deeper in our toolbox, we can find a few performance tricks for helping slow eaters. If we spend time reading our JMS vendor's documentation, we can get a feel for the possible tools we could use. For example, some vendors have support for throttling, which effectively slows down producers if consumers are lagging behind. We might as well use what's already available to our advantage—we paid for it! Once our MDBs are efficiently consuming messages, we need to make sure they aren't eating more than their fair portion. This is the subject of our next antipattern.

6.12 *Antipattern: Eavesdropping*

As messages fly around in a message-based system, consumers must pick and choose the messages they'll consume. The potential for information overload increases with each new message producer participating in the system. A consumer eating a relatively small portion of messages today may be faced with significantly larger portions tomorrow.

Take, for example, a publish/subscribe scenario with subscribers eavesdropping on a high-traffic topic. As more and more messages are sent to that topic, the subscribers may experience an abysmal signal-to-noise ratio. Similarly, in a point-to-point scenario, receivers consuming messages from a high-volume queue may be burdened with handling low priority work. Developing custom message filtering logic in each message consumer is both time consuming and prone to error. It also makes it difficult to uniformly improve message filtering logic and performance.

As a work-around, multiple destinations (topics and queues) can be set up to partition messages according to their intended use. In other words, we can break up coarse destinations into multiple fine-grained destinations for more selective listening. For example, we could configure two queues for our order processing system: one for standard orders and the other for premium orders. However, the process of setting up special interest destinations starts to fall apart at some point, and ultimately leads to a proliferation of topics and queues, which must be administered and managed. This work-around also places the burden on message producers to send only relevant messages to each destination. Message consumers are in turn burdened with registering interest in only the appropriate destinations necessary to get all the information they need.

6.12.1 *Solution: Use message selectors*

Message selectors are one way for message consumers to easily tune out messages they don't need or want to hear. Each message consumer can be configured with a unique message selector, much as we use mail and news filters to receive only information we're interested in reading.

A message's filtering can be based only on its headers and properties, not on the payload it carries. The SQL-92 conditional expression syntax—which makes up SQL WHERE clauses—is used to declare the filtering criteria. The JMS provider filters messages, so the process is automatic from the consumer's perspective.

The use of message selectors is one way to easily design *queue specialization* into a message-based system. Referring back to our example order processing system, we can see it may make good business sense to handle premium orders differently than standard orders. Rather than creating two different queues—one for standard orders and another for premium orders—a single queue could be used by all message consumers interested in orders. We could then create two different types of OrderRequest handlers modeled as MDBs: a standard order handler and a premium order handler.

Assuming an OrderRequest message contained the total price of the order as a message property, the standard order handler would be created with a message selector on that property so the standard order handler would only see orders on the queue with a total price up to $1,000. The premium order handler's message selector would restrict its view of the queue to only those orders that exceeded $1,000. We could then vary the size of the respective MDB instance pools independently. For example, the premium order handler's pool might be increased to improve the throughput of fulfilling premium orders. Figure 6.10 illustrates the flow of messages when message selectors are used to handle premium orders differently than standard orders.

Using the same example, each subscriber of OrderStatus messages could use message selectors to select the messages they receive. Messages that didn't match the selection criteria for a given subscriber wouldn't be delivered to that subscriber. Each subscriber would pick up a good, clean signal without any of the noise.

How and where messages are filtered is an implementation detail of the JMS provider. Any specific JMS vendor's implementation may apply the message selection logic in the server-side message router or in the client-side consumer's JVM.

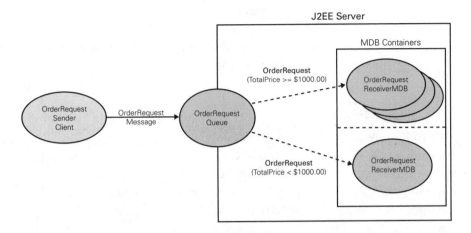

Figure 6.10 Message selectors can be used to improve signal quality by filtering messages based on header and property values. Rather than having to eavesdrop on all messages for fear of missing an important message, consumers can be created with unique message selectors. This allows the QoS to be varied according to the business value of the message being handled by a pool of MDB instances.

Depending on the implementation, message selectors may create a measurable drag on performance. In general, however, filtering on the server side is less expensive and may actually improve performance by minimizing network traffic for unwanted messages. In any event, it pays to have performance benchmarks and automated tests that can continually check whether performance is going off the rails. Running these tests can help determine objectively how the performance of message selectors stacks up against custom message filtering logic in each message consumer.

At the end of the day, anything that can be done with message selectors can also be achieved using multiple destinations. The use of message selectors over multiple destinations ultimately boils down to striking a balance between resource management and performance.

Now, let's apply what we've learned by setting up a message selector.

6.12.2 *Declaring message selectors*

Message selectors are declared for each message consumer when the consumer is created. With MDBs, no extra coding is necessary. The message selection criteria simply are declared in the XML deployment descriptor. The MDB container creates all MDB instances in the pool with the same message selection criteria.

Assuming an `OrderRequest` message contains a property defining the total cost of the order, adding the following XML snippet to the standard XML deployment descriptor (`ejb-jar.xml`) causes only those orders exceeding $1,000 to be delivered to the MDB instances managed by this container:

```
<message-selector>
  <![CDATA[TotalPrice > 1000.00]]>
</message-selector>
```

That's all there is to it! Of course message selectors can be arbitrarily complex, depending on the number of message properties and the conditional logic involved. Using a CDATA section around the message selector text means the text won't be subjected to XML parsing. Therefore, we won't need to escape all the logical operators to appease the XML parser.

6.12.3 *Going beyond message selectors*

Many JMS vendors have value-add features for going beyond message selectors. If you choose to take these paths, just remember that you're straying away from portability. Fortunately, with MDBs we can take advantage of these extensions at deployment time. That is, we usually won't have to change any code to put these extensions in or take them out. The deployment descriptor conveniently includes all configuration details.

As we learned, the JMS specification restricts message selectors to filtering, based on a message's headers and properties. In other words, we can't filter a message by inspecting its payload. In response, many vendors have added proprietary extensions to the message selector syntax to support content-based routing. For example, many vendors can use XPath to filter either proprietary XML message types or a `TextMessage` containing XML.

Another proprietary extension for message filtering is the use of wildcard topic names. By using a dot notation when naming topics, we can set up a hierarchy of information. Consumers can then easily subscribe to groups of messages. Take, for example, a financial application that sends stock quote updates to either the STOCKS.NYSE.IBM or STOCKS.NASDAQ.SUNW topics. If consumers want to subscribe to all NASDAQ prices, they simply register interest in the STOCKS.NASDAQ.* topic. Alternatively, they can listen to a specific stock by registering interest in the STOCKS.NASDAQ.SUNW topic, for example.

Up to this point we've covered many antipatterns related to the design of applications using JMS and MDBs. As a parting shot, let's look at a final antipattern, one that usually reveals itself at the end of your development process.

6.13 *Antipattern: Performance Afterthoughts*

We've touched on performance in many ways throughout this chapter. However, just because some antipatterns had performance side effects doesn't mean we should focus on performance too early. Premature optimization is speculative at best. On the other hand, casting performance absolutely to the wind is a recipe for disaster. Every design decision we make, including the selection of a JMS vendor, ultimately has the potential to affect performance. Our path deviates away from a successful deployment each time a decision is made without objectively measuring its performance implications.

Although the JMS specification defines two messaging models and various QoS features that may influence performance, the specification does not address the performance implications of these decisions. This lapse gives JMS vendors a lot of room to compete and tailor their product offerings to shine in certain deployment scenarios. Indeed, vendors have different strengths and weaknesses. It's entirely possible that a vendor's implementation designed specifically to excel in certain scenarios may fall down in other scenarios. And then there's the code we write!

Simply measuring the time it takes a JMS server to transport a single message from a producer to a consumer doesn't give us a full picture of performance. The performance of an individual message's delivery cycle may be markedly different when the JMS server is under load—for example, delivering fat, persistent messages to multiple consumers. Without a rough measure of success based on realistic usage patterns, the measurements are useless.

6.13.1 *Solution: Measure early and often*

Our defense against performance-related antipatterns is a solid foundation of automated tests that validate our application's performance requirements. When faced with decisions that may affect performance, these automated tests can be rerun to objectively measure any impact. As our application's design takes shape, we'll get confidence by continually running its performance tests to measure progress. If a change improves performance, we can raise the bar by modifying the tests to use the new benchmark. If performance degrades, we can undo whatever changes were made and try again.

Automated performance tests can also be used as a yardstick when evaluating different JMS implementations in terms of their performance. Before making an investment in a specific JMS vendor's implementation, we should create a few benchmarks. We should start by using a simple driver that can be configured easily to produce/consume arbitrary numbers of messages and report performance metrics for each action. Because the performance of messaging models will vary between vendors, we need to make sure the test is indicative of our application's needs. Then we can proceed to write automated tests that use the test rig to simulate a representative use case and automatically check that performance is within tolerable limits.

Given the variation in vendor implementations and design decisions, performance cannot be treated as an afterthought without facing potentially dire consequences. Writing performance tests early and running them often illuminates unforeseen bottlenecks and reduces the effects of downstream thrash tuning. The following list represents factors that should be considered when writing and running performance tests:

- **Message throughput** The number of messages a JMS server is able to process over a given period of time can be a telling metric. It quantifies the degree to which an application can scale to handle more concurrent users and a higher message volume.

- **Message density** The average size of a message impacts the performance and scalability of an application. Smaller messages use less network bandwidth and are generally easier for the JMS server to manage.

- **Message delivery mode** Persistent messages must first be stored in nonvolatile memory before being processed by the JMS server. Effective tests must produce messages representative of the production system to get an accurate picture of production performance.

- **Test under realistic load scenarios** Load testing with multiple users often illuminates bottlenecks that aren't evident in a single producer/consumer scenario. Write tests that measure the message throughput capable under average and peak concurrent user loads. Consider both the ratio of users to actual JMS connections, and the resources required.

- **Production rate versus consumption rate** If the rate at which messages are produced exceeds the rate at which messages are consumed, the JMS server must somehow manage the backlog of messages. Watch for any significant disparities between the send rate and the receive rate.

- **Go the distance** Endurance testing over an extended period of time can identify problematic trends such as excessive resource usage or decreased message throughput. Running performance tests overnight, for example, may highlight problems that may be encountered when the system goes live.

- **Know your options**   JMS vendors generally support proprietary runtime parameters and deployment options for tuning the performance and scalability of their product offering. Know what options are available out-of-the-box so that the JMS provider can be configured to yield optimal performance and scalability relative to your application.

- **Monitor metrics**   Some JMS vendors include an administrative console for monitoring internal JMS metrics such as queue sizes and message throughput. Monitor these metrics to gain insight into the usage patterns of your application. If an API is available for obtaining these metrics programmatically, such as through JMX, write tests to check continually whether the metrics are within tolerable ranges.

- **Chart metrics**   Simple charts serve as early warning systems against undesirable performance trends. For example, plotting the number of messages processed as a function of time will help pinpoint where message throughput plateaus. When using point-to-point messaging, plotting the queue size over time will clearly indicate when messages are being backlogged.

Automated performance tests are invaluable for their ability to keep all these considerations continually in check. Don't settle for having to manually recheck performance every time you make a change. Invest early in tests that check their own results and run them often to gain confidence. You'll be glad you did!

6.14 *Summary: Getting the message*

JMS is easy to use and extremely powerful, yet subtle implications must be carefully considered when using JMS to build message-based applications. In this chapter, we discussed several common pitfalls as we developed an example order processing system glued together with asynchronous messaging. In many cases, we were able to side-step problems by applying relatively simple refactorings. In other instances, we avoided potential problems altogether by understanding the consequences of design decisions and planning accordingly.

Although many antipatterns discussed in this chapter are applicable to JMS in general, we specifically put MDBs under the microscope. As first-class EJB components making their debut in EJB 2.0, MDBs enable asynchronous access to server-side business logic and resources. Moreover, they simplify the development of message consumers that can scale to handle high-volume message traffic. Nevertheless, designing and configuring MDBs to meet the challenges of today's business needs requires attention to detail. As we watch MDBs mature to include support for other messaging technologies, we'll likely bear witness to new MDB antipatterns.

Many antipatterns we discussed in this chapter are related to performance. JMS is used primarily as a glue technology to integrate multiple applications through the exchange of portable messages. As such, the quality of a message-based application is measured according to the message throughput it can reliably scale to handle. The important lesson to be learned from these antipatterns is to size and test your application early and often to ensure a successful deployment.

6.15 *Antipatterns in this chapter*

This section covers the Fat Messages, Skinny Messages, XML as the Silver Bullet, Packrat, Immediate Reply Requested, Monolithic Consumer, Hot Potato, Slow Eater, Eavesdropping, and Performance Afterthoughts antipatterns.

FAT MESSAGES

DESCRIPTION
> Using the same message type for all situations and not designing messages for their intended consumers leads to bloated messages.

MOST FREQUENT SCALE
> Application

REFACTORED SOLUTION NAME
> Message dieting

REFACTORED SOLUTION TYPE
> Software

REFACTORED SOLUTION DESCRIPTION
> Design messages to carry just enough information to allow their consumers to autonomously handle the messages. Send references to data when sending the data itself is size prohibitive.

ANECDOTAL EVIDENCE
> "This message contains a plethora of information, just in case consumers need it."

SYMPTOMS, CONSEQUENCES
> The messaging pipes are clogged with fat messages, and message throughput suffers.

SKINNY MESSAGES

DESCRIPTION

Messages that don't contain enough information burden their consumers with making extra remote calls to get more information.

MOST FREQUENT SCALE

Application

REFACTORED SOLUTION NAME

Put some meat on the bones.

REFACTORED SOLUTION TYPE

Software

REFACTORED SOLUTION DESCRIPTION

Err on the side of sending a bit too much information. Add state information to references to let consumers decide when and if to load referenced data.

ANECDOTAL EVIDENCE

"Why is the application spending all of its time I/O blocked?"

SYMPTOMS, CONSEQUENCES

Asynchronous communication breaks down into synchronous communication to clarify the intent of messages. Misuse of references causes contention of a shared resource and ends up being slower than a fatter message.

XML AS THE SILVER BULLET

DESCRIPTION

Filling messages with XML by default in the name of flexibility and portability

MOST FREQUENT SCALE

Application

REFACTORED SOLUTION NAME

Use XML on the edges.

REFACTORED SOLUTION TYPE

Software

REFACTORED SOLUTION DESCRIPTION

Use XML messages to communicate with applications beyond your control. The `MapMessage` has similar flexibility and portability when communicating with application within your control.

ANECDOTAL EVIDENCE

"XML is the only way to make this message portable." "All the cool developers are using XML."

SYMPTOMS, CONSEQUENCES

Messages containing XML may incur unnecessary overhead that limits message throughput. Message handling logic isn't explicit or type-safe.

PACKRAT

DESCRIPTION
>Storing all messages, regardless of whether delivery must be guaranteed

MOST FREQUENT SCALE
>Application

REFACTORED SOLUTION NAME
>Save only the important messages.

REFACTORED SOLUTION TYPE
>Software

REFACTORED SOLUTION DESCRIPTION
>Consider the ramifications of losing a message before deciding to guarantee its delivery.

ANECDOTAL EVIDENCE
>"Let's be safe and store all messages by default."

SYMPTOMS, CONSEQUENCES
>Storing all messages limits message throughput and unnecessarily burdens the JMS server.

IMMEDIATE REPLY REQUESTED

DESCRIPTION
>Using JMS for a synchronous request/reply style of communication

MOST FREQUENT SCALE
>Application

REFACTORED SOLUTION NAME
>Use synchronous communication technologies where appropriate.

REFACTORED SOLUTION TYPE
>Software

REFACTORED SOLUTION DESCRIPTION
>If a request/reply style of communication is needed, consider using Java RMI or SOAP.

ANECDOTAL EVIDENCE
>"How can I return a result once the consumer handles the message?"

SYMPTOMS, CONSEQUENCES
>Undesirable coupling between producers and consumers, negating the benefits of asynchronous messaging

MONOLITHIC CONSUMER

DESCRIPTION

Inlining business logic in the class that consumes a message

MOST FREQUENT SCALE

Application

REFACTORED SOLUTION NAME

Delegate.

REFACTORED SOLUTION TYPE

Software

REFACTORED SOLUTION DESCRIPTION

Design the message consumer to simply crack the message then forward the message's data to a separate class defining the actual business logic.

ANECDOTAL EVIDENCE

"I can't test the business logic without starting the JMS server." "That's too hard to test." "Our system's only API is through asynchronous messaging."

SYMPTOMS, CONSEQUENCES

Business logic is tightly coupled to the use of JMS and can only be accessed by sending it a message.

HOT POTATO

DESCRIPTION
A message is continuously tossed back and forth between the JMS server, and a message consumer that won't acknowledge it has received the message.

MOST FREQUENT SCALE
Application

REFACTORED SOLUTION NAME
Acknowledge the message receipt, not its result.

REFACTORED SOLUTION TYPE
Software

REFACTORED SOLUTION DESCRIPTION
Consumer should always acknowledge that they've received a message. This acknowledgment should not be dependent on the success of the business logic handling the message. Log failures in business logic to a separate error queue.

ANECDOTAL EVIDENCE
"Where did all these messages come from?"

SYMPTOMS, CONSEQUENCES
The JMS server is burdened with attempting to redeliver messages that no consumer will ever acknowledge.

SLOW EATER

DESCRIPTION

Message consumers that take a relatively long time to consume a message negatively affect message throughput

MOST FREQUENT SCALE

Application

REFACTORED SOLUTION NAME

Eat as fast as you can.

REFACTORED SOLUTION TYPE

Software

REFACTORED SOLUTION DESCRIPTION

Measure the consumption rate of messages as an early warning system against bottlenecks. Optimize the code paths of message consumers as necessary.

ANECDOTAL EVIDENCE

"We have to frequently increase the size of the message-driven bean instance pool." "The message queues continue to grow unchecked."

SYMPTOMS, CONSEQUENCES

Message throughput is negatively affected when the production rate is greater than the consumption rate.

EAVESDROPPING

DESCRIPTION
Listening in on high-traffic message queues and topics for fear of missing an important message

MOST FREQUENT SCALE
Application

REFACTORED SOLUTION NAME
Use message selectors.

REFACTORED SOLUTION TYPE
Software

REFACTORED SOLUTION DESCRIPTION
The use of message selectors lets consumers tune out messages they aren't interested in hearing. Specialized message consumers can handle high-priority messages with a better QoS.

ANECDOTAL EVIDENCE
"This consumer keeps getting spammed with unwanted messages."

SYMPTOMS, CONSEQUENCES
Message consumers are burdened with handling throw-away messages and high priority work is intermixed with low priority work. Network and CPU utilization increases.

PERFORMANCE AFTERTHOUGHTS

DESCRIPTION

Focusing on performance without requirements or engaging in premature optimizations without a baseline

MOST FREQUENT SCALE

Application

REFACTORED SOLUTION NAME

Measure early and often.

REFACTORED SOLUTION TYPE

Process

REFACTORED SOLUTION DESCRIPTION

Gather performance requirements early and often. Build automated performance tests that continuously validate performance criteria. Use performance tests to benchmark JMS vendors based on your application's requirements.

TYPICAL CAUSES

Poor planning

ANECDOTAL EVIDENCE

"We will have plenty of time to performance tune at the end of the development cycle." "We'll let our QA department measure performance." "We're using a reputable JMS server, so it should scale well."

SYMPTOMS, CONSEQUENCES

Repeated delivery of poorly performing software, redesign of critical use cases late in the development cycle, and last-minute tuning activities that are ineffective.

Part 3

EJB persistence

W hen the summer rains flood the creeks in the Texas hill country, experienced kayakers start seeing all kinds of unfit watercraft appear on the local creeks. The owners of the craft, which range from nearly rotten canoes to swimming lounge chairs, are visibly unprepared. Most have no helmet, and few have adequate life vests. Approaching the creek this way is inherently dangerous, and we frequently try to keep inexperienced boaters away, usually with little success. Invariably, we find the unsafe watercraft downstream, wrapped around the rocks and the trees that make navigation difficult under the best of circumstances.

Some of the watercraft that we might see on Austin creeks would be quite at home in swimming pools, but have no place on area creeks. Similarly, the component-oriented design of EJB is not well suited for persistence. In chapter 7, we discuss antipatterns related to EJB persistence. We explore common traps like application joins and filters. In chapter 8, we go one step further, recommending alternatives to EJB entity beans. We present a simple example solved with EJB, JDBC, and JDO, and then weigh the advantages and disadvantages of each approach. Our goal here is to get you out of that swimming pool float and into something more appropriate for the EJB development creeks that you'll find yourself navigating.

Bitter entities

7

This chapter contains
- Antipatterns related to entity beans
- Application joins and filters
- Rules for building efficient primary keys

After weeks of intense political campaigning in Connecticut, my sister sweeps down the Park City, Utah slope. The snow is much lighter and fresher than she usually sees in the East. The refreshing cold tickles her cheeks as she rips down the immaculate run. She had planned to spend the day skiing the easier runs as a warm-up, but after witnessing the intensity of the sweeping Park City runs, she can't help herself: she heads for the fun stuff.

It's all coming back to her nicely. Her edges deliciously carve up the steep gully when she sees the little mogul ahead. Feeling confident, she gets ready for the jump. She squares her shoulders, feels the pressure of acceleration on the balls of her feet, and as it eases up, tightens quads and calves to propel herself into the air. Only when it's too late and she's in the air does she realize her timing is off.

7.1 Understanding entity bean antipatterns

Since the initial EJB specification was released, entity beans have been a topic of great controversy. Entity beans are fraught with mixed messages and contradictions and continue to cause great confusion. Between the 1.1 and 2.0 releases, sweeping modifications (or, arguably, rewrites) were made to the specification's entity bean portion. These changes added to the confusion. Many argue that entity beans should be used rarely, if at all. (In fact, chapter 8 will outline some of these arguments.) Our overwhelming consensus is that EJB entity beans are problematic at best and fatally flawed at worst.

But what if you want to stick with entity beans? You may not buy our arguments, or you may have no choice in the matter on your project. If you must use entity beans, you'll find this chapter is a guide to avoiding the common antipatterns in the latest EJB specification. We will table the controversy and look at how best and—more importantly—how not to implement entity beans.

7.1.1 Understanding the entity bean antipattern landscape

We will discuss three major types of antipatterns in this chapter. Some can be addressed with impartial solutions, and we'll talk you through the strengths and weaknesses of each one. Here are the areas that we'll address:

- **Object model antipatterns**   Several antipatterns in this chapter discuss situations that predominantly arise when using entity beans to implement a persistent domain object model.

- **Database design antipatterns**   We won't discuss database design in detail, but the use of keys is critical. The Rusty Keys antipattern addresses the misuse and length of keys.

- **Application logic antipatterns**   Often, the design of a framework or application forces you to make poor decisions. Application joins and filters fall in this category, and we'll consider them as well.

Some of these antipatterns are not limited to EJB, but can be found in nearly every persistence framework. However, we find that EJB offers a particularly ripe environment for each antipattern covered here.

7.2 Antipattern: Face Off

If you were to code your application with the simplest possible design, you might decide that directly accessing your entity beans from another application layer is okay. You'd quickly find that communication costs—and serialization costs—would destroy your application's performance. Face Off occurs when you access persistent entities directly from a distributed tier. The Face Off antipattern is probably the biggest pitfall an EJB developer will encounter when using any kind of persistence architecture. Fortunately, most good EJB developers quickly recognize this antipattern and implement one of the well-known workarounds.

Face off can occur whenever an entity bean is used but is most pronounced when entity beans are used for fine-grained persistent storage, as with a persistent domain object model. Face off is the practice of directly invoking entity bean methods from EJB client code, without using a session bean façade.

Because entity beans can be accessed remotely, looking up an entity bean directly from the client and interrogating its persistent data directly is tempting. At first glance, this simple design seems easier than wrapping a façade around the entity bean. However, façade-less access to entity beans can have disastrous effects on the performance and the transactional integrity of a system.

Take, for example, a system with a `Person` entity bean that represents user data in the database. Say this bean has five persistent properties—`firstName`, `lastName`, `phone`, `fax`, and `email`. We will discuss accessing this entity bean directly from client code, then look at what happens when we interpose a session bean façade between the entity bean and the client.

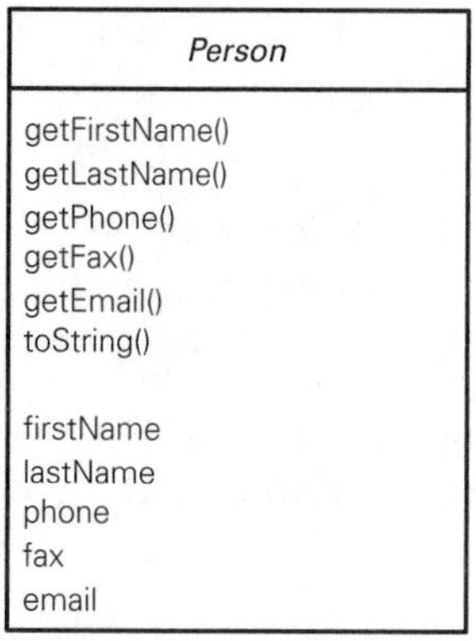

```
          Person

getFirstName()
getLastName()
getPhone()
getFax()
getEmail()
toString()

firstName
lastName
phone
fax
email
```

Figure 7.1
This Unified Modeling Language (UML) diagram is a domain model for a Person class. It's a reasonable design in some cases, but it's easy to abuse. Accessing a component like this directly from a remote client can result in poor performance due to round tripping.

7.2.1 Network round-tripping chokes applications

Imagine that we want to display a list of all Person objects in the database. To do so, we look up the home interface for the entity bean and invoke a finder method on it. Then, given the resultant list of Person objects, we iterate through each one, spitting out information to an output stream.

Arguably this design (figure 7.1) may not be the best for our client code, because we should be separating the presentation from the business logic. We'll leave that antipattern to be addressed elsewhere. For now, let's focus on the communication cost.

Accessing the persistent data in an entity bean directly from a client will lead to network thrashing. The design simply requires too many network round-trips to do all but the most basic operations. *Bitter Java* introduced this antipattern in 2002, but many other books discussed the problem in various forms. We cannot say this strongly enough: In many cases, the number of network round-trips determines application performance success or failure. Solve any network communication problems, and you will be well on your way to good performance. Listing 7.1 shows an entity bean design that suffers from excessive round-tripping.

Listing 7.1   Our flawed test client makes 5*n* + 1 trips to the EJB container

```
InitialContext context = new InitialContext ();
Object personHomeOb = (PersonHome) context.lookup ("Person");
PersonHome personHome = (PersonHome)
    PortableRemoteObject.narrow (personHomeOb, PersonHome.class);
```
Obtain the entity bean home interface

```
Collection people = (Collection) personHome.findAll ();

Person person;
```
Get a list of all Person beans from it

```
for (Iterator iter = people.iterator (); iter.hasNext (); )
{
    person = (Person) iter.next ();                    Each method involves a
    System.out.println ("Person: ");                  round-trip back to the bean
    System.out.println ("    first name: " + person.getFirstName ());
    System.out.println ("    last name: " + person.getLastName ());
    System.out.println ("    phone: " + person.getPhone ());
    System.out.println ("    fax: " + person.getFax ());
    System.out.println ("    email: " + person.getEmail ());
}
```

This client code is massively inefficient. As the number of records (or persistent fields in `Person`) increases, performance quickly degrades. In case this degradation is not obvious, figure 7.2 illustrates the bottlenecks that network communications and overhead create in the application. Each field access in our example will incur a network round-trip. So, our test program will make $5n + 1$ trips to the EJB container, where n is the number of `Person` records in the database and 5 is the number of fields that we retrieve from the `Person` bean. (The finder method also makes one extra trip— $+ 1$.) If our `Person` entity bean had a one-to-many relationship to a set of addresses or projects, the number of database round-trips would multiply quickly.

7.2.2 *Losing transactional integrity*

A slightly subtler problem with the Face Off antipattern is the loss of transactional integrity when bean methods are accessed directly. Because of the EJB specification's declarative transaction management capabilities, a developer may assume that the following code snippet would modify a `Person` entity bean instance in a single atomic unit of work.

Listing 7.2   Nontransactional update of an entity bean

```
public void updatePerson (Object personKey, String phone, String fax)
{
    InitialContext context = new InitialContext ();
    Object personHomeOb = (PersonHome) context.lookup ("Person");
    PersonHome personHome = (PersonHome)
        PortableRemoteObject.narrow (personHomeOb, PersonHome.class);

    Person person = personHome.findByPrimaryKey (personKey);     Look up
    person.setPhone (phone);  Update the phone number            a Person
    person.setFax (fax);                                         entity bean
}                             Update the  fax number
                             in a separate transaction
```

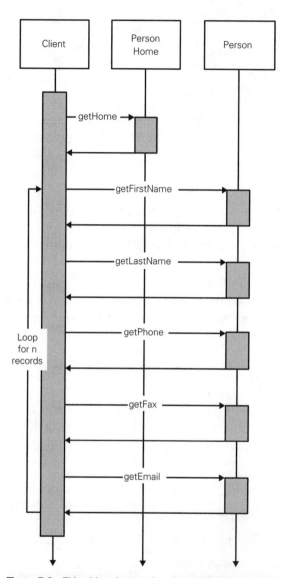

Figure 7.2 This object interaction diagram shows the interactions between the client and the server. The total number of round-trips is the number of fields multiplied by the number of persistent records. The problem is worse than this OID indicates because the get calls are within a tight loop. We can reduce the overhead to a single network round-trip.

In the nontransactional update in listing 7.2, the `setPhone()` and `setFax()` methods are both transactional, but these two methods will be invoked in different transactions. Consequently, the phone number may be incorrectly updated, leaving the entity bean in a transactionally inconsistent state. If the client crashes between this operation and the next one, or if the fax number modification fails, then the phone number will be updated, but the fax number will not. This problem is a different consequence of the Face Off antipattern, although the solutions to both are similar.

7.2.3 *Solution: A Session Façade*

Fortunately, the solution to both the round-tripping and transactional consequences is simple and effective: a session façade. Let's discuss the impact of a session façade on round-tripping first.

Obviously, we can improve the initial network cost of $5n+1$ network round-trips. Looking at the client code we can see that we need to make at least one network round-trip—to obtain the list of `Person` objects to process—but we should also be able to eliminate the $5n$ round-trips altogether. We must simply transmit all the data that we intend to process the first time that we access the bean. Though our application receives the same number of bytes, the overhead that we eliminate will be enormous.

We'll use a Session Façade between the client and the entity bean to consolidate our round-trips. We'll use a DTO, also called `Person`, to move data from our façade. DTOs are simple objects used to organize and hold the data for all `Person` records that will be retrieved. Our façade contains a method that returns DTOs. We can create these DTOs on the session bean side by copying data from the `Person` entity beans to a DTO that we'll then return to the client (listing 7.3).

Listing 7.3 Our improved test client makes a single round-trip to the EJB container

```
InitialContext context = new InitialContext ();        Obtain the session
Object pmHomeOb = (PersonManagerHome)                   bean façade home
              context.lookup("PersonManager");                 interface
PersonManagerHome personManagerHome = (PersonManagerHome)
     PortableRemoteObject.narrow (pmHomeOb, PersonManagerHome.class);

Collection people = (Collection) personManagerHome.findAll ();  ◁─┐
                                                           Get a list of
Person person;                                          all Person objects
```

```
for (Iterator iter = people.iterator (); iter.hasNext (); )
{
    person = (Person) iter.next ();                    Person is a DTO, not an EJB
    System.out.println ("Person: ");                  The code in the loop is local
    System.out.println ("    first name: " + person.getFirstName ());
    System.out.println ("    last name: " + person.getLastName ());
    System.out.println ("    phone: " + person.getPhone ());
    System.out.println ("    fax: " + person.getFax ());
    System.out.println ("    email: " + person.getEmail ());
}
```

Our revised client code looks just the same, except that we look up a session bean, not an entity bean, in JNDI. The bean code is a bit more complex in this situation because we must introduce a session bean and a `Person` data transfer class in addition to the `Person` entity bean. Figure 7.3 shows the impact of our improvements. Ironically, we've added a layer, but we've improved the performance significantly. The Session Façade consolidates $5n + 1$ round-trips to a single round-trip. In practice, a façade can make an even more dramatic impact than we've shown, because a single façade can also package composite objects, such as a person, an address, and other necessary items for an invoice.

7.2.4 *Using a façade for transactional integrity*

Putting a session bean façade in front of the entity bean also resolves our transactional integrity issue. In a façade scenario, the client code will invoke a single session bean method. Provided that this session bean method has the correct transaction mode, the container will set up a transaction for this session bean method and all the entity bean methods involved in the update (`setPhone()` and `setFax()` in listing 7.2) will participate in this single transaction.

Alternately, this problem can be addressed by manually manipulating the container's `UserTransaction` from the client code to ensure that the transaction begins before any changes take place and commits after all changes are complete.

For a more complete discussion of this transactional aspect of the Face Off antipattern, see chapter 8.

7.2.5 *Using local interfaces*

The addition of local bean interfaces in the EJB 2.0 specification provides EJB developers with the tools to develop entity bean models immune to the Face Off antipattern. A bean's local interface can be used only within a single application server. Remote clients cannot misuse beans with a local interface.

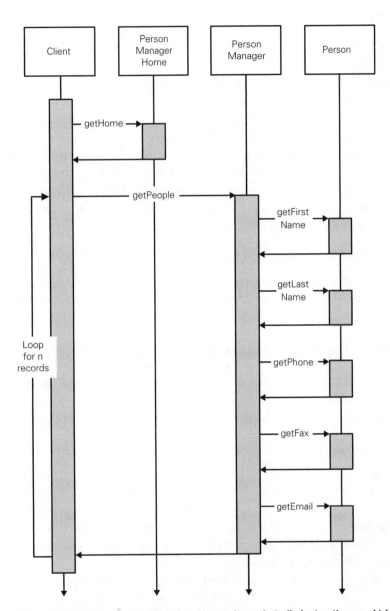

Figure 7.3 Using a Session Façade adds one layer, but eliminates the round-tripping problem in figure 7.2. The bold line indicates distributed communications. The façade in this case reduces the total round trips from 5n + 1 (where 1 is the number of person objects) to 1.

To take things a step further, a bean can have a local interface, a remote interface, or both. So you can create a bean that is accessible solely to other beans deployed to the same container to provide remote access to only a subset of the bean methods. By doing so, you can prevent others from remotely invoking fine-grained methods, instead requiring that fine-grained data access be performed through the appropriate session bean facades.

So, you can see that the session bean façade pattern can eliminate both the performance and transaction problems that can crop up if a client accesses beans in an overly fine-grained manner. This commonly occurs when using entity beans to implement a domain object model, because an object model is typically fine-grained. However, this antipattern can occur in other situations as well—in fact, it can occur even if you exclusively use session beans.

With clever use of local interfaces, you can ensure that others cannot abuse your entity beans. This is the ideal solution to the Face Off antipattern, as it allows you to delegate the antipattern enforcement to the compiler. By withholding remote access to fine-grained methods, you force client code to use your entity beans in the correct manner.

7.3 *Antipattern: Ham Sandwich; Hold the Ham*

> *As soon as she's in the air, she senses that she's in trouble. She lands awkwardly. Her inside edge catches and throws the rear of her right ski violently to the left. Before the binding releases, she hears the snap, and the damage is done. She can walk without pain, but she knows the knee will need to be surgically repaired. Only now does she see how she took on too much mountain, too aggressively, and too soon.*

That a persistence framework should leave most of the persistence coding to the bean developer seems incredible. Yet that's the way that most of us used EJB 1.x, if we used it at all—a tough endeavor. For many of us, like my sister's experience in Park City, undertaking persistence coding can be biting off too much. The choice between BMP and CMP when implementing an entity bean is an important one—from the standpoint of development time, maintenance simplicity, and the ability to leverage the persistence work done by the container vendor. The persistence choice should be a simple one, eased by the selection guideline presented in section 7.3.1. However, because of changes made between the 1.x and 2.x versions of the EJB specification, the waters are a bit muddied.

7.3.1 *The choice between BMP and CMP*

Entity beans were originally designed with the assumption that the entity bean developer would perform the work of moving an entity's persistent data from its backing store into the container. So the EJB specification team focused on setting up the contracts for BMP to ensure that developers would have a sufficient set of APIs for performing this translation. In the original specification, CMP was a small addition that allowed developers to transfer the process of mapping persistent data into a backing store to the container. The original CMP added little real value to the entity bean, aside from simplifying the process of storing and retrieving the persistent fields in an entity bean.

Additionally, using CMP forced entity bean developers to live with the generally immature object-relational (OR) mapping capabilities offered by container vendors. So, in general, the industry shied away from CMP, using bean-managed persistence in conjunction with an OR mapping tool or custom SQL. When choosing between BMP and CMP in the 1.x specification, BMP was usually the better choice.

With the advent of the EJB 2.0 specification, CMP underwent a dramatic redesign. Some weaknesses in the original specification have been addressed, and the CMP specification has been greatly expanded. Given these improvements, the situation has reversed: It is now better to stay away from bean-managed persistence and, instead, take advantage of the power of the CMP 2.0 specification, when special requirements don't force you to choose otherwise. This recent change has made the inappropriate use of BMP more common than one would expect since developers learned that CMP with EJB 1.x caused more problems than it solved and that impression has endured despite the specification changes. Let's take a look at some of those problems.

- **BMP complicates database portability** BMP requires that the entity bean developer communicate directly with the data store. Often, developers choose to implement the marshaling of data between a data store and an entity bean by using JDBC to talk directly to an SQL database. In this situation, portability among different SQL databases is unlikely because SQL dialects vary greatly among database vendors.

- **BMP does not typically match the performance of container-managed persistence** BMP entity beans often suffer from performance problems when loading and storing data. BMP implementations frequently include all data for an entity bean when loading the object. This is known as *eager loading*. The opposite—loading data on an as-needed basis—is known as *lazy loading*. You often want to eager-load a commonly used subset of the persistent data and lazy-load the other fields. Similarly, BMP implementations usually flush all data to the data store on commit, instead of simply writing the fields that have actually changed. This practice can lead to wasteful data transfer, reindexing of unchanged data, and even to spurious execution of database triggers. This problem can become significant if your entity beans have many fields or have a few large fields, such as image or document data.

- **CMP 2.x is much less restrictive than CMP 1.x**   The original EJB specification required that all persistent fields be declared as publicly accessible fields in a CMP entity bean. Given this restriction, the container had to load all data when the entity bean was first loaded, and either write all data back to the data store on commit or perform costly (from both a memory and a CPU cycle standpoint) state comparisons to detect fields that changed at commit. So CMP 1.x entity beans and common implementations of BMP entity beans shared the same problem—eager-loading data and flushing too much data on commit.

- **BMP cannot express relations among beans**   BMP entity beans are isolated from other entity beans at the container layer. That is, the EJB container does not have a concept of relationships between BMP entity beans. So if you traverse any relationships, you've got to do it in application logic. With BMP, you must manually establish these relations by writing infrastructure code—a practice that the EJB specification is specifically supposed to isolate from the business logic tier. At best, this means that you must undergo the tedium of manually performing the appropriate SQL to maintain these relations. At worst, you might decide not to write this tedious process, either because of fears of introducing bugs or maintenance issues, or because of project time constraints. In addition, compromises in the project design might be made.

- **Loading multiple results according to an application-defined filter is a tragic flaw for BMP beans**   The only way to load an entity bean is to use a finder method. If you want to write a finder method that returns all `Person` entity beans whose last name starts with the letter J, you must execute the appropriate SQL query to obtain the primary keys of all matching rows, and then return from the finder method a list of all *primary key* objects for the entity beans matching the query. The container will then look up these objects by primary key. If the objects aren't in cache, the container will go back to the database to fetch the data corresponding to the returned primary key. This conclusion is disastrous since each finder method execution may actually involve a variable amount of SQL queries—one to find the primary keys and another for each primary key returned by the SQL statement. However, when writing containers, developers often shy away from the IN keyword (which efficiently tests for membership), instead issuing an individual SQL statement for each entity bean! So loading a set of 100 objects may result in upwards of 101 SQL statements.

- **BMP does not offer a standardized query syntax**   The only way for client code to look up a set of entity bean instances is to execute a finder method on that entity bean's home interface. For BMP entity beans, these finder methods must be hand-coded by the bean developer to return the appropriate data. This practice is limiting in that queries are fixed at compile time and are not defined in any standardized manner, making maintenance and future development work more difficult. Further, BMP finder methods do not provide any facilities for caching query results. So, unless the bean developer takes special steps to cache query results—which is a complex problem at best—each finder method will result in a query against the database. Each finder is created, regardless of whether or not any data has changed in the database since the query was last run. Additionally, when a BMP entity bean accesses data in a relational database, we run into portability complications again because different relational databases have different variations of SQL.

- **BMP is harder**   The strongest argument for CMP is that BMP is harder. When you can, let the computer do the work.

7.3.2 Solution: Choose CMP when possible

It seems too obvious: you should always make decisions based on the best possible current information. However, like many antipatterns, this one is rooted deeply in history. Differences between the 1.x version of CMP and the current version are so significant because they have caused a complete change of course—CMP now has significant advantages over BMP, unlike previous versions. A number of weaknesses remain in the CMP specification. We will table these issues for now and address them in greater depth in chapter 8.

Table 7.1   Choosing between CMP and BMP

Choose CMP if...	Choose BMP if...
• You want to minimize the hassle of storing persistent entity data in a database. • You want to have portability among different relational databases. • You want to be able to perform EJB Query Language (EJB QL) queries to find entity beans. • You plan on taking advantage of container-managed relationships, either for performance reasons or for object model design reasons.	• You need your entity beans to access data in esoteric back-ends not supported by CMP vendors. • You need considerable control over the loading and storing of data not provided by the CMP specification. Be sure to review the capabilities of your application server before deciding that you need this type of control, as application servers using CMP 2 can take care of many common needs such as delayed loading.

Table 7.1 shows a few good reasons to choose between CMP and BMP. In general, you should use BMP only if you have requirements that CMP can't handle. For example, if you have a data store that CMP does not support, then you may want to consider BMP. If you find yourself in this situation, you may also want to consider developing a CMP plug-in for your application. The main application-server vendors publish proprietary APIs for developing such plug-ins. The downside here is that you must write a plug-in for each application server you want to use, limiting portability among application servers. On the other hand, you will be able to take advantage of the advanced facilities available only in the CMP specification, such as EJB QL support and container-managed relationships.

Let's look closer at the flip side of persistence, and see how CMP solves some of the problems we mentioned earlier.

- **CMP improves portability**   CMP resolves the portability issue by delegating the responsibility for database communication to the container. So, the container must ensure that it supports all idiosyncrasies of SQL's different dialects. This means that beans written and tested against an Oracle database stand a fighting chance of working with a SQL Server or DB2 database with absolutely no bean code changes.

- **Current implementations of CMP have better performance than BMP**   The EJB 2.0 CMP specification rectifies some earlier performance concerns by stating that CMP entity beans must declare abstract bean-like setters and getters for each persistent field to be managed by the CMP implementation. This is in contrast to the public field approach in the EJB 1 CMP specification. The EJB container is now responsible for creating a concrete implementation of the abstract entity bean class. This implementation must include implementations of these abstract accessor methods. These vendor-created methods have the opportunity to perform sophisticated fetch algorithms, such as lazy loading of certain fields, adaptive prefetching based on runtime usage statistics, or simpler detection of data changed in a transaction. By using the CMP 2.0 specification, we can easily avoid the performance problems commonly found in BMP entity beans implementations.

- **CMR enable efficient relationship management in the database and container** CMP entity beans can define CMR in much the same way as they declare simple container-managed fields. This allows a CMP entity bean to delegate relation traversal to the container. This greatly simplifies the process of defining relations among entity beans, reducing the likelihood of errors by eliminating the infrastructure code involved in relation traversal and trimming the amount of time needed to code, test, and maintain these relations. Also, this simplification makes relationships between entity beans available to bean developers who otherwise would avoid the complexity.

- **CMP has better performance through better key management** CMP resolves the $n + 1$ performance problem because the container is responsible for both executing the full query and creating the `findByPrimaryKey()` method. So, the container has the opportunity to perform database queries that return multiple results efficiently, only executing a single SQL query for a given EJB QL statement.

- **EJB QL provides a standard query language** The CMP specification defines EJB QL as a standardized declarative query language that can be used to find objects that match a given filter. A bean developer needs only to define an abstract finder method and a corresponding EJB QL definition in the bean's deployment descriptor. The container then creates a concrete implementation of the finder method that translates the EJB QL definition to an SQL query. This improves code readability and maintenance by providing a standard that everyone on a team understands and uses, and improves the portability of queries. From a performance standpoint, when using EJB QL, the container has the opportunity to do advanced caching of queries, potentially resulting in significant performance improvements. Using a cache for queries when possible will make your application faster, because it will spend less time communicating with the database, and more scalable, because the overall load on the database will be lessened.

For many reasons, the case for CMP is now convincing. Perhaps the most compelling reason to use CMP is a much simpler one: CMP code is easier to write, easier to manage, and easier to maintain. It decouples your application code from the database; you don't have to specify the individual table and field names in your application code.

7.4 *Antipattern: Application Joins*

Enterprise applications often involve relationships between different entity beans. For example, a system might have a one-to-many relation between `Person` and `Address`—a `Person` entity can relate to multiple `Address` entities. When you persist those beans to a data store, you can let the database or the application manage the relationship. The application usually can't process the relationship nearly as fast as the database.

A relational database can evaluate joins in concise, efficient terms, but we often implement them in the application tier instead, leading to poor performance. Java is simply not optimized for data lookups. Performing a join in Java kills any possibility of database tuning and indexing that might otherwise accelerate the query. When a relational database processes a join, it uses sophisticated technology to optimize query access plans and, consequently, minimize the number of direct data comparisons.

7.4.1 *Solution: Delegate joins to the database*

The problem caused by application joins can often be addressed by pushing the joining operations down to the database tier. For example, if you want to find all `Person` beans who have a certain type of account, you don't want to load all instances into memory and loop through, doing a string comparison on each instance's account's type. A far better approach would be to translate the join into SQL (or whatever underlying query language your database supports) and let the database do the filtering work.

When you see this antipattern, it's usually related to the old EJB 1.x specification, which did not support CMR. Many legacy EJB programs use these techniques, and many programmers still do application joins, often by habit.

The CMR and EJB QL support added to CMP entity beans has done wonders to reduce the occurrence of application joins. These new additions to the specification provide bean developers with higher-level tools for creating joins, so the developer can rely on the EJB container to create efficient SQL to perform the necessary, low-level database work.

7.4.2 *Common examples of application joins*

Some situations that commonly lead to application joins are obvious and simple to avoid; others like those listed below are subtler and sometimes not possible to resolve.

- **Application-defined relation in CMP entity bean** Whenever possible, applications that use CMP should express any relations between entity beans in terms of a CMR field. By doing this, the entity bean has maximum opportunity to take advantage of any optimizations in the container to cache relations or otherwise ensure optimal materialization of the relationship.

- **Cross-data-store relation** One major service provided by an EJB container is the capability to execute transactions that span multiple data stores. This means that, for example, a custom inventory system can perform transactions with a third-party procurement system or with a sales database.

  However, the cross-data-store transactions are often limited—a database cannot usually create relations to data in a different data store. So while you can perform transactions that span multiple databases, you typically cannot create CMR that span databases. Therefore, you must create and maintain such relations in the application logic of the bean. This type of an application join is usually unavoidable. In this situation, the performance hits associated with application joins must be accepted, because no lower level exists that can be used to express this relation.

  When creating cross-data-store relations, bear in mind that your application must handle the relationship properly. Consider both lazy-load of the relation, and caching the relation information, if possible, to minimize the frequency of joins. Eager loading is typically only helpful if, by loading multiple parts of an object at the same time, you can achieve efficiencies of scale. Because relations between different data stores are typically handled on a one-off basis, usually no advantage exists to eager loading. Further, eager loading will impose a performance penalty if an object is loaded when the eager-loading relation is not necessary.

- **BMP relation** You must implement relations between BMP entity beans in the application logic; absolutely no mechanism exists to delegate this work to the container. Relations among BMP entity beans behave in the same way as cross-data-store relations because it's unlikely that the database can be used to help out with these types of relations.

  As with cross-data-store relations, caching and lazy loading of BMP relations can significantly help performance issues. Better yet, migrate the BMP entity bean to use CMP, if possible.

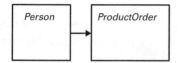

Figure 7.4 This UML diagram shows a one-to-many relation between the Person and ProductOrder entity beans. This is a relationship that might be conditional on runtime parameters, such as whether the product has been shipped to the customer. These types of relationships are limited for many different reasons.

This antipattern is trivial, but appears broadly in EJB applications, even on EJB 2.x application servers. We mention it here because it's so prominent. Next, we'll examine a similar, but far more subtle, antipattern—application filters.

7.5 *Antipattern: Application Filters*

A filter, in the relational language SQL, is the WHERE clause. Like joins, filters belong on the database when it's possible to put them there. Databases process filters many times faster than applications for several reasons. First, applications that use their own filters instead of database filters retrieve more rows from a database than those that don't. Second, relational databases are optimized to filter, through features like indices and specialized optimizers. For example, an accounting system might retrieve a list of all PurchaseOrder objects that have not cleared and search that list for other criteria. Some application filters will be easy to avoid. Others are much more subtle. In the next section, we'll look at several different types of application filters.

7.5.1 *Understanding the types of application filters*

Object-oriented programming encourages implementation hiding and layered programming. Blissful ignorance makes for cleaner code, but also fertile ground for antipatterns. Our desire to produce elegant, layered software can cause us to produce beautiful code that runs like a crippled sloth. As a rule, filters belong in the database. Let's take a detailed look at the different types of filters that you're likely to encounter. Some, you can work around. In other cases, you'll just have to bite the performance bullet.

Dynamic relations.

Often, Java developers will attempt to create a relation between persistent objects that is conditional on a runtime parameter. For example, consider a system that has a one-to-many relation between Person and ProductOrder. You can express it in UML, as we have done in figure 7.4.

You might decide to parameterize this relation with information about whether or not the `ProductOrder` has been shipped. In other words, you might want to change the relation accessor method to be

```
public Collection getProductOrders(boolean shipped)
```

And you might want the values of this method to differ, depending on the boolean value passed to the method.

This is not a relation; this is a filter. Conceptually, you should store relations between classes in a `Collection`, without any additional runtime information. If the application dictates that a method such as `Person.getProductOrders(boolean shipped)` is necessary, then you should implement a method to do the filtering and document it as an application filter. Better yet, you should use two separate relations—`shippedProductOrders` and `unshippedProductOrders`.

Even a well-written dynamic relation usually circumvents any caching that an EJB container can do because the conditional processing occurs in the application code domain. Ideally, the application creates the dynamic relation by performing an SQL query that passes the filters through to the relational database as SQL. More often, however, dynamic relations run as an in-memory application filter that operates on the complete relation. So, in our example, the check to see if the product order has shipped might be executed in Java. In that case, the database returns the entire collection of product orders placed by a given person, even if only five of the product orders in question matched the condition. That's far too inefficient.

Dynamic queries

Dynamic queries are queries defined at runtime that cannot be known in advance. For example, any application that allows a user to search for data by combining boolean filters into a boolean expression will generate SQL that contains a variable number of conditions in the WHERE clause, each joined together by either AND or OR operators. Static SQL queries can use parameterization to allow for runtime modifications, but the query's structure itself cannot be modified. Dynamic queries must be created at runtime. These types of queries are problematic in EJB because EJB QL queries must be defined at deploy time. You cannot assemble an EJB QL statement that satisfies the structural requirements of a dynamic query.

You have two possible workarounds at your disposal to allow dynamic querying of CMP entity beans. On the one hand, you can dynamically create an SQL query to determine the primary keys of the entity beans that match the filter. This is not ideal because your system will be polluted with SQL statements, which, as discussed earlier, can lead to portability problems, both between different relational database vendors and with nonrelational databases. The other workaround is to perform part or all query filtering in memory. This approach can be prohibitively slow, but avoids the portability issues in the previous solution.

Which solution is better depends on the specifics of your application. In particular, you must consider the portability requirements, the performance requirements, and the expected data size of the collections to be filtered.

Loop filters

When looping over a data set, either in a for or while loop, or in a recursive construct, programmers will often perform conditional checking and may skip data entries that do not match given constraints. These types of conditional checks can evolve frequently into the functional equivalent of a dynamic relation or dynamic query. Continuing the example, you might be working on an application that prints all purchase orders for a given customer and decide that you'd like to add the capability of printing only those purchase orders that have not yet been shipped. This conditional check might be put around the code that prints the order (listing 7.4).

Listing 7.4   Dynamic filter hidden in loop

```
public void printPurchaseOrders (Person person, boolean onlyUnshipped)
{
    ProductOrder po;
    for (Iterator iter = person.getProductOrders().iterator ();          ◁
        iter.hasNext();)                          Loop over each ProductOrder
        {
        po = (ProductOrder) iter.next ();
        if (onlyUnshipped && !po.isShipped ())    ◁  Print only those that have
            print (po);                              not yet been shipped. This
    }                                                is our filter!
```

When working on an existing project, beware of introducing application filters this way. These problems are hard to spot unless you are looking for them, because no performance degradation exists within the system, as such. Upon adding the if condition in the for loop, the algorithm will run in more or less the same time (depending on how slow the print method is) but will do considerably less work. Look at it this way: If the print method is fast, it may print out zero purchase orders, but it will still take the same amount of time to execute as if it had printed all the purchase orders. So, unless your project's unit tests do performance checking (see chapter 9 for details) *and* you modify that performance test to reflect the fact that the new method should run faster, this inefficiency could easily make it into a production system.

The antipatterns discussed here are predominantly relevant only for entity beans that implement a persistent object model. In the next sections, we'll introduce two common antipatterns that apply to all entity beans, regardless of how the entity bean is used. The antipatterns can occur in entity beans that implement an object model and in entity beans that are more traditional distributed components.

7.6 *Antipattern: Rusty Keys*

When a seasoned database developer is brought onto an EJB project, her initial reactions can be absolutely priceless. EJB projects written by developers with no database experience will often do things in exactly the wrong way, from a database standpoint. You saw hints of this above in the application joins and filters antipatterns, where the database's power was not leveraged when it could have been. However, the most offensive database abuse commonly seen in an EJB project is the Rusty Keys antipattern. This antipattern is second only to the Face Off antipattern in terms of the damage it is likely to do. Unfortunately, it is also seldom recognized and, therefore, a more pervasive antipattern than the Face Off antipattern. The Rusty Keys antipattern is easy to identify—you need look no further than your entity beans' primary keys. If your primary key is not short, then you've got a big problem.

At the most basic level, entity beans are about persistent data. An entity bean differs from a session bean in that some representation of the entity bean persists over time, regardless of the application server's state. Typically, this data is stored in a relational database. Therefore, when designing an entity bean, all the power and restrictions of relational databases must be taken into consideration. The fundamental rule of databases—so fundamental that it usually goes without saying—is that the primary key should be as short as possible. Many other important rules exist in the relational database world, but they tend to be guidelines rather than rules, and many of them actually conflict with each other. But any database expert knows that primary keys *must* be short.

A primary key is a unique identifier of a row in a table. As such, it is used by a database whenever any operation is performed on a given row. A Relational Database Management System (RDBMS) must be able to do a handful of things extremely quickly. Foremost of these quick tasks is the join. RDBMSs are heavily dependent on indices as the fundamental accelerators. Let's look at a few places where a database typically uses primary key information:

- In the simplest case, the primary key is used to select data. To do this, a database must compare a requested primary key value to the primary keys in a table. This comparison is typically implemented using either a hashing algorithm or tree, depending on index type, to improve search performance. A longer primary key will require more computation to hash or compare than a shorter primary key.

- Performance optimizations for common joins use knowledge about relations between foreign keys and primary keys to build fast lookup tables. Like most other types of data, RDBMSs cache index fields to boost performance. When your key fields are too long, they chew up the caching space, called index buffers, with too few entries.

- Databases usually allow indexing on non-primary-key data in a table to improve the performance of searching for rows that match arbitrary column filters. This task might involve simple indexing of a numeric column or sophisticated text processing of large text columns. Regardless, the index will again store information about which primary keys match which filter or search parameters.

The speed of all these types of operations is dependent on primary key size. Short primary keys will result in faster processing; longer primary keys will require more CPU cycles to perform comparisons and lookups. More importantly, because primary key information plays such an important role in database architectures, this data is often stored in special areas of memory, called index or join buffers. The length of the primary key data will dictate how big this storage space must be and how much data it can hold. Because many primary keys are implemented as a key field, the information in a key can be repeated many times in the index buffer.

7.6.1 *Solution: shorten your primary key*

Fortunately, a simple fix to this antipattern exists. Simply replace long primary keys with shorter ones. If your application requires too many different columns—or exceptionally long columns—for a primary key, then you should think about creating an artificial primary key instead. Most persistence strategies use this approach. If you feel that you cannot reduce the size of your primary key because, for example, you are using a Social Security number to identify employee records, then consider creating a shorter surrogate key. This type of key has no business value; it is used strictly to provide a short, efficient key for database applications.

We've mentioned the term *short* a couple of times. This begs the question: how long is too long? Unfortunately, no clear-cut answer exists, but table 7.2 offers a few guidelines. The ideal size of your primary key depends on several factors, including the amount of data you anticipate putting into the table and the particulars of your database vendor. In general, 4 bytes (or 32 bits) is a good starting place. A 32-bit primary key provides room for a considerable number of records but is short enough to allow for fast comparisons in most database architectures. In fact, going below 32 bits is often not that helpful. Most CPUs these days are designed with 32-bit registers, meaning that many CPU instructions will take the same amount of time to process 10-bit values as it would take to process 32-bit values. Of course, this processing time also depends quite a bit on the database, the hardware, and the operating system you are using. Bear in mind that the Java `long` type is a 64-bit type, so 32 bits is not sufficient if you plan on using a `long` in Java.

Table 7.2   Guidelines for the creation of primary keys

Acceptable (small) primary key types		Unacceptable (big) primary key types	
Java	**SQL**	**Java**	**SQL**
int	NUMERIC	String	VARCHAR(1024)
long	INT	Date	TIMESTAMP
short	TINYINT	Serialized object	BLOB
byte	BIGINT		
char	CHAR(1)		

Strings are perhaps the most common long primary key type seen in entity beans. This antipattern has been propagated by the masses of sample code that uses clever-looking item code or a purchase order number such as 32-XZ8G or OGN-5703810. These values may look great in sample code, but programmers have a nasty habit of reusing sample code, so these string-based primary keys have found their ways into all sorts of entity beans.

In addition, many algorithms for persistence frameworks use a concept called a global unique identifier (GUID). If you generate these algorithms with a combination of time stamps and character keys, then your primary key is probably too long.

7.7 *Antipattern: Revolving Doors*

One important consideration when working with potentially multithreaded applications is re-entrancy. A re-entrant algorithm is one in which the same code operates on the same data simultaneously in multiple threads. More specifically, an EJB application is re-entrant if multiple clients can simultaneously access the same bean in the same transactional context.

This simultaneous access raises many problems with thread safety and transaction isolation. Therefore, the EJB specification prohibits re-entrant behavior, specifying that it is illegal for multiple clients to perform simultaneous operations on a given bean in a given transactional context. Unfortunately, this prohibition can also impose inconvenient limitations on business logic.

If your business algorithms involve multiple tightly coupled objects acting in concert to perform a calculation, it is likely that you will run into re-entrancy problems when implementing these algorithms with entity beans. A side effect of this prohibition is that it is forbidden for bean A to invoke a method in bean B, which, in turn, invokes a method in bean A. This behavior is not semantically re-entrant—that is, from the client perspective, all EJB rules were followed. However, the container cannot possibly differentiate between this situation and true re-entrant code. (Technically, containers could detect this situation, but it's prohibitively expensive because the various beans involved in the EJB call stack may be on physically separate machines.)

For session beans and message-driven beans, the container can easily uphold this requirement—re-entrancy is simply forbidden on the grounds that it is not necessary for typical session bean or message-driven bean uses. Operations on these types of beans normally represent coarse-grained business processes. So designing tightly coupled session beans or message-driven beans is not common practice.

However, the situation is different for entity beans. Entity beans often represent fine-grained object models, so some amount of entity bean coupling is common. You can easily imagine a system that might use re-entrant code: Say you have two entity beans, `PurchaseOrder` and `LineItem`. To compute the total cost of a purchase order, your business logic dictates that you perform the following steps:

`PurchaseOrder.getTotalCost()` invokes `LineItem.getLineItemCost()` for each `LineItem` in the order.

`LineItem.getLineItemCost()` invokes `PurchaseOrder.getDiscount()` to determine what, if any, discount to apply to the line item cost.

As you can see in listing 7.5, these two seemingly innocuous steps are re-entrant! This is analogous to our A invokes B invokes A description and is quite commonplace in non-EJB development.

Listing 7.5 This code snippet from PurchaseOrder and LineItem demonstrates re-entrant behavior

```
public float getTotalCost ()
{
    float price = 0;
    LineItem item;
    for (Iterator iter = getLineItems ().iterator (); iter.hasNext (); )
    {
        item = (LineItem) iter.next ();            This method invokes a
        price += item.getLineItemCost ();     ⟵┘  method in LineItem ...
    }
}
public float getLineItemCost ()                    ... which invokes a method
{                                                              in PurchaseOrder
    return getPrice () * (1 - getPurchaseOrder ().getDiscount ());  ⟵
}
```

Unfortunately, no one clear-cut solution exists to this problem. Instead, two partial solutions exist, each with its own associated problems.

7.7.1 Solution 1: Refactor to avoid re-entrancy

The problems in our simple purchase order example could be resolved with a little clever refactoring. We could change the method signature for LineItem.get-LineItemCost() to have a parameter for the discount code, thus avoiding the re-entrancy problem altogether (listing 7.6).

Listing 7.6 Code snippets from a refactored PurchaseOrder and LineItem that avoid re-entrant behavior

```
public float getTotalCost ()
{
    float price = 0;
    float discount = getDiscount ();
    LineItem item;
    for (Iterator iter = getLineItems ().iterator (); iter.hasNext (); )
    {
        item = (LineItem) iter.next ();                 This method passes
        price += item.getLineItemCost (discount);  ⟵┘  discount to LineItem...
    }
}
public float getLineItemCost (float discount)  ⟵┐  ... which no longer re-enters
{                                                 │  PurchaseOrder
    return getPrice () * (1 - discount);
}
```

This refactoring solves our problem because the container will no longer detect a possible re-entrant situation and, therefore, won't throw any exceptions. However, the refactoring is a bit ugly. The requirements the EJB server imposes are seemingly arbitrary and hard to enforce on the Java language syntax—always a bad thing.

7.7.2 *Solution 2: Disable the container's re-entrancy checking*

Unfortunately, running into more complex re-entrant situations is common, especially when working on an existing project, in which major refactoring might not be an option. The EJB specification provides a mechanism to disable re-entrant code checks for a particular entity bean, by setting the `reentrant` element in the bean's deployment descriptor to `True`.

If you decide to go with strictly local interfaces, then disabling re-entrancy is a safe workaround. However, this method instructs the container to disable re-entrant code checking altogether, which is dangerous if you allow remote access to your entity beans. The bean developer and the author of the client code must ensure that no damaging re-entrant situations occur. Obviously, this is an error-prone situation, and is thus not a path to be taken lightly. So, while this solves our problem without forcing us to make ugly hacks or major refactorings, this solution forces us to do things in an ostrich-like stick-our-heads-in-the-sand manner—we are fixing the problem by ignoring it and hoping that no re-entrant situations occur in code.

7.7.3 *Solution 3: Lobby the EJB specification team*

What we really need is a third behavior for re-entrant applications. Hypothetically, with sophisticated bytecode analysis, an application server could detect those seemingly re-entrant situations that are not dangerous and flag them so that additional information is passed among application servers in these situations. This additional information, which we discarded as inefficient, would be acceptable in this case because it would only be communicated among the different JVMs when potentially re-entrant situations are encountered. So we would be able to make a compromise in terms of network efficiency when necessary. In other situations, we could use the faster, but less flexible, option of disabling re-entrancy.

However, specification teams tend to be relatively slow-moving bodies, and other more significant outstanding issues remain with the EJB specification. A change to re-entrant behavior any time in the near future seems unlikely.

7.8 Summary

In this chapter, we've examined common entity bean antipatterns easily resolvable within the confines of the EJB specification. A few antipatterns have historical undertones: Most EJB models now use a Session Façade because this information is widely available, and most existing BMP applications have roots in old code or habits formed under the EJB 1.x specifications. We looked at application joins and filters, which are properly placed in the database. Finally, we looked at keys and re-entrant code, as well as workarounds to both. An understanding of these anti-patterns will help you create and maintain entity beans that take full advantage of the EJB specification's power.

In the next chapter, we'll discuss antipatterns that do not have solutions in the EJB domain, and we'll look at alternate technologies that can be used to resolve these issues. The solutions presented in these two chapters will equip you with techniques that can be used to address a wide variety of persistence needs.

7.9 *Antipatterns in this chapter*

This section covers the Face Off, Ham Sandwich; Hold the Ham, Application Joins, Application Filters, and Rusty Keys antipatterns.

FACE OFF

DESCRIPTION

Entity beans are accessed directly from the client using the entity bean remote interfaces.

MOST FREQUENT SCALE

Project

REFACTORED SOLUTION NAME

Session bean façade

REFACTORED SOLUTION TYPE

Technology

REFACTORED SOLUTION DESCRIPTION

Entity beans should be hidden behind session bean façades that define business operations. In this solution, business logic that needs to directly manipulate data must be deployed in the form of session beans.

ANECDOTAL EVIDENCE

"Our persistence framework uses CMP, so our client code accesses entity beans in order to perform business logic."

SYMPTOMS, CONSEQUENCES

Directly accessing entity beans from client code often leads to performance penalties and unexpected transaction consequences.

HAM SANDWICH; HOLD THE HAM

DESCRIPTION
BMP entity beans give you very little, compared to their limitations and to what the container-managed persistence specification provides.

MOST FREQUENT SCALE
Project

REFACTORED SOLUTION NAME
Full-featured persistence frameworks

REFACTORED SOLUTION TYPE
Technology

REFACTORED SOLUTION DESCRIPTION
BMP entity beans provide woefully little support for common object-relational persistence needs. You should use container-managed persistence or a non-EJB persistence framework instead of BMP if you are using entity beans just to access data in a relational database.

ANECDOTAL EVIDENCE
"BMP gives us more control over our persistence needs, so we're using it for all our relational database data access."

SYMPTOMS, CONSEQUENCES
Using BMP when CMP (or a non-EJB persistence technology) would work often results in complicated and error-prone entity bean implementations that do not take advantage of all the same techniques that a more complete persistence framework would employ.

APPLICATION JOINS

DESCRIPTION

The association between two different database entities represented by entity beans is made in application logic, rather than by using container-managed relationships.

MOST FREQUENT SCALE

Project

REFACTORED SOLUTION NAME

Container-managed relationships

REFACTORED SOLUTION TYPE

Technology

REFACTORED SOLUTION DESCRIPTION

The CMP specification provides the ability to model relationships between entities in such a way that the container can take care of maintaining the relationship. This allows the developer to deal with relationships between entity beans, using regular Java field traversal semantics.

ANECDOTAL EVIDENCE

"The relation between `Person` and `Address` is established using the `Person` primary key. So, I'll put a field in `Address` to store the `Person` primary key, and look up the associated `Person` object by ID as necessary."

SYMPTOMS, CONSEQUENCES

Application joins typically result in abysmal performance and complicated entity bean code.

APPLICATION FILTERS

DESCRIPTION

Commonly used data filters that are implemented in Java code

MOST FREQUENT SCALE

Project

REFACTORED SOLUTION NAME

Database queries

REFACTORED SOLUTION TYPE

Technology

REFACTORED SOLUTION DESCRIPTION

Databases are designed with querying and filtering in mind. Any significant filtering performed in Java code should be moved to the database tier if possible. For CMP solutions, this means that querying should be done using EJB QL when possible.

ANECDOTAL EVIDENCE

"I only want to display users located in the commonwealth of Massachusetts, so I'll just put in an `if` statement that checks the user's address's state code."

SYMPTOMS, CONSEQUENCES

Massive performance penalties caused by transmitting too much data from the database to the JVM, and by the JVM spending lots of time churning through the filter without taking advantage of any database indices

RUSTY KEYS

DESCRIPTION
Poor primary key choice can cripple a database

MOST FREQUENT SCALE
Project

REFACTORED SOLUTION NAME
Well-chosen primary keys

REFACTORED SOLUTION TYPE
Technology

REFACTORED SOLUTION DESCRIPTION
Using synthetic fields (ones that have no meaning at the application level) or well-chosen, short application fields can boost database performance and help prevent data limitations or costly refactoring down the road.

ANECDOTAL EVIDENCE
"I'm making a financial application for a U.S.-based bank. All users have a Social Security number. So, I'll just use the string field that stores the Social Security number as the primary key."

SYMPTOMS, CONSEQUENCES
Often, entity bean developers decide to use application-defined fields as primary key fields. This can lead to two types of problems. First, compound or large single-column primary keys are typically not as fast from a database standpoint as are single, short primary keys. Second, the evolution of a project might cause application-defined primary keys to no longer be unique.

Bitter alternatives

This chapter contains

- Inherent problems with entity beans
- A survey of persistence alternatives to entity beans
- A comparison of entity beans, JDBC, and JDO

We watch with some amusement as Eric drags his battered and ancient Corsica kayak to the put-in. By contrast, Stephen, who is taking time away from Olympic training to paddle with us, shoulders his feather-light fiberglass slalom boat down to the river easily. The kayak is beautiful, with razor sharp edges and a nose that looks like the point of a dagger. I glance over his shoulder at the Tellico, which is running a little low this year, and wonder how a glass boat will hold up over the river's protruding rocks. I shrug. Surely Stephen can keep his boat and his body out of trouble. I am sure I'll be paddling for my life, but an Olympian should be able to handle this class IV run with no problem. We should instead be concerned about Eric. He often panics on rivers like this one, and we aren't sure he'll even remember to hang onto his paddle—or control his bladder—when he reaches the lip of fourteen-foot Baby Falls.

Stephen controls his boat with breathtaking precision over the early eight-foot ledges. His lines and movements are precise, but he generally watches from the bank as we play in each microeddy or hydraulic. We line up like baby ducks and slide over Baby Falls with ease, though Eric flips and rolls at the bottom. Next is bony Diaper Wiper, named for the shallow muddy and rocky bottom, that dirties most well-positioned boats. Stephen slides through with ease, but we all cringe when the bottom of his kayak crackles audibly as it scrapes over the rocks. We approach Jarrod's Knee, named for the broken body part of a local boater. Eric lines up and most of his boat slips over the ledge. Then we hear a loud crunch and look up to see Eric's stern stationary at the top of the drop, revealing the situation that every kayaker dreads the most—the vertical pin.

8.1 Understanding entity bean alternatives

This chapter will be a little different from most others that you'll find in Manning's *Bitter* books. We won't really illustrate how to use or misuse a major EJB feature. Instead, we'll show you why EJB entity beans should be avoided and suggest alternatives. If you're strongly committed to entity beans, then we invite you to skip this chapter and move on to the next one. (You won't be tested, and you won't need this information to understand the rest of the book.) If you're open to exploring entity bean alternatives, then read on.

In chapter 7, we discussed antipatterns caused by common, but avoidable, misuses of the entity bean specification. In this chapter, we will focus on problems not easily solved within the realm of EJB entity beans. To provide a clear view of the landscape, we'll present a simple application that supports persistent objects with three different alternatives: EJB CMP, JDBC, and object-oriented persistence frameworks. Against that backdrop, we'll fully explore several entity bean alternatives and examine some entity bean specification weaknesses that these alternatives can address.

In chapter 2, we began to present a case against EJB entity beans. Let's recall the foundation of that case:

- EJB entity beans are awkward and complex.
- EJB persistence is too coarse-grained, requiring container services (with potentially significant overhead) that most persistent objects simply do not need.
- EJB have critical idiosyncrasies that complicate modeling.

As discussed in chapter 2, entity beans are typically used for data persistence. While they do provide other services—including failover, security, and transaction awareness—these additional services are irrelevant to this discussion. We don't mean to imply that these services aren't valuable. We're simply saying the way you use entity beans doesn't benefit from those services. To side-step the pitfalls unearthed in chapter 7, adept EJB developers universally wrap entity beans in façades. Thus, the client is prevented from interacting directly with an entity bean. The façade is then responsible for providing distribution, security, transaction, and fail-over services to the client (figure 8.1). Consequently, this best practice relegates entity beans to one important job—object persistence. As such, we should compare entity beans to other object persistence frameworks and consider several key factors that address the problems we've seen with entity beans.

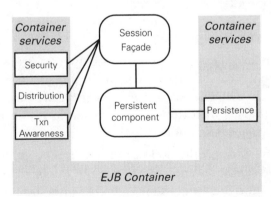

Figure 8.1 Security, distribution, transactional awareness, and failover are all available to the EJB entity bean, but most clients access entity beans through a Session Façade. For this reason, these services are irrelevant to the discussion about the merits of EJB entity beans, for all of the most practical purposes.

With any troubled framework, a time arrives when you have to decide whether to apply more Band-Aids, do major surgery, or pull life support and start over. Different pain tolerances and motivations make this decision inherently difficult, but here we'll opt to start over. Rather than apply one more Band-Aid to significant problems inherent to EJB entity beans, in this section, we'll focus on other frameworks. We will look at the restrictions that these alternatives impose upon us, and we'll assess whether—and when—they should be used in place of entity beans. We'll discuss the goals of each technology and then look at a brief feature comparison. We will consider the following issues for each technology:

- **J2EE integration**   How does this technology integrate with other J2EE technologies? The JCA and JTA are two components of J2EE that are particularly appropriate points of integration for persistence frameworks.

- **Security**   Security refers to support for EJB-style declarative security policy configuration. With most modern EJB applications, a session façade provides security services.

- **Remote access**   Remote access refers to the EJB capability to make transparent method invocations on remote objects. As we discussed in chapters 2 and 7, support for these features in a persistence framework can actually makes life harder by increasing communications costs and adding complexity.

- **JCA**   A relatively new part of the J2EE standard, JCA defines a standardized means of configuring, managing transactions for, and connecting to a data source. Persistence frameworks that are JCA-compliant will be considerably easier to deploy into a J2EE container and more likely to seamlessly plug in to a greater number of J2EE containers.

- **JTA**   JTA provides a standard means of interaction between a transaction manager and transactional data sources. Persistence frameworks that support JTA can participate in distributed transactions and can synchronize their transaction boundaries with the global transaction boundaries declared in an EJB deployment descriptor.

- **Simplicity**   Developers need to ask themselves how much they will have to learn to use a given API. A simple system is one that a user can be reasonably expected to pick up in a short amount of time with little or no training and adequate documentation. A complex API has a steep learning curve and requires a good deal of experience to use effectively.

- **Java language alignment**   We also need to know how much a given technology differs from the Java language specification. Whereas with simplicity, we must ask how much we have to learn, here the question is: How much do we have to *unlearn* in order to use a given API? An API closely aligned with the Java language will not require any paradigm shifts on your part; one not closely aligned with the Java language will require you to think in different ways than you normally would when programming in Java.

- **Deployment flexibility** Does this technology place any limitations on the deployment architecture? In particular, can applications written with this technology be used both within and without an application server? What types of data store decisions must be made up-front?

Although these are the major connection points into J2EE, they represent only part of the story. This chapter also covers your ability to code efficiently and build persistence frameworks at a good pace.

8.2 *Using EJB persistence*

We talked about the history of CMP and EJB in the previous two chapters. To summarize, CMP uses the container to provide a coarse-grained persistence strategy. That means that each CMP bean handles distribution, security, transactions, and database synchronization. We've also shown that these services are relatively expensive. Furthermore, we've seen that entity beans are EJB components and not plain Java objects. As such, they come with a whole set of restrictions and programming conventions. Keeping that in mind, table 8.1 illustrates how CMP entity beans stack up against key persistence framework criteria.

Given our space constraints, we can't build a representative application complex enough to do this comparison justice, but we can, at least, present a simple one. We're guessing you've grown bored with the often-cited EJB examples that model the "real world." So, in the spirit of this book, we'll choose objects in the adventure sport domain. Let's look first at code that persists a kayak object modeled as a CMP entity bean and provides efficient access through the customary session façade. The façade is not doing much for us, but keep in mind that EJB will give us distribution, security, and transactional awareness, among other services.

First, let's look at the three Java files needed to define the Kayak EJB. We edited these program listings for size, removing some comments and optimizing formatting for space. Additionally, we've removed distracting functionality not strictly necessary for creating a Kayak EJB instance, such as finder methods and DTO mappings. We'll address these concepts later.

Table 8.1 Evaluation of CMP entity beans

CMP entity beans	
J2EE integration—Security	Yes
J2EE integration—Remote access (to entity logic)	Yes
J2EE integration—JTA	Yes
J2EE integration—JCA	Not applicable—the underlying data store to which the data is persisted may be JCA-compliant
Simplicity	Very difficult to learn with many pitfalls
Java language alignment	Many Java language features, such as inheritance and pass-by-reference, are not supported or are treated differently Some language features can be emulated at the application level
Deployment flexibility	Requires an EJB container Can be used with many types of data stores, including RDBMS and OODBMS

8.2.1 Implementing CMP

Fortunately, CMP 2.0 has reduced the amount of code needed to implement a CMP entity bean. Listing 8.1 shows the implementation class for our Kayak entity EJB.

Listing 8.1 KayakEJB.java

```java
package com.bitterejb.boatshop;

import javax.ejb.*;
import java.rmi.*;

/**
 *  Container-managed persistence entity bean that implements the Kayak
 *  domain object.
 */
public abstract class KayakEJB implements EntityBean {

  private EntityContext context = null;

  public abstract Long getId();
  public abstract void setId(Long id);
  public abstract boolean getIsRented();
  public abstract void setIsRented(boolean rented);
  public abstract String getRenter();
  public abstract void setRenter(String renter);
  public abstract String getLocation();
```

Persistent attributes

```
      public abstract void setLocation(String location);
      public abstract int getCapacity();                          Persistent
      public abstract void setCapacity(int cap);                  attributes
      public abstract boolean getHasRudder();
      public abstract void setHasRudder(boolean rudder);

      public Kayak toDataTransferObject () {    A DTO controls communication costs
            Kayak k = new Kayak ();
            k.setId (getId ());
            k.setIsRented (getIsRented ());
            k.setRenter (getRenter ());
            k.setLocation (getLocation ());
            k.setCapacity (getCapacity ());
            k.setHasRudder (getHasRudder ());
            return k;
      }

      public Object ejbCreate(Long id, String location,     Constructor
                            int cap, boolean rudder)         handles only
        throws CreateException {                             initialization

        setId(id);
        setIsRented(false);
        setRenter(null);
        setLocation(location);
        setCapacity(cap);
        setHasRudder(rudder);
        return null;
      }


      public void ejbPostCreate(Long id, String location, int cap,
        boolean rudder)
        throws CreateException { }

      public void setEntityContext(EntityContext c) {
        context = c;
      }
                                                          Remaining methods
      public void unsetEntityContext() {                  manage the EJB
        context = null;
      }
      public void ejbRemove() throws RemoveException { }
      public void ejbActivate() { }
      public void ejbPassivate() { }
      public void ejbStore() { }
      public void ejbLoad() { }
  }
```

While the KayakEJB class is fairly simple, it does not look much like a POJO—a plain ol' Java object. The first two annotations highlight all of listing 8.1's interesting semantics. The rest of the code merely appeases the EJB container, which means we're carrying around a whole lot of baggage. To persist this simple business object, you're forced to learn to build and access EJB entities efficiently, using a relatively complex framework. You're also well advised to understand the life cycle of the EJB and the semantics of the container in which it lives.

We should note, too, that much of this code could be automatically generated, but that's not the point. The inherent complexity still has a cost—a developer still must understand, maintain, and possibly debug the code. For a class this simple, that process is not too much to ask, so we'll move on. However, keep in mind that this complexity can erode productivity as the size of the application increases over time.

Next on our agenda is the local interface. Using this interface, the session façade can directly access a `KayakEJB` bean instance within the same JVM. Listing 8.2 shows the local interface to our Kayak entity EJB.

Listing 8.2 KayakLocal

```
KayakLocal.java
package com.bitterejb.boatshop;

import javax.ejb.*;

/**
 *  Local interface to the Kayak EJB.
 */
public interface KayakLocal extends EJBLocalObject {
  public abstract Long getId();
  public abstract boolean getIsRented();
  public abstract void setIsRented(boolean rented);
  public abstract String getRenter();
  public abstract void setRenter(String renter);
  public abstract String getLocation();
  public abstract void setLocation(String location);
  public abstract int getCapacity();
  public abstract void setCapacity(int cap);
  public abstract boolean getHasRudder();
  public abstract void setHasRudder(boolean rudder);
  public abstract Kayak toDataTransferObject();
}
```

The local interface is simple enough. We just define the interface that we'll use to access the individual bean—an inconvenience, but again, automating the interface code generation is relatively easy.

Moving on, let's take a look at the `KayakLocalHome` interface. Now, we start to layer on complexity. We need to understand a little more about how the EJB container manages entity bean instances. In this case, the `home` object allows us to find kayaks in our boat shop. The `home` object also allows us to create individual kayaks and add them to our database. Fortunately, the container provides the method implementation for us. Listing 8.3 shows the local home interface for our `Kayak` entity EJB.

Listing 8.3   KayakLocalHome

```
package com.bitterejb.boatshop;

import javax.ejb.*;
import java.rmi.*;
import java.util.*;

/**
 *  Home interface to the local Kayak EJB.
 */
public interface KayakLocalHome extends EJBLocalHome {

  public Collection findByRenter(String renter) throws FinderException;

  public Collection findAll() throws FinderException;

  public KayakLocal findByPrimaryKey(Long id) throws FinderException;

  public KayakLocal create(Long id, String location, int capacity,
    boolean rudder)
    throws CreateException;
}
```

`KayakLocalHome` is simply the interface for creating and finding kayaks. The container provides the implementation of this interface for us. So far each layer is easy. However, as we layer on additional code and see the added potential for programming error, we may start to wish that we'd brought a simpler, old-school boat onto this river.

8.2.2   Adding the DTO and facade

Now we need to tune the design to add our façade and DTO. Because we'd rather deal with objects than with primitives, we'll want to use a DTO. Recall that DTOs allow you to send entire objects, rather than primitives, back to the client, improving usability and saving communication costs. Our DTO, then, is a simple kayak class with primitive attributes. Listing 8.4 shows the Kayak DTO.

Listing 8.4   Kayak

```
Kayak.java:
package com.bitterejb.boatshop;

import java.io.*;

/**
 *  Kayak data transfer class.
 */
public class Kayak
  implements Serializable {

  private Long      id;
  private boolean    isRented;
  private String     renter;
  private String     location;
  private int        capacity;
  private boolean    hasRudder;

  public Long getId() { return id; }
  public void setId(Long id) {  this.id = id; }

  public boolean getIsRented() {  return isRented; }
  public void setIsRented(boolean rented) { isRented = rented; }

  public String getRenter() { return renter; }
  public void setRenter(String renter) { this.renter = renter; }

  public String getLocation() {  return location; }
  public void setLocation(String location) { this.location = location; }

  public int getCapacity() { return capacity; }
  public void setCapacity(int cap) {  capacity = cap; }

  public boolean getHasRudder() { return hasRudder; }
  public void setHasRudder(boolean rudder) { hasRudder = rudder; }

  public String toString () {
    return "kayak id: " + id + "; location: " + location
      + "; capacity: " + capacity + "; renter: " + renter
      + "; rudder: " + hasRudder;
  }
}
```

Notice that the DTO looks exactly as what we'd ideally hope our persistent object would, if the persistence framework could persist the object transparently. With CMP, however, the DTO is only a small part of this persistent implementation. Indeed, if you're coding all this by hand, then you're breaking a serious sweat by now. Hopefully, you're using a tool to autogenerate the code. But don't be fooled! Code generation is the easy part. Once the code has been spewed out, you must maintain it. Inevitably, you'll end up trying to debug this EJB someday (although, of course, you might conveniently chalk it up to a mistake made by your rookie cube mate).

We're only halfway home. Remember, we need to wrap the entire model with a Session Façade because direct access to the entity beans will require unacceptable communication costs. The session bean serving as a façade should create a Kayak-EJB entity bean instance based on specified input parameters and return a Kayak DTO to the client. Listing 8.5 shows the session façade to our Kayak entity EJB.

Listing 8.5   BoatshopEJB

```java
package com.bitterejb.boatshop;

import javax.ejb.*;
import java.util.*;
import java.rmi.*;
import javax.naming.*;

public class BoatshopEJB implements SessionBean {        Session Façade class

   private SessionContext context = null;
   private static long   seed = System.currentTimeMillis ();

   public Kayak createKayak (String location, int capacity,     ◁──┐  Method
      boolean rudder)                                              │  to create
      throws RemoteException, CreateException, NamingException {   │  a kayak

      KayakLocal kayak = getKayakLocalHome ().create
         (new Long (seed++), location, capacity, rudder);   ◁──┐  This is not a very
      return kayak.toDataTransferObject ();                     │  good way to
   }                                                            │  create an id

      private KayakLocalHome getKayakLocalHome ()     Get local home
         throws NamingException {
         InitialContext ic = new InitialContext ();
         return (KayakLocalHome) ic.lookup ("KayakLocal");
      }

   public void setSessionContext (SessionContext c) {
      context = c;
   }

   public void ejbCreate () { }
   public void ejbRemove () { }
   public void ejbActivate () { }
   public void ejbPassivate () { }
}
```

Figure 8.2 illustrates the application design. The previous listings provided persistence and a DTO. Listing 8.5 is a client of the persistent object, allowing a single access point for the framework. We can use this unified interface to provide security, distribution, and transactional awareness. The home interface manages the data store; the EJB object implements each persistent instance; and the façade provides a distributed access point.

To keep this chapter brief (and make sure you stay awake), we've omitted the `BoatshopRemote.java` and `BoatshopRemoteHome.java` interface listings. They will be the same for all implementations discussed in this chapter—after all, that is the whole point of the session bean façade.

Keep in mind that this technique is not a good way to create an index. A better approach would be to use a sequence generator that uses a database table and a high-low style algorithm to atomically check batches of IDs and dole out these IDs

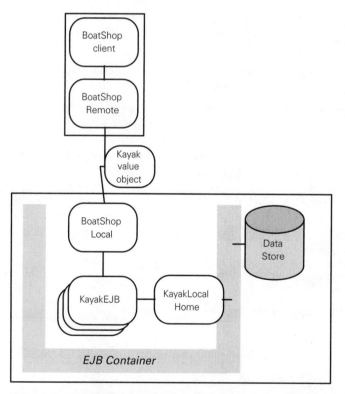

Figure 8.2 The persistent entity, KayakEJB, is only a very small part of our overall design. The home interface actually manages the data store, and provides interfaces to create, destroy, and find kayaks. The clients actually access the business logic through a Session Façade. The Session Façade communicates with the kayak DTO.

as needed. However, implementing this approach is out of this book's scope. Ideally, identity generation is a good example of a service that your persistence framework should provide for you.

8.2.3 *Including deployment details*

You will recall that EJB strives to separate deployment decisions from implementation decisions. To merge the classes we developed into a CMP entity bean and a session bean, we must write an EJB deployment descriptor that outlines features of the beans. Listing 8.6 shows the deployment descriptor for our Kayak entity EJB.

Listing 8.6   Deployment Descriptor

```
ejb-jar.xml
<!DOCTYPE ejb-jar
  PUBLIC '-//Sun Microsystems, Inc.//DTD Enterprise JavaBeans 2.0//EN'
  'http://java.sun.com/j2ee/dtds/ejb-jar_2_0.dtd'>
<ejb-jar>
  <enterprise-beans>
    <session>
      <!-- The JNDI name of the bean.  -->
      <ejb-name>Boatshop</ejb-name>

      <!-- Class configuration for the bean -->
      <home>com.bitterejb.boatshop.BoatshopRemoteHome</home>
      <remote>com.bitterejb.boatshop.BoatshopRemote</remote>
      <ejb-class>com.bitterejb.boatshop.BoatshopEJB</ejb-class>

      <session-type>Stateless</session-type>
      <transaction-type>Container</transaction-type>
    </session>

    <entity>
      <!-- The JNDI name of the bean.  -->
      <ejb-name>Kayak</ejb-name>

      <!-- Class configuration for the bean -->
      <local-home>com.bitterejb.boatshop.KayakLocalHome</local-home>
      <local>com.bitterejb.boatshop.KayakLocal</local>
      <ejb-class>com.bitterejb.boatshop.KayakEJB</ejb-class>
      <persistence-type>Container</persistence-type>
      <prim-key-class>java.lang.Long</prim-key-class>
      <reentrant>False</reentrant>

      <!-- Container-managed persistence info -->
      <cmp-version>2.x</cmp-version>
      <abstract-schema-name>Kayak</abstract-schema-name>

      <cmp-field><field-name>id</field-name></cmp-field>
      <cmp-field><field-name>location</field-name></cmp-field>
      <cmp-field><field-name>isRented</field-name></cmp-field>
```

```
      <cmp-field><field-name>renter</field-name></cmp-field>
      <cmp-field><field-name>capacity</field-name></cmp-field>
      <cmp-field><field-name>hasRudder</field-name></cmp-field>

      <primkey-field>id</primkey-field>
    </entity>
  </enterprise-beans>
  <assembly-descriptor>
    <container-transaction>
      <method>
        <ejb-name>Boatshop</ejb-name>
        <method-intf>Remote</method-intf>
        <method-name>*</method-name>
      </method>

      <trans-attribute>Required</trans-attribute>
    </container-transaction>

    <container-transaction>
      <method>
        <ejb-name>Kayak</ejb-name>
        <method-intf>Local</method-intf>
        <method-name>*</method-name>
      </method>

      <trans-attribute>Mandatory</trans-attribute>
    </container-transaction>
  </assembly-descriptor>
</ejb-jar>
```

The use of deployment descriptors is actually a strength of EJB. All deployment details are neatly separated in a separate XML configuration file. You might argue that the deployment details are growing too complex, but in general, the flexibility here outweighs the complexity. And, again, the creation of the deployment descriptor can be automated.

Okay, *now* we're done. Take a moment and review all the code. Keep in mind that our simple problem—persist and retrieve simple kayak objects—caused us to write all this code. You'll likely be generating some of this code, but that fact alone will not isolate you from the complexity. You'll continue to see the files as you build, debug, or step outside the traditional EJB box, as sometimes you must. Yet without looking from a different vantage point, you'll find seeing and appreciating the existing alternatives can be difficult. Indeed, sometimes we get so heads-down in a technology that we can't look past traditional approaches. So, let's pop our heads up and take a look around at useful alternatives.

8.2.4 *Rolling your own with BMP entity beans*

In chapter 7, we saw how, in the EJB realm, public opinion has been leaning against BMP and toward CMP for persistence needs. Nevertheless, BMP entity beans still play an important part in the EJB specification for the following reasons:

- CMP does not support many complex relational database schemas. Many enterprise applications must integrate with existing applications that rely on a given existing schema.

- Many proprietary or legacy enterprise information systems do not have CMP support. In these situations, CMP cannot be used.

- Other special requirements, ones that step beyond traditional CMP limitations, may require BMP.

So, how does BMP stack up? We know it dumps a whole lot of work and complexity in your lap—you have to take on the role of the container. Otherwise, a BMP bean looks like a CMP bean. Table 8.2 tells the story.

Table 8.2 BMP, like CMP, provides deep services through the EJB container, including distribution, security, and management for transactions. BMP is even more difficult to learn, and does not support key Java language extensions, but the flexibility can make it more attractive than CMP for performance reasons or to support additional data stores.

BMP Entity Beans	
J2EE integration—Security	Yes, with remote interfaces; no, with local interfaces
J2EE integration—Remote access (to entity logic)	Yes, with remote interfaces; no, with local interfaces
J2EE integration—JTA	Yes
J2EE integration—JCA	Not applicable It depends on the underlying implementation
Simplicity	Very difficult to learn with many pitfalls More complex than CMP because persistence methods must be implemented by the developer
Java language alignment	Many Java language features such as inheritance and pass-by-reference are not supported or are treated differently. Some language features can be emulated at the application level.
Deployment flexibility	Requires an EJB container Can be used with many types of data stores, including RDBMS and OODBMS

The sample code for persisting a Kayak using BMP is similar to the CMP example earlier, except that the developer must write the data storage and retrieval code. For the sake of your sanity and space constraints, we'll leave this as an exercise for the curious.

One considerable advantage to BMP entity beans over straight JDBC (described in section 8.3) is that the EJB container handles many facets of object life cycle automatically. The entity bean developer is responsible only for implementing the methods that deal with the entity bean persistence. The container takes care of issues such as determining when to load or store a particular instance and caching objects for performance improvements.

Despite the container's good intentions with BMP, we conclude that the disadvantages outweigh the few advantages. You have to take on all the complexity and many restrictions of a CMP domain model, and then layer on all the work usually done by the container. As a reward, you lose many performance optimizations of CMP. Indeed, it's a zero-sum game. For more details, flip back to section 7.3 and read "Ham sandwich, hold the ham."

8.3 *Simplify with JDBC*

Contrary to what most salespeople will tell you, many programming projects do not need an object-oriented persistence framework of any kind. A significant number of programmers are going back to basics and using POJOs with JDBC and a Session Façade for their persistence needs. After all, if you're simply building a glorified user interface to a database, then why use a persistence framework at all? Furthermore, many feel that persistence frameworks may be too difficult to tune, since they do not give you complete control of the underlying SQL ultimately generated.

For these reasons, any discussion of data persistence in Java must include JDBC. Providing a standard means of communicating with SQL databases, JDBC is a stable and mature specification. As such, it's a viable alternative for simpler projects and those that are relational in nature.

The JDBC standard was developed to provide Java developers with a standard way to execute SQL statements against a relational database and to efficiently process the data returned from SQL queries. JDBC supports transactions, and JDBC drivers can be integrated into a container-managed transaction. This integration with the container allows the JDBC transaction boundaries to transparently synchronize with the boundaries defined in a bean's deployment descriptor. However, JDBC has no standard support for complex Java types. Additionally, JDBC does not support any distributed-object concepts addressed by the EJB specification. It is designed purely as a means to access relational databases from Java programs. Many times, that's enough. Table 8.3 scores JDBC against our persistence criteria.

Table 8.3 JDBC allows good flexibility but forces developers to look elsewhere for security, distribution, and transaction support. The usage is simple, but relational databases and object-oriented programs process data in fundamentally different ways.

JDBC	
J2EE integration—Security	No
J2EE integration—Remote access (to entity logic)	No
J2EE integration—JTA	Yes, provided that the JDBC driver supplies an XADataSource
J2EE integration—JCA	Yes
Simplicity	JDBC is the simplest of the persistence alternatives. Basic usage is well understood for traditional relational problems, and simple enough for many object-oriented problems. For complex object-oriented problems, algorithms with SQL and JDBC can get unbearably complex.
Java language alignment	No. SQL is a relational language. Data returned by JDBC calls is in tabular form—rows with columns—instead of objects. It only supports primitive data types.
Deployment flexibility	No container requirements In general, SQL is used with RDBMS.

JDBC is an ideal persistence choice for projects that involve a considerable amount of proprietary database code and for projects closely aligned with a relational model, rather than an object-oriented model. For example, you might choose JDBC for persistence if you perform most of your business logic in stored procedures and only use a thin Java layer for data presentation. Similarly, if your application is a thin user interface for an existing relational database or a relational reporting application, then JDBC is likely the right choice. Don't underestimate the number of applications that fit this description—they're all over the place. JDBC offers plenty for many simpler object-oriented applications or components, as well.

8.3.1 *Implementing a simple JDBC model*

Let's look at how we would implement the routines necessary to insert a new Kayak object into a relational database, starting with a simple Kayak DTO—a POJO (listing 8.7). Most of our complexity will involve translating between this object and the relational format required for the database code.

Listing 8.7   Kayak POJO

```
Kayak.java:
package com.bitterejb.boatshop;

import java.io.*;

/**
 *  Kayak class.
 */
public class Kayak
  implements Serializable, Cloneable {

    private Long       id;
    private boolean    isRented;
    private String     renter;
    private String     location;
    private int        capacity;
    private boolean    hasRudder;

    public Long getId() { return id; }
    public void setId(Long id) {  this.id = id; }

    public boolean getIsRented() {  return isRented; }
    public void setIsRented(boolean rented) { isRented = rented; }

    public String getRenter() { return renter; }
    public void setRenter(String renter) { this.renter = renter; }

    public String getLocation() {  return location; }
    public void setLocation(String location) { this.location = location; }

    public int getCapacity() { return capacity; }
    public void setCapacity(int cap) {  capacity = cap; }

    public boolean getHasRudder() { return hasRudder; }
    public void setHasRudder(boolean rudder) { hasRudder = rudder; }

    public String toString () {
      return "kayak id: " + id + "; location: " + location
        + "; capacity: " + capacity + "; renter: " + renter
        + "; rudder: " + hasRudder;
    }
}
```

That's not much different from our DTO in listing 8.6. This DTO actually fills a similar role. We'll map this object onto an inbound SQL insert or update string. We could also map the object onto an outbound database query.

8.3.2 *Implementing the JDBC Façade*

We now have the equivalent of our DTO. Next, we need to make modifications to the session bean to perform the insert via direct JDBC calls. Here, we're basically moving our persistence directly into the façade layer. Keep in mind that there is more than one way to skin a cat. This approach is the most straightforward for our example. Again, we'll forego writing the remote and home interfaces for the session bean. Listing 8.8 shows the session bean used to insert new kayak objects using JDBC.

Listing 8.8   BoatshopEJB.java, JDBC version

```java
package com.bitterejb.boatshop;

import javax.ejb.*;
import java.util.*;
import java.rmi.*;
import javax.naming.*;
import java.sql.*;
import javax.sql.*;

/**
 *  Stateless session bean that can insert Kayak objects.
 */
public class BoatshopEJB implements SessionBean {

  private SessionContext   context = null;
  private static long   seed = System.currentTimeMillis ();

  public Kayak createKayak (String location, int capacity,
    boolean rudder)
    throws RemoteException, CreateException, NamingException {

    Kayak kayak = new Kayak ();
    kayak.setId (new Long (seed++));
    kayak.setLocation (location);
    kayak.setCapacity (capacity);
    kayak.setIsRented (false);
    kayak.setRenter (null);
    kayak.setHasRudder (rudder);

    insert (kayak);
    return kayak;
  }

  private void insert (Kayak k)
    throws CreateException, NamingException {

    DataSource ds   = null;
```

Create and insert a Kayak Java object

The code uses native Java objects

Insert maps the relational kayak object onto an SQL string

```
    Connection conn    = null;
    PreparedStatement ps = null;
    try {
      ds = (DataSource) new InitialContext ().lookup ("java:/DefaultDS"); ◁──
      conn = ds.getConnection ();
      ps = conn.prepareStatement ("INSERT INTO KAYAK"
        + "(ID, LOCATION, ISRENTED, RENTER, CAPACITY, HASRUDDER) "
        + "VALUES(?, ?, ?, ?, ?, ?)");

      ps.setLong (1, k.getId ().longValue ());

      String s = k.getLocation ();
      if (s == null)
        ps.setNull (2, Types.VARCHAR);
      else
        ps.setString (2, s);

      ps.setBoolean (3, k.getIsRented ());

      s = k.getRenter ();
      if (s == null)
        ps.setNull (4, Types.VARCHAR);
      else
        ps.setString (4, s);

      ps.setInt (5, k.getCapacity ());

      ps.setBoolean (6, k.getHasRudder ());

      ps.executeUpdate ();

    } catch (SQLException sqe) {
      throw new CreateException (sqe.getMessage());
    } finally {
      if  (ps != null)
        try { ps.close (); } catch (Exception e) {}

      if (conn != null)
        try { conn.close (); } catch (Exception e) {}
    }
  }

  // Misc EJB Methods
  public void setSessionContext(SessionContext c) {
    context = c;
  }

  public void ejbCreate() { }
  public void ejbRemove() { }
  public void ejbActivate() { }
  public void ejbPassivate() { }
}
```

The datasource name is embedded in code

Using this approach, the session bean layer must manage the database. As you can see, this management is much less complex for simple inserts, deletes, and even basic queries. Less code needs to be written than with the EJB alternative. The downside is that, whenever you use SQL directly, you're building a tighter coupling to your database. That is, the session bean must know how to access the database tables and columns, and then map the results into kayak objects. Nevertheless, we can conclude that for such simple applications, the value that an EJB entity bean adds is probably not worth the cost in complexity or performance.

Don't misunderstand the conclusion we've just made. We are not advocating building a full persistence layer from scratch with SQL. We're talking about using SQL tactically to populate your objects. The requirements for a real persistence framework are not clear with such a simple example, but as you add layers of transactions, complex object relationships, and object interaction, the database code and the resulting SQL become much more complex.

How do you know when your application has become complex enough to require a persistence framework? You simply pay attention to your pain and read the code. If you find yourself spending unbearable amounts of time dealing with the intricacies of SQL and relational database integration, you might be ready for a full persistence framework. If you find your code looks more and more procedural and that the database integration layer prevents you from designing simpler, object-oriented applications, then you definitely should consider a data persistence layer.

8.3.3 *Deploying a Session Façade for JDBC*

Because we're not using an entity EJB, our deployment descriptor only references a single bean—our `BoatshopEJB` session bean. All other deployment details, unfortunately, are embedded in the code.

Listing 8.9   Deployment descriptor ejb-jar.xml

```
<!DOCTYPE ejb-jar
   PUBLIC '-//Sun Microsystems, Inc.//DTD Enterprise JavaBeans 2.0//EN'
   'http://java.sun.com/j2ee/dtds/ejb-jar_2_0.dtd'>
<ejb-jar>
  <enterprise-beans>
    <session>
      <!-- The JNDI name of the bean.   -->
      <ejb-name>Boatshop</ejb-name>
```

```
      <!-- Class configuration for the bean -->
      <home>com.bitterejb.boatshop.BoatshopRemoteHome</home>
      <remote>com.bitterejb.boatshop.BoatshopRemote</remote>
      <ejb-class>com.bitterejb.boatshop.BoatshopEJB</ejb-class>

      <session-type>Stateless</session-type>
      <transaction-type>Container</transaction-type>
    </session>
  </enterprise-beans>
  <assembly-descriptor>
    <container-transaction>
      <method>
        <ejb-name>Boatshop</ejb-name>
        <method-intf>Remote</method-intf>
        <method-name>*</method-name>
      </method>

      <trans-attribute>Required</trans-attribute>
    </container-transaction>
  </assembly-descriptor>
</ejb-jar>
```

Listing 8.9 shows just part of the code needed to fully implement a mechanism for storing objects in a database using pure JDBC. Our JDBC solution can only insert new objects. We must write corresponding `update()`, `delete()`, and `load()` methods for each class in our domain object model. Of course, for a simple application like this, the code would not be difficult to add or maintain.

For complex problems, an intelligent JDBC-based solution may grow to include a sophisticated loading mechanism to support many desirable loading features, such as lazy loading relations and large fields or efficient loading of large result sets. However, implementing these types of features, while essential for a real comparison, would require quite a bit of coding, and the end result would end up looking like one of the solutions that we'll talk about next—object persistence frameworks. The goal of this example is to demonstrate what the code might look like when the requirements of the project match the criteria in table 8.4.

JDBC and SQL were not designed with the problem of object persistence in mind, so when looking at this example, don't forget that our code is not really appropriate for JDBC. However, this code example is representative of how many application developers use JDBC in enterprise applications today. While we should be careful to remember that JDBC and SQL are valuable technologies with significant advantages of their own, the problems faced by enterprise application developers trying to persist a domain object model are not always ones for which JDBC is ideally suited.

Table 8.4 If you decide not to use EJB entity beans, you'll probably wind up choosing between an object persistence framework and straight JDBC solutions. The decision between JDBC and an object persistence framework is a simple one that depends on the nature of the application and complexity of the data access layer.

Decision	Technology choices	Selection criteria
Choose	JDBC over object persistence frameworks	• Business logic is predominantly implemented in custom stored procedures • Data model is relational, not object-oriented • The problem is simple • The problem is relational in nature (e. g., reporting, database population)
Choose	Object persistence frameworks over JDBC	• Data model is complex and object-oriented • You plan on establishing relations among classes in your object model • Object model uses inheritance heavily

8.4 Using object persistence frameworks

CMP is basically a persistence framework that works on the level of coarse-grained components. JDBC, in contrast, persists data at the field granularity level. For example, with JDBC, you load and store all individual fields in an object into a row or set of rows in the database. Because Java is object-oriented, we should consider object persistence frameworks that address the persistence problem at the object granularity level.

With object persistence frameworks, you load and store entire objects,[1] which is more natural for most object-oriented applications. Object persistence frameworks usually take care of the details of loading and storing data automatically, so all you need to do is use familiar Java language syntax to access the data in your database. When you're working with a complex domain model, this approach is simpler than JDBC, where you must manually convert between objects and raw data stored in result sets.

8.4.1 Surveying the object persistence landscape

Within the realm of object persistence frameworks, you've got several viable options. Your choice of an individual framework will depend on your application's requirements, your skills, and your preference. You can think of the object

---

1 Most object persistence frameworks support lazy loading semantics, so while you conceptually load entire objects, the framework might load only a certain set of fields initially and lazy-load larger or less frequently used fields.

persistence landscape along two separate axes. First, the potential data stores define how data is physically stored. More interestingly, the interfaces define how you interact with the data store. Let's look at the major categories along each axis.

The data store

This axis answers the question, "How do you persist your data?" Object-oriented systems store objects and links between those objects. Relational database management systems store data in related tables.

- **Object-oriented database management systems (OODBMS)** represent data in the database as lists of objects, rather than as tables containing rows and columns. In a famous paper called "The Design of a Robust Persistence Layer for Relational Databases," Scott Ambler concluded that object-oriented databases are nice but no match for relational databases. Still, some applications, like CAD systems, are inherently object-oriented. It pays to consider OODBMS for these types of problems. Vendors, such as Poet, Progress, and Versant supply the key OODBMS products in the Java space.

- **Relational DBMS (RDBMS)** represent databases as rows in a table. While this approach is not inherently object-oriented, it is ubiquitous. RDBMSs are highly efficient, due to a clean mathematical model and decades of practical experience and academic study. We understand how to maintain, tune, code, and administer them. It's meaningless to discuss alternatives that don't work well with relational databases.

Interfaces to the data store

To us, the critical question is this: How does your application access data in the data store? Object-oriented frameworks, for the most part, use techniques that strive for as much transparency as possible. The major distinction is proprietary versus open. Proprietary solutions can provide more flexibility; standards are more interoperable. Let's look at a breakdown of the differences between object-oriented and persistence frameworks:

- **Object-relational mapping frameworks** (OR mappers) can convert between an object and the corresponding row-set in a set of tables in a relational database. These frameworks specialize in providing an object-oriented domain model and building the "glue" code that connects domain models to a database. The better frameworks are efficient. They also have highly flexible mapping technology that can adapt to a wide variety of relational schemas. OR mappers became much muddier when Oracle bought the industry's leading OR mapper, TopLink. At this point, it's not clear if Oracle will continue to support rival databases or application servers as well as it has in the past, but several good products are more than capable. CocoBase is the main alternative to TopLink in this space, and several open source OR mappers exist. Castor is the most popular open alternative, but Hibernate is also gaining in favor.

- **Standardized object persistence frameworks**   Some alternatives attempt to provide a standard mapping to both object-oriented databases and relational databases. Within this group, the alternative with the most momentum is JDO. Most implementations have surprisingly nimble mapping technology, good performance, and perhaps one of the cleanest programming interfaces. Some JDO implementations ship with a database back end, and some focus on relational mapping. The standardization of the JDO specification by the Java Community Process board members provides us with a convenient common ground to use for discussion of object persistence tools. Strong support for JDO exists from OODBMS vendors and from third-party OR mapping products, but relational database vendors themselves

Many of the Java object-oriented persistence frameworks are remarkably similar. They all provide fine-grained persistence, with clean, object-oriented interfaces. For convenience, we'll use JDO in this book, but most arguments that we'll make also hold true for other persistence frameworks and mapping technologies.

8.4.2 *Understanding JDO*

The JDO specification defines a set of abstract APIs for transactional persistence of objects. JDO does not make any assumptions about the actual physical data store used by an implementation, because the JDO standard is not written just for relational databases or object databases. Instead, the design focuses on generic, flexible implementations for any transactional data store. JDO implementations exist for relational databases and object databases, as well as legacy enterprise information systems. Increasingly, large commercial Java projects—including projects with Credit Suisse, Nokia, and Pacific Gas & Electricity—have demonstrated the success of JDO. To keep our discussion clear, we will not consider extensions to the standard that some JDO products may include.

One important design pattern that we will bundle into this object persistence framework category is the Data Access Object (DAO) pattern described in *Core J2EE* and other sources. The DAO pattern isolates data access from the underlying data store. The JDO standard is, in many ways, the logical conclusion of the DAO pattern—it is an abstract API for accessing objects stored in arbitrary databases. JDO allows the same decoupling of underlying data technology from object persistence as does the DAO pattern. Table 8.5 measures JDO against our performance criteria.

Table 8.5 JDO is an example of an object-oriented persistence framework. JDO does not offer security or remote access services, but these features are usually provided through a Session Façade within EJB solutions. JDO's key benefits lie in its light weight and its simplicity, combined with superior Java alignment.

Java Data Objects (JDO)	
J2EE integration—Security	No
J2EE integration—Remote access	No
J2EE integration—JTA	Yes
J2EE integration—JCA	Yes
Simplicity	Basic and complex object models are equally simple to use in JDO. Some of the more advanced JDO options require a good understanding for proper usage. JDO does add some deployment complexity.
Java language alignment	Yes JDO objects behave just like regular Java objects. JDO Query Language (JDOQL) uses Java boolean expression syntax.
Deployment flexibility	No container requirements Can be used with many types of data stores, including RDBMS and OODBMS

8.4.3 Implementing a simple model with JDO

Now, let's look at how to insert a new `Kayak` object using JDO (listing 8.10). Our object is a POJO, but the persistence framework will add persistence in a postcompile processing step. Notice that the JDO implementation is considerably simpler than both the EJB and JDBC implementations. Also, notice that the JDO domain object is doubling as the DTO in this example.

Listing 8.10 kayak.java, JDO version

```
package com.bitterejb.boatshop;

import java.io.*;

/**
 *  Kayak class.
 */
```

```
public class Kayak                                      The persistent Kayak class
   implements Serializable, Cloneable {                 is a simple Java object

   private Long       id;
   private boolean    isRented;
   private String     renter;
   private String     location;
   private int        capacity;
   private boolean    hasRudder;

   public Long getId() { return id; }                    Persistent attributes
   public void setId(Long id) {  this.id = id; }          are expressed in
                                                          pure Java object
   public boolean getIsRented() {  return isRented; }
   public void setIsRented(boolean rented) { isRented = rented; }

   public String getRenter() { return renter; }
   public void setRenter(String renter) { this.renter = renter; }

   public String getLocation() {  return location; }
   public void setLocation(String location) { this.location = location; }

   public int getCapacity() { return capacity; }
   public void setCapacity(int cap) {  capacity = cap; }

   public boolean getHasRudder() { return hasRudder; }
   public void setHasRudder(boolean rudder) { hasRudder = rudder; }

   public String toString () {
      return "kayak id: " + id + "; location: " + location
        + "; capacity: " + capacity + "; renter: " + renter
        + "; rudder: " + hasRudder;
   }
}
```

Kayak.java is a pure Java object, with nothing added and nothing lost. As Java developers, we want our persistent object to look exactly like this. The persistence framework completely and transparently manages persistence for us. The magic happens behind the scenes. JDO-based implementations typically run either their source or, more often, the compiled bytecode, of their domain object model through a tool that enhances the source or bytecode to add persistence.

Admittedly, this process is regarded as risky by some, and can lead to complex build situations. For example, obfuscation programs often work by manipulating bytecode after compilation. So, if you choose to use bytecode enhancement with JDO (rather than source enhancement) and an obfuscator, you must take care to run the enhancer before the obfuscation process. Further, some people feel that bytecode should only be modified by compilers and application servers, and not by other tools. So, you should educate yourself on these issues if they are important to you, and ensure that whatever technology you choose provides you with alternatives (such as source code enhancement with JDO) to anything that you are uncomfortable with.

8.4.4 *Implementing the JDO model's façade*

Next, we need to make modifications to the session bean to account for using JDO. We use the persistence manager factory to manage the lifecycle of our persistence objects (listing 8.11).

Listing 8.11 BoatShopEJB.java, JDO version

```
package com.bitterejb.boatshop;

import javax.ejb.*;
import java.util.*;
import java.rmi.*;
import javax.naming.*;
import javax.jdo.*;
/**
 *  Stateless session bean that can insert Kayak objects via JDO
 */
public class BoatshopEJB implements SessionBean {

  private SessionContext   context = null;
  private PersistenceManagerFactory   factory = null;
  private static long   seed = System.currentTimeMillis ();

  public Kayak createKayak (String location, int capacity,
    boolean rudder)
    throws RemoteException, CreateException, NamingException {

    Kayak kayak = new Kayak ();
    kayak.setId (new Long (seed++));
    kayak.setLocation (location);
    kayak.setCapacity (capacity);
    kayak.setIsRented (false);
    kayak.setRenter (null);
    kayak.setHasRudder (rudder);

    PersistenceManager pm = factory.getPersistenceManager ();
    pm.makePersistent (kayak);
    pm.close ();

    return kayak;
  }

  public void setSessionContext(SessionContext c)
    throws EJBException {
    context = c;

    try {
```

The JDO persistence manager inserts a kayak

Caches a reference to persistence manager factory

```
        InitialContext ctx = new InitialContext ();
        // Cache a reference to a PersistenceManagerFactory.
        factory = (PersistenceManagerFactory) ctx.lookup
            ("java:comp/env/jdo/PersistenceManagerFactory");
    } catch (NamingException ne) {
        throw new EJBException (ne);
    }
  }

  public void ejbCreate() { }
  public void ejbRemove() { }
  public void ejbActivate() { }
  public void ejbPassivate() { }
}
```

Again, we have left out the remote and home interfaces for the session bean.

This interface is every bit as simple as the JDBC implementation and is much simpler than the comparable EJB implementation. The interface also carries none of the overhead associated with distribution, security, or transactional awareness, and rightfully so—those features are already managed by the session façade.

8.4.5 *Deploying the solution*

The deployment descriptor is the same as for the JDBC application (listing 8.12). The deployment data for the JDO objects, which handles relational mapping and database connection information, is now in a separate file:

Listing 8.12 Deployment descriptor ejb-jar.xml

```
ejb-jar.xml
<!DOCTYPE ejb-jar
  PUBLIC '-//Sun Microsystems, Inc.//DTD Enterprise JavaBeans 2.0//EN'
  'http://java.sun.com/j2ee/dtds/ejb-jar_2_0.dtd'>
<ejb-jar>
  <enterprise-beans>
    <session>
      <!-- The JNDI name of the bean.  -->
      <ejb-name>Boatshop</ejb-name>

      <!-- Class configuration for the bean -->
      <home>com.bitterejb.boatshop.BoatshopRemoteHome</home>
      <remote>com.bitterejb.boatshop.BoatshopRemote</remote>
      <ejb-class>com.bitterejb.boatshop.BoatshopEJB</ejb-class>

      <session-type>Stateless</session-type>
      <transaction-type>Container</transaction-type>
    </session>
  </enterprise-beans>
</ejb-jar>
```

```
<assembly-descriptor>
  <container-transaction>
    <method>
      <ejb-name>Boatshop</ejb-name>
      <method-intf>Remote</method-intf>
      <method-name>*</method-name>
    </method>

    <trans-attribute>Required</trans-attribute>
  </container-transaction>
</assembly-descriptor>
</ejb-jar>
```

In addition to the EJB deployment descriptor, we must also write a JDO metadata file to identify the classes in the system that are part of the persistent domain object model (listing 8.13):

Listing 8.13   JDO descriptor boatshop.jdo

```
boatshop.jdo:
<!DOCTYPE jdo
   PUBLIC '-//Sun Microsystems, Inc.//DTD Java Data Objects Metadata 1.0//EN'
   'http://java.sun.com/dtd/jdo_1_0.dtd'>
<jdo>
  <package name="com.bitterejb.boatshop">
    <class name="Kayak" />
  </package>
</jdo>
```

Realistically, this information belongs in the deployment descriptor, and this is our first hint that JDO is not a first-class citizen in the EJB kingdom. It's a tiny detail, and one that we deal with gladly for the advantages that JDO brings.

8.4.6   Comparing the options

Let's review the three solutions. Two of the solutions—object persistence and JDBC—have clear and compelling niches. For certain applications, JDBC is a simple and logical choice. For relational problems such as reporting and user interfaces that are tightly coupled to a database design, using JDBC makes sense. For simple models, JDBC is also a reasonable choice. As you start to add more difficult conditions, JDBC can break down. Complex object models, demanding performance requirements, interlaced transactional requirements, or shifting database designs can quickly push your application needs beyond the capabilities of JDBC.

Object persistence solutions, including relational mappers and object-oriented database management systems, are well equipped to handle demanding and complex object models. They dramatically simplify coding. The downside is that tuning the performance of a relational database engine is much more difficult when you go through an intermediate database interface. However, object persistence vendors are making significant strides in that direction by adding features such as synchronized distributed caches and lazy loaders. These features can strip much of the stress off the database layer.

We can clearly see that the EJB CMP entity bean implementation is the most complex of the three solutions. Ironically, most of this complexity supports features that a persistence layer does not need: role-based security, distribution, and transactional awareness at the object level. CMP code is much more complex than the alternatives and doesn't even fully support Java concepts such as abstract classes and inheritance. Chatty communications with the container add considerable overhead. It's tough to think of an EJB CMP implementation that another persistence alternative could not manage. In the next section, we'll look at a few problems specific to the EJB CMP framework.

The flimsy plastic of Eric's boat flexes and bends, and the snubbed nose finally slides off the rock, just as it's designed to do. Relieved, we continue, but each kayak scrapes and drags through the rocky slot until Stephen makes his run. This time, from the bottom of the drop, the party can see the sharp nose wedge deeply between two rocks. Stephen shifts his weight to slide the boat free, but it only wedges tighter. Eventually, the nose gives way and his slender boat folds in half. Luckily, Stephen works his legs free and swims away. His skills as an Olympian are not enough to overcome a simple fact: On this day, he does not have the right tool for the job.

8.5 *Antipattern: Persistent Problems*

Few decisions stay with an application longer than the choice of a persistence framework. Unfortunately, many developers and managers make this decision by default, choosing a persistence framework based on the persistence solution provided by their application server. An unstated rule seems to guide many developers: EJB persistence must occur through entity beans. However, the overhead and inflexibility of the entity bean architecture makes the framework impractical for many implementations. In reality, you're likely to spend far less by choosing a persistence framework based on an application's needs, even if you have to buy additional software or training to make it happen. Software development costs simply dwarf shrink-wrapped software costs in all but the most extreme instances. You'll want to consider the shortcomings of EJB entity beans. We're not saying that the EJB entity frameworks are completely inadequate for any task. We just believe that if you do decide to use EJB entity beans, you should do so with your eyes wide open.

8.5.1 *Generic entity bean weaknesses*

Let's review a few arguments we made in chapter 2. The entity bean specification provides four major services: declarative and distributed transactions, declarative security, scalability and fail-over support, and data persistence. When you look closely, you'll notice a significant mismatch between the way persistence is used and the way the other three services are typically used—the latter are fine, and the former is coarse. Figure 8.3 shows an example. You'll probably want coarse-grained services for an invoice, but fine-grained persistence for the objects within the invoice. In fact, you'll probably often want your coarse-grained services at an even higher level. This imposes a num-

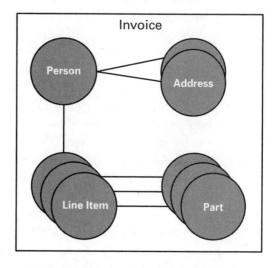

Figure 8.3 **This invoice is a coarse-grained object, composed of many fine-grained objects. The invoice contains a person with a billing and shipping address, and a list of invoice items, each with a part. You want persistence at the fine-grained level, but other services such as distribution and transaction integrity at a higher level.**

ber of architectural limitations inherent in the entity bean specification. These limitations are at the root of most entity bean antipatterns, including those discussed in chapter 7.

8.5.2 *Inheritance and polymorphism*

As you know, *inheritance* is the capability of an object-oriented programming language for one class to specialize or extend a base class. *Polymorphism* is the capability of an object-oriented programming language for a subclass to override a method's behavior in one of its superclasses. Java supports both inheritance and polymorphism. Many architectures require these capabilities as well. However, the entity bean specification does not properly support these concepts. Writing an entity bean that extends a parent entity bean is possible. However, when executing an entity bean finder method, the container returns only objects of the same class as the entity bean's object interface.

In our boat rental example, the domain object model comprises three classes: `Boat`, `Kayak`, and `Canoe`. `Kayak` and `Canoe` both extend `Boat`. You may want to define a `findAllBoats` method that can provide a list of all `Boat` objects in the database. Entity beans can't represent this relatively simple domain object model—the `Boat` entity bean cannot define a finder method that returns anything other than `Boat` entity beans. Worse, `Boat` is not actually a full-fledged entity bean in the way that we've emulated inheritance in our examples. No entry exists in the deployment descriptor for `Boat` because we do not want `Boat` objects to be created; it's an abstract class.

One common workaround to this problem is to establish a convention of writing a method that finds one list of all `Kayak` objects and another list of all `Canoe` objects, and returns the combination of these lists. This workaround presents three major problems:

- **The method that does this work must know about all its subclasses** This means that every time you add a new subclass of `Boat`, you must also modify this method to add the new type lookup. This technique does not scale well from a development standpoint and requires that anyone extending `Boat` has access to the source for this method.

- **Returned results are grouped by subclass** It may be that you want to sort all `Boat` objects—regardless of subclass—by storage location. To do this in an architecture that uses the subclass-assembly finder technique described earlier, you would have to perform a costly application sort, which would be better performed in the database than in the Java application.

- **Results in higher cost and higher incident of defects** The complexity of this solution increases the likelihood of bugs and the cost of both maintenance and initial development.

In our example, the code for this workaround might look like that in listing 8.14:

Listing 8.14   EJB inheritance

```
/**
 *  Lists all boats in the database.
 */
public Collection list ()
   throws RemoteException, FinderException, NamingException {

   Collection boats = getKayakLocalHome().findAll ();
   boats.addAll (getCanoeLocalHome().findAll ());

   BoatLocal boat;
   Collection returnBoats = new ArrayList (boats.size ());
   for (Iterator iter = boats.iterator (); iter.hasNext (); )
   {
     boat = (BoatLocal) iter.next ();
     returnBoats.add (boat.toDataTransferObject ());
   }
   return returnBoats;
}
```

Many other techniques and patterns emulate different parts of true polymorphism and inheritance. For example, the pattern that we chose does not map to databases that use inheritance structures. Other patterns that rely on delegation to emulate inheritance can support complex inheritance structures in databases, but are even more unwieldy to code than our examples.

This begs the question: Why do we have to jump through all of these hoops at all? Java doesn't have these problems. In the words of Martin Fowler, a famous modeler, "Entity beans don't bring enough to the party to offset the drinks they consume." No workarounds are nearly as full-featured or simple as the Java language's basic support.

The lack of true polymorphism is a bigger strike against entity beans than you might guess if you're just casting a passing glance. Polymorphism simplifies code, but with EJB, architectures that lean heavily on polymorphism will become complex and slow. Maintenance and future development of such systems are difficult as well—the maintainers must be aware of the conventions and assumptions decided upon when the system was first written. The crux of the problem is this: You've now got to worry about translating from your component model to the Java language! What's next, Object-EJB mappers?

To illustrate the absurdity of the situation, compare listing 8.15 to listing 8.14 written using JDO:

Listing 8.15   Inheritance using JDO

```
/**
 *  Lists all boats in the database.
 */
public Collection list ()
  throws RemoteException {

  PersistenceManager pm = factory.getPersistenceManager ();
  return (Collection) pm.newQuery (Boat.class).execute ();
}
```

Notice that listing 8.15 presents a single query. We won't have to write it as we add new types of boats. Had we performed an ordering on the query, our results would not have been grouped by subclass as in the previous example. Our code is simpler, more flexible, and more powerful, just as object-oriented programming intended it to be.

8.5.3 *Query language flexibility is often critical*

Let's shift gears a little and move into the realm of query language. EJB QL is a query language defined in the EJB 2.0 specification for performing queries on container-managed persistence entity beans. It is an object-based query language that looks much like a subset of SQL.

The addition of EJB QL in the EJB 2.0 specification offers a big improvement over earlier versions, which provided no common syntax for performing queries. Still, you'll want to be aware of weaknesses in EJB QL that make it insufficient for many advanced applications.

Deploy-time definition

EJB QL queries must be defined at deploy time. Therefore, queries cannot be dynamically generated based on user input or other dynamic state. EJB QL queries can be parameterized at runtime, but this ability is not a replacement for true dynamic query generation. For example, data-intensive systems often need to generate queries on the fly based on the constraints expressed by the user.

CMP only

EJB QL is defined within the scope of CMP entity beans. So you cannot use EJB QL to find entity beans defined using BMP. This is an inconvenient limitation because it is based on the assumption that CMP is sufficient for all persistence needs. As discussed previously, CMP has not yet reached a point where you can necessarily rely on it to map to existing database schemas.

Limited relation support

EJB QL can only traverse those types of relations supported by container-managed relationships.

Alternate 1—JDBC and SQL

JDBC fully supports any SQL that your underlying relational database supports. For the most part, JDBC is tied to relational, SQL-based systems. (JDBC drivers exist for other types of storage systems, but are relatively uncommon.) This connection is limiting in that applications written to use JDBC can only run on relational databases. However, because relational databases dominate the data store marketplace, tying an application to JDBC is not that big of a deal. More limiting is the nonportable nature of many common SQL operations. Most relational databases deviate considerably from ANSI SQL. This difference can lead to applications that can operate only against a particular database or that behave slightly differently when using different databases.

SQL is an expressive and powerful query language, and a wealth of knowledge and resources is available regarding the design of relational queries. When dealing with complex query processing on relational data sets, SQL is indispensable. However, using SQL for simple queries can be problematic. In general, Java application developers are more comfortable thinking in object terms than in relational terms and will sometimes create inefficient queries or queries that do not do exactly what the developer intended.

Alternate 2—Object persistence and object query languages

Object persistence frameworks such as JDO typically support a query language more sophisticated than EJB QL. Like JDBC, queries can usually be generated dynamically at runtime. Additionally, most object persistence tools have more mature relation support than the EJB QL specification, supporting concepts such as maps and many-to-many relations.

However, the queries supported by object persistence frameworks are usually limited by the relationships defined in the domain object model. This limitation makes these languages easier to understand for Java developers, as they are typically more comfortable with an object model. Yet, if you need to perform complex relational queries and you decide to use an object persistence tool, make sure that it can handle the query types you anticipate using.

8.5.4 DTOs require non-EJB solutions for local entities

One common pattern used in conjunction with session bean façades is the DTO pattern. Because entity beans can only be used by an EJB client in a remote manner, and because the session bean façade pattern is designed to keep all entity bean access within the EJB container, we need a non-EJB mechanism to allow the EJB client code to access the domain object model represented by entity beans on the server. The DTO pattern dictates that you write a normal Java class for each class in your persistent domain object model. Then, whenever a session bean needs to return a domain object model part, it converts the entity beans that it wants to return into the corresponding DTOs and returns these DTOs instead.

The standard DTO pattern is something of an antipattern itself, made necessary as a consequence of other EJB issues. Implementing the DTO pattern adds yet another set of classes to those needed for the entity bean specification and opens up the possibility for errors when copying data to and from DTOs.

Alternate 1—JDBC

JDBC-based systems may or may not need DTOs, depending on how JDBC is used in the system. If your JDBC solution maps data from the database into objects, then these objects could be designed to double as DTOs as described next.

Alternate 2—Object persistence

Object persistence technologies such as JDO present an elegant solution to the coding requirements added by the DTO. Because it is possible to use these persistence technologies outside the context of an application server, a session bean façade that uses JDO or a comparable technology for domain object model persistence instead of entity beans can just return the domain objects themselves, eliminating the need to have DTOs altogether. This approach reduces the complexity of session bean coding because the extra step of performing a DTO-to-entity bean mapping is not necessary. We've seen this in action in the sample Kayak creation code beginning in listing 8.1. Both the EJB and JDBC versions had to do an extra step of copying the data into a DTO, but the JDO implementation was able to use the Kayak object as both the DTO and the persistent object.

8.5.5 *Container-bound persistence*

Using entity beans for data persistence forces you to deploy your application into a container. Doing so is not desirable. You'll often find advantages in designing a system to be as flexible as possible from an implementation and deployment standpoint. If you do, you'll allow deployment decisions to be made as necessary at deployment time rather than up-front as a consequence of the chosen technologies.

The Fast Lane Reader pattern (J2EE Blueprints Patterns) presents one common example in which this flexibility is wanted. The Fast Lane Reader pattern suggests that, to improve performance of read-only parts of an enterprise system, you might consider bypassing the EJB container and instead read data directly from the database. The pattern suggests that you use the DAO pattern (Core J2EE) to access the data in the database. As described in section 8.4.2 , the DAO pattern is essentially a specialization of a general-purpose object persistence framework. So, if you use an object persistence framework for persistence needs within the container, and that framework does not rely on a container to operate, then you can easily use the exact same code to implement the Fast Lane Reader pattern. This approach is valuable because it prevents the read-only classes from becoming out-of-sync with the transactional classes, since the same classes can be deployed into both the read-only and the container environments.

Another situation in which maintaining deployment flexibility can be advantageous occurs when developing an application for external customers. Writing such an application so it can be deployed in a manner defined by your clients can be valuable. Some clients might want the application to run in a clustered environment, while others—due to varying hardware and software resources—might want to run it stand-alone, without an EJB container. If your application relies on a container to persist data, the latter option won't be available to you.

8.6 *Solution: Do not "inherit" a persistence architecture—choose it*

If you want to be successful, you must consider each major component of your architecture carefully. The critical criteria in choosing a persistence framework are J2EE integration, security, JCA integration, JTA integration, simplicity, Java language alignment, and deployment flexibility. We mention these again because they each play a large role in your application's eventual success or failure. Simplicity with J2EE integration, including JCA and JTA, makes your application easier to write and manage. Deployment flexibility makes your code easier to scale, easily enabling both single-server and clustered implementation. Language alignment protects your investment and makes code much easier to test and refine. Of course, you must also consider the political realm: EJB is the most strategic environment because it has the best political support. However, no decision is politically safe if it doesn't meet your needs. To succeed, you must clearly and carefully analyze your alternatives and make the best choice.

8.7 Summary

In this chapter, we argued that EJB entity beans are not the best way to handle persistence. EJB entity beans present several fundamental problems that are difficult to bypass:

- Entity beans are more difficult than alternatives to code and maintain.
- Entity beans are not closely aligned with Java.
- Entity beans enforce the use of many coarse-grained services, adding too much overhead.

These antipatterns are best resolved using alternate persistence mechanisms. We looked at two basic alternatives. The first alternative uses JDBC with POJOs, wrapped in a Session Façade. This approach creates a simple and scalable alternative appropriate for many applications. However, when domain object models get too complex, the JDBC solution can break down.

The second alternative is to use an object persistence framework, which is suitable for complex domain models. The alternatives presented here provide persistence services and only persistence services—they do not solve any other problem inherent in the EJB specification. Decoupling these services is a good thing and necessary for good performance. Because persistence and other services should not be tightly coupled, using a tool that addresses only persistence is often ideal, provided that that tool can be used in conjunction with the EJB specification. This pairing offers the best of both worlds—all the advantages of EJB plus a persistence model that does not impose design-time or deploy-time limitations on a project.

Entity beans should be reserved for situations when remotely accessible persistent components are necessary. More often than not, efficient, well-designed enterprise applications do not access their domain objects in this fashion. Instead, applications typically need only remote access to business methods in a façade. Remote method calls are not usually made on the domain objects themselves. The domain objects may be accessible by business methods that return them, in the guise of DTOs, but all distributed operations are performed through session beans or message-driven beans.

When starting an enterprise project, it is critical that you choose technologies that will meet the project requirements. To do this, you must understand the technologies available for persistence and the problems inherent in each approach. You should use a persistence framework chosen because of the business needs of the project, instead of using an inherited framework because it comes free with your application server.

In chapter 10 we'll consider a few finer points of component development and show you how to efficiently build and deploy your applications. Chapter 9 will show you how to automate your performance tuning.

8.8 *Antipatterns in this chapter*

This section covers the Persistent Problems antipattern.

PERSISTENT PROBLEMS

DESCRIPTION
Few decisions stay with an application like the choice of a persistence framework, but many development teams inherit a framework, like EJB entity beans, without making a total evaluation of the alternatives.

MOST FREQUENT SCALE
Organization

REFACTORED SOLUTION NAME
Evaluate solutions; don't inherit one.

REFACTORED SOLUTION TYPE
Technology

REFACTORED SOLUTION DESCRIPTION
Consider the business needs of the application. Make sure that a "default" choice is up to the challenge. Insist on customer references, with a deployed application of the size, scope and nature of a problem similar to the one that you're attacking.

ANECDOTAL EVIDENCE
"We're doing J2EE, so we guess persistence is EJB CMP entity beans."

SYMPTOMS, CONSEQUENCES
Cost overruns, inadequate flexibility, inadequate scalability.

Part 4

Broader topics

In Arkansas, we gaze at the rain-swollen Little Missouri River. We look forward to running this Ozark jewel, which is rarely this high. Our egos, too, are swelled. This river, now merely the promise of a fun diversion, would have been well beyond our skill level a mere two years ago. As we suit up, we plan our run, discussing strategy and safety issues. I notice a partner frantically scrambling through our gear and realize that we've forgotten to pack a spray skirt. The function of a skirt is to seal water out of the kayak. After eight hours of driving, we'll have no run today.

In Arkansas, we painfully learned that issues like packing and strategizing can be as important as fundamental skills like paddling. The same holds true of EJB development. Part 4 of *Bitter EJB* addresses secondary issues like tuning and packaging.

   In chapter 9, we discuss the importance of good performance tuning techniques. We emphasize the need for an automated test suite and the importance of testing before making assumptions about performance. In chapter 10, we discuss the issues of building, testing, and packaging an application. We look into tools like XDoclet and Ant that make the build process easier to automate. And we underscore the importance of running automated tests. In chapter 11, we peek into the future of EJB, pointing to technologies that may play a crucial role in the future of EJB.

Bitter tunes

9

This chapter covers
- Definitions of performance
- Antipatterns related to the EJB performance tuning process
- A JUnitPerf tutorial
- Tuning an example EJB application using JUnitPerf tests
- A step-by-step performance testing methodology
- Techniques for automating performance testing

It's early in the morning, and I'm locked in tightly to my new snowboard, staring anxiously down the impossibly steep slope. I'm a skier who's grown increasingly addicted to the freedom of snowboarding, and I've learned quickly. But I'm having a tough time getting to the next level—the confident level of the elite boarder. With a twist of the hips, I accelerate downhill. I mechanically hammer through a couple of turns, reacting to each tiny groove and bump in the ungroomed morning snow. My brain gradually falls behind, and my body only barely keeps up with the descent. I'm in a purely reactionary mode now, with my eyes tracking the terrain only inches in front of me. I fear that I may be unable to stop, and I certainly can't keep up this reckless pace. I wonder if I will even see the crash come.

In this chapter, we'll tour a few common pitfalls related to the EJB performance tuning process. We'll focus on developing a disciplined performance testing methodology driven, not by irrational fears or wild speculation, but by automated tests whose objective results aren't distracted by emotion. By continually measuring the performance of our code—and the impact of our changes to it—these tests will help us stay ahead of the pain endured when undetected performance problems sneak into our code.

Ah, but tuning isn't a development activity, you say. Configuring the application for its operational environment is a job suited for those other geeks—the operations folks strolling safely around the lodge—not those of us still on the mountain. Well, we could pass the buck that way, but letting performance tuning roll too far downhill is an incredibly inefficient way to develop software. At best, it introduces a costly delay in the feedback cycle between making a change intended to improve performance and seeing whether that change actually did any good. At worst, failure to start measuring performance early invites the danger that significant problems will crop up later, when redesigns are no longer economical. Instead, to maximize our time and ensure a successful rollout of our application, we must obtain immediate results on early performance testing.

In this chapter, we will consider an EJB application that suffers from poor performance. The application will employ a familiar antipattern that will serve as a crash test dummy for our performance testing methodology, letting us focus on tuning the application and measuring the impact of that tuning. Each time we ratchet the performance gear a notch, we'll receive immediate data that indicates unambiguously whether we've truly improved performance. By taking the guesswork out of the tuning process, we'll increase our confidence, allowing us to tackle new performance requirements without fear.

9.1 *Measures of success*

Before we shift into high gear, let's first nail down a definition of performance as a measurement. In general, two ways exist for viewing performance: response time and throughput. We tune and test applications differently, depending on the aspect on which we're focusing our improvements.

9.1.1 *Response time*

The *response time* of our application refers to the speed at which the application is able to service a given request, such as a user requesting a web page through a browser. The request may be serviced by any number of resources in our application, including servlets, EJB, a database, or a legacy system. We can manage certain types of resources by placing a limit on the maximum number of concurrent requests each resource can safely handle. That is, managed resources are control valves that help us throttle the application for consistent performance and stability. Consequently, each time a request requires the use of a managed resource, it may need to wait in a queue until the resource is available.

Take, for example, a limited resource familiar to most enterprise developers—database connections. Figure 9.1 (a) shows a database connection servicing a request for data. In this case, the database connection pool is sized with ample available connections capable of servicing requests without queuing. So no cost is incurred in waiting for a database connection to become available. In contrast, figure 9.1 (b) shows a queue of active requests waiting to be serviced by a single database connection. In this case, the size of the database connection pool is not able to keep up with the number of new requests without queuing. Step right up… and take a number!

From figure 9.1, we can infer that the response time of a request will include any time spent waiting in the request queue for an available database connection. The response time may also include any network latency in obtaining a database connection via a remote call. Furthermore, as concurrent requests for a database

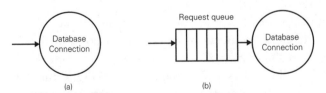

Figure 9.1 Database connections are examples of managed resources that may cause incoming requests to be queued before being serviced. Queuing incurs additional response time overhead.

connection increase, more requests will be queued, waiting for the connection. Therefore, to characterize the response time of our application accurately, we must take two essential measurements: the response time for a single request and the response time for the same request under a load of concurrent requests.

In section 9.7.2, we'll roll up our sleeves and write automated tests that measure the response time of a use case from our application. By continually running these tests, we should gain confidence, knowing that any optimizations we make have indeed improved response time. For now, let's begin by considering the possible measurements of such tests.

9.1.2 Throughput

While response time focuses on the speed of a specific request, *throughput* measures the number of requests our application can service in a given amount of time. For EJB applications, throughput is typically measured as the number of business transactions per second (tps). What constitutes an average business transaction is certainly application-specific, so throughput metrics always must be taken in appropriate context. For example, our application might be capable of processing 10 product catalog queries per second, with each query returning an average of five products.

From a slightly different angle, we use throughput as an indicator of our application's potential to scale. *Scalability* is a measure of a load's affect on our application's performance. For example, if we say that our application can scale to handle five concurrent users, then we're referring to the application's ability to maintain a linear (not exponential) average response time for each user, while under the stress of a five-user load.

Applications that scale well can deliver increasingly higher levels of throughput by adding resources, such as more hardware or more connections within a pool. When the average response time of a business transaction becomes intolerable under load, the application has reached its *maximum effective throughput*. Stressing the application beyond this point by piling on a heavier load will further degrade its responsiveness.

Revisiting our example of database connections as managed resources, figure 9.2 shows how a database connection pool can be used to work off requests efficiently. As the number of concurrent requests increases, the single database connection in figure 9.2 (a) will eventually hit a wall. Try as it might, the connection won't be able to keep up with the number of pending requests in the queue. Consequently, the request queue will continue to grow, adding to the response time of all waiting requests. By tuning the size of the database connection pool to include two

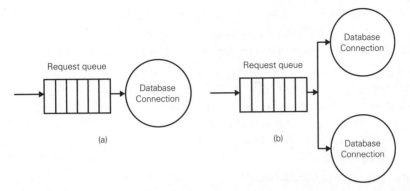

Figure 9.2 Pooling limited resources, such as database connections, is a common technique for improving an application's throughput. By increasing the size of the connection pool, a scalable application can take advantage of these additional resources to deliver better performance.

available connections, as shown in figure 9.2 (b), more requests can be serviced in a given amount of time. All other things being equal, figure 9.2 (b)'s connection pool will double the application's throughput depicted in figure 9.2 (a).

When attempts to get an application to scale prove frustrating, or even downright impossible, bottlenecks are the usual suspects. In general, a bottleneck is any chokepoint that restricts throughput. When a bottleneck is suspected, load testing tools are called to the rescue. Load testing tools are invaluable. They first put a load on an application, then shine light on any bottlenecks that rear their ugly heads. In section 9.7.5, we'll capture a nasty little bottleneck in the wild by writing an automated load test. Before we do, however, we must discuss an antipattern everybody knows but nobody likes to talk about: Premature Optimization.

9.2 Antipattern: Premature Optimization

Making a chunk of seemingly slow code faster can be quite satisfying. You can get a thrill from strutting your programming prowess and seeing immediate performance improvements. However, that thrill can cloud your judgment. Time passes in a flash as performance tweaking takes over, often resulting in an overly complex tangle of code that might get run only once in a blue moon. But when that code does run—man, is it fast!

Nobody is immune to the allure of Premature Optimization. We've been both victims of and witnesses to its use. Premature Optimization can take many forms: a speculative architecture decision, the choice of a particular design, a change in the runtime environment, or convoluted code.

Low-level code optimizations tend to attract your attention first. The trouble is, in most cases, the code paths you decide to optimize aren't called frequently enough to justify the time spent tuning the code. To make matters worse, the risk of wasting time optimizing arbitrary code paths increases with the code base size. Sure, you can always find a chunk of code that can be made faster, but it's usually the wrong one. Although you want your code to be reasonably efficient at all times, you gamble each time you blindly optimize code at the expense of code clarity and precious development time. Indeed, code clarity is often compromised as a result of optimization.

Premature Optimization has another insidious side effect. Tweaking code to make it faster tends to break something that's already working. That is, as you contort the code to squeeze out the last little bit of performance, you inevitably make compromises that can come back to bite you big later. Alas, your code won't win any awards for producing the wrong result quickly.

9.2.1 *Tuning EJB applications blindfolded*

EJB applications are especially unforgiving when you tune them in the dark. They inherently use at least one other resource, such as a database. As such, any arbitrary EJB method may spend more time blocked, waiting on a resource, than actually using the CPU. In that case, optimizing code won't show any significant performance improvement.

The runtime environment of an EJB application is also particularly fertile ground for the Premature Optimization antipattern. You must consider the virtual machine, database, and application server versions, as well as a dizzying array of internal tuning parameters for each version. If you try to get all these parameters adjusted for optimal performance before understanding their effect on your application, you incur at least two costs. First, you divert time away from those activities that really pay the bills. Second, you can complicate deployment unnecessarily by assuming that certain configuration parameters must be used.

Another reason EJB applications are prone to Premature Optimization is the myriad design decisions that must be weighed against performance. Indeed, it's easy to speculate on possible optimizations from the design perspective. Once you swerve onto that path, you may waste a significant amount of development time before you see any possible gain. Table 9.1 describes a few premature high-level design optimizations prevalent in EJB applications, along with their potential consequences.

At the end of the day, time spent tuning one area of our application is time not spent tuning another. It's a game of opportunity cost. Without a deep understanding of your application and the behaviors of its users, arbitrary

Table 9.1 Premature design optimizations in EJB applications may degrade performance and increase complexity. Deferring these types of optimizations until deemed necessary and beneficial is a better use of our time and resources.

Premature Optimization	Potential consequences
Entity beans	If your business object doesn't require concurrent read and write access while retaining stringent transactional integrity, then the use of an entity bean may incur unnecessary complexity and performance overhead. A servlet or session EJB using JDBC is often sufficient.
Stored procedures	Although stored procedures allow your database to do the heavy lifting, the business logic they encapsulate is tightly coupled to the database schema and may be written in a proprietary language that's difficult to maintain. Designing a business logic layer in your middle tier generally is easier to develop and maintain.
Bean-managed persistence	BMP entity beans may suffer from hard-coded SQL, difficult-to-maintain database logic, and $n + 1$ database calls to load n bean instances. Entity beans using container-managed persistence generally are more efficient and easier to develop, if used properly.
Custom primary key generator	If not designed carefully, custom primary key generators may require synchronization that becomes a scalability bottleneck. Better scalability, with less work, may be realized by using automatic primary key generators already provided by your database. To help, JDBC 3.0 includes new methods to facilitate the retrieval of automatically generated fields.
Caches	If the data in your cache is changing more often than it's being used, then the number of cache hits may not justify the complexity of caching while preserving data integrity.
Custom resource pools	The use of custom resource pools in the name of better performance may prevent your application server from managing resources effectively. Stability may deteriorate unless the pools already provided by your server are used.

optimizations are pure speculation. However, by first identifying the most valuable optimizations, whether at a high or low level, you can concentrate your efforts where they're most needed.

9.2.2 Solution 1: Plan, but don't act (yet)

Performance requirements are the solution for Premature Optimization. Without well-defined goals, you'll try forever to optimize every line of code you write to mitigate a performance backlash. However, by defining measurable goals for performance-critical use cases, you can optimize pragmatically, based on patterns in user behavior and data usage. Your energy is focused on solving the most critical performance issues first.

In our experience, the best performance gains are realized when following the advice given in the simple motto, "make it run, make it right, make it fast." Notice that this advice speaks to the order in which you take action, not necessarily the order in which you consider the necessity of those actions. In other words, you should take action to improve performance only when not doing so would preclude you from delivering a successful application. The earlier you know what determines success, the better.

Knowing when to take action isn't always clear-cut. We're constantly trying to strike a delicate balance between optimizing the code we write today and building an application that can achieve expected levels of performance. On one hand, you want to keep the code efficient without racking up too much time tuning. On the other hand, you need to consider the performance requirements of your application early and often. If you don't keep in mind how your decisions might impact performance, chances are when you finally do look up, you'll be aimed straight for a tree. Nevertheless, you can avoid possible disasters by expending effort to improve performance only when you've gathered sufficient evidence to let you prioritize and focus on optimizations that will truly make a difference.

If you defer performance tuning until it's proven to be a high-yield investment, you'll have a chance to validate your design with working code and tests. At this point in the development cycle, you will be able to understand the design well enough to consider the potential benefits of global and local optimizations toward meeting performance goals. Better yet, with a solid foundation of tests, you will be able to tune safely, knowing that the tests will fail if tweaking code causes existing functionality to break. In the meantime, writing well-factored, modular code puts you in a position to tune economically down the road, if necessary.

9.2.3 *Solution 2: Write well-factored, modular code*

Until performance improvements are necessary, write code that is as simple and clean as possible. The time you'll save if you write the simplest and cleanest code as a matter of course can be used later to optimize those few places where code accidentally gets complex and laden.

If you find opportunities to improve performance, remember that simple designs that use well-factored, modular code are more amenable to performance tuning than more complicated designs. In general, well-factored code is easier to change. And code that's easy to change is easier to tune. By encapsulating implementation details, modular components can respond to change, allowing us to change their underlying code without breaking their clients. Moreover, well-factored, modular code exposes succinct methods that serve as excellent starting points for optimizing a particular code path. Take, for example, the method in listing 9.1 responsible for withdrawing an amount from a bank account, designed as an entity EJB.

Listing 9.1   Code that is not well factored is also difficult to tune

```
public double withdraw(int accountId, double amount)
  throws Exception {

    InitialContext context = new InitialContext();            Find the
                                                               specified
    Object homeRef = context.lookup("AccountHome");           account
                                                               by its ID
    AccountHome accountHome =   (AccountHome)PortableRemoteObject.
      narrow(homeRef, AccountHome.class);

    Account account = accountHome.findByPrimaryKey(accountId);

    account.setBalance(account.getBalance() - amount);        Withdraw the
                                                               specified amount
    return account.getBalance();                              of money
}
```

Notice how all the logic is inlined in the method. If we were to run a code profiler on this code, we would find it difficult to ascertain which piece of logic—finding the appropriate account or withdrawing the specified amount—consumes the most time. The profiler would merely decompose the overall method time into the individual execution times of each method invoked. However, we'd like to know which coarse-grained code path could benefit most from tuning. To make this monolithic method easier to read, let's refactor it a bit, as shown in listing 9.2.

Listing 9.2   Well-factored code enables a code profiler to help you tune effectively

```
double withdraw(int accountId, double amount) {
                                                       Find the specified
    Account account = findAccount(accountId);          account by its ID

    return account.withdraw(amount);          Withdraw the specified
}                                             amount of money
```

Our refactoring organized the inlined code into two distinct methods: find-Account() and withdraw(). In applying this refactoring, not only have we made the code simpler and more modular, we've also enabled the code profiler to help us. The code profiler can now quantify the individual cost of each code path and point us directly to the starting point of the most expensive path. And, as an added bonus, once we optimize a particular method, that method can be used by other components in our application, providing better performance many times over.

Now, let's consider what would happen if, instead of building performance into our design, we attempt to bolt on performance after the design is finished.

9.3 Antipattern: Performance Afterthoughts

Developing applications that perform well requires prior intent. If performance is important, it must be baked in to the application, not bolted on afterwards. We learned this lesson the hard way a few years back. (And one of us has the hairline to prove it!) The database we were using had a serious bottleneck in its locking strategy. When used with applications that read more data than they wrote, the database was lightning fast. Yet whenever multiple concurrent users attempted frequent database updates, this particular database was clearly the wrong tool for the job. Unfortunately, we didn't know the bottleneck existed until it was too late. Although we knew from the beginning that the application needed to scale in order to be successful, we didn't plan for scalability early enough. We assumed that the application would scale, and if it didn't, we figured we would have time later to refactor the application's design to be more scalable. Building a prototype that demonstrated a few performance-critical use cases under load would have alerted us earlier to the impending doom.

Just because you're using EJB technology doesn't mean you can disregard performance concerns. It's true that any worthy EJB container will help you manage resources for the best possible performance. However, perfuming a poorly performing application with the scent of EJB won't keep the flies away.

We can increase our application's probability of success by using simple designs tactically with well-factored, modular code, but that, too, is no substitute for strategically planning for performance. This presents a conundrum. If we delay considering performance until right before the application goes live, it's usually too little too late. Then again, we don't want to speculate on performance at the expense of rapidly delivering valuable software. The answer to this problem lies in continuous planning and measurement.

9.3.1 Solution: Plan early and often

To counterbalance premature optimization, we need to plan proactively for performance. That's not to say we should attempt to predict future performance demands and carve a plan in stone. We'll be sorely disappointed when, as often happens, things don't go according to that plan. Indeed, our perspective inevitably will alter as we learn more about our application and its users. Consequently, the performance plan is subject to frequent change. Planning for performance requires that we constantly consider the current state and goals of our application, by taking measurements and making course corrections throughout the project.

As the delivery date approaches, no doubt we'll know which aspects of our application suffer from poor performance. Furthermore, we'll have more accurate estimates of the production load on our application and the respective hardware necessary to handle that load. Performance plans may change as a result of this information, and we should consider this a good thing.

In the meantime, the performance planning process will help us head off potential problems at the earliest opportunity. If we continually plan for performance, we'll be able to see obstacles in the terrain ahead and react in time to avoid a crash. Let's consider the following guidelines for performance planning:

1   *Understand the application's usage patterns*   Users generally expect different levels of service, depending on the feature of the application they are using at the time. Users expect some use cases to respond rapidly and understand when others are slower. A web user, for example, expects to navigate a product catalog quickly. Yet, when an online order is placed, the same user will accept a delayed order confirmation via email. Understanding patterns in user behavior, and the data and resources required to support that behavior, provides invaluable input into the performance planning process.

2   *Prioritize performance requirements*   To maximize your time and dollars, you should satisfy the performance requirement with the highest business value first. For example, optimizing a product catalog for maximum responsiveness when browsed under load is arguably a better investment than optimizing your email server for faster order confirmation. Once the top performance requirement has been demonstrated successfully, you can work on the next highest priority requirement. Rinse and repeat.

3   *Write automated performance tests*   Performance tests that unambiguously define and validate the performance requirements of your application are essential in helping you meet desired performance goals. Without a target, you'll never know when you've hit the mark. Good performance tests express objective exit criteria in an executable format. In other words, running these tests will help you decide if tuning is necessary, and, if so, when tuning should stop. Tests also prevent tendencies to overoptimize based on speculation or commit too early to designs and infrastructure that seem to promise improved performance.

4   *Build modular components*   Components that hide their implementation insulate the rest of the application from changes made to improve

performance. Using these components, you can start with a simple algorithm that works, even if it may incur a few extra seconds of overhead. As you learn more about your application and its uses, you can easily swap in a new, blazingly fast algorithm or data structure, for example.

5   *Revise plans based on feedback*   Once performance goals have been identified and prioritized, you must demonstrate performance as early as possible to get feedback. You'll want to know sooner rather than later if you're making design decisions that may prohibit your application from meeting user demands. If you feed this information back into the planning process, you can steer the design to meet your performance goals continually. You can respond more readily to change, rather than dutifully marching to an inflexible master plan.

6   *Understand your EJB server's configuration options*   In your haste to tear the wrapper off your new EJB server, a few finer features may go unnoticed. Server vendors differentiate themselves from their competitors, providing different knobs and levers you can twist and pull to improve performance. If you understand the available options, you'll know when to leverage rather than build for successful performance. Study and investigate the contents of the box. Then experiment and see what happens. Your tests will announce impending danger if your application starts to sputter.

7   *Schedule the availability of production hardware*   Your plan should include testing on production-quality hardware as soon as possible. Indeed, how your application performs for real users is what matters most ultimately. Everything else is just preparation.

Remember, it's not the plan that's important, but the planning. With that in mind, let's get down in the trenches with a real, live application.

9.4   *Grist for the tuning mill*

Let's say we've accepted a mission to develop yet another online product catalog. Our customer group—those folks defining the requirements of our application—has decided that users want to browse a list of all products for a particular category within a product catalog. The initial user interface will be an HTML browser, but it's imperative that the catalog browsing service be available to other types of distributed clients. This requirement is not unlike the others we've been delivering, from which a service-oriented architecture has emerged.

We conclude that the simplest approach would be to publish a remote façade that encapsulates the business logic of querying a product catalog. We dub it the catalog service. A stateless session bean seems like the logical choice given our architecture and experience, so let's make it the centerpiece of our design.

9.4.1 *Putting an EJB to the test*

Before diving into the implementation of our catalog service, let's start by writing a test. Why? Well, how else will we know what code to write? If we write a test first, we'll have an example of the catalog service's intended use. In addition to demonstrating the intent of the catalog service, the test can validate automatically that the catalog service returns the correct results. Once the test passes, we're done!

Listing 9.3 shows the JUnit test, which queries for all products in the snowboard category of the product catalog. (Note: a full tutorial on JUnit goes beyond the scope of this chapter. The *JUnit Primer*[1] will help get you up and running quickly.)

> **Listing 9.3 Unit testing the product catalog service**

```
public class CatalogTest extends TestCase {

    public CatalogTest(String name) {
        super(name);
    }

    public void testGetProducts() throws Exception {

        String snowboardCategory = "Snowboard";

        Catalog catalog = (Catalog)getCatalogHome().create();

        Collection products =
            catalog.getProductsByCategory(snowboardCategory);

        assertEquals(25, products.size());

        Iterator productIter = products.iterator();
        while (productIter.hasNext()) {
            ProductDetails product = (ProductDetails) productIter.next();
            assertEquals(snowboardCategory, product.getCategory());
        }

        catalog.remove();
    }
}
```

---

1 http://www.clarkware.com/articles/JUnitPrimer.html

The test case has a single test method, `testGetProducts()`, that starts by using the `Catalog` home interface to create a remote reference to a `Catalog` session bean instance. The `Catalog` remote interface represents a façade—a black box from the client's perspective—that finds products in a catalog. Using the remote `Catalog` reference, the test then queries for all products in the snowboard category. We expect exactly 25 products in this category because before running the test we created 25 example products in the snowboard category of the product catalog database. Iterating over the resulting collection of products, the test validates that the catalog service only returns the products in the snowboard category.

Excellent! Now there's just one problem: We have to get the test to pass.

9.4.2 *Passing the test*

To get the test to pass, we have to write the code for the `Catalog` EJB. All EJB components require a remote interface, home interface, and bean class. We won't actually show the code here because, frankly, the implementation doesn't matter. Instead, we'll just show the design of one possible solution. Our priority should be to begin by writing clean and simple code. We won't worry about performance here. We just want to validate that our design is usable and our code produces the correct results, thus avoiding the risk of overspending on performance too early. Running the test from the remote client's perspective gives us confidence that the catalog service is working as we expect. We can change and tune the underlying code without the fear that existing functionality might silently break. If it does, the test will surely let out a scream.

Under the hood in the `Catalog` bean class, we code the bean to use JDBC to query our product table directly through a database connection. The values in our database table are then packaged and returned to the client in a collection of light-weight `ProductDetails` DTOs. In future use cases, administrative users may update the products in a catalog. This updating might require a more complex persistence mechanism, for example, the type of persistence afforded by an entity bean. We'll cross that bridge when we get there. Right now we're concerned only with retrieving read-only product information, so a simple stateless session bean wired up to the database will do just fine. Figure 9.3 shows a UML sequence diagram illustrating the interaction of our recently built components.

Notice that all business logic occurs on the server side, behind the façade of the `Catalog` interface. As such, our design is modular. If performance becomes an issue, we can tune the code behind the `Catalog` interface without adversely affecting its remote clients. That's reassuring because we have a sneaky suspicion that tuning may be in our immediate future.

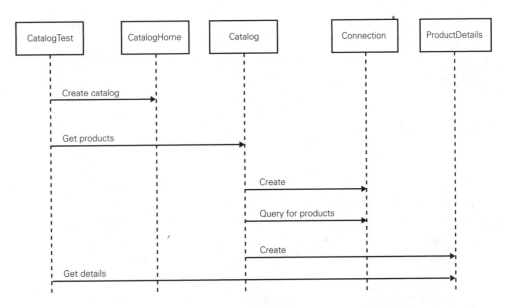

Figure 9.3   The Catalog stateless session bean, wired directly to the database, is used to query the catalog for all products in a product category. The test stands in for a client, demonstrating a usage scenario and validating that expected results are returned.

We've written just enough code to get the test to pass. We've made it work and made it right. Now, let's make it fast.

9.4.3   *Specifying response time as a measure of success*

Up until now, we've written simple code so that the test would pass. In doing so, we certainly didn't forget the hard-earned wisdom we gained designing distributed systems over the years. Rather, we made a concerted effort to determine the workability of our design and code first, before speculating on performance.

With much pride, we demonstrate the new catalog service to our customer, who is delighted. After kicking the tires a bit, our customer hunkers down at our test machine and proceeds to press the button that lists the snowboard category products over and over again. Our customer likes the fact that the new catalog service is working this soon in the schedule, so now we're ready to start polishing. The customer consensus is that the service just isn't fast enough; we need to improve performance.

The average response time of the web page to query and list 25 products is approximately 1.4 seconds. We think we can do better than that with a little tuning, but we need a way to measure success. So we ask our customer group to write a new performance requirement. We watch as they scratch their heads and mumble a bit, but finally they draft a performance:

> *The average response time of the catalog web page listing up to 25 products should not exceed 1 second.*

Great, now we have a goal!

9.4.4 *Seeing light at the end of the tuning tunnel*

To satisfy our new performance requirement, we need to shave off about a half-second of the response time, then stop tuning before we hit the point of diminishing returns. However, we're not sure whether to start chiseling in the presentation layer or the business logic layer. We want to focus our attention on tuning the sections of code that contribute the most overhead to the overall response time. Guessing would be a fool's game, so we put our trusty code profiler on the case to hunt down the busiest code. Table 9.2 shows the results:

Table 9.2   Using a code profiler takes the guesswork out of tuning by identifying hot spots worth optimizing. Always seek the advice of a code profiler before attempting to tune code.

Method	Total time (ms)
CatalogEJB.getProductsByCategory()	1327.0
CatalogServlet.service()	10.0
CatalogEJB.getConnection()	10.0
CatalogEJB.runQuery()	15.0
	1362.0

The code profiler identifies the CatalogEJB.getProductsByCategory() method as the major contributor to the total response time. Well, that rules out tuning the presentation layer for any observable gain in performance. The top contributor is the EJB method, not the servlet method that presents its results. The profiler results also rule out tuning the database interaction. The time it takes to obtain a database connection and execute the SQL query is insignificant compared to the business logic in the EJB.

We have no question that the culprit is the code in the EJB that transforms database rows into products. But when we're done tuning, how will we know we've made good progress? What if our tuning activities cause performance to take a step backward? Fear begins to envelop us as we're reminded of endless hours spent with the subject of our next antipattern—Thrash-tuning.

9.5 *Antipattern: Thrash-tuning*

I am barely a third of the way down the hill, contemplating disaster, when something finally clicks. Instead of focusing on every slight ripple in the snow, I concentrate only on obstacles that might impact my balance or my course down the mountain. I'm able to keep my eyes further ahead, improving my ability to plan and react. With this improvement I husband my waning strength better, saving it for the biggest challenges—like that tree just ahead! I've entered the zone that my mentors so often describe.

If you're always looking at your feet, you can't anticipate what's up ahead. And if you can't anticipate, you can't determine whether your microadjustments are making any progress toward the ultimate goal. Before long, you're bound to diverge hopelessly off course.

Thrash-tuning is a nasty habit born out of undisciplined performance tuning. You know the drill: change a tuning parameter here, tweak some code there, then run the application. *Is it faster? No, it actually seems to be slower! Interesting. Now which change caused that to happen?* Lacking clear knowledge, you repeat the cycle, over and over again.

Without a baseline to measure against, Thrash-tuning is entirely unpredictable. You may spend days tuning in circles with only a minor improvement to the application's overall performance. Sometimes you get lucky and increase performance by a single order of magnitude in a quick round of thrashing, but you'll soon find that's the exception. As a general rule, Thrash-tuning can consume hours or days of your life, without amounting to much good.

The following are common ways to invoke the curse of Thrash-tuning:

- **Changing more than one thing at a time**   In the rush to get the most bang for your tuning buck, you change multiple things at once, but doing so makes the individual contributions of those changes indistinguishable from each other. Multiple changes also makes backing out a change that degrades performance difficult.

- **Forgetting to measure between changes**   Without quantifiable evidence that a particular change improves performance, you can't clearly determine its impact. Performance goals always seem to be just beyond your grasp.

- **Not knowing when to stop**   Remember, Thrash-tuning is a habit and a particularly hard one to kick. You may find yourself tuning endlessly. Performance tests are the cure, telling you when enough is enough.

If these scenarios sound all too familiar, you're not alone. Both novice and veterans alike have suffered similar fates at the hands of EJB applications. The sheer number of opportunities for improving EJB performance makes falling into a vicious tuning cycle deceivingly easy. At one end of the spectrum, you can change deployment descriptors quickly to dynamically influence performance. At the opposite end, you can apply high-level design patterns, using general knowledge gained from distributed computing.

The difficulty lies in choosing an approach and measuring its impact in isolation. A solution applied in hopes of improving performance for one aspect of our application may cause unwanted secondary effects in other areas. Consequently, performance tuning quickly turns into a delicate balancing act. We become painfully aware that multiple controls often exist for performance with complex interactions. Each new interaction increases the odds that making a change—one that theoretically should improve performance—may not make a difference.

Besides being incredibly frustrating, when thrash-tuning runs rampant, it has the potential to rob us of enormous amounts of development time. The more you scratch it, the more it itches. A sure-fire way to stop this irritation is to use a sound methodology with information derived from automated performance testing.

9.5.1 *Solution: Use a performance testing methodology*

The only defense we've found against falling prey to Thrash-tuning is the use of tests to gather evidence first, before making an attempt to improve performance. We've tried predicting whether an optimization would improve performance, and yet, after hours of navel gazing, we remained undecided. Although not as therapeutic as navel gazing, writing tests that measure the impact of changes has given us much better success.

To ensure that you're always ratcheting forward toward optimal performance, current performance must be automatically compared to a baseline. Doing so keeps the performance of your application from going off the rails. If you use a methodology like the following, your performance stays on track, never more than one change away from the last baseline:

1. Begin with clean and modular code that's easy to understand and modify, and driven by tests that express its intentions and expectations.

2. Choose quantifiable performance goals for the code.

3. Profile the code to identify hot spots with the highest return on investment.

4. Write and run an automated test that baselines current performance.

5 Make a change intended to improve performance.

6 Run the automated test again to measure the gain (or loss) in performance.

7 Repeat as often as necessary until the application meets its performance goals.

Notice that we use a test to measure both before and after a tuning change is made. The test tells us if the tuning did any good. If not, we can back out the change to arrive safely at the last good baseline. Bear in mind that we might need to give caches, pools, and other performance-enhancing mechanisms a chance to warm up before taking a measurement. Otherwise, the observed performance may be thrown off by a cold start. In other words, the test environment has to be predictable, and the tests must be repeatable.

This easy-to-use formula really shines when applied incrementally to solve the most pressing performance problem at any given time. Once performance has improved in one area, and a test is in place to keep that problem continually in check, you can repeat the formula with the next most important performance problem.

We'll use this methodology to confidently tune our catalog service throughout the remainder of this chapter. In fact, we've already taken the first steps toward our goal. We wrote clean and modular code to make our test pass. Demonstrating our results to our customer prompted them to draft a realistic performance requirement we can measure. Before beginning to hack and slash, we used a profiler to find high-yield tuning opportunities. Now we're ready to begin tuning so that we can deliver on the goal our customer has given us. First, let's make sure we get started on the right foot by avoiding the tedium of manual testing.

9.6 *Mini-antipattern: Manual Performance Testing*

When we first turned over our catalog service to our customer, we watched as they poked and prodded, and we noticed that they grew weary of manually hitting the web page to assess performance. A couple times, they had to redo tests because the manual process wasn't followed consistently. Clearly, we need a more efficient and less error-prone testing strategy. As the suite of performance tests grows, running them all manually just doesn't scale. So many tests to run, so little time. Our team has earned a reputation for cranking out high-quality features like clockwork. To live up to that great reputation, we can't drag ourselves to the test lab to play the role of simulated web users every time we change something that impacts performance. That's what computers are for!

When push comes to shove and deadlines loom, manual tests are always the second thing (right after documentation, of course) that gets selectively ignored. Peril usually isn't too far behind. The next time we tune something without the safety of automated tests, our confidence will wane, and we'll fall back into a Thrash-tuning cycle again. Our stress goes up, the number of defects increases, and pretty soon we're burnt out.

9.6.1 Solution: Automate performance testing

Automated performance tests are like canaries in a coal mine. If we keep them running, they'll continue to measure whether performance goals are being met in the face of change. If a change causes performance to backslide, well, we'll know it at the poor birdie's expense.

Good performance tests offer many advantages, including

- automatically checking their own results
- providing immediate feedback in the form of a simple pass or fail status
- retaining their value over time through repeated testing of expectations
- running continuously without manual intervention
- instilling confidence to change code with impunity

At the least, we should run our performance tests once a day as a sanity check. If we're actively tuning code or changing the runtime environment, we should run them more often. The repeatability of the tests will prove our application's readiness for production.

A plethora of tools already exists for performance testing automation. Apache JMeter,[2] for example, is an open source desktop application that measures the performance of an application's behavior under load. Traditionally used to test web applications, over time JMeter has been made more extensible. You can now write custom extensions to put almost any server, network, or object under load. JMeter is also highly configurable; it includes a collection of test listeners for graphically visualizing performance. It can also be configured to include test assertions. For example, you can assert that a request for a web page returns within a specified amount of time. Yet, although JMeter is a valuable tool for performance testing, it falls short of our goals for automation. Specifically, the test results must be manually inspected each time the tests are run. While we could

---

2 http://jakarta.apache.org/jmeter/

probably extend JMeter to satisfy our desire for automation, instead we opt to use a complementary tool.

In this chapter we'll use JUnitPerf, an open source performance-testing tool that wraps existing functional tests written in JUnit. We choose JUnitPerf because it allows us to write tests that automatically check their own results and provide immediate feedback with an unambiguous pass or fail status. JUnitPerf is also tightly integrated with JUnit, so our performance tests can be run automatically alongside our functional JUnit tests.

9.7 *Automated performance testing with JUnitPerf*

We've already validated the feasibility of our EJB design with working code and a functional test. Making it fast enough to please our customer is our next order of business. However, we don't want to risk breaking functionality by complicating our code with performance optimizations. To be useful, the catalog service has to work right and perform well at the same time. Let's explore how JUnitPerf can keep both these interests in check.

9.7.1 *JUnitPerf overview*

JUnitPerf[3] is an open source set of JUnit extensions for automated performance testing. JUnitPerf tests transparently wrap standard JUnit tests and measure their performance. In other words, we can build upon our existing functional test to make sure the code continues to work right. The JUnitPerf tests tell us if the code is fast enough. If a performance test doesn't meet expectations, the whole test fails. If the functional test fails, the performance test fails. Conversely, if the performance test passes, then we have confidence that tuning didn't cause existing functionality to break. Table 9.3 describes the major JUnitPerf classes and interfaces.

Because JUnitPerf tests can run any class that implements JUnit's Test interface, we could use JUnitPerf to measure the performance of any test conforming to this interface. In this section, we use it to wrap the JUnit test we wrote earlier for our catalog service. We could also use JUnitPerf to run HttpUnit tests and measure the performance of our entire web application, for example. Another option might be to use JUnitPerf to run Cactus tests to validate our catalog service's business logic from within the EJB container.

---

3 http://www.clarkware.com/software/JUnitPerf.html

Table 9.3   JUnitPerf is a collection of classes and interfaces for performance testing JUnit tests.

Class/Interface	Description
TimedTest	Runs a JUnit test and measures its elapsed time. A TimedTest is constructed with a specified maximum elapsed time. By default, a TimedTest will wait for the completion of its JUnit test and then fail if the maximum elapsed time was exceeded. Alternatively, a TimedTest can be constructed to immediately fail when the maximum elapsed time of its JUnit test is exceeded.
LoadTest	Runs a JUnit test with a simulated number of concurrent users and iterations. The load can be incrementally ramped by registering a Timer instance to control the delay between the additions of each concurrent user.
Timer	An interface implemented by classes that define timing strategies to optionally control the delay between additions of users in a LoadTest.
ConstantTimer	A Timer with a constant delay.
RandomTimer	A Timer with a random delay and a uniformly distributed variation.

But that's another day. Right now, our customer is getting nervous. Let's put our money where our mouth is with an automated response time test for the catalog service.

9.7.2   Testing response time

Recall that we're staring down the barrel of a response time of approximately 1.4 seconds to display 25 products on a web page. We won't sleep well until the response time is under 1 second. Luckily, we know what to do. The code profiler indicated earlier that optimizing the CatalogEJB.getProductsByCategory() method would be the smart move. How will we know when we're done? Well, when a performance test passes, of course.

We want to write a test that will fail if the response time of our use case exceeds 1 second. To do that, we create a JUnitPerf TimedTest instance that wraps our existing CatalogTest.testGetProducts() test case method. Listing 9.4 shows the JUnitPerf test used to validate our performance expectations.

Listing 9.4   Testing the response time of the catalog service

```
public class CatalogResponseTimeTest {

  public static Test suite() {

    long maxTimeInMillis = 1000;

    Test test = new CatalogTest("testGetProducts");
    Test timedTest = new TimedTest(test, maxTimeInMillis);
    return timedTest;
```

```
    }

    public static void main(String args[]) {
      junit.textui.TestRunner.run(suite());
    }
  }
```

As a convenient way to run our test, our test defines a `suite()` method called by the JUnit test runner in the `main()` method. We run the `CatalogResponseTime-Test`, and it fails with the following output:

```
.TimedTest (WAITING):
    testGetProducts(com.bitterejb.catalog.ejb.CatalogTest): 1352 ms
F
Time: 1.352
There was 1 failure:
1) testGetProducts(com.bitterejb.catalog.ejb.CatalogTest)
Maximum elapsed time exceeded! Expected 1000ms, but was 1352ms.

FAILURES!!!
Tests run: 1,   Failures: 1,   Errors: 0
```

All right, we knew that would happen. We just wanted to see if the test was really measuring anything. The test expected the response time to be less than 1 second, but sure enough, it measured the same response time as observed by our customer—1.4 seconds. Now we have a solid baseline from which to work. We should be able to optimize code, improving the response time until the test passes. If the test doesn't eventually pass, we'll need to start turning the performance knob in the other direction or look for another knob to turn.

Be aware of a subtle "gotcha!" when writing JUnitPerf tests. The response time measured by a `TimedTest` includes the elapsed time of the `testXXX()` method and its test fixture—the `setUp()` and `tearDown()` methods. Therefore, the maximum elapsed time specified in the `TimedTest` should be adjusted accordingly to take into account any cost of the existing test's fixture.

9.7.3 *Tweaking code*

To get the test to pass, we follow the code profiler's advice and optimize the logic that created `ProductDetails` objects from the rows in our database. The SQL query is sufficiently fast, according to the profiler, so nothing is gained barking up that tree. After optimizing, we run the `CatalogResponseTimeTest` again, and it gives us the following output:

```
TimedTest (WAITING):
testGetProducts(com.bitterejb.catalog.ejb.CatalogTest): 751 ms

Time: 0.751

OK (1 test)
```

Hey, that did the trick! The test tells us that we made good progress. Had the test failed, we could have continued to optimize until it passed.

After showing off the improved catalog service to our customer, we add this test to our suite of performance tests. As we go forward, the automated test will continue to keep the response time of this use case in check.

9.7.4 *Specifying scalability as a measure of success*

At this point we know how long it takes for one user to get a list of 25 products using the catalog service. How long will the same process take if our application is under the stress of multiple concurrent users? Until now we haven't thought much about scalability, but we're confident that our simple design won't let us down. Here's where the rubber meets the road.

Our customer is impressed with our track record of meeting goals, and now is ready to hand us a new challenge. Performance planning early and often has enabled the customer to accurately estimate the expected load on the production system. The customer now wants to improve upon our performance success by writing a new performance requirement, which states:

The response time of the catalog web page listing up to 25 products should not exceed 1 second under a load of five concurrent users.

In other words, the catalog service should scale to handle five concurrent users while consistently maintaining the single-user response time we demonstrated earlier. That's a tall order. Let's use JUnitPerf to see how far off the mark our application currently is.

9.7.5 *Testing response time under load*

We have an automated JUnitPerf test that measures single-user response time. We'd like to use a similar testing technique to put this test under a load of five concurrent users while measuring each user's response time. We want the test to fail if any user's response time exceeds one second. Then we can follow our performance testing methodology to tune until the test passes.

To do so, we write a JUnitPerf test that creates a LoadTest instance passing in a TimedTest instance and a number of concurrent users. The TimedTest in turn wraps our existing `CatalogTest.testGetProducts()` test case method. Listing 9.5 shows the JUnitPerf test used to validate our scalability expectations.

Listing 9.5   Testing the scalability of the catalog service

```
public class CatalogLoadTest {

  public static Test suite() {

     long maxTimeInMillis = 1000;
     int concurrentUsers = 5;

     Test test = new CatalogTest("testGetProducts");
     Test timedTest = new TimedTest(test, maxTimeInMillis);
     Test loadTest = new LoadTest(timedTest, concurrentUsers);
     return loadTest;
  }
  public static void main(String args[]) {
     junit.textui.TestRunner.run(suite());
  }
}
```

We run the `CatalogLoadTest` , which fails with the following output:

```
. . . . . . . . . .
TimedTest (WAITING):
testGetProducts(com.bitterejb.catalog.ejb.CatalogTest): 771 ms
TimedTest (WAITING): testGetProducts(com.bitterejb.catalog.ejb.CatalogTest):
   1372 ms
F
TimedTest (WAITING): testGetProducts(com.bitterejb.catalog.ejb.CatalogTest):
   1963 ms
F
TimedTest (WAITING): testGetProducts(com.bitterejb.catalog.ejb.CatalogTest):
   2584 ms
F
TimedTest (WAITING): testGetProducts(com.bitterejb.catalog.ejb.CatalogTest):
   3255 ms
F
Time: 3.40
There were 4 failures:

1) testGetProducts(com.bitterejb.catalog.ejb.CatalogTest)
   Maximum elapsed time exceeded! Expected 1000ms, but was 1372ms.
2) testGetProducts(com.bitterejb.catalog.ejb.CatalogTest)
   Maximum elapsed time exceeded! Expected 1000ms, but was 1963ms.
3) testGetProducts(com.bitterejb.catalog.ejb.CatalogTest)
   Maximum elapsed time exceeded! Expected 1000ms, but was 2584ms.
4) testGetProducts(com.bitterejb.catalog.ejb.CatalogTest)
   Maximum elapsed time exceeded! Expected 1000ms, but was 3255ms.
```

. . .

```
FAILURES!!!
Tests run: 5,  Failures: 4,  Errors: 0
```

Ouch! Our application can't scale beyond one user. Notice that the first user's response time is within the 1-second limit, but the other users' response times bust the threshold. Worse yet, the response times increased for each successive user, indicating that our application has a bottleneck restricting its ability to scale.

So we fire up the code profiler and run the `CatalogLoadTest` to obtain clues. The code profiler doesn't let us down. Table 9.4 shows what the profiler finds when the catalog service is under load.

Table 9.4   Running a profiler on the catalog service under load reveals contention for a database connection. Load testing tools help illuminate scalability bottlenecks.

Method	Average time (ms)
`CatalogEJB.getProductsByCategory()`	716.0
`CatalogServlet.service()`	10.0
`CatalogEJB.getConnection()`	1248.0
`CatalogEJB.runQuery()`	15.0
	1989.0

The `CatalogEJB.getConnection()` method that was only taking around 10 milliseconds in our initial run of the code profiler is now taking up the majority of the overall response time. Let's tune that method while continuing to test the single-user response time.

9.7.6   *Using a connection pool to increase throughput*

Based on the evidence provided by the code profiler, we conclude that a single database connection is the limiting factor to scaling our application. Consequently, requests for a connection are being queued. Each successive user's response time in turn rises above the desired threshold.

In this case, pooling database connections is a low cost, high reward change sure to improve scalability. Before you start rolling your eyes over yet another example demonstrating the virtues of connection pooling, allow us to explain. We realize connection pooling is the poster child for many discussions on performance. Indeed, it's a well-known performance problem, and that's exactly why we're using it here. We want the problem—and the solution—to be familiar so

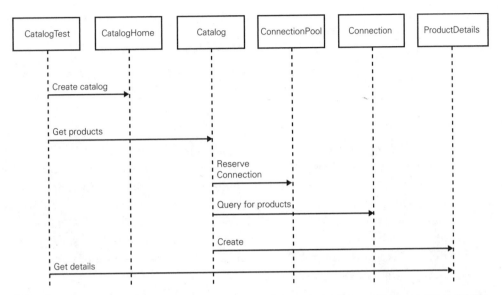

Figure 9.4 **Refactoring the catalog service to use a database connection pool improves the scalability without sacrificing code complexity.**

you can focus on how to test it. It's not about the connection pool; it's about the technique to discover it.

It's also worth noting that we've run across more than one improperly sized connection pool. Worse yet, we've seen custom connection pools that were implemented incorrectly. (Yet another victim of the Not Invented Here antipattern.) In other words, just because you're using a connection pool doesn't necessarily mean you get instant scalability. You have to test for that, so let's get back to the technique.

Instead of synchronizing access to a single database connection shared by multiple users, we refactor our Catalog EJB to use a database connection pool. We then configure the pool size to five active connections to improve scalability. Figure 9.4 shows a UML sequence diagram illustrating the use of the database connection pool.

Now we run the CatalogLoadTest again, and it passes with the following output:

```
. . . . .
TimedTest (WAITING): testGetProducts(com.bitterejb.catalog.ejb.CatalogTest):
    751 ms
TimedTest (WAITING): testGetProducts(com.bitterejb.catalog.ejb.CatalogTest):
    812 ms
```

```
TimedTest (WAITING): testGetProducts(com.bitterejb.catalog.ejb.CatalogTest):
    822 ms
TimedTest (WAITING): testGetProducts(com.bitterejb.catalog.ejb.CatalogTest):
    831 ms
TimedTest (WAITING): testGetProducts(com.bitterejb.catalog.ejb.CatalogTest):
    811 ms

Time: 0.972

OK (5 tests)
```

Outstanding! Our scalability test is passing, and the underlying functional test continues to pass. This tells us that refactoring to use a database connection pool didn't break anything. As we expected, the refactoring actually improved scalability. Because requests don't need to be queued before being serviced, the response times are fairly consistent for each concurrent user. The test validates our design as able to handle five concurrent users without any specific user experiencing a delayed response time. If, in the future, the response time of any user increases beyond the limit set in our load test, the test will fail.

9.7.7 *Testing throughput*

We may end up with performance requirements expressed as throughput rather than as response time under load. For example, we might want to write an automated test to measure the total amount of time elapsed while servicing all five concurrent users. Using JUnitPerf, we simply reverse the order in which we create the tests, this time wrapping the LoadTest in a TimedTest, as indicated in listing 9.6.

Listing 9.6 Testing the throughput of the catalog service

```
public class CatalogThroughputTest {

  public static Test suite() {

    long maxTimeInMillis = 1000;
    int concurrentUsers = 5;

    Test test = new CatalogTest("testGetProducts");
    Test loadTest = new LoadTest(test, concurrentUsers);
    Test timedTest = new TimedTest(loadTest, maxTimeInMillis);
    return timedTest;
  }

  public static void main(String args[]) {
    junit.textui.TestRunner.run(suite());
  }
}
```

The `CatalogThroughputTest` will fail if the catalog service is unable to process at least five catalog queries per second. After refactoring to use a database connection pool, the `CatalogThroughputTest` passes with the following output:

```
.....
TimedTest (WAITING): LoadTest (NON-ATOMIC): ThreadedTest:
  testGetProducts(com.bitterejb.catalog.ejb.CatalogTest)(repeated): 972 ms

Time: 0.972

OK (5 tests)
```

Now that we've written JUnitPerf tests to measure both response time and throughput, let's put all the numbers together into a performance model.

9.8 Modeling performance

Using our existing JUnitPerf tests, we can ramp up the user load to sketch out a model that represents our application's overall performance. Doing so will answer questions in the performance planning process like, "Will our application scale to meet the demands of 10, 100, or 1,000 concurrent users?"

As an example, figure 9.5 shows the average response time as a function of the number of concurrent users. The figure example compares the use of a database connection pool with 10 active connections to that of a single shared database connection.

Notice that with a single database connection the application cannot maintain a linear response time as the number of concurrent requests increases. That is, as more users attempt to use the application, their observed response times are elongated. In contrast, using a database connection pool allows the application to service requests to up to 25 users at a relatively constant response rate.

Figure 9.6 shows the throughput as a function of the number of concurrent users. This figure also compares the use of a database connection pool with 10 active connections to that of a single shared database connection.

Notice that, regardless of the number of concurrent users, the bottleneck caused by a single database connection limits the throughput to one catalog query per second—the application's maximum effective throughput. In contrast, by configuring the connection pool with 10 active connections, the application is able to consistently process almost 10 catalog queries per second. The application can scale to handle at least 25 concurrent users with only 10 shared connections.

Models such as these are great information radiators. You can look at them quickly and know how your application performs. Many performance testing

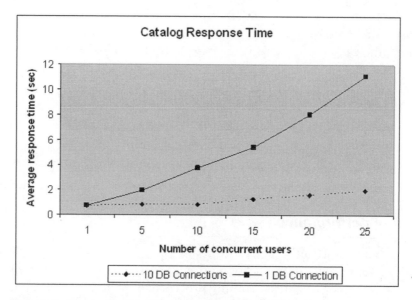

Figure 9.5   The use of a database connection pool, as indicated by the dotted line, yields a fairly constant response time for up to 25 concurrent users. With a single shared connection, as indicated by the solid line, the response time curve is exponential.

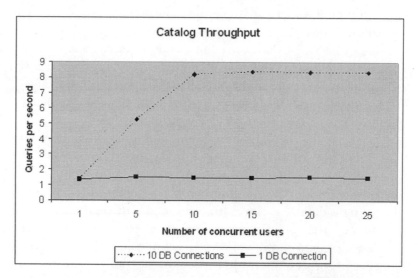

Figure 9.6   The use of a database connection pool, as indicated by the dotted line, delivers a throughput roughly equivalent to the number of active connections in the pool. With a single shared connection, as indicated by the solid line, the throughput bottoms out at one query per second.

tools, including JMeter, will automatically generate charts of this sort. Use them to your advantage.

9.9 *Mini-antipattern: Stage Fright*

If we don't test our application's performance early and often in a production-like environment, when the curtain goes up, the application may fall down in front of its live audience. Often we assume that, when an application meets its performance goals in development, it will perform equally well for its intended audience. We're usually disappointed.

To simulate realistic production traffic and usage patterns, we need to test our application's performance with representative data, tool versions, workloads, network latency, and hardware capacity. Tests that merely simulate users continually buying Chihuahuas from our online pet store won't cut it. We'll be in for an unwelcome surprise when a real user tries to buy a furry friend not already cached in the middle tier.

9.9.1 *Solution: Practice on stage*

To alleviate the fear and risk of embarrassment on stage, practice is our only recourse. Running performance tests in a production-staging environment as soon as possible, and keeping those tests running, will give us the confidence we need. The best approach to practicing for a production setting is to write tests that address our worst fears. What will happen when 10 users log in at the same time? We won't know until it happens, but we do know it's better to have it happen when we're practicing. Writing a passing login test under a 10-user load goes a long way toward boosting our confidence for the big show. In other words, tests let us safely play "what if" games with performance. By simulating a load, they can help us determine the amount of hardware we'll need to support our expected user load.

We need to give our application a dress rehearsal by testing under realistic scenarios. We'll use the same version of the virtual machine, application server, database, and other tools that will be deployed in the production environment. If caching and pooling is used to boost performance, then we can let the application warm up before running the performance tests. In other words, our tests should measure the actual performance, as observed by real users, to the maximum extent possible.

Once we've done our best to design and tune for performance under realistic loads, no substitute exists for tuning an application in production. Don't underestimate the value of a tool that can monitor a live performance. Usage patterns in a live system may behave differently than expected.

9.10 *Summary: Tuning with confidence*

In this chapter, we looked at several antipatterns that commonly plague the EJB performance tuning process. In our quiet moments, when we're sure nobody is listening, we've probably all admitted to ourselves that we've been bitten by the need for speed. However, now that we've resolved to put speed in its place, we want to avoid these antipatterns by adopting an approach that's best summarized in the carpenter's motto: measure twice, cut once.

Before tuning to improve performance, we profiled our code to find hot spots. We then measured the performance again with a failing performance test written using JUnitPerf. Only after reviewing this evidence did we attempt to change code or the runtime environment to improve performance. We also put our trust in our gauges—automated tests that specify the performance requirements set by our customer. We leveraged these tests, using them as the qualifying measure of success, to ensure that our application's performance continually improved.

The methodology proposed for side-stepping the pitfalls encountered in this chapter is applicable to any type of performance tuning activity—EJB or otherwise. The bottom line: When making a case for or against applying changes in the name of performance, don't assume facts not already in evidence. Test first, then tune with confidence.

9.11 Antipatterns in this chapter

This section covers the Premature Optimization, Performance Afterthoughts, Thrash-tuning, Manual Performance Testing, and Stage Fright antipatterns.

PREMATURE OPTIMIZATION

DESCRIPTION
Good programmers frequently try to optimize every line of code and speculate in the name of performance, without considering which code/design elements are actually performance problems.

MOST FREQUENT SCALE
Application

REFACTORED SOLUTION NAME
Performance test automation

REFACTORED SOLUTION TYPE
Process, technology

REFACTORED SOLUTION DESCRIPTION
Use the simplest code/design that will work. Establish concrete criteria and run automated performance tests against the criteria to establish the need for performance tuning. Tune only problem areas. Write well-factored and modular code that's easy to tune later, if necessary.

ANECDOTAL EVIDENCE
"It works fine, but I suspected future performance problems so I spent the afternoon making it fast." "All of my code is a little tough to read, but it's very fast." "That design/technology is going to be too slow."

SYMPTOMS, CONSEQUENCES
Fewer development cycles are left for customer requirements or meaningful optimization when unforeseen problems arise. Design and code becomes unnecessarily complex and difficult to maintain. Functionality breaks when it's tweaked to be faster.

PERFORMANCE AFTERTHOUGHTS

DESCRIPTION

Attempting to bolt performance on to an application at the end of the development cycle rather than bake it in from the beginning

MOST FREQUENT SCALE

Application

REFACTORED SOLUTION NAME

Continuous performance planning

REFACTORED SOLUTION TYPE

Process

REFACTORED SOLUTION DESCRIPTION

Gather performance requirements early and often. Build automated performance tests that continuously validate performance criteria. Performance tests help to define exactly which areas do not meet criteria to focus testing efforts. Make any necessary course corrections throughout the project based on quantifiable measurements.

TYPICAL CAUSES

Poor planning

ANECDOTAL EVIDENCE

"We will have plenty of time to performance tune at the end of the development cycle." "It's a good design. We do not need to tune for performance." "We'll let our QA department measure performance." "We're using Enterprise JavaBeans, so it should scale well."

SYMPTOMS, CONSEQUENCES

Repeated delivery of poorly performing software, redesign of critical use cases late in the development cycle, and last-minute tuning activities that are ineffective

THRASH-TUNING

DESCRIPTION

Performance tuning is difficult without a solid baseline or when multiple configuration parameters are changed at once between measurements. Attempting performance tuning in these conditions makes it difficult to gauge progress and correct problems, lengthening the overall cycle time and giving the appearance of thrashing.

MOST FREQUENT SCALE

Application

REFACTORED SOLUTION NAME

Good performance methodology

REFACTORED SOLUTION TYPE

Process

REFACTORED SOLUTION DESCRIPTION

A sound performance testing methodology and a good testing environment are the primary keys. Baseline measurements are mandatory to gauge progress. All tests should start from a common configuration and changes should be made one at a time. Focus on performance problems demonstrated by failed tests.

ROOT CAUSES

Haste, inadequate performance testing tools

ANECDOTAL EVIDENCE

"It feels faster, don't you think?" "When are we done tuning?" "What did we change to make it slower?"

SYMPTOMS, CONSEQUENCES

Inefficient performance testing and tuning, longer than expected performance tuning cycles, and unclear results of performance improvements

MANUAL PERFORMANCE TESTING

DESCRIPTION

Manually running performance tests every time something is changed doesn't scale and the tests aren't easily repeatable

MOST FREQUENT SCALE

Organization

REFACTORED SOLUTION NAME

Automated performance testing

REFACTORED SOLUTION TYPE

Process, technology

REFACTORED SOLUTION DESCRIPTION

Use a performance testing tool like JUnitPerf to build automated tests. Let a computer run the tests continuously and consistently.

TYPICAL CAUSES

Inadequate performance testing tools

ANECDOTAL EVIDENCE

"I don't have time to run that test." "I can't repeat the results of the test from run to run."

SYMPTOMS, CONSEQUENCES

The time it takes to run tests manually increases the pressure to fall back into a thrash-tuning cycle. Performance problems aren't detected consistently.

STAGE FRIGHT

DESCRIPTION

Failure to test software in its production environment with representative data, tool versions, workloads, network latency, and hardware capacity

MOST FREQUENT SCALE

Application

REFACTORED SOLUTION NAME

Production environment testing

REFACTORED SOLUTION TYPE

Process

REFACTORED SOLUTION DESCRIPTION

Test application performance in settings as close as possible to the production environment.

TYPICAL CAUSES

Pride, ignorance

ANECDOTAL EVIDENCE

"We don't have time to test in production. The system is going live tomorrow!" "Don't worry. This is good code. It should work fine in the production environment." "It was fast on my development machine."

SYMPTOMS, CONSEQUENCES

Software that performs well in development environments, but fails miserably in production settings

10

Bitter builds

This chapter contains

- Antipatterns related to build infrastructure
- Arguments for the automation of build tasks
- Problems, such as redundancy, solved by XDoclet
- Reasons for test-first development

We're a small crew of four sailing in the Atlantic. Our eyes are focused on the storm clouds to the south of us. What direction are they moving in and just how strong a storm is brewing? I had not checked the weather prediction before leaving. My three companions are inexperienced sailors, but I know enough to be wary. As we watch, the weather front rolls over us and the wind and waves suddenly pick up in force. The boat keels to starboard as we struggle to furl in the headsail. It is now a small triangle fluttering taughtly, but our main is untrimmed and it is overpowering the boat. My inexperienced crew cannot figure out how to take a reef—they cannot even identify the reefing sheet. They are moving like tipsy sailors on the heaving deck, and when one of them slips and falls on his knee, the thud makes up my mind: We're going to do what all sailors hate, take down all sails and start up the engine. With a barely audible vroom over the sound of the waves, the engine starts. We breathe easier.

EJB development has proven to be a complex and time-consuming process. Building object-oriented code is demanding in the best circumstances, but dealing with class loading issues, implementing multiple classes per bean, writing deployment descriptors, and deploying to an Application server all take time and energy away from the task at hand—developing business logic. Unit testing and integration headaches further impede making headway. In this threatening storm, manual power isn't enough anymore.

Fortunately, EJB development tools have finally begun to mature, negating any need to suffer under these rote processes, regardless of any integrated development environment (IDE) you or your peers choose. Code generation tools make implementing EJB as easy as writing the bean implementation class, then auto-generating everything else with simple metadata, a la Javadoc. Automated build tools iron out the wrinkles associated with performing regular builds and deployments, helping you stay on track and keep your schedule.

Neglect these tools at your own risk. If your development process consists of more than making a code change and running a single command to build, deploy, and verify that the code works, you're working too hard. You're also taking yourself away from the context of your business problem, slipping off your business's logic development hat and slapping on a build guru beret. When making small changes and executing tests over and over again, these context switches can easily lead to costly mistakes, taking you out of your most productive zone. The time spent executing manual build and deployment tasks can seriously add up, pushing deadlines and even breaking your spirit. Waiting for long builds or server restarts, just to verify the functionality of a bean implementation, wastes valuable development time. The longer you wait for the results of a unit test, the more likely you are to switch over and check e-mail or the latest news on Slashdot. These small distractions add up very quickly to murder productivity.

In this chapter, you'll see the cost of manual development, and learn the secrets that others have long known: how you build something is almost important as what you build. We'll introduce the tools and techniques that great EJB programmers use to automate testing, streamline builds, and generate code.

10.1 Wrapping big packages without bows

The EJB specification defines the ejb-jar format as the interface between application developers and assemblers and the container provider. An ejb-jar file is the deployable unit for the EJB architecture. The J2EE architecture specifically enables EJB container implementers to support loading and reloading ejb-jar files dynamically, independent of other deployed units like other enterprise applications, EJB, and web applications.

An ejb-jar package contains one or more beans, their classes and a deployment descriptor. The application developer constructs the initial ejb-jar file with a basic deployment descriptor. An application assembler takes ejb-jar files and edits the deployment descriptors: satisfying dependencies, configuring security, etc. The EJB container then deploys the final ejb-jar file.

10.1.1 Understanding an example EJB

Let's start by examining a trivial stateless session bean implementation and identifying the components necessary to make it deployable. First, we have the bean implementation class (listing 10.1). The bean implementation class resides only on the server and contains the actual business logic—the meat—for our EJB:

Listing 10.1   Example bean implementation

```
package ejb;

import javax.ejb.*;

public class ExampleBean implements SessionBean {
    public String trim(String s) {
        return s.trim();
    }

    public void ejbCreate()
      throws CreateException {}
    public void ejbActivate()
      throws EJBException {}
    public void ejbPassivate()
```

```
      throws EJBException {}
    public void ejbRemove()
      throws EJBException, RemoveException {}
    public void setSessionContext(SessionContext context)
      throws EJBException {}

}
```

The second component of a stateless session bean implementation is the home interface which must be deployed on both the client and server. The EJB container will implement the home interface stub, enabling clients to obtain a different stub, which implements the actual business interface (listing 10.2):

Listing 10.2   Example bean home interface

```
import javax.ejb.*;

public interface ExampleHome extends javax.ejb.EJBHome {

  public ejb.Example create() throws javax.ejb.CreateException,
    java.rmi.RemoteException;

}
```

Third, we have the bean's component interface. Like the home interface, the component interface must be deployed to the server as well as the client. The component interface exposes the actual business logic to the client (listing 10.3):

Listing 10.3   Example bean component interface

```
import javax.ejb.*;

public interface Example extends javax.ejb.EJBObject {

  public String trim(String s) throws java.rmi.RemoteException;

}
```

Last, we have the deployment descriptor—the `ejb-jar.xml` file. The deployment descriptor (listing 10.4) tells the container how to deploy the bean and contains the out-of-band information—like transaction semantics and security restrictions—that can't be determined from the bean implementation:

Listing 10.4   Example deployment descriptor

```
<?xml version="1.0" encoding="UTF-8"?>

<!DOCTYPE ejb-jar PUBLIC
  "-//Sun Microsystems, Inc.//DTD Enterprise JavaBeans 2.0//EN"
  "http://java.sun.com/dtd/ejb-jar_2_0.dtd">

<ejb-jar>
  <enterprise-beans>
    <session >
      <display-name>Example</display-name>
       <ejb-name>Example</ejb-name>
       <home>ejb.ExampleHome</home>
       <remote>ejb.Example</remote>
       <ejb-class>ejb.ExampleBean</ejb-class>
       <session-type>Stateless</session-type>
       <transaction-type>Container</transaction-type>
     </session>
    <container-transaction >
     <method>
       <ejb-name>Example</ejb-name>
       <method-intf>Remote</method-intf>
       <method-name>trim</method-name>
       <method-params>
          <method-param>java.lang.String</method-param>
       </method-params>
     </method>
     <trans-attribute>Required</trans-attribute>
    </container-transaction>
  </enterprise-beans>
</ejb-jar>
```

10.1.2 *Organizing your directory structure*

Having a well-defined set of conventions for EJB naming, packaging, and storage can go a long way toward helping developers easily identify and develop EJB, and automating the EJB build and deployment process. The "Sun Naming Conventions for Enterprise Applications" (http://java.sun.com/blueprints/code/namingconventions.html) provides you with a good starting point.

First, you need to decide where to store the EJB source files. We've found that the easiest way is to store EJB source files with the rest of the application source files and to use a packaging convention to separate them. For example, if your current module is in the package `com.mycompany.example`, you would store the EJB implementation and interface files in the `com.mycompany.example.ejb` package.

Doing so lets you easily identify and extract the EJB classes from the other common classes, and prevents potential naming collisions.

For example, if you are working with all EJB implementation classes, a naming collision might arise. If you name your EJB implementation classes using a standard convention, `<Name>Bean.java`, and operate on all files in our source tree following this convention, you will get plain JavaBeans as well. Storing the EJB files in a separate package lets you filter all source files that follow the naming convention and appear in packages containing the `ejb` package distinction.

Table 10.1 EJB classes are much easier to manage when you give them appropriate names. These suggestions are conventions that will help you identify the critical EJB types. With this approach, you will not have to worry about naming collisions, and can easily identify the purpose of an EJB.

Class naming convention	Description
Remote<Name>	Remote component interface
Remote<Name>Home	Remote home interface
Local<Name>	Local component interface
Local<Name>Home	Local home interface
<Name>Bean	Bean implementation

Before local interfaces came along, most naming conventions did not have the `Remote` prefix on the class names. Using the separate `ejb` package for EJB classes allows you to work equally well with these legacy implementations.

10.1.3 Filling the EJB JAR

An `ejb-jar` file is a Java Archive (JAR) file containing the beans' implementation classes, home and component interface classes, primary key classes for entity beans, and deployment descriptors. The `ejb-jar` file must either contain or reference classes on which the EJB depends. The standard EJB deployment descriptor is stored in the `META-INF/ejb-jar.xml` file. The `META-INF` directory may contain vendor-specific descriptors as well. The `ejb-jar` references dependent classes outside of the `ejb-jar` using the `Class-Path` attribute in the JAR file's manifest file. For example, if an `ejb-jar` depends on classes stored in two other JAR files named `common.jar` and `client.jar`, the `ejb-jar` should specify this dependence in the `META-INF/MANIFEST.MF` file (listing 10.5):

Listing 10.5 Example MANIFEST.MF file

```
Manifest-Version: 1.0
Class-Path: common.jar client.jar
```

Next, you package up each ejb-jar file into another JAR called an enterprise application archive (EAR) file. An EAR file contains one or more ejb-jar and web application archive (WAR) files as well as any other JARs commonly referenced by these EAR components. The EAR file has a descriptor of its own, META-INF/application.xml, which lists all contained EJB and WAR files.

The specification also supports an optional EJB client JAR. An EJB client JAR contains the beans' home and component interfaces and also contains or references the classes upon which that these interfaces depend, such as custom exceptions. The ejb-jar file references this file in its manifest file's Class-Path attribute. For example, if the bean implementation returns a custom java.util.Map implementation called MyMap, the MyMap class goes in the ejb client JAR file. The interface may say that it returns Map as opposed to MyMap, however the client will still need the MyMap implementation in its classpath at runtime.

10.1.4 *Loading classes*

How exactly the container loads component classes has long been a source of confusion. Understanding this loading is core to successful, error-free deployment. Java class loaders are required, by specification, to follow a hierarchical architecture, starting with the system class loader at the root. Each class loader has a parent class loader. When asked to load a particular class, the class loader first checks with its parent loader, and if the parent loader cannot load the desired class, the child loader attempts the load itself. A given class loader can see only classes made available to itself and class loaders higher in the hierarchy. This setup enables Java applications to isolate different parts of the application securely.

Class loaders in different branches of the class loader hierarchy—that is, neither class loader is a parent or ancestor of the other—may load different versions of the same class. This technology makes applets possible. Though a web browser only uses a single virtual machine, each applet gets a different class loader, completely isolating classes from different domains. This allows two different domains to load separate versions of the same third-party library and prevents code from one domain from affecting another, maliciously or by accident.

The J2EE architecture uses class loaders to deploy multiple enterprise applications into a single virtual machine. In a J2EE application, each EAR file gets a

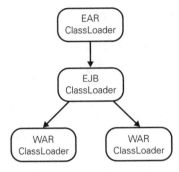

Figure 10.1
This diagram shows the major components of the J2EE class loader architecture, which takes advantage of loaders to enable deploying multiple enterprise applications into a single virtual machine. Each EAR file gets a separate loader; the application has a single EJB class loader; and each WAR file gets a loader of its own, which delegates to the EJB loader.

separate class loader. Next, the application has a single EJB class loader, which delegates to the EAR class loader parent. All EJB in an EAR file are loaded through the same EJB class loader. Last, each web application or WAR file gets its own class loader, which delegates to the EJB class loader.

The container loads classes stored in the `ejb-jar` or WAR files in their respective class loaders. JARs referenced in the `Class-Path` attribute in the `MANIFEST.MF` file of the EJB or WAR files are loaded in the EAR class loader.

Essentially, a J2EE application shares all classes stored in referenced JAR files between all components of the J2EE application. EJB share the same class loader and thus the same classes as well. This means that two EJBs in the same application cannot have different versions of the same class file. If you need two versions of the same class, you must deploy them in separate EARs and access each via its remote interfaces. WARs, on the other hand, have dedicated class loaders. Two WAR files can have different versions of the same third-party JAR file stored in the `lib` directory (If the WAR file references the JAR in its `Class-Path` attribute, the JAR will be loaded into the EAR class loader and thus will be visible to both web applications.)

Why would we want to share classes? Sharing classes may or may not be desirable. If two components have unique copies of the same class, they cannot pass by reference. Trying to cast a class instance from one component to the next will result in a `ClassCastException` or even a `ClassNotFoundException` if the class isn't visible to the component's class loader. The only way to pass instances back and forth between two components is through serialization. Using a remote interface implicitly has this effect. On the other hand, having separate copies of a class can be desirable as well. If two components share the same class, they also share that class's static state. For example, in the case of the GoF Singleton pattern, both components would share the same instance. If you don't need or desire components to share the same instance, you should deploy them separately.

10.2 Antipattern: System Loaded Application Classes

Because deployment associated with class loaders is complex, you may be tempted to take the easy way out. When you put all classes on the global classpath, you are asking the system to load everything through the system class loader. However, don't take the path of least resistance. Storing application classes on the system classpath can lead to development and deployment problems and can often skirt real issues.

First, as long as an instance of a class is present, that instance references its class, which in turn references its class loader. If a third-party library loaded through the system class path holds onto an instance of an application class, the EAR loader for that application can never get collected. If you try to hot deploy your application, the container would simply throw away the old EAR class loader and create a new one, and the third-party JAR would keep our loader from getting garbage collected. Essentially, you load two instances of your application at the same time. Each time you redeploy, the process will repeat until you run out of memory or another limited resource.

Secondly, during development, if you make a change to a class loaded through the system class loader, you have to restart the entire application server. Restarting an application server can take many seconds and even minutes. If you develop and deploy frequently, these delays can add up quickly.

10.2.1 Solution: Follow the J2EE guidelines

The solution is to follow the patterns laid out for the J2EE architecture and store all applications and third-party JARs in the EAR file. This approach will enable fast redeploys, smooth development, and reliable production systems.

EJB containers are supposed to shield applications from third-party classes as much as possible, but the truth is that some don't. We've run into this problem with XML parser implementations and database driver versions. If you experience these problems, follow your vendor's guidelines for adding third-party JAR to the application server's class path. If the versions of the third-party JARs used by the application server cause problems for your application, chances are that your versions may cause problems for the Application server.

10.3 Antipattern: EJB Code Duplication

The cost of many EJB architecture benefits is that you must maintain multiple files per bean. For each bean, you need—at minimum—the implementation class, the component interface class, the home interface class, and the deployment descriptor. Add business delegates, service locators, and DTOs, and things can get really hairy. If a method signature changes in your bean implementation, you must duplicate the change in at least two other places, changing the signatures in the component interface and deployment descriptors to match. Adding and changing EJBs quickly becomes a monotonous task as you chase down dependencies all over the place.

10.3.1 *Solution: Autogenerate the EJB classes*

A number of tools have surfaced to target just this problem XDoclet (http://xdoclet.sourceforge.net/) is just one of them. XDoclet builds on the Javadoc architecture, using Javadoc tags in the bean implementation class to dictate the building of the component interface, home interface, and deployment descriptor as well as such classes as business delegates and DTOs. Essentially, we can implement an entire EJB so that it can be deployed on multiple vendors from a single location. Let's revisit our earlier example bean implementation with the XDoclet tags added (listing 10.6):

Listing 10.6 Example bean implementation with XDoclet tags

```
package ejb;

import javax.ejb.*;

/**
 * Example bean implementation.
 *
 * @ejb.bean
 *    type="Stateless"
 *    name="Example"
 *    jndi-name="ejb/Example"
 *    display-name="Example"
 */
public class ExampleBean implements SessionBean {
    /**
     * @ejb.interface-method
     *    view-type="remote"
     * @ejb.transaction
     *    type="Required"
     */
    public String trim(String s) {
        return s.trim();
    }
    /**
     * @ejb.create-method
```

```
     *     role-name="Administrator"
     */
    public void ejbCreate()
      throws CreateException {}
    public void ejbActivate()
      throws EJBException {}
    public void ejbPassivate()
      throws EJBException {}
    public void ejbRemove()
      throws EJBException, RemoveException {}
    public void setSessionContext(SessionContext context)
      throws EJBException {}


}
```

A simple XDoclet Ant target (listing 10.7) executes XDoclet against all bean implementations in your source tree, auto-generating local and remote interfaces, standard deployment descriptors, and vendor-specific deployment descriptors for WebLogic and JBoss. XDoclet can also generate business delegates, data transfer objects, and other utility classes.

Listing 10.7   XDoclet Ant target

```
<target name="xdoclet ">
    <ejbdoclet sourcepath="${src.java.dir}"
               destdir="${src.java.dir}"
               ejbspec="2.0">
        <fileset dir="${src.java.dir}">
            <include name="**/ejb/*Bean.java"/>
        </fileset>
        <remoteinterface/>
        <homeinterface/>
        <localinterface/>
        <localhomeinterface/>
        <deploymentdescriptor/>
        <weblogic/>
        <jboss/>
    </ejbdoclet>
</target>
```

10.3.2 Solution: Autogenerate the manifest

Let's say you want to reference all of your third-party JARs and your common JARs from your EJB and web components. You can do so using the Class-Path attribute in the component's MANIFEST.MF file. One approach would be to implement a custom Ant task, but we've found that this can leave you in the "chicken before the egg" scenario. You must compile your Ant task using our build script, but you also need your task class in your build script. You could maintain classes used in your build separately. However, for simple cases like this, we prefer to dodge this overhead and code the task implementation directly into our build file. Ant's `script` task enables just this. The `script` task takes code from the task body and executes it using a scripting engine such as BeanShell (http://beanshell.org). Listing 10.8 generates a list of JAR files from the lib directory and outputs a MANI-FEST.MF file that can be used in constructing the EJB and web components. Now, adding a third-party JAR to our project is as simple as dropping it in a directory.

Listing 10.8 Script to autogenerate the MANIFEST.MF file

```
<target name="build.manifest">
    <mkdir dir="${manifest.dir}"/>              ⟵┘  Create a directory for
                                                     the manifest if necessary
    <fileset dir="${lib.dir}" id="lib.fileset"/>  ⟵┐
    <dependset>       Check if we've added any new JARs   Create a fileset with
        <srcfileset refid="lib.fileset"/>                 all of the third-
        <targetfileset dir="$manfest.dir}"                party JARs
                    includes="MANIFEST.MF"/>
    </dependset>
    <script language="beanshell"><![CDATA[       ⟵  Start a script using
        import java.io.*;                            BeanShell as the
        import org.apache.tools.ant.types.*;         language
        import org.apache.tools.ant.*;

    // output file names from FileSet instance to
    // PrintWriter.
    void outputFileNames(FileSet set, PrintWriter out) {  ⟵  Output the
        DirectoryScanner scanner =                            file names
            set.getDirectoryScanner(project);                 from a
        String[] files = scanner.getIncludedFiles();          fileset
        for (int i=0; i < files.length; i++)
            out.print(" " +
                new File(files[i]).getName());
    }

    // if the manifest file does not exist, create it.
    String manifestFileName =
        project.getProperty("manifest.dir") +           Look up the the
        "/MANIFEST.MF";                                  third-party JAR
    FileSet libFileSet =                                 fileset
        (FileSet) project.getReference("lib.fileset");  ⟵
    File manifest = new File(project.getBaseDir(),   ⟵┐  Create
        manifestFileName);                                MANIFEST.MF
    if (manifest.createNewFile()) {  ⟵
        System.out.println(                          If the file doesn't
            "Building manifest: " + manifest);       already exist, create it
```

```
            PrintWriter out = new PrintWriter(
                new FileWriter(manifest));
            out.print("Manifest-Version: 1.0\n");
                                                          Print the
            // output classpath manifest entry.          Manifest-Version
            out.print("Class-Path:");                     attribute
            outputFileNames(libFileset, out);

            // close manifest file.
            out.print("\n\n");
            out.close();
        }
    ]]></script>
</target>
```

10.3.3 Solution: Autogenerate the EAR descriptor

The EAR descriptor file is stored in META-INF/application.xml. The application.xml file references the components contained in the EAR file. We would use the application.xml file in listing 10.9 to deploy our EJB example along with a basic web application:

Listing 10.9   Example application.xml file

```
<?xml version="1.0" encoding="UTF-8"?>

<!DOCTYPE application PUBLIC
    '-//Sun Microsystems, Inc.//DTD J2EE Application 1.2//EN'
    'http://java.sun.com/j2ee/dtds/application_1_2.dtd'>

<application>
    <display-name>example</display-name>
    <module>
        <web>
            <web-uri>example.war</web-uri>
            <context-root>/example</context-root>
        </web>
    </module>
    <module>
        <ejb>example-ejb.jar</ejb>
    </module>
</application>
```

As you can see, we could autogenerate this file using the same pattern as we used to generate the MANIFEST.MF file. In fact, the build on our current project does just that. My build environment generates one or more WARs and one ejb-jar file. The name of the application here is *example*. We name the default web application after the application name and construct a name for the `ejb-jar`, using it as well. We use the WAR name to determine the `context-root` for the web application. These conventions may not apply to all projects; however, our pattern makes tweaking the generation on a per-project basis trivial.

10.4 *Antipattern: Build Guru*

A build guru used to be a critical member of the project team, in charge of launching and integrating periodic builds. Today, tools and techniques have evolved to the point that a build guru is not necessary. Stating the case more strongly, you have an antipattern if your project needs a build guru or a specific IDE to perform the build. Everyone should be able to cook up the software, at any time and any reasonable location. Indeed, even a computer should be able to cook up the software on a scheduled interval without human intervention. Building code should be like breathing, as code is the lifeblood of the application.

We once worked on a project developing software for medical insurance providers. Those familiar with the domain can tell you that the business logic here can be daunting. Our team developed the application using an IDE and had no single build file and, to top it off, the interdependencies were so rampant that we had to deploy the entire application to test a single component. The development process consisted of making a small change, then "pointing and clicking," deploying each component separately. This process was far from ideal. First of all, being tied into a single IDE was not fun, especially for those of us who were more productive in other environments. Second, the build process took ten times longer than necessary. Needless to say, as the application got more complex, deadlines slipped more and more. The development time scaled linearly with the application size when it should have stayed constant. Moreover, the more components we had to deploy, the greater the odds were that we would slip up and the longer we were out of context. This made staying in the development "zone" difficult.

We worked on another project for a credit card company. The build script consisted of a hodgepodge of shell scripts scattered throughout the source tree. No single build file existed. As each developer added a new component, a new build script was also added. This was nice while we were working on a single deployment because the build times were very fast, but the approach fell to pieces when it came time to deploy. Deploying to production was an all-day affair as we ensured that everything was built and deployed, frequently deploying multiple times before we got everything right.

10.4.1 Solution: Use Ant for heavy lifting

As the storm howls around us, we combat the wind and the waves. Even with the engine at full throttle, we are barely making headway against them. We divide our attention between the effort of steering back to port and the sound of the straining engine. We cast a nervous glance at the radio, realizing that we may be in over our heads.

Unlike pleasure sailors on an open sea, programmers aren't squeamish about turning their ship's control over to the engine room. With this antipattern, Ant (http://ant.apache.org) was the engine that powered us out of the storm. After struggling against the wind, my team got its act together on the project for the credit card company, moving to a single, atomic build and EAR-based deployment and still keeping reasonable build times. Deployments took minutes and worked unfailingly. We got our Saturdays back and built our client's confidence in the project at the same time. Ant comes with a variety of scripts, called tasks, geared toward almost any aspect of development and deployment that comes to mind, including building `ejb-jar` and EAR files. Also, extracting the paths and other relative references out into Ant properties enabled us to execute the build in any environment, even directly from many IDEs.

Ant provides many options for building `ejb-jar` files. Listing 10.10 takes classes and a deployment descriptor as input and generates an `ejb-jar` file containing the EJB implementation and interface classes. We can build a common JAR, using the remaining classes—that is, excluding classes in a package named `ejb`—and include this file in the `MANIFEST.MF` file's `Class-Path` attribute:

Listing 10.10   Example EJB Ant target

```
<target name="ejb">
    <mkdir dir="${build.ejb.dir}"/>    Create a directory for the ejb-jar file
    <ejbjar srcdir="${build.class.dir}"    ◁┐ Point to the directory containing
                                              the compiled class files

             descriptordir="${descriptor.dir}"    ◁┐ Point to the directory with
                                                      the descriptors

             manifest="${build.config.dir}/MANIFEST.MF"    ◁┐
                        Point to the MANIFEST.MF file to use
```

```
            basejarname="${name}-ejb">
                <include name="ejb-jar.xml"/>
            </ejbjar>
        </target>
```

Pick a name for the ejb-jar file

Point to the deployment descriptor

Adding a new EJB to your application is now a simple matter of adding the bean implementation source file to the source tree. XDoclet autogenerates the remaining EJB files and Ant builds them into an `ejb-jar` file. Ant's `ejb-jar` task also allows for more complicated scenarios. Specifically, you can build an `ejb-jar` for each EJB or a JAR for each deployment descriptor. I personally like to stick with a single `ejb-jar` unless multiple files are absolutely necessary.

Some vendors provide EJB precompilers. After creating the `ejb-jar` file, we run the EJB compiler against it and get another level of compile time checking. For example, the EJB compiler may verify that the interface and implementation methods line up and that all the necessary life cycle callbacks have been implemented. The EJB compiler may also generate client stubs for the EJB interfaces. Ant's `ejbjar` task provides support for many EJB compilers using nested tasks.

In the next sections, we'll move away from code generation and build automation. We'll enter the realm of testing, focusing on solutions that let you automate tests.

10.5 *Antipattern: Running with Scissors*

Writing code without tests is like running with scissors. The further you run, the more likely you are to fall. When (not *if*) you do, you're bound to experience pain. EJB pose no exception. Logic embedded in EJB implementations should be tested as much (if not more) and as efficiently as logic embedded in plain old Java classes. Unit testing EJBs should not require redeploying the application or even having an application server running.

10.5.1 *Solution: Test with impunity*

The mysteriously cool nature of EJB can make testing a little daunting but, remember, ultimately bean implementations are just plain Java classes. We do not need to completely build and deploy them to test them. Simply instantiating a bean implementation class and invoking methods on it provides more flexibility than invoking the bean through the component interface. Essentially, testing a bean by deploying it only verifies that the container works, something we can hope that the vendor has already done. Listing 10.11 instantiates and tests our example EJB:

Listing 10.11   Example EJB test case

```
package ejb;

/**
 * Unit test for example EJB.
 */
public class ExampleTest extends junit.framework.TestCase {

    public ExampleTest(String name) {
        super(name);
    }

    public void testTrim() {
        ExampleBean bean = new ExampleBean();
        bean.ejbCreate();
        assertEquals("test", bean.trim(" test  "));
        bean.ejbRemove();
    }

}
```

As you can see, the unit test merely instantiates and invokes methods on a bean instance. The unit test calls the life cycle methods just as the container might, and can even go so far as to mock the `SessionContext` object, satisfying whatever dependencies the component may have on it. We can also test the correctness of our bean's behavior under normal conditions, noting if it throws an exception when not configured properly. If our EJB accesses resources via JNDI, we can use a simple in-virtual machine JNDI implementation and bind the necessary mock implementations into it. When considering database access, you can either mock out a `DataSource` altogether or use an embedded database implementation such as HSQL (http://hsql.sourceforge.net/).

JUnit, the test framework used in listing 10.12 also has convenient Ant targets to facilitate running unit tests. With a simple target, we can execute every unit test in our source tree or choose just one test specified on the command line:

Listing 10.12   JUnit Ant target

```
<target name="test">
  <junit dir="${test.dir}"
         showoutput="yes"
         printsummary="yes">
    <property name="test" value="*"/>
```

```
      <batchtest todir="${test.results.dir}">
        <fileset dir="${src.java.dir}">
          <include name="**/${test}Test.java"/>
        </fileset>
      </batchtest>
      <formatter type="xml"/>
    </junit>
  </target>
```

To execute all available tests, we simply type `ant test`. To execute only our example test, we would type `ant test -Dtest=Example`, running any test class named `ExampleTest` in any package.

10.6 Antipattern: Integration Hell

An EJB application contains many moving parts. We want assurance that the gears consistently line up. We've been on projects that put off integration until the last minute. Each developer worked independently until a couple days before we were due to go to production. Without fail, we needed more than two days to get everyone's code working together, and we always came close to missing our deadline.

On another project, we integrated on a weekly basis. Even this wasn't often enough. We usually spent a day and a half untangling after the team of 18 brought their individual code together all at once. Open issues always persisted when we finished.

The longer we put off integrating with other developers' code, the farther we move from each other and the harder bringing a project back together will be. We've found that things tend to go much more smoothly—and integration takes a lot less effort—if we integrate multiple times a day. The problem is that no team member wants to bear the monotony of building and deploying three times a day, nor should they.

10.6.1 Solution: Integrate early, often, and automatically

We've started using CruiseControl (http://cruisecontrol.sourceforge.net/) to manage automatic builds. CruiseControl runs on a separate server, periodically pulling the project from source control and building and deploying it. Cruise-Control checks for updates in the source control. If an update has been made, it builds. If not, it waits quietly until the next interval. CruiseControl executes the build, using your existing Ant script, and runs the unit tests. If the build or unit tests fail, CruiseControl sends email to the team, publicly humiliating the build breaker who either failed to check everything or test that the code didn't break existing functionality. Mercifully, CruiseControl will restart a failed build after a predefined amount of time.

At any time, team members can go to the website hosted by the CruiseControl web application and see the results of all previous builds. They can see the updates checked in, the compilation errors, and the unit test results, all through a nice HTML interface. Everyone knows the status of the build in source control and knows, too, the changes others have made with almost no effort. Furthermore, you can use Ant to autogenerate a Javadoc for the project, so your documentation will always be consistent with the build.

10.7 *Summary*

When using EJB, you'll find spending a little time streamlining the build process can yield surprisingly successful results—increasing developer efficiency and the predictability of projects. Doing so can also boost developer morale, since these results create plenty of time for the fun stuff. In this chapter, we saw how a manual build process can distract us from the more difficult application development challenges. We also looked at the use of code generation with XDoclet to relieve the duplication of effort inherent in EJB programming. We also covered the integration of extreme programming practices like continuous integration and automated tests into our build process.

In *Bitter EJB*'s final chapter, you'll find a conclusion of our thoughts about EJB antipatterns. We'll review the weak points of the EJB frameworks and present the authors' suggestions for improvements. Finally, we'll consider the role that antipatterns should play in the future of EJB.

10.8 *Antipatterns in this chapter*

This section covers the System Loaded Application Classes, EJB Code Duplication, Build Guru, Running with Scissors, and Integration Hell antipatterns.

SYSTEM LOADED APPLICATION CLASSES

DESCRIPTION

All classes are dumped into the default class path, leaving the system loader to handle all class loading.

MOST FREQUENT SCALE

Application

REFACTORED SOLUTION NAME

J2EE application guidelines

REFACTORED SOLUTION TYPE

Process, software

REFACTORED SOLUTION DESCRIPTION

Store all application and third-party EJB in the EAR. Changes in a class deployed this way require a restart to the application server.

TYPICAL CAUSES

Laziness, ignorance

ANECDOTAL EVIDENCE

"We can't get Hot Deploy to work. After we try it a couple of times, we get strange errors."

SYMPTOMS, CONSEQUENCES

Often, the system has difficulty garbage-collecting the loader.

EJB CODE DUPLICATION

DESCRIPTION

EJB forces you to duplicate code across the interface, program files, deployment descriptors, and various implementation files.

MOST FREQUENT SCALE

Application

REFACTORED SOLUTION NAME

Autogenerate code with XDoclet or template driven alternatives.

REFACTORED SOLUTION TYPE

Technology

REFACTORED SOLUTION DESCRIPTION

Template technologies like XDoclet can take a common description of a class (such as Javadoc tags) and generate multiple sources from the same target, eliminating the need for creating duplicated code.

TYPICAL CAUSES

Ignorance

ANECDOTAL EVIDENCE

"For EJB, it seems like I always write the same line of code five times."

SYMPTOMS, CONSEQUENCES

High maintenance costs and high initial development costs.

BUILD GURU

DESCRIPTION
A single developer is responsible for running and maintaining periodic builds.

MOST FREQUENT SCALE
Application

REFACTORED SOLUTION NAME
Let Ant do the heavy lifting

REFACTORED SOLUTION TYPE
Technology

REFACTORED SOLUTION DESCRIPTION
Build tools, like Ant, make it much easier to create and automate builds, so that each member of a team can initiate and manage a build as often as it is required.

TYPICAL CAUSES
Laziness, ignorance

ANECDOTAL EVIDENCE
"I'll build it later. It's too hard."

SYMPTOMS, CONSEQUENCES
Integration occurs infrequently, or the build process (not the code) frequently breaks. The build process has many steps or dependencies.

RUNNING WITH SCISSORS

DESCRIPTION
You develop software without automated unit tests.

MOST FREQUENT SCALE
Application

REFACTORED SOLUTION NAME
Automate tests with Ant and JUnit

REFACTORED SOLUTION TYPE
Process, software, technology

REFACTORED SOLUTION DESCRIPTION
Create test cases first. Automate them with a tool like JUnit, and integrate them into the build.

TYPICAL CAUSES
Laziness, ignorance

ANECDOTAL EVIDENCE
"It worked when I checked it in." or "I forgot to test that part."

SYMPTOMS, CONSEQUENCES
The team is afraid to refactor obviously broken or inefficient code for fear of breaking the system. Quality suffers. Testing does not catch obvious bugs. Regression is a significant problem.

INTEGRATION HELL

DESCRIPTION

Infrequent integrations are expensive.

MOST FREQUENT SCALE

Application

REFACTORED SOLUTION NAME

Integrate early, often, and automatically

REFACTORED SOLUTION TYPE

Process, software, technology

REFACTORED SOLUTION DESCRIPTION

Development teams need discipline, and tools, to effectively integrate with greater frequency. Once teams start integrating more often, they find that it gets much easier.

TYPICAL CAUSES

Laziness

ANECDOTAL EVIDENCE

"No thanks, we'll wait."

SYMPTOMS, CONSEQUENCES

The longer that you take between integrations, the more expensive it gets.

11

A bittersweet future

This chapter contains

- A look at EJB's past and near future
- Suggestions for the next step of EJB architectures
- A glimpse at promising technologies like AOP

I'm on the face of the cliff, two thirds of the way up the Cathedral Ledge. In the past, climbers would scar cliff faces by drilling deeply into the rock to set permanent bolts. Today, things are a little different. We use the natural features of the cliff to wedge or clamp our safety ropes in place. The approach is not always as secure, but it conserves our climbing playgrounds. Today, my protection so far has been spotty at best. I seriously doubt that my last three anchors will hold. I'm coming to the critical move. Up to this point, I've been a little sloppy, trusting the grip in my hands more than the balance and placement of my feet. That's a sure recipe for disaster, and the next move won't give me any room for error. It's a difficult static move that will take every ounce of strength in my fingers. I take two deep breaths and then I commit, hoping that my anchors will hold. But even if they do, I don't want to count on my partner to spot me.

11.1 *Marking our place in history*

In *Bitter EJB*, we've taken a look at the critical problems that EJB developers face each day. Plain, old-fashioned ignorance causes some antipatterns to germinate. Those are easy to solve. But others arise from deeply rooted problems in the EJB specification. The state of the art needs to improve to ensure the long-term viability of EJB. In this chapter, we'll briefly address the future of EJB. Much of this future has yet to be written. Up to now, we've put our trust in promising, but precarious, anchors while carefully traversing the wall.

11.1.1 *Early mistakes*

As you've seen, early EJB marketing was far more successful than the actual frameworks. EJB 1.0 was nowhere near ready for prime time. Omissions in a 1.0-level technology are understandable and normally would not do much damage. However, EJB providers oversold their technology, and the result was a set of highly publicized failures. The problems were not trivial ones, as we can see in this brief review:

- The caretakers of EJB bickered over whether persistence would be added to EJB. In the end, persistence was added as an optional extension. Aggressive vendors, like IBM, picked it up, while others, like Oracle, opted to wait for more safety rope.

- CMP could not perform or scale nearly well enough. BMP implementations added all existing JDBC overhead, without providing the characteristic simplicity.

- EJB security was not fully mature, so customers were left to integrate security into their applications on their own, or choose proprietary solutions.

- EJB did not provide an alternative for performing asynchronous communication. Ironically, messaging would have been a much better fit for the EJB component model than persistence, which was finalized in the EJB 1.1 specification. Messaging was inexplicably delayed until the EJB 2.0 specification.

- The deployment strategy was proprietary, difficult to manage, and difficult to understand. Instead of using some form of configuration file, EJB technology used serialized objects.

- Productivity tools were scarce at best.

To be blunt, the inventers released EJB before it was ready and sold individual products as if they were mature. As a result, the technology as a whole ultimately lost both respect and its early momentum in the marketplace. The next two releases of EJB partially or completely resolved most major problems and established EJB as the platform of choice for web-enabled enterprise applications. Nothing else comes close as a platform. EJB integrates enterprise concerns—managing synchronous and asynchronous transactions—with an unmatched level of integrated security, performance, and scalability.

Today, you're probably getting mixed signals regarding the market strength of EJB. On one hand, the community is strong and impressive enterprise applications are appearing. One of the best ways to judge a technology is by the strength of its third-party community. In the case of EJB, you need look no further than TheServerSide. TheServerSide.com community receives 250,000 new viewers and two million page hits every month. That's a staggering number, and it's only the tip of the iceberg for EJB. You can also find vibrant and mature markets for third-party components, tools, books, periodicals, and consultants.

J2EE—and EJB by extension—is now the default development environment on the server tier for today's most successful enterprise applications. J2EE applications are appearing in numbers. One look at the customer references on the home pages for major commercial Application servers will convince you that customers are building real enterprise applications. The clustered deployments made popular by static web applications are now moving into the realm of traditional distributed enterprise applications. You could argue that we are only now realizing the benefits promised years ago by supporters of CORBA and DCE.

On the other hand, a vocal minority is starting to speak out against EJB, and is opting for alternative technologies to use in its place. These trends suggest a departure from the EJB-everywhere approach that was heavily sold in the late 1990s. For example, growing technologies like JDO and proprietary relational mappers are providing an alternative to EJB for persistence. In addition, some new research suggests that aspect-oriented programming (which we introduce in more detail in section 11.2.1) may be a much better technology for the crosscutting concerns that enterprise programmers frequently face. Finally, many new developers are adopting POJOs to handle all but the most severe enterprise development issues.

This dissention is natural, and healthy. Competitive pressure and open criticism from an open community can drive the Java platform in ways that a private enterprise cannot. In the end, EJB's success or failure will depend upon its ability to serve its intended community. As it stands, EJB is a niche product that serves only the most advanced enterprise applications. With some rework, it could grow to be more of a mainstream server-side enterprise application technology. Without significant rework, EJB will continue to serve only a fairly specialized niche. Let's look at the types of enhancements that EJB needs to make to address the concerns of its user base.

11.2 Plotting the next moves

You've seen how the EJB specification team has addressed some early concerns. It has dramatically improved the performance of entity beans and rapidly addressed deployment flexibility problems that plagued early EJB applications. The specification team needs to move swiftly to continue the evolution toward a modern, efficient framework suitable for today's users. That's going to take uncharacteristic cooperation and teamwork within the whole community. Some of the technology's founders must admit that EJB has some core weaknesses that need to be addressed—and addressed quickly.

11.2.1 Into the future

For all the progress that we've made with EJB, the specification is starting to look a little dated. A few component-oriented architectures have failed in the past because they force the developer to accept a whole lot of overhead for a package of services, whether or not the services are needed. The situation is much like going to a dishonest mechanic. You may walk in wanting only an oil change, but if you're not careful, you may leave with a rebuilt transmission and a tune up as well. Instead, EJB needs to evolve to an autonomous collection of services that can be adopted or not, as necessary. That suggests that the EJB specification team should abandon the component-oriented model as it stands today and move toward a platform containing optional services, with a much more transparent persistence model at the core. As we'll see below, JBoss has already begun to move in this direction. Also, users need to be able to consume services in a way that fits the design of their application. Persistence is a great example of the failings of a component-oriented approach for fine-grained services (as we discussed in chapter 2).

If component-oriented software is not the answer, aspect-oriented programming (AOP) might present a solution in certain circumstances. AOP allows you to intercept the program execution at critical points like method execution, and add behaviors to support crosscutting concerns. As such, AOP is a much more natural model for the types of problems that EJB is intended to solve. Transactions, persistence, security, logging, distribution and synchronization are all crosscutting concerns that aspect-oriented programming manages well.

Figure 11.1 is borrowed from Manning's *AspectJ in Action*. The figure illustrates how an aspect-oriented system takes crosscutting concerns and weaves them into a final system. With AOP, you develop applications in a three-step process:

1 Gather requirements that identify crosscutting concerns.

2 Implement concerns independently.

3 Specify the re-composition rules that allow the system to weave concerns together to form your final system.

You can see that this type of development would fit enterprise applications extremely well. The JBoss Application server is already moving in that direction, with method interceptors and an architecture that leverages AOP models to its benefit.

Of course, research into AOP is young, and you're likely to see that AOP is no silver bullet, either. We still don't have a compelling AOP language, and the best

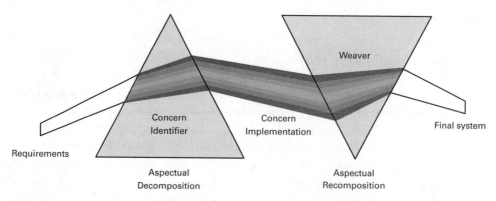

Figure 11.1   Aspect oriented programming (AOP) is built to handle the types of crosscutting concerns that are important to enterprise developers, like persistence, exceptions, distribution and transactions.

transition path from EJB is not clear. Let's consider the ways in which the specification team might make a transition:

1　They could choose to move aggressively in the direction of AOP, scrapping the cumbersome container in favor of a library of aspects addressing enterprise concerns, and providing a framework that enables tools or users to support the aspectual recomposition. You would see extreme changes in the Java language that supports this new paradigm.

2　The specification team could take a more conservative approach, enabling AOP but not forcing that development paradigm. This type of strategy could move container services away from the container and allow services to be organized and consumed as aspects. You would also likely see method interceptors that provide convenient attachment points for AOP crosscutting concerns. Once underway, the correct AOP development environments could evolve independently.

One still cloudy supposition is becoming clearer: The EJB container may be an idea whose time has passed. We may have reached a time to shift away from the component-oriented approach toward a model that lets the programmer choose the services that she needs to get the job done and consume those services more efficiently. Without such an approach, EJB will be saddled with deployment complexity, little flexibility after deployment, and less than optimal performance.

11.2.2　*Fix persistence*

Many developers who say that they do not like EJB mean that they do not like entity beans. The EJB persistence story started off with a utopian distributed domain model idea. You could put domain object A on one machine, domain object B on another, and they would interoperate with complete location transparency. After they realized that this approach wouldn't fly (because of something called a network), the developers complicated their domain model with an endless chain of quick patches and compromises, trying desperately to make it work. The problem is that all the original limitations and none of the benefits remain.

We need to start over. It seems that entity beans completely monopolize the EJB spec. Why waste all that time implementing a fundamentally flawed technology? The answer is political—vendors have invested too much only to see entity beans fail. However, as an industry, we need to recognize that EJB persistence is broken. We also need to demand a fix—and use alternatives until we get one.

When we heard the outcry over the PetStore performance benchmark (see chapter 1), we noticed that little of the discussion centered on EJB persistence. As currently defined, entity beans lead to uncertainty, demand frequent and painful workarounds, and often result in poor performance. A reworked persistence framework should embrace the following ideas:

- A better persistence strategy needs to start with a finer grained service. Coarse-grained services can and should be attached elsewhere.

- A revised framework needs to focus solely on providing persistence to Java objects with all their complexity. Inheritance and abstract interfaces are critical.

- A revised framework needs to be more transparent.

- A revised framework cannot impose arbitrary restrictions. Currently, the specification asks users to avoid a warped version of re-entrance. That demand makes modeling much more difficult.

Realistically, the EJB specification team could start with a cleaner persistence framework like JDO. Doing so would put them much closer to an ultimate working solution. Better yet, the team should learn from the mistakes of the past and start from scratch with a cleaner, simpler notion of persistence.

11.2.3 *Fix the deployment strategy*

Metadata is information about a given class, interface, object, or component. Deployment descriptors are essentially a way to provide metadata about a class at deploy time. The deployment descriptor approach had its benefits but, like the component-driven architecture, it is showing its age. The complexity of deployment descriptors grows with every release and won't be likely to get any easier. To shift to another strategy, EJB will have to provide a richer metadata capability.

Ideally, the metadata capability should be built into the base Java programming language. Such a proposal has already been suggested in the form of Java Specification Request (JSR) 175. By adopting this request, the EJB specification team could move toward a richer, simpler strategy for dealing with metainformation, without the need for complex deployment descriptors. JSR 175 may be adopted soon in a future Java release. This move would go a long way toward improving EJB tools and simplifying the platform, in general.

11.2.4 *Putting the economic house in order*

To date, the Java programming language is still proprietary: a private company, not a standards body, controls it. Further, like much of the computer industry, Sun has shown serious weakness lately. To succeed, EJB will also need better economic strength from Sun or a move toward standardization. To make the current model work, Sun must be viable and strong, with enough resources to support the community process and Java specification. A floundering Sun would present a potentially significant danger to the Java community as a whole. If weakened, Sun might try to exert more control, attempting to leverage the Java platform for more direct financial gain at the cost of the overall strength of Java. Keep in mind that others, notably IBM, offset this danger through significant investments in Java development and legal control over many frameworks. Still, the gatekeeper, to a large extent, is Sun.

To be fair, the Java Community Process has come a long way since its inception. Several critical extensions to Java frameworks have come from JSRs that were not introduced by Sun. This is a step in the right direction. We must keep swinging the pendulum toward a standardized platform for the good of the entire industry.

Don't underestimate your ability to make an impact on the overall process. You can participate in any JSR about which you feel passionately. Several well-reasoned arguments from smaller companies, and even independent consultants, have made an impact on the overall direction of a JSR and, by extension, the EJB framework. If you do decide that you'd like to participate, make sure that you've got the requisite skills to understand the core issues and build a solid argument. Failing that, work with a mentor who does understand and participate in the process.

11.3 Antipatterns and next moves

Since *Bitter Java* was published in 2002, you've seen antipatterns play an ever-increasing role in the EJB community. From the PetStore benchmarks to the Java persistence questions raised by many vocal Java spokespeople, the community is starting to look at failure as an opportunity to learn. It is our hope that books like this one will improve Java by encouraging frank and open discourse. In the end, the strength of the Java platform lies ultimately in the community. We will determine where Java goes from here. As we participate in the Java Community Process's increasingly visible public debate and vote with our pocketbooks for products that work for us, we can determine the products that will succeed.

> *As I look down the 400-foot vertical drop, I understand that my next moves will be for keeps. My choices are clear. If I trust my partner to support me now, I can reach the summit. If not, I turn around and climb back down the face to return and conquer this peak another time. I look at the cliff face and think.*

Bitter tales

This appendix contains

Chapter 1 of Bruce Tate's best-selling *Bitter Java*, published in April 2002 by Manning Publications Co. It is offered as an introduction to antipatterns.

On a cold day in Eastern Tennessee, my kayak is perched precariously atop a waterfall known as State Line Falls. The fall has a nasty reputation among kayakers. One of our team is walking this one. He was injured and shaken up last year at the same spot. This time around he wants no part of it.

From the top, there is no clue of the danger that lurks around the bend, but we know. We have been thinking ahead to this rapid for several days. We have read about what I cannot yet see. Five truck-sized boulders guard four slots. The water rushes through the slots and plunges to the bottom of the fall. I will see the entire waterfall only seconds before I go over it. Most of the water lands on boulders barely covered by two feet of water. Three of the four slots are reputed to be too violent and dangerous for your mother-in-law. Through the fourth, the river rips into the narrows and picks up speed. It drops sharply over the lip and crashes onto the jagged rocks 16 feet below. I am a programmer by trade, a father of two, and a kayaker of intermediate skill. I have no business going over a Class V waterfall described in guidebooks as "marginal." But here I am, looking for the landmarks. I pick my slot, sweep left, and brace for the soft landing—or the crash. I am in free fall.

A.1 A Java development free fall

The sales team was strong. They got all the right sponsors, lined them up, and marched them into the executive's office. They all said the same thing. The development cycle times were outrageous. Each project was longer than the last, and the *best* project overshot deadlines by 85 percent. It did not take the CIO long to add up the numbers. The cost overruns ran well into seven figures.

The answer was Java. The lead rep presented a fat notebook showing references from everywhere: the press, the news, and three major competitors. The proposed tools won awards and added to the outrageous productivity claims promised by even the most conservative vendors. They never cited the downside or training requirements. In early 1996, hardly anyone did. The sales team brought in the big gun: a proof-of-concept team that quickly hammered out an amazingly robust prototype in a short time. The lead rep had practiced the close many times, but in this case, the deal was already sealed. She was able to get even more of the budget than she expected. After all, a product and language this easy and this similar to C++ should not require much training, so she got most of that allocated budget too.

But a year and a half later, the lead programmer was sitting behind a desk in the middle of the night while the sales rep celebrated her third National Circle sales award in Hawaii. In truth, the programmer seemed genuinely happy to be there. He knew that he was in over his head, and he needed help badly. He could see that clearly now. When the project started, the programming team had just enough time to learn the syntax of the new language. They had been using an object-oriented language for four years without ever producing an object-oriented design. Their methodology called for one large development cycle, which provided very little time to find all of the mistakes—and even less time to recover. The insane argument at the time was that there was no time for more than one iteration.

As a member of the audit team dispatched to help the customer pick up the pieces, I was there to interview the programmer. My team had composed a checklist of likely culprits: poor performance, obscure designs, and process problems. We had written the same report many times, saving our customers hundreds of thousands of dollars, but the interviews always provided additional weight and credibility to back up our assertions.

"Is your user interface pure HTML, then?" I asked.

"Yeah," the programmer replied. "We tried applets, but that train crashed and burned. We couldn't deal with the multiple firewalls, and our IT department didn't think they would be able to keep up with the different browser and JVM configurations."

"So, where is the code that prints the returning HTML?"

He winced and said, "Do you really want to go near that thing?" In truth, I didn't want any part of it. I had done this long enough to know that this baby would be too ugly for a mother to love, but this painful process would yield one of the keys to the kingdom. As we reviewed the code, we confirmed that this was an instance of what I now call the Magic Servlet antipattern, featured in chapter 3. The printout consisted of 30 pages of code, and 26 were all in a single service method. The problem wasn't so much a bad design as a lack of any design at all. We took a few notes and read a few more pages. While my partner searched for the code fragment that processed the return trip, I looked for the database code. After all, I had written a database performance book, and many of the semiretired database problems were surfacing anew in Java code.

"Is this the only place that you connect to the database?" I asked.

"No," he answered. "We actually connect six different times: to validate the form, to get the claim, to get the customer, to handle error recovery, to submit the claim, and to submit the customer." I suppressed a triumphant smile and again reviewed the code. Connection pooling is often neglected but incredibly powerful. In chapter 7, the Connection Thrashing antipattern shows how a method can spend up to half of its time managing connections, repeating work that can usually be done once.

I also jotted down a note that the units of work should be managed in the database and not the application. I noticed that the database code was sprinkled throughout, making it difficult to change this beast without the impact rippling throughout the system. I was starting to understand the depth of the problem. Even though most of these audits were the same, at some point they all hit me in the face like a cold glass of water.

Over the next four hours, we read code and drew diagrams. We found that the same policy would be fetched from 4 to 11 times, depending on the usage scenario. (The caching antipatterns at this customer and others prompted discussions in chapter 5, where you'll learn about the caching and serialization techniques that can make a huge difference.) We drew interaction diagrams of the sticky stuff and identified major interfaces. We then used these diagrams to find iteration over major interface boundaries and to identify general chatty communications that could be simplified or shifted.

We left the customer a detailed report and provided services to rework the problem areas. We supplied a list of courses for the programmers and suggested getting a consulting mentor to solidify the development process. When all was said and done, the application was completed *ahead* of the revised schedule and the performance improved *tenfold*. This story actually combines three different customer engagements, each uglier than this one. I changed some details to protect the names of the guilty, but the basic scenario has been repeated many times over the course of my career. I find problems and provide templates for the solutions. While most of my peers have focused on design patterns, I find myself engaged with *antipatterns*.

A.1.1 Antipatterns in life

> *On the Watauga River, with all of the expectations and buildup, the run through State Line is ultimately anticlimactic. I land with a soft "poof" well right of the major turbulence. The entire run takes less than 20 seconds. Even so, I recognize this moment as a major accomplishment.*

How could a journeyman kayaker successfully navigate such a dangerous rapid? How could I convince myself that I would succeed in light of so many other failures? I'd learned from the success and failure of those who went before me. The real extremists were those that hit rock after rock, breaking limbs and equipment, while learning the safest route through the rapid. I see a striking similarity between navigating rivers and writing code. To make it through State Line Falls, I simply did three things:

- *I learned to use the tools and techniques of the experts.* As a programmer, I attend many conferences to learn about best practices, and to find the new frameworks and tools that are likely to make a difference on my projects.

- *I did what the experts did.* I learned the easiest line and practiced it in my mind. We can do the same thing as programmers, by using design patterns detailing successful blueprints to difficult architectural problems.

- *I learned from the mistakes before me.* The first time down a rapid, it's usually not enough to take a good plan and plunge on through, torpedoes be damned. Good plans can go bad, and it's important to know how to react when they do. As a programmer, I do the same thing. I am a huge fan of "merc talk," or the stories told around the table in the cafeteria about the latest beast of a program. This is the realm of the antipattern.

When I was told how to run State Line Falls, I asked what-if questions. What should my precise angle be? How can I recover if I drift off that angle? How far left is too far? What's likely to happen if I miss my line and flip? I got answers from locals who had watched hundreds of people go down this rapid with varying degrees of success. The answers to these questions gave me a mental picture of what usually happened, what could go wrong, and what places or behaviors to avoid at all cost. With this knowledge, I got the confidence that it took to run the rapid. I was using design patterns and antipatterns.

A.2 *Using design patterns accentuates the positive*

Design patterns are solutions to recurring problems in a given context. A good example is the Model-View-Controller design pattern introduced in chapter 3. It presents a generic solution to the separation of the user interface from the business logic in an application. A good design pattern should represent a solution that has been successfully deployed several times. At State Line Falls, when I read about the successful line in guidebooks and watched experienced kayakers run the rapid, I was essentially using design patterns. As a programmer, I use them for many reasons:

- *Proven design patterns mitigate risk.* By using a proven blueprint to a solution, I increase my own odds of success.

- *Design patterns save time and energy.* I can effectively use the time and effort of others to solve difficult problems.

- *Design patterns improve my skill and understanding.* Through the use of design patterns, I can improve my knowledge about a domain and find new ways to represent complex models.

Embracing design patterns means changing the way we code. It means joining communities where design patterns are shared. It means doing research instead of plowing blindly into a solution. Many good sources are available.

Books

This is a sampling of books from the Java design pattern community and the definitive source for design patterns (*Design Patterns: Elements of Reusable Object-Oriented Software*). As of this writing, five or more are under development, so this list will doubtlessly be incomplete. Amazon (http://www.amazon.com) is a good source for finding what's out there.

- *Design Patterns: Elements of Reusable Object-Oriented Software*, by Erich Gamma, Richard Helm, Ralph Johnson, and John Vlissides (The Gang of Four)
- *Refactoring: Improving the Design of Existing Code*, by Martin Fowler, Kent Beck (contributor), John Brant (contributor), William Opdyke, and Don Roberts
- *Core J2EE Patterns*, by John Crupi, Dan Malks, and Deepak Alur
- *Concurrent Programming in Java: Design Principles and Patterns*, by Doug Lea
- *Patterns in Java, Volume 3: A Catalog of Enterprise Design Patterns Illustrated with UML*, by Mark Grand
- *Data Structures and Algorithms with Object-Oriented Design Patterns in Java*, by Bruno R. Preiss
- *Java Design Patterns: A Tutorial*, by James William Cooper

A.2.1 Design patterns online

Manning Publications has a series of author forums for discussion. These authors discuss server-side architectures, Java programming techniques, Java ServerPages (JSP), Extensible Markup Language (XML), and servlets. The author of this book also has an online community to discuss Java antipatterns.

Manning authors

- Manning author forums: http://www.manning.com/authoronline.html
- Java antipatterns: http://www.bitterjava.com

Java vendors

- IBM: http://www-106.ibm.com/developerworks/patterns/
- Sun: http://java.sun.com/j2ee/blueprints/

A.2.2 *UML provides a language for patterns*

The design pattern community has exploded in recent years partially because there is now a near universal language that can be used to express patterns. Unified Modeling Language (UML) brings together under one umbrella several of the tools supporting object-oriented development. Concepts such as scenarios (use cases), class interactions (class diagrams), object interface interaction (sequence diagrams), and object state (state diagrams) can all be captured in UML. Though this subject is beyond the scope of this book, there are many good UML books, tools, and resources as well.

Books

- *UML Distilled: A Brief Guide to the Standard Object Modeling Language*, by Martin Fowler and Kendall Scott
- *Enterprise Java with UML*, by C. T. Arrington
- *The Unified Modeling Language User Guide*, by Grady Booch, et al.

Tools

- Rational: http://www.rational.com
- Resource center at Rational: http://www.rational.com/uml/index.jsp
- TogetherJ from Together Software: http://www.togethersoft.com

A.3 *Antipatterns teach from the negative*

AntiPatterns: Refactoring Software, Architectures, and Projects in Crisis by William J. Brown, et al., is an outstanding book dedicated to the study of antipatterns. The antipattern templates that follow each chapter in this book come from Brown's text. In it, the authors describe an antipattern as "a literary form that describes a commonly occurring solution to a problem that generates decidedly negative consequences." The words that caught my attention are *commonly occurring solution* and *decidedly negative consequences*. Many others have presented some of the negative examples in this book as the right way to do things. Some, like the Magic Servlet, are forms of programs published in tutorials, created by wizards, or captured in frameworks. As for negative consequences, anyone who has followed software engineering closely knows that a high percentage of software projects fail. The *AntiPatterns* text cites that five of six software projects are considered unsuccessful. Java projects are not immune. Earlier this weekend, I heard about a canceled Java project using servlets and JSPs at a Fortune 100 company that will be replaced with a new project using CICS and C++!

Some of the madness in our industry is caused by outright malice. Some vendors sell software that they know isn't ready or doesn't work. Some managers resist change and sabotage projects. Some coworkers take shortcuts that they know they will not have to repair. Most of the time, though, it is simple ignorance, apathy, or laziness that gets in the way. We simply do not take the time to learn about common antipatterns. Ignorant of software engineering history or the exponentially increasing cost of fixing a bug as the development cycle progresses, we might kid ourselves into thinking we'll take a shortcut now and fix it later.

A.3.1 *Some well-known antipatterns*

As programmers, we will run across many antipatterns completely unrelated to Java. For the most part, we will not go into too many of them, but here are a few examples to whet your appetite:

- *Cute shortcuts.*   We've all seen code that optimizes white space. Some programmers think that the winner is the one who can fit the most on a line. My question is, "Who is the loser?"

- *Optimization at the expense of readability.*   This one is for the crack programmers who want you to know it. In most cases, readability in general is far more important than optimization. For the other cases, aggressive comments keep things clear.

- *Cut-and-paste programming.*   This practice is probably responsible for spreading more bugs than any other. While it is easy to move working code with cut and paste, it is difficult to copy the entire context. In addition, copies of code are rarely tested as strenuously as the originals. In practice, cut-and-paste programs must be tested *more strenuously* than the originals.

- *Using the wrong algorithm for the job.*   Just about every programmer has written a bubble sort and even applied it inappropriately. We can all find a shell sort if pressed, and if we understand algorithm analysis theory, we know that a bubble sort is processed in $O(n^2)$ time, and a simple shell sort is processed in $O(n\log(n))$ time, which is much shorter for longer lists.

- *Using the wrong class for the job.* In object-oriented languages, we've got to choose between classes like tables and arrays that have similar function but different characteristics. If our algorithm calls for random access of a collection, using a b-tree or hash table will be much faster than an array. If we're going to frequently index or enumerate the collection, an array is faster.

A.3.2 *Antipatterns in practice*

The study and application of antipatterns is one of the next frontiers of programming. Antipatterns attempt to determine what mistakes are frequently made, why they are made, and what fixes to the process can prevent them. The practice is straightforward, if tedious. The benefits are tremendous. The trick to the study of antipatterns is to:

1 *Find a problem.* This might be a bug, a poor-performing algorithm, or unreadable method.

2 *Establish a pattern of failure.* Quality control is a highly specialized and valued profession in manufacturing circles. A good quality engineer can take a process and find systemic failures that can cost millions. Software process can create systemic failure, too. The Y2K bug was a systemic failure of a very simple bug that was created and copied across enterprises hundreds of millions of times. Sometimes, the pattern will be related to a technology. Most often, process problems involve people, including communications and personalities.

3 *Refactor the errant code.* We must of course refactor the code that is broken. Where possible, we should use established design patterns.

4 *Publish the solution.* The refactoring step is obvious but should be taken a bit further than most are willing to go. We should also teach others how to recognize and refactor the antipattern. *Publishing the antipattern is as important as publishing the related solution.* Together, they form a refactoring guide that identifies the problem and solves it.

5 *Identify process weaknesses.* Sometimes, frameworks or tools encourage misuse. Other times, external pressures such as deadlines may encourage shortcuts. We must remember that a process must ultimately be workable by imperfect humans. In many cases, education may be the solution.

6 *Fix the process.* This is the most difficult, and most rewarding, step. We effectively build a barrier between our healthy enterprise and the disease. Here, we take a hard look at what's broken. In simple cases, we fix

the problem. In more extreme cases, we might need to establish a risk/ reward analysis and win sponsorship to fix the problem.

Figure 1.1 illustrates the antipattern process.

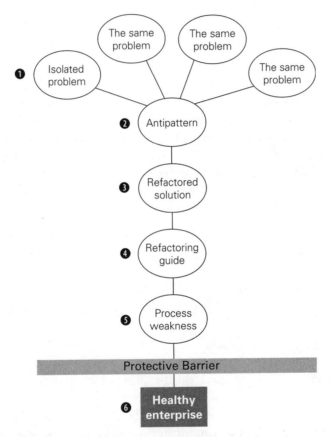

Figure 1.1 The antipattern process involves finding a problem ❶, establishing a pattern and publishing an antipattern ❷, refactoring the solution ❸, building a guide so that the problem can be resolved and fixed en masse ❹, identifying process weaknesses ❺, and building a barrier between the healthy enterprise and the antipattern ❻.

A.3.3 *Antipattern resources*

The antipattern community is gathering momentum, looking for things that break in a methodical way and capturing those experiences. Some engines use pattern recognition to find bugs from software *source code*. Many programmers are

starting to publish *bug patterns* for common programming mistakes. The http://
www.bitterjava.com site has some links to Eric Allen's series "Bug Patterns."

The design pattern community also has a counterpart: the *antipattern* community. This group is interested in learning from common experience and capturing
that knowledge in a uniform, methodical way.

AntiPatterns: Refactoring Software, Architectures, and Projects in Crisis brings these
concepts together better than any other source I have seen. With Brady Flowers,
who contributed the Enterprise JavaBeans (EJB) examples for this book, I had
started to do bitter Java sessions at conferences before we found *AntiPatterns*.
When we found it, we immediately fell in love with the ideas expressed in this
book. Most of the book's antipatterns went beyond theory and explained the cultural conditions prompting a problem. The book is extraordinarily useful to programmers who strive for excellence. We hope to take these concepts into the Java
community to continue the momentum that *AntiPatterns* has created. We will go
beyond generic antipatterns and dive into those that are most prevalent to the
Java community. These are some online resources for antipatterns:

- The authors have an online source for Java antipatterns. You can find it at
  http://www.bitterjava.com. On the site, we will attempt to provide you with
  articles, discussion boards, and useful links.

- The http://www.antipatterns.com site has articles, events, and message
  boards.

A.4 *Antipattern ideas are not new*

Should developers spend more time on the study of antipatterns or design patterns? I will answer this with another true adventure story. Throughout the better
part of this past century, mountain climbers across the world had an ultimate goal:
to scale Mt. Everest, the highest summit in the world. Over time, mountaineers
tried many different approaches that would allow political passage to the mountain, solid expedition logistics, and the best chances for success. Two routes go
through Tibet. George Mallory was an early British mountain climber, famous for
saying he climbed Everest "Because it is there." He made his attempts on the north
face, over terrain called the North Col. The other northern route was considered
much too dangerous for early mountaineers. Edmund Hillary, who became the
first to climb Everest, eventually succeeded on the southern face, through Nepal.
That route is called the South Col route. After the first ascent, expeditions climbed
this dangerous mountain with greater regularity and greater margins of safety.

They began to unlock the secrets of operating at high altitude and to find where the inevitable danger spots were likely to be. They began to understand when the summer monsoons directed the jet stream away from Everest to provide a window of acceptable weather. They learned to leave their tents at midnight so that they would not be trapped on the summit in the afternoon, when the weather frequently deteriorated. They were using design patterns.

Inevitably, people started to guide trips up the mountain with increasing success. Many debated that some of the paid clients did not have the appropriate skills to be on the mountain and would not be able to handle themselves in the event of an emergency. These criticisms turned out to be prophetic. Two expeditions led by the strongest guides in the world got trapped at the top of Everest through a series of poor decisions and bad luck. An afternoon storm killed many of them, including three of the six guides and several of the clients. Jon Krakauer made this incident famous in the book *Into Thin Air.* The design patterns were able to get them to the top but were unable to get them safely back down. Good application of climbing antipatterns, like avoiding the top of the mountain at dangerous times and holding fast to a prescribed turnaround time, could have made the difference.

A.4.1 *Learning from the industry*

In many real-world situations, the principles of design patterns and antipatterns are combined. In heath care, aggressive preventive care (design patterns) is combined with systematic diagnostics of health-related issues (antipatterns). In manufacturing, quality certification programs like ISO 9000 (design patterns) are combined with aggressive process analysis, problem identification, and continuous improvement (antipatterns). Road signs are combined to point out good driving behaviors like "Pass on left" and hazards like "Watch for falling rock." In many other fields, the two practices go hand in hand. Software engineers should try to combine these two approaches.

A powerful movement in the quality industry, from the late '70s through the '80s, sought to involve front-line assembly workers in the quality process. These teams were tightly integrated with quality professionals. The teams, sometimes with light-handed management direction, would identify problems and contribute a block of time weekly toward solutions to those problems. My father, Robert G. Tate, Jr., became so attached to this process that he left a high-level position at Dover Elevators to pursue a consulting career installing "quality circles" around the world. He found that something magical happened with the involvement of the actual blue-collar plant floor. The relationships changed. Management, quality control, and the product builders began to work together. The process was remarkably simple:

- Quality circles would form for the purpose of solving quality problems.
- Participants would become involved in the identification and solution of quality problems.
- Management would empower them to deal with quality problems directly.
- Participants were educated to perform these tasks.

Many of the quality groups showed staggering returns. Other programs, such as Zero Defects, also thrived. Awards and accreditations, like Malcolm Baldrige and ISO 9000, gathered steam. The United States again discovered the value of quality.

In a very real sense, this book represents the same ideas that we see in other areas and places them in the context of Java application development. We are taking responsibility for bringing quality code to the desk of the common programmer. We want to identify places where our assembly line is broken. We want to spot holes in process and procedure that can cripple our customers or even ourselves down the road. We want to *know* when major systematic problems, like the routinely late turnaround times on Everest, occur. We then want to systematically solve them and save others from repeating our mistakes. Most of this book deals with antipatterns that are already well entrenched in Java programs, processes, and programmers. We should now talk briefly about the discovery process.

A.4.2 Detective work

Experienced, conscientious programmers find most antipatterns. While teaching the instincts of a detective may be difficult, I can provide some rules of thumb from my consulting experience. These tips represent the places and methods that I use to find antipatterns hiding in a customer's process, or my own.

Bug databases contain a bounty of wealth

Most organizations already track quality metrics in the form of bug databases. We can look to establish patterns based on keyword searches and spot checks. Are we seeing a pattern of memory leaks? If so, misconceptions or frameworks could be a source of bad behavior. Are the change lists for view-related maintenance particularly long? If so, this could point to tight coupling. Are certain objects or methods particularly vulnerable to bugs? If so, they might be refactoring targets.

Early performance checks can point out design flaws

Sanity checks for performance early in a process can point to design flaws. Some of these might be isolated incidents. Some, even at an early stage, are likely to be common enough to warrant special attention. Internet applications are particularly vulnerable to communication overhead. Several of the antipatterns in this book deal with round-tripping, or making many communications do a relatively isolated task. Sloppy programming, including many of the issues in chapter 9, can also cause performance problems, especially in tight loops.

Frequent code inspections and mentors help

Beginners and early intermediates can be a common source of antipatterns. Pairing them with more experienced programmers and architects for code reviews and mentoring can head off many bad practices before they start. At allmystuff, the engineering department did a nice job of mentoring the solutions development staff, which typically consisted of weaker developers with better customer skills. Even a five-minute code inspection can reveal a surprising amount of information. Are the methods too long? Is the style readable and coherent? Are the variable names appropriately used? Does the programmer value her intelligence above readability?

End users are unusually perceptive

Later in my career, I began to appreciate the impact of end-user involvement at all stages of development. I found that end users can be brutally honest, when we allow them to be. When I began to truly listen to feedback, I could tell very early if my team would need to bear down or change direction. Too often, we ask for the questions and listen only if we hear what we want or expect.

Outsiders can use interviews

The most powerful tool for someone outside a development organization is the interview. People are put off when we try to propose answers without asking questions. Getting them to open up in an interview is usually not difficult but may occasionally be troublesome. When we are digging for trouble, people are much more perceptive if they perceive that we are helping to solve problems and not looking for someone to blame. Interviews are most useful if we can script at least a set of high-level questions, as well as anticipate some low-level questions.

Establishing a pattern

By itself, a problem is only a bug. We should already have processes and procedures for identifying and fixing bugs. Indeed, many of my father's customers had adequate measures for detecting and removing bad products from the line. The problems with these reactive approaches are twofold. First, we will never find all of the bugs. Second, if we do not fix the machinery or the process, we will create more bugs! After we have established a pattern, we need to elevate it from bug to antipattern.

A.4.3 Refactoring antipatterns

After we find a problem and establish a pattern, our strategy calls for refactoring it to form a better solution and process. Here, we are overlapping the realms of design patterns and antipattern. My intuition is that this combination is part of what is missing in the software quality industry. The combination of design patterns and antipatterns is practical and powerful. Poor solutions can be identified through antipatterns and redesigned into more proven and practical alternatives using design patterns. The process of continually improving code through restructuring for clarity or flexibility and the elimination of redundant or unused code is called *refactoring*.

Many experts advocate the rule "If it isn't broke, don't fix it." In the realm of software development, following this rule can be very expensive, especially at the beginning of a program's life cycle. The average line of code will be changed, modified, converted, and read many times over its lifetime. It is folly to view a refactoring exercise as time wasted without considering the tremendous savings over time. Instead, refactoring should be viewed as an investment that will pay whenever code is maintained, converted, read, enhanced, or otherwise modified. Therefore, refactoring is a cornerstone of this book.

A.5 Why Bitter Java?

In the Java community, the study and promotion of design patterns, or blueprints for proven solutions, has become well established and robust. The same is not true of the antipattern. As an architect and consultant, I have seen an amazing sameness to the mistakes that our customers tend to make. While the problem of the month may change slightly in a different domain or setting, the patterns of poor design, culture, and even technology stay remarkably consistent from one engagement to the next. I strongly believe that the study of antipatterns inherently changes the way we look at the software process. It keeps us observant. It makes us communicate. It helps us to step beyond our daily grind to make the fundamental process changes that are required to be successful.

Most of the antipatterns in *Bitter Java* have a relatively limited focus compared to the more general antipatterns in the *AntiPatterns* text. Each is applied to the server-side programming domain, which is popular right now and young enough to have a whole new set of common mistakes. Our hope is that this book will continue the evolution of the study of antipatterns and bring it into the Java community.

A.5.1 *The* Bitter Java *approach*

Bitter Java will take a set of examples, all related to a simple Internet message board, and redesign them over many chapters. Each iteration will point out a common antipattern and present a refactored, or redesigned, solution that solves the problem. In many cases, there may still be problems in the refactored solution. In most cases, these problems are addressed in later chapters. The others are left as an exercise for the reader. Regardless, the focus of the antipattern is to refactor a single problematic element.

The focus of *Bitter Java* is on server-side programming. The base architecture uses common server-side standards of servlets, JSPs, Java connectors, and EJBs. Where possible, the solutions are not limited to any vendor, though EJB implementations are currently platform specific.

A.5.2 Bitter Java *tools*

Based on my experience, I have chosen VisualAge for Java, WebSphere, and DB2 because the software and support are readily available to the authors. All of the implementations stress open Java designs and software architectures. Free, open alternatives to our software include:

- The home page for Java, with pages for base toolkits and specifications for J2EE extensions, can all be found at http://java.sun.com.
- A free servlet container, for the execution of servlets and JSPs either in a stand-alone mode or with a web server, can be found at http://jakarta.apache.org/tomcat/.
- A free web server can be found at http://apache.org.

BEA Systems' WebLogic also supports all of the classes and constructs used in this book, though they have been tested only on the original toolset. We do use the IBM database drivers (and I feel that the native database driver is almost always the best option), but we do not use the IBM-specific framework for databeans or serv-let extensions, opting for the open counterparts instead.

A.5.3 *The Bitter Java organization*

Bitter Java presents some background information in chapters 1 and 2, and subsequent chapters present a series of antipatterns. The patterns are collected into themes. Chapters 3 and 4 focus on a design pattern called Model-View-Controller, and an associated Java design pattern called the Triangle. Chapters 5 and 6 concentrate on optimizing memory and caching. Chapters 7 and 8 concentrate on EJBs and connections. Chapters 9 and 10 address programming hygiene and good performance through scalability. The chapters are organized in the following manner:

- Background material for the chapter.
- A basic description of the antipattern, including some of the root causes and problems.
- Sample code illustrating the use of an antipattern.
- One or more refactored solutions.
- Sample code illustrating the refactored solution.
- A summary containing the highlights of the chapter.
- A list of all antipatterns covered in the chapter.

Antipatterns and templates

Each antipattern is presented twice: once in the main text, and once in template form at the end of each chapter. The templates that we have chosen, both within the chapters and at the end of most chapters, are based on the templates suggested in the *AntiPatterns* book. Those in the chapter text choose a minimalist organization with the keyword *antipattern* followed by its name in a heading, followed by some background material. Finally, we present a refactored solution following the *solution* keyword. At the end of each chapter is a more formal template, following the conventions in *AntiPatterns*. In this way, we make this initial contribution to the initial collection of Java antipatterns.

If you are looking for particular technologies or techniques, this is where to find them:

Table A.1 The technologies and techniques in *Bitter Java* are presented in an order that suits the ongoing refactoring of a set of examples. This table can help you navigate to particular concepts that might interest you.

Technologies	Chapter
JSP design and composition	3, 4
Servlet design and composition	3, 4
JDBC, database programming	3, 4, 5, 6, 7
Connections framework	7
XML antipatterns	7
Web services	7
EJBs	8
Caching	5
Model-view-controller	3, 4
Performance antipatterns, tuning, and analysis	10
Antipatterns and the development process	1, 2, 11
Connection pooling	6
Coding standards and programming hygiene	9

For the programming examples, http://www.manning.com/tate/ has the complete code for all of the examples, as well as forums for discussing the topics of the book. The code in the book will be in the Courier style:

```
code = new Style("courier");
```

Where possible, long programs will have embedded text to describe the code. In other places, there may be in-line code that looks like this. Most of the programming samples are based on VisualAge for Java, version 4, and WebSphere Studio version 4. Most Java examples are based on JSP 1.1 and on Java 1.2. We'll tell you if the version is different. Some of the code examples for the antipatterns are for instructional purposes only and are not running programs. We have compiled and tried all of the good programming examples. They work.

A.5.4 *The* Bitter Java *audience*

Bitter Java is not written like a traditional technical manual or textbook. To keep things lively, we will mix in real-life adventure stories at the beginning of each chapter, with a programming moral later in the chapter. We hope that the style will engage many, and it might put off a few. If you are a reader who likes to cut to the chase, you will probably want to skip to chapter 3, and you may even want to skip the story at the front of each chapter. If you are looking for a dry reference with little extraneous content, this book is probably not for you.

The skill level for bitter Java is intermediate. If you have all of the latest Java design pattern books and have bookmarks for all of the key design pattern communities, this book is probably not for you. If you do not yet know Java, then you will want to try some introductory books and then come back to this one. If, like most Java programmers, you are an intermediate who could use some advice about some common Java pitfalls, then this book *is* for you. Those who have converted to Java from a simpler language, a scripting language, or a procedural language like C may find this book especially compelling.

Finally, *Bitter Java* is intended to be at a slightly lower level of abstraction than project management books, or the first *AntiPatterns* text. We intend to introduce code and designs that do not work and to refactor them. From these, we will show the low-level impact of process flaws, a failure to educate, and shortcuts. From this standpoint, architects and programmers will find appropriate messages, but they may find following the examples challenging. Project managers may also find some compelling thoughts, though the programming content may be slightly advanced. For both of these communities, antipattern summaries are listed at the end of each chapter in a concise template based on those in the original *AntiPatterns* text.

A.6 *Looking ahead*

Bitter Java is about programming war stories. Books like *The Mythical Man Month,* by Fredrick P. Brooks, have left an indelible impression in the minds of a whole generation of programmers. We aim to do for Java programmers what Brooks did for project managers. *Bitter Java* is about the quest for *imperfection.* We are not looking for isolated examples. We are looking for problems in process and culture, demonstrated by technically flawed designs. We are setting out to find the repeated mistakes that have bite. We are recording some of the useful mythology of the Java programmer.

In the next chapter, we will focus on the current landscape of the industry and why it is so ripe for antipatterns. Next, we will look at basic server-side designs and some antipatterns that plague them. Then, we will focus on common problems with resources and communication. Finally, we will look at advanced antipatterns related to enterprise Java deployments. So, settle down with this cup of bitter Java. We hope that when you're done, your next cup will be a smoother, more satisfying brew.

Bitter basics

This appendix contains
- An introduction to Enterprise JavaBeans

Only a few short years ago, development teams sweated and toiled to build custom system-level architectures—often inescapably riddled with bugs—to support their business applications. Although proprietary offerings speckled the middleware market, the portability and interoperability of these products left a lot to be desired. Developers wasted time rewriting logic to work with each different application server vendor's implementations; debugging code that had little to do with the actual business problems at hand; and retooling when requirements outgrew initial expectations. The problems cried out for another level of abstraction, one that would allow developers to concentrate on their own specific requirements. Enter EJB.

A number of proprietary offerings allowed developers to explicitly access system-level services through standard APIs. However, an explicit model has a significant downside: it comingles the system APIs with the business logic. EJB, on the other hand, abstract out the business logic by allowing the application server to intercept bean calls and implicitly invoke system-level services. In the EJB model, only business logic is placed in the bean implementations, and the container invokes system-level services based on separate declarative configuration information. This approach also allows the system-level aspects of your application to be configured at deployment time without modifying or recompiling source code.

Physically, the EJB architecture consists of a relatively concise specification and a small set of Java interfaces; both may be downloaded for free at Sun's EJB website (http://java.sun.com/ejb). The specification defines developer roles in the EJB architecture and contracts that actors in these roles are required to follow. The Java interfaces represent the physical code contract between the application server provider and the bean developer.

The spirit behind EJB is that bean developers can compose business logic leaving the system-level details to the container vendors who, in turn, make their money selling runtime environments in which the beans can live. The container implements a number of system-level services. Many of these services remain almost completely out of sight and out of mind for bean developers. The EJB architecture lays a foundation for bean providers to develop business logic without worrying about synchronization, transactions, resource management, state management, persistence, security, or other system-level details. If any of these services fall under your project's requirements, EJB may be for you.

B.1 Developing in the EJB architecture

The specification defines EJB as a distributed-component architecture. An EJB, a special Java component, lives in an EJB container. Third-party vendors customarily provide an EJB container as part of an Application server. An EJB encapsulates business logic—that is, code directly related to the purpose of your application. For example, if your application books kayaking trips, the business logic might include scheduling a trip for a user and sending out a confirmation email. Monitoring the transaction, ensuring that all steps complete successfully, qualifies as system logic. As an EJB developer, you can implement your business logic and let the container transparently manage system-level services for you.

Unlike many other Java technologies and APIs that we've come across, the EJB architecture does not begin and end on the Java interfaces. In fact, the interfaces' sheer flexibility often tends to obscure the interfaces' purposes. You may sometimes be required to declare methods or implement behaviors not detailed in the EJB interfaces themselves. Other times, implementing a certain method or behavior may be erroneous. A thorough understanding of the rules surrounding the EJB architecture—the contracts and rules between the bean provider, the container provider, and the bean client—is key to successfully developing for the platform.

B.1.1 Getting acquainted with the cast, the bean triad

The EJB specification defines three distinct types of beans: session, entity, and message-driven. Each bean type has a contract (or a rule set) and a specific purpose. You can use combinations of this bean triad to address almost any middleware requirement. Let's look first at an overview of each bean type, then we'll focus on the EJB architecture as a whole, describing bean type-specific caveats as necessary.

Modeling services with session beans

Session beans model services. They perform tasks on behalf of the client and are often closely related to your project's use cases—those specific tasks that the actors or clients in your application set out to perform. For example, if one of your use cases calls for scheduling a trip with an extreme sports company, your session bean would model a booking agent that contains methods to inquire about availability and schedule trips.

Session beans come in two flavors: stateless and stateful. These types refer to the beans' ability to *remember* information from one request to the next. The session bean type you choose depends on factors such as the service your bean is modeling, the type of client accessing the bean, and the characteristics of the environment in which the bean lives. (For example, you will need to know whether the bean and the client are running on the same machine or communicating over a network.)

When we first started developing with session beans, we found the stateful variety to be more intuitive as their development correlates closely with that of normal Java objects. Essentially, a stateful session bean provides a means for clients to lease memory on the server. The client can create the object and operate on it much as it would on a local object. The stateful session bean instance lives on the server until the creating client explicitly removes it or the Application server causes it to expire after a pre-set length of idle time.

Stateless session beans are less intuitive than their stateful siblings. Imagine a Java object that cannot retain client-specific information from one method call to the next. Why on earth would you want to use this? The answer is simple—scalability. A stateful session bean instance can be used for only one client for the entire session. The application server is obligated to maintain this instance until the client removes it and possibly until the idle timeout. If you have a lot of clients, stateful beans can consume resources—memory to hold the instance and CPU cycles to retrieve the specific instance when needed—quickly. In the stateless model, however, the application server can redirect the client's request to any arbitrary bean instance, even on another machine. The Application server can grow and shrink a pool of stateless session bean instances as needed, using memory only when necessary and transparently failing over when exceptional conditions arise.

Persisting data with entity beans

Entity beans provide a framework for mapping data from a persistent store to Java interfaces. They allow middleware developers to decouple their application logic from their persistence APIs. This means you can swap relational database vendors easily or even migrate from a relational database to an object-oriented database without modifying your business logic. Where session beans are transient, entity beans are durable and persist across server restarts and even crashes. In the same way that session beans correlate well with use cases, you can compare entity beans with the objects that your application logic manipulates—your application's domain objects.

Continuing the extreme sports trip booking example, you would use entity beans to model either the user that booked the trip or the trip reservation. If your application data was persisted in a relational database, you may have one table to hold user information and another table to hold information on scheduled trips.

You could map an entity bean to each table. The individual entity bean instances map one-to-one to the table rows. The entity bean logic maps the fields in the persistent store with methods in a Java interface.

Entity beans come in two flavors, those using BMP and those using CMP. The developer is responsible for the persistence logic in a BMP entity bean. For example, if a relational database backs a BMP entity bean, the bean developer implements the SQL for creating objects, accessing an object's fields and querying for objects.

The EJB container automatically manages the persistence logic for CMP entity beans. Although CMP has its limitations, it is a rapidly maturing technology. If possible, CMP is definitely the advisable road to take. First, CMP abstracts the persistence details from the entity bean. A CMP entity bean user can reconfigure a bean backed by a relational database to use an object-oriented database without modifying even the entity bean logic—not to mention the business logic that uses the entity bean. CMP also gives the container more control over the persistence details, increasing its ability to optimize updates and cache data. Many application server vendors even provide functionality to automatically set up the database tables based on CMP entity beans.

Processing asynchronous messages with message-driven beans

JMS provides a framework for asynchronous message passing. Whereas a normal method call blocks until the processing finishes, JMS enables you to fire off a message and immediately go about your business without waiting for a return value.

A JMS-based system consists of two types of actors: producers and consumers. Producers send messages to JMS destinations where a consumer pulls and processes the message. JMS supports two production-consumption models: point-to-point and publish-subscribe.

In the point-to-point model, each message is processed only once. The JMS destination type is referred to as a queue. Producers put messages on a queue in the same location used by a consumer to pull and process the messages. The publish-subscribe model supports multiple consumers or subscribers that can subscribe to a JMS destination called a topic. The JMS server removes a message from the topic once all subscribers have had a chance to process it.

Message-driven beans provide a convenient means to implement JMS consumers. A message driven bean operates as and plays by similar rules as a stateless session bean. However, a bean client directly invokes methods on a session bean while a message-driven bean only implements the method that the container fires in response to messages on a JMS destination. One goal of the JMS architecture is to keep developers from worrying about multithreaded programming; message-driven beans help to further alleviate synchronization concerns.

B.1.2 *Know your host, the EJB container*

EJB live in a runtime environment provided by the EJB container. The container bridges the bean client interface and the actual bean implementation, both of which are defined by the bean provider. The container uses this bridge to intercept bean method invocations, allowing the application server to hook system-level tasks at the beginning and end of method invocations. The EJB specification makes services such as transaction management mandatory, while others such as hot deployment are left to vendors' devices.

Container services

- **Remote Method Invocation (RMI)**   Because EJB is fundamentally a distributed architecture, EJB are typically meant to be remotely accessible. The EJB container abstracts these details. Clients can access EJB components remotely using Java RMI, a pure Java to Java network protocol, or CORBA-IIOP, a platform- and language-independent protocol that slightly predates RMI. In the EJB 2.0 specification, container support for IIOP is mandatory. This exposes your bean's functionality to other CORBA-compliant applications including the Microsoft COM architecture among others. The container also ensures that the values you pass back and forth across the remote interface abide by the rules of the underlying transport mechanism. For example, parameters and return values must be serializable.

- **Java Naming and Directory Interface (JNDI)**   The EJB container provides a JNDI service. JNDI is a flexible API used to bind and retrieve objects and other data using URL-like keys. The EJB container makes beans and system resources such as database and JMS connection factories available through a special implementation of the JNDI class called `InitialContext`. Depending on the vendor's implementation, the information in the InitialContext can be accessed locally or remotely or shared across a cluster. Containers typically bind EJB references under the "java:comp/env" context. However, as of the EJB 2.0 specification, this is not required.

- **Object life cycle management**   The EJB container manages the life cycles of EJB components. The container creates, caches, pools, and disposes of EJB instances, optimally servicing client needs. The container also reads and persists data at appropriate times. This is a key reason to use entity beans over custom JDBC.

- **Transactions** EJB containers automatically manage transactions. A transaction is a programming concept used to simplify application reliability. Among other capabilities, EJB containers can ensure that your process's view of the application's state stays consistent for the transaction's duration; that the processes in your application do not interfere with each other; and that your entire unit of work either executes successfully or not at all.

- **Hot deployment** Guaranteed uptime and reliability in enterprise applications is a must. Consequently, many application servers allow for hot deployment of EJB components. In other words, you can add, remove, and reload beans while the application server is running. Combined with transactions, hot deployment allows you to modify a bean's implementation without adversely affecting a client's request midstream.

- **Server management/monitoring, logging** Application servers provide robust sets of tools to monitor and manage the state of your server and bean instances. Vendors provide tools to easily configure beans and system resources, to monitor system performance and resource usage, and to audit application events such as client access, transaction failures, system exceptions, and outages, etc.

- **Concurrency** A key and powerful concept within the EJB architecture is thread management. The container simplifies bean development by guaranteeing that all access to a bean instance will be single-threaded. This guarantee completely alleviates any need to use synchronization primitives inside bean implementations. Application servers manage concurrent access to EJB components in a number of ways including synchronizing access to bean instances or creating multiple bean instances to which client requests can be delegated. The exact synchronization strategy used depends on the type of bean and the application server's implementation.

- **Clustering** Many EJB application servers support clustering. You can run duplicate application instances on the same or different machines. This will make your application more scalable and able to process a larger number of client requests via load balancing. Your application will also be more reliable, because you can fail over to other server instances if a server instance goes down. Application servers support many different heterogeneous and homogeneous, multitiered configurations. Typically, homogeneous configurations are the most easily managed and scalable, as every server will share the same configuration. Consequently, the need for expensive invocations over the network is eliminated.

- **Resource management** The container makes system resources such as database connection, JMS queues and topics, and JCA adapters available to your application via JNDI bindings. The container creates, manages, and pools such resources and ensures that access correlates with transaction contexts.

- **Security** In addition to the default security mechanisms provided by the Java platform, the EJB architecture allows you to limit access to EJB types and individual methods based on declarative user roles. The container also makes a user's authentication information available to your business logic automatically to facilitate programmatic security.

Remote method invocation (RMI)

RMI is fundamental to the EJB architecture. Remote EJB invocations in a pure Java environment depend on a core Java technology, RMI. In RMI, remotely accessible objects implement the `java.rmi.Remote` interface. An RMI compiler generates a stub and skeleton for the object. The client invokes methods on the stub; the RMI subsystem marshals the call across the network to the skeleton running on the server. The skeleton delegates the method call to your actual implementation and marshals the return value back across the network to the client (figure B.1). From the client's perspective, the invocation works similarly to that of a local call. One exception is that the remote interface throws a `RemoteException`, signaling potential failure points due to network or I/O exceptions and enabling the client to react politely to such conditions.

While values passed within the same virtual machine are passed by reference—for example, a pointer to your instance—parameters and return values passed across a remote interface are serialized. As a result these are passed by value; modifications to an instance on one end will not be reflected on the other. Any objects that pass through a remote interface must implement the `Serializable` interface. When an object is serialized, the entire object map—every object that the object references—is serialized and passed as well. For this reason, you should try to minimize coupling between objects that will be passed across a remote interface or serialized in general. This approach will help manage the amount of data passed across the network and will reduce the transfer of duplicate information across a set of invocations.

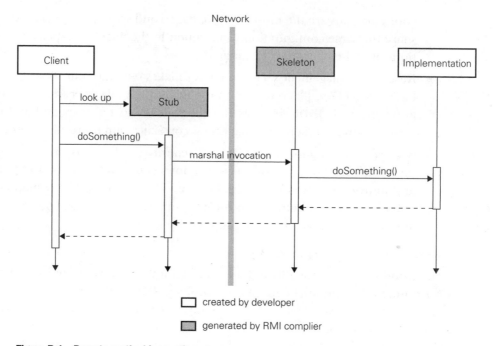

Figure B.1   Remote method invocation sequence

CORBA is a platform and language independent predecessor to RMI. An explicit goal of the EJB specification is to support integration by existing architectures. In this spirit, the 2.0 specification mandates that containers support CORBA interfaces to EJB as well as the RMI counterparts.

IIOP is the underlying communication protocol used by CORBA. RMI-IIOP combines the compatibility of CORBA with RMI's ease of use. Applications can also use RMI-IIOP for intervendor communications. RMI-IIOP sacrifices some functionality for the sake of interoperability. For example, in RMI you can upcast remote objects directly. In contrast, objects retrieved via RMI-IIOP—possibly from a JNDI registry—must be upcast using the `java.rmi.PortableRemoteObject.narrow()` method. This method adds the necessary Java class definition information lost during the IIOP transmission. Client code in a J2EE environment should always favor the narrow method over the direct upcast to ensure interoperability.

B.2 *Crafting enterprise beans*

Let's briefly review: The three types of EJB can be used to model your middleware application's parts. Session beans are used for your application's logic. Entity

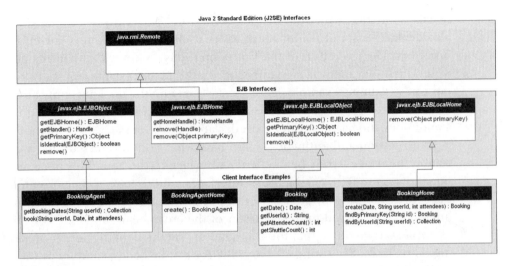

Figure B.2 EJB client interface class diagram

beans represent your application's data. Message-driven beans process asynchronous events.

As we mentioned earlier, session beans come in two flavors: stateful and stateless. To access and implement either type of session bean, you must follow that type's unique set of rules. In addition, entity beans have two implementation types relating to the persistence delegation models. A developer must explicitly implement the persistence logic for an entity bean using BMP, while the container automatically handles persistence logic for entity beans using CMP.

B.2.1 Defining the client interfaces

The EJB client (possibly another EJB) invokes bean methods and abstractly controls the bean instance's life cycle via a well-defined set of interfaces. Session and entity beans use a home and client Java interface combination while message-driven bean clients communicate using JMS.

Session and entity bean clients look up the bean's home interface using JNDI. The home interface provides bean clients with a starting point, offering a way to loosely control a bean's life cycle. For example, when a client calls the remove() method for a session bean, the container may actually pool the bean instance for use in a later request, rather than actually making it available for garbage collection.

Entity bean clients create, query, and remove instances through the home interface. When a client creates an entity bean, the entity is created in the persistent store. When the client calls the remove() method on an entity bean, the container deletes the entity's data from the persistent store. The entity bean's home interface also declares a set of finder methods that clients use to query for entity bean instances. The operation of the finder methods compares to that of a SELECT in SQL. The finder method signature follows the findXXX() pattern. Let's return to our trip-scheduling example. Here findByUser() on the booking entity home interface would return the collection of booking entities associated with a given user. At a minimum, the bean provider must declare a findByPrimaryKey() method.

Both session and entity beans also have what's often referred to as a client or remote interface—your bean client's interface to the actual instance and functionality (figure B.2). Session bean interfaces tend to have service-oriented methods—for example, "book a trip" or "post a message." Methods in entity bean interfaces correspond to the elements of the entity bean models. In our booking example, this might be "get the trip date" or "set the booking agent" on the booking entity bean. See listings B.1 and B.2 for source code examples of the session and entity bean interfaces, respectively.

Message-driven beans do not define a standalone Java interface. Clients invoke message-driven beans indirectly using JMS messages. This, in turn, means that the container keeps complete control over the message-driven bean life cycle.

Listing B.1 Stateless session bean client interface example

```java
import java.rmi.RemoteException;
import java.util.*;
import javax.ejb.*;

/**
 * Stateless session bean client interface example.
 */
public interface BookingAgent extends EJBObject {

  /**
   * Get bookings for a user ID.
   * @param userId User's ID.
   * @return Collection of Date instances.
   */
  public Collection getBookingDates(String userId)
    throws RemoteException;

  /**
   * Book a trip.
   * @param userId ID of the user booking the trip.
   * @param date Trip date.
   * @param attendees Number of attendees.
   */
  public void book(String userId, Date date, int attendees)
  throws BookingException, RemoteException;
```

```
}
import java.rmi.RemoteException;
import java.util.*;
import javax.ejb.*;

/**
 * Stateless session bean home interface example.
 */
public interface BookingAgentHome extends EJBHome {

  /**
   * Mandatory no-parameter create() method.
   */
  public BookingAgent create() throws RemoteException,
    CreateException;

}
```

Identifying persistent objects with primary keys

Like records in a relational database table, primary keys uniquely identify entity bean instances. The primary key for an entity bean may be a primitive type or a complex object. A primary key class must implement Serializable and follow the rules of serialization. Primary key objects are used between the client and container as well as between the container and bean implementation to identity entity bean instances.

Choosing local vs. remote interfaces

One of the most difficult elements of building an EJB model is controlling the high communications costs. Often, you must choose the right mechanism and timing to communicate between major objects. To a beginner, the need to make rapid decisions can seem overwhelming. Fortunately, EJB 2.0 offers a few additional tools to guide you through the maze. In EJB versions 1.0 and 1.1, all beans had explicitly remote interfaces. In other words, all invocations were *supposed* to use RMI, whether or not the client and the bean were running in the same virtual machine. All bean home and client interfaces extended the EJBHome and EJBObject Java interfaces, respectively. This proved to be a significant performance bottleneck and many vendors implemented localized performance optimizations, often fudging the contract between the container and bean client.

EJB 2.0 introduced the idea of explicitly local interfaces. Beans providing local interfaces extended the EJBLocalHome and EJBLocalObject Java interfaces rather than their remote counterparts. Beans and clients running in the same virtual machine could now communicate efficiently and still reap the benefits of the other system-level services provided by the container. Why two interfaces? A few subtle, but crucial, differences exist between the implementations of remote and local interfaces. First and foremost, remote interfaces communicate using RMI or RMI-IIOP. Parameters and return values are passed-by-value. In other words, the method and the caller have completely separate copies of the objects. Local interfaces, on the other hand, pass-by-reference; the method and the caller have references or pointers to the same object in memory (which is why the bean and client must be running in the same virtual machine). Secondly, remote invocations are vulnerable to a host of errors and issues you don't see in local invocations. The remote bean client should be aware of and able to politely respond to unexpected conditions such as network outages and I/O errors. Conversely, local bean clients are much simpler; they typically only need to account for application exceptions. Lastly, when designing the interface, the bean provider must balance performance and functionality. Providing a finer grained interface gives the client more flexibility but increases the overhead of remote calls. A coarser interface consolidates much of the overhead in remote invocations, but can limit the bean client's deployment options.

For the most part, we use local interfaces for entity beans and remote interfaces for session beans. Entity bean interfaces inherently provide convenient, fine-grained access to entity fields and are not well suited to remote invocations. Session bean interfaces, on the other hand, tend toward the coarse-grained, service-oriented end and are therefore conducive to remote invocation. Even if your session bean and client will initially run within the same virtual machine, the overhead of a remote interface is minimal in most situations. You will save in development and testing time and effort when scaling to a clustered environment. Entity beans with local interfaces can be used internally in your session bean implementations.

> **Listing B.2   CMP entity bean client interface example**

```
import java.util.*;
import javax.ejb.*;

/**
 * CMP entity bean client interface example.
 */
public interface Booking extends EJBLocalObject {

  /** Scheduled date for the booked trip. */
  public Date getDate();

  /** User that booked the trip. */
```

```
    public String getUserId();

    /** Number of attendees. */
    public int getAttendeeCount();

    /** Number of shuttles needed. */
    public int getShuttleCount();

}

import java.util.*;
import javax.ejb.*;

/**
 * CMP entity bean home interface example.
 */
public interface BookingHome extends EJBLocalHome {

  /** Used to create a booking. */
  public Booking create(Date date, String userId,
    int attendees);

  /** Locate Booking instances by primary key. */
  public Booking findByPrimaryKey(String id)
    throws FinderException;

  /** Locate Booking instances by user ID. */
  public Collection findByUserId(String userId)
    throws FinderException;

}
```

Comparing remote instances

When comparing two objects for equality in a local environment, you typically use either the equality operator, ==, which compares two primitive values or object references for equality, or the equals() method, which typically compares two in-memory objects for equivalency. This model does not necessarily work in a distributed setting as two different client stubs may reference the same or equivalent objects in another virtual machine and memory space. EJB clients can use the isIdentical() method on a bean's client interface to compare remote instances.

For example, given two EJBObject stubs foo and bar that refer to the same EJB instance on the server, (foo == bar) may return false whereas (foo.isIdentical(bar)) could return true.

Note that, unlike stateful session beans and entity beans, stateless session beans have no identity. A call to isIdentical() for two EJBObject's referring to the same stateless session bean type will always return true.

B.2.2 *Implementing the business logic*

The EJB implementation class implements one of three bean type-specific interfaces and contains the actual implementation logic. Unlike conventional Java classes and interfaces, the EJB implementation does not implement the client interface directly. This model decouples the class interfaces and allows the container to safely hook all access to your bean instance, starting and stopping transactions, verifying security credentials, and implicitly performing other system-level services. Your bean implementation should never directly implement the client interface. Subtle bugs could surface if a request undermined the container's control and invoked your bean directly, a possibility if your bean inadvertently passed a reference to itself as a method parameter or return value. See figure B.3 for a class diagram of our example bean implementations.

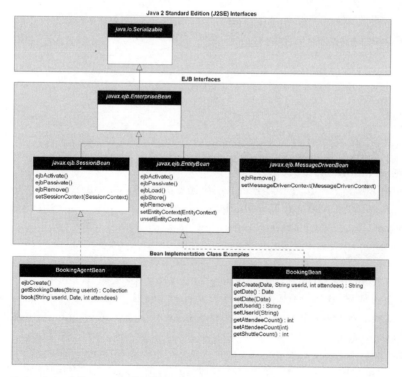

Figure B.3   EJB implementation class diagram

Listening to the container

The three bean types implement a given set of callback methods used by the container to notify the bean instance of life cycle events. The container invokes these methods at specific points in the EJB's life.

Implementing session beans

All session beans implement a variant or variants of an `ejbCreate()` method. The container invokes one of these methods when it creates the bean instance. Stateless session beans always have one, no-parameter `ejbCreate()` method. Stateful session beans can implement `ejbCreate()` methods with or without parameters so long as they correspond with the `create()` methods in the session bean's home interface. The bean implementation class uses the parameters to initialize the bean's state. See listing B.3 for the source code example for our booking agent session bean implementation.

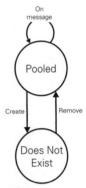

**Figure B.4
Stateless
session bean life
cycle diagram**

The container calls the `ejbRemove()` before the end of a bean instance's life. The session bean implementation releases any resources at this time. Note that, in the event of significant bean or server error, the container may never invoke `ejbRemove()`; bean implementations should account for this condition.

The container may create and destroy stateless session bean instances at will (figure B.4). However, with stateful session beans, the container may serialize and deserialize instances to conserve resources—more specifically, to conserve memory. The specification refers to this practice as passivation, and the converse function as activation. The container calls `ejbPassivate()` before passivation or serialization and `ejbActivate()` after activation or deserialization. The stateful session bean implementation should release transient resources such as database connections or open sockets upon passivation and restore these same resources upon activation.

Stateful session beans can also optionally implement the `SessionSynchronization` interface. This provides the implementation with another set of callback methods used to send transaction life cycle notifications. For example, a stateful session bean can restore its state in the event that a transaction aborts (figure B.5).

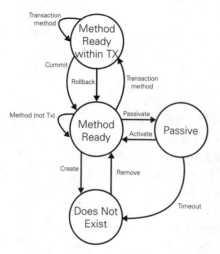

Figure B.5
Stateful session bean life cycle diagram

Listing B.3   Stateless session bean implementation example

```
import java.util.*;
import javax.ejb.*;

/**
 * Stateless session bean implementation class example.
 * Note: Does not explicitly implement bean client interface.
 */
public class BookingAgentBean implements SessionBean {

  /** Session context instance. */
  private SessionContext sessionContext;

  /** Called by container before invocation. */
  public void setSessionContext(SessionContext sessionContext) {
    this.sessionContext = sessionContext;
  }

  /** Called by container after creation. */
  public void ejbCreate() throws CreateException {}

  /** Possibly called by container before removal. */
  public void ejbRemove() {}

  /** Not actually used in stateless session beans. */
  public void ejbActivate() {}

  /** Not actually used in stateless session beans. */
  public void ejbPassivate() {}

  public Collection getBookingDates(String userId) {
    // Query database for list of booking dates
    // and return a Collection of Date instances.
    // ...
```

```
    return null;
  }
  public void book(String userId, Date date, int attendees)
  throws BookingException
  {
    // Add a booking to the database.
    // Throw a BookingException if there is a
    // scheduling conflict.
    // ...
  }

}
```

Implementing entity beans

The purpose of the ejbCreate() and ejbRemove() methods in the entity bean implementation differs from that of the session bean counterparts. Entity bean ejbCreate() methods may accept parameters as well. The entity bean ejbCreate() method creates an object in the persistent data store and returns the object's primary key. The container calls the ejbRemove() method to remove the object from the persistent store. The bean implementation must implement one ejbCreate() method for each create() method in the client interface. Entity beans are not required to implement any create() methods. The bean implementation must also implement one ejbPostCreate() method for each ejbCreate() method; both methods must have the same parameters. The container invokes ejbPostCreate() after calling the ejbCreate() method and associating your instance with an EJBObject—in other words, after your bean is client-accessible.

While entity beans using BMP return a primary key object from the ejbCreate() method, entity beans using CMP should return null. The container will create the object in the persistent store and generate the primary key.

Entity beans using BMP must implement two additional container callback methods, ejbLoad() and ejbStore(). These methods allow the container to synchronize an entity bean instance's data with a data store. The container uses ejbLoad() to tell the entity bean instance to load its data from the store, possibly for the first time, or to synchronize the beans data at the beginning of a transaction. The container uses ejbStore() to tell the bean instance to persist its data to the store. The container invokes each of these two callback methods at a time that depends on several factors, including your vendor's implementation, your bean's transaction configuration, and your caching settings, if any.

The container uses the ejbActivate() and ejbPassivate() methods to prepare an in-memory entity bean instance for creation and removal. For a new object, the container will invoke the `ejbActivate()` method before calling `ejb-Load()` for the first time. This allows the bean implementation to set up any transient resources needed for the `ejbLoad()` implementation. When a container removes an instance from memory (without removing the object from the persistent store), it will call `ejbStore()` to ensure that all data has been persisted and then call `ejbPassivate()` to release resources (figure B.6).

The bean provider is responsible for implementing the finder methods for BMP entity beans. Though the finder methods declared in the home interface and the actual bean implementation have a one-to-one correspondence, the method names and return values are slightly different. Specifically, finder method names in the bean implementation are prefixed with an `ejb`. In addition, while the finder method in the client interface returns a collection of `EJBObject` instances or remote stubs, the finder method in your implementation class returns a `Collection` of primary keys. Using the minimally required `findByPrimaryKey()` method as an example, the corresponding finder method implementation would be called `ejbFindByPrimaryKey()`.

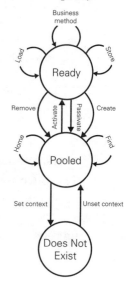

Figure B.6
Entity bean life cycle diagram

Entity bean implementations using CMP depart significantly from other EJB bean implementations (listing B.4). First, the implementation class for a CMP entity bean is declared abstract. Each persistent field also has a set of abstract getters and setters. For example, for the user ID field in our booking entity, we would have an abstract `getUserId()` and `setUserId()` method pair. The container subclasses your bean's implementation class, implementing the field accessors as well as the finder methods. You declare finder method functionality for CMP beans separately from your business logic, using EJB QL. EJB QL is syntactically comparable to a limited version of SQL. However, EJB QL is not tied to relational databases.

EJB 2.0 also introduced the notion of CMR. If you use local interfaces and CMP, you can configure relationships between your entity beans. For example, you could have a one-to-many relationship constraint between two entity bean types, much as you would between two tables in a relational database. This feature allows you to model complex data maps using entity beans and abstracts out this relationship management logic from the data store, further decoupling your application logic from the underlying persistence mechanism (listing B.4).

Listing B.4   CMP entity bean implementation example

```
import java.util.*;
import javax.ejb.*;

/**
 * CMP entity bean implementation example.
 */
public abstract class BookingBean implements EntityBean {

  /** Create implementation. */
  public String ejbCreate(Date date, String userId,
     int attendees)
  {
    setDate(date);
    setUserId(userId);
    setAttendeeCount(attendees);

    // return null because this bean uses CMP.
    return null;
  }

  /** Scheduled date for the booked trip. */
  public abstract Date getDate();
  public abstract void setDate(Date date);

  /** ID of user that booked trip. */
  public abstract String getUserId();
  public abstract void setUserId(String userId);

  /** Number of attendees. */
  public abstract int getAttendeeCount();
  public abstract void setAttendeeCount(int attendees);

  /** Number of shuttles needed. */
  public int getShuttleCount() {
    // Calculate the number of shuttles needed based
    // on the number of attendees.
    return -1;
  }

}
```

Implementing message-driven beans

When it comes to container callback methods, message-driven beans are most closely comparable to stateless session beans. Message driven bean implementations have a no-parameter `ejbCreate()` method called when the instance is created and an `ejbRemove()` method called when the instance gets destroyed (figure B.7).

Message-driven bean implementation classes implement the JMS `MessageListener` interface in addition to the `MessageDrivenBean` interface. The `MessageListener` interface contains a single `onMessage()` method that accepts a JMS Message as a parameter. The container fires the `onMessage()` method in response to messages on the JMS destination to which the message-driven bean is bound.

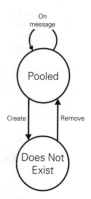

Figure B.7
Message-driven bean life cycle diagram

Controlling the runtime with the bean context

One aspect common to all three bean type implementations is their method of container runtime communication. Each bean implementation declares a callback method that the container uses to associate a context with the instance, specifically `setSessionContext()`, `setEntityContext()`, and `setMessageDrivenContext()` for session, entity, and message-driven beans, respectively. Bean implementations use the context object to get authentication information on the client or to access the transaction manager.

Session and entity beans can use the context object to obtain their corresponding `EJBObject` or client interface or their `EJBHome` object. Additionally, entity beans get the primary key object through the context object.

Throwing the right exception

The EJB architecture breaks exceptions into two different classes—system and application exceptions. The container handles each class in a different fashion. Understanding exceptions and how the container reacts to them is an often-underrated key to effectively developing EJB components.

System exceptions signify fatal, unexpected system-level errors. These include `RemoteException`, `EJBException`, `RuntimeException`, and subclasses therein. An I/O error that occurs while transferring data over the network qualifies as a system exception, as does an unchecked null pointer. When a system exception occurs, the EJB specification requires that the container dispose of the bean instance that threw the exception and rollback the currently running transaction. However, the specification does award the container a lot of flexibility in recovering from system exceptions. For example, if a network I/O error occurs, the container may transparently reattempt the request; the client may be none the wiser.

Application exceptions signify application-specific events, such as field validation errors or, in the case of our trip scheduling application, a scheduling conflict. When an application level exception occurs, both the bean instance and the running transaction stay intact. The specification requires that the container throw application exceptions back to the client. The specification also declares default application exceptions. `CreateException` are thrown when an error occurs in the `ejbCreate()` method. Finder methods in entity beans throw `FinderException` if an error occurs during an entity bean query.

B.2.3 *Playing it safe with transactions*

Transactions, a key benefit of the EJB architecture, allow a developer to reliably and atomically execute a task. For example, in our extreme sport trip scheduling application we could ensure that a trip was scheduled and that the client's credit card was charged. If we ran into a scheduling conflict, the credit card would not get charged. If the credit card were declined, the trip would not get scheduled. A powerful feature of the EJB architecture is the container's ability to automatically handle transactions, even across multiple systems.

The EJB specification allows for two transaction situations, BMTs and CMTs. Beans with BMTs have the code to start and commit transactions explicitly embedded in the business logic, whereas the container automatically starts and commits CMTs.

Using CMTs, you can configure transaction attributes separate from your application logic down to a method-level granularity. You can configure bean methods to start a new transaction, run in an existing transaction, suspend an existing transaction, or even throw an exception if the client tries to invoke the method while running a transaction. CMTs award you a lot of flexibility and should be used whenever possible.

BMTs should be used only in the rare case where you have to run multiple individual transactions in a single method or, as with stateful session beans, when you need the transaction to span multiple method invocations. More often than not you can implement both cases in a different, but equally clear, manner using the more powerful and flexible CMTs.

Transactions naturally come with a bit of overhead and tend to consume resources easily. As a general rule, transactional tasks should be surgically fine to avoid robbing other clients of resources unnecessarily. A transaction's completion should almost never depend upon a human user's interaction.

B.2.4 *Configuring the bean*

EJB descriptors are XML files that tell the application server which classes comprise your bean. They also tell the application server how to configure your bean. A single descriptor can hold configuration information for multiple beans (listing B.5). The XML document type definition for the standard descriptor `ejb-jar.xml` can be downloaded at http://java.sun.com/dtd/ejb-jar_2_0.dtd.

Most application servers also require vendor-specific descriptors. For example, you may have a `weblogic-ejb-jar.xml` file containing the WebLogic-specific configuration information. The definitions for these proprietary descriptors vary from server to server.

You can edit descriptors by hand. However, most application servers and EJB development tools include tools to produce and modify the descriptors for you. Using such tools ensures validity in your descriptors, preventing potential issues and possibly even streamlining the development process.

Listing B.5 Deployment descriptor example

```
<?xml version="1.0"?>

<!DOCTYPE ejb-jar PUBLIC
  '-//Sun Microsystems, Inc.//DTD Enterprise JavaBeans 2.0//EN'
  'http://java.sun.com/dtd/ejb-jar_2_0.dtd'>

<ejb-jar>
  <enterprise-beans>
    <session>
      <ejb-name>BookingAgent</ejb-name>
      <home>BookingAgentHome</home>
      <remote>BookingAgent</remote>
      <ejb-class>BookingAgentBean</ejb-class>
      <session-type>Stateless</session-type>
      <transaction-type>Container</transaction-type>
    </session>
    <entity>
      <ejb-name>Booking</ejb-name>
      <local-home>BookingHome</local-home>
      <local>Booking</local>
      <ejb-class>BookingBean</ejb-class>
      <persistence-type>Container</persistence-type>
<prim-key-class>java.lang.String</prim-key-class>
<reentrant>False</reentrant>
<cmp-version>2.x</cmp-version>
<abstract-schema-name>Booking</abstract-schema-name>
      <cmp-field>
    <field-name>userId</field-name>
      </cmp-field>
      <cmp-field>
    <field-name>date</field-name>
      </cmp-field>
      <cmp-field>
    <field-name>attendees</field-name>
      </cmp-field>
```

```
      <query>
         <query-method>
<method-name>findByUserId</method-name>
<method-params>
   <method-param>java.lang.String</method-param>
</method-params>
         </query-method>
         <ejb-ql>
<![CDATA[
         SELECT OBJECT(a) FROM Booking AS a WHERE userId = ?1
]]>
         </ejb-ql>
      </query>
   </entity>
</enterprise-beans>
<assembly-descriptor>
   <container-transaction>
     <method>
       <ejb-name>BookingAgent</ejb-name>
         <method-name>*</method-name>
     </method>
       <trans-attribute>Required</trans-attribute>
   </container-transaction>
   <container-transaction>
     <method>
       <ejb-name>Booking</ejb-name>
         <method-name>*</method-name>
     </method>
       <trans-attribute>Required</trans-attribute>
   </container-transaction>
  </assembly-descriptor>
</ejb-jar>
```

B.2.5 *Packaging it*

All EJB are packaged in an `ejb-jar` file. An `ejb-jar` is essentially a JAR file containing all classes for the bean's interfaces and implementation, all the bean's dependent classes, and the bean's XML descriptors. A JAR file is simply a zip file with a `META-INF` directory and a manifest file. A single `ejb-jar` file may contain one or multiple EJB components.

You can also distribute a separate client `ejb-jar` file, though the specification does not require it. When you package the server and client components separately, you can reference the client JAR file in a `Class-Path` entry in your ejb-jar's manifest file:

```
/META-INF/*.xml        descriptors
/mypackage/*.class     bean classes
```

B.2.6 *Invoking your beans from a client*

Invoking an EJB may be a bit daunting at first (it was for us) but is fundamentally a cut-and-paste task. With session and entity beans, the client follows the following steps:

1 Create an `InitialContext` instance.

2 Look up the EJB's home object in the context.

3 Cast the home object using the `narrow()` method.

4 For session beans, call a `create()` method. For entity beans, call a `create()` method or lookup an `EJBObject` instance using a finder method.

5 Invoke methods on the `EJBObject`.

6 If you are using stateful session beans, remember to call the `remove()` method and help the container conserve resources.

Listing B.6 provides source code for looking up and invoking our BookingAgent example session bean.

Listing B.6 EJB client code example

```
// get a client stub.
InitialContext context = new InitialContext();
Object homeObject = context.lookup("BookingAgent");
BookingAgentHome agentHome = PortableRemoteObject.narrow(
  homeObject,
  BookingAgentHome.class
);
BookingAgent agent = agentHome.create();

// book a trip.
Date date = ...;
agent.book("bitterejb", date, 20);
```

To invoke a message-driven bean, simply send a JMS message to the proper destination.

bibliography

Ambler, Scott. "The Design of a Robust Persistence Paper for Relational Databases." Newmarket, Ontario: Ambysoft, 1997–2003.

Beck, Kent; Fowler, Martin, *Planning Extreme Programming*. Reading, Mass: Addison-Wesley, 2000.

Brooks, Fredrick P, *Mythical Man Month*. Reading, Mass: Addison-Wesley, 1995.

DeMichiel, Linda G., specification lead, *Enterprise JavaBeans^{TM} Specification Version 2.0*. Palo Alto, Ca: Sun Microsystems, 2001.

Eckstein, Robert, Editor, *Java Enterprise Best Practices*. Cambridge, MA: O'Reilly & Associates, Inc., 2002.

Fowler, Martin, *Refactoring: Improving the Design of Existing Code*. Reading, Mass.: Addison-Wesley, 1999.

Fowler, Martin; Rice, David; Foemmel, Matthew; Hieatt, Edward; Mee, Robert; Stafford, Randy, *Patterns of Enterprise Application Architecture*. Reading, Mass.: Addison-Wesley, 2002.

Hunter, Jason, *Java Servlet Programming*. Cambridge, MA: O'Reilly & Associates, Inc., 2001.

Laddad, Ramnivas, *AspectJ In Action*. Greenwich, CT: Manning Publications, 2003.

Matena, Vlada; Hapner, Mark, *Enterprise JavaBeans^{TM} Specification Version 1.0*. Palo Alto, Ca: Sun Microsystems, 1998.

Matena, Vlada; Hapner, Mark, *Enterprise JavaBeans^{TM} Specification Version 1.1*. Palo Alto, Ca: Sun Microsystems, 1999.

Monson-Haefel, Richard, *Enterprise Java Beans*. Cambridge, MA: O'Reilly & Associates, Inc., 2000.

Monson-Haefel, Richard; Chappell, David, *Java Message Service*. Cambridge, MA: O'Reilly & Associates, Inc., 2002.

Moore, Geoffrey A.; McKenna, Regis, *Crossing the Chasm*. New York, NY: HarperBusiness, 2002.

Roman, Edward; Ambler, Scott; Jewell, Tyler, *Mastering Enterprise JavaBeans*. New York, NY: John Wiley & Sons; 2nd edition, 2001.

Shankland, Stephen, *Java Jigsaw*. San Francisco, CA: c/net news.com, March 25, 2002.

Tate, Bruce, *Bitter Java*. Greenwich, CT: Manning Publications, 2002.

Terry, Shaun, *Enterprise JMS Programming*. New York, NY: John Wiley & Sons, 2002.

Sullins, Benjamin; Whipple, Mark, *EJB Cookbook*. Greenwich, CT: Manning Publications, 2003.

Yourdon, Edward. *Death March: The Complete Software Developer's Guide to Surviving Mission Impossible Projects*. Englewood Cliffs, NJ: Prentice Hall, 1999.

index

A

abstract
  persistence layer 69
administration 38
Adobe PDF 108
allmystuff 369
alternative technologies
  and EJB 350
alternatives
  to EJB 29
  to entity beans 246
Amazon 5, 361
Ambler
  Scott 268
Ant 5, 17, 335, 338
  target 338
antipattern 5, 124, 369
  See also mini-antipattern
  Application Filters 230, 243
  Application Joins 228, 242
  books 362
  Build Guru 337, 345
  cache 359
  community 365
  Conversational Baggage 157
  Custom DTO 73, 79
  Customers in the Kitchen
    66, 79
  Database Connection
    Hog 101
  and design patterns 359–360,
    366
  detective work 368
  Eager Iterator 103, 124
  Eavesdropping 195, 209

  EJB Code Duplication 332,
    344
  and EJB future 355
  entity beans 214
  Face Off 215, 217, 240
  Fat Messages 165
  Golden Hammer 12, 20
  Golden Hammers of Session
    State 143, 158
  Ham Sandwich 222, 241
  Hot Potato 191, 207
  in industry 367
  Integration Hell 341, 347
  Killer System Exceptions 97,
    123
  Local and Remote Interfaces
    Simultaneously 60, 78
  Magic Servlet 358, 362
  Narrow Servlet Bridges 113,
    125
  on line 361, 366
  Packrat 179, 205
  Performance
    Afterthoughts 199, 210,
    296, 320
  Persistent Problems 275, 284
  Premature Optimization 291,
    319
  Revolving Doors 235
  Round-Tripping 369
  Running with Scissors 339,
    346
  Rusty Keys 233, 244
  seasoned developers and 12
  Session Hodgepodge 152,
    160

  Sledgehammer for a Fly 30,
    51
  Slow Eater 194, 208
  Swallowing Exceptions 94,
    122
  System Loaded Application
    Classes 332
  System Loaded Applicaton
    Classes 343
  Tangled Threads 86, 121
  Thrash-tuning 303, 321
  well-known 363
  XML as the Silver Bullet 177,
    204
antipattern Monolithic
  Consumer 188, 206
AntiPatterns text 363, 366,
  371–372, 374
Apache 33, 371
application design 16
  and EJB 18
application exceptions 92, 97
application filters 230, 232, 243
  types 230
Application Filters
  antipattern 230, 243
application joins 228, 233, 242
  examples 229
Application Joins
  antipattern 228, 242
Application servers
  overspending 5
  pooling threads 86
application tier
  designing 57
application.xml 336

application-defined relation 229
architects 369, 374
arrays 364
AspectJ 352
Aspect-Oriented Programming
    (AOP) 93, 352
    and crosscutting
        concerns 352
    process 352
asynchronous
    APIs 25
    communication 350
    messages 380
asynchronous messaging 163
    excessive coupling and 182
    layering and 190
attributes
    persistent 250–251
authentication 42, 84
autogenerate
    EAR 336
    EJB class 333
    EJB code 325
    manifest 334
automated tests 17

B

B2B 178
Baldrige, Malcolm 368
BEA 5, 371
bean-managed persistence
    See BMP
behavior
    and session beans 85
benchmarking 10
best practices
    and EJB 1.0 7
    and PetStore 11
Bitter Java 5
BLOB
    SQL 235
blocked I/O 88
BMP 11, 222, 239, 259, 385
    defined 380
    drawbacks 223
    evaluation 259
    and relationships 224
    vs. CMP 223
BMP relation 229
BMT 99

bottleneck 217, 291
    example 312
    horror story 296
bubble sort 363
bug patterns 366
bugs 363, 365, 368
build 324
    case study 337
build environment 17
Build Guru
    antipattern 337, 345
bulk accessors 70
Business Delegate 71
business logic 377
by reference
    passing 54

C

C 374
C++ 357, 363
caching 11, 14, 39, 67, 359
    component level 33
    and iterators 107
calls between JVM
    and parameters 56
Castor 105
    JDO 269
central directory 8
checked exception 97
choice
    of persistence framework 275
choosing
    a persistence architecture 282
CICS 363
class diagrams 362
class loader 325, 330
    and EAR files 331
    and WAR files 331
ClassCastException 331
ClassNotFoundExceptions 96
Class-Path 329
client interfaces 385
client JAR
    EJB 330
client stub factory 116
cluster
    and EJB 85
clustering 16, 382

CMP 222, 246, 254, 267, 349,
    385
    advantages 225
    and EJB 43
    and EJB QL 280
    complexity 275
    defined 380
    dynamic query
        limitations 231
    evaluation 250
    example 250
    history 223
    in EJB 2.0 43
    and performance 226
    vs. BMP 223, 259
CMP vs. BMP
    decision matrix 226
CMR 8, 45, 227–228
coarse-grained
    remote interfaces 64
    services and persistence 47
CocoBase 269
code inspection 369
code profiler 295
    aided by well-factored
        code 295
    example output 302
code reviews 369
collisions 67
combining
    local and remote
        interfaces 62
comments 363
Commons Logging 33
communication overhead 369
comparing
    remote instances 389
complex
    entity beans 247
complexity 16, 27, 32, 38–39
    and EJB inheritance 277
    and entity beans 253
    for JDBC 34
complexity graph 15
component
    architecture 378
    inheritance 29
    interface 327
component-oriented
    architectures 351
    and persistence 60

concurrency 382
Concurrent Programming
    books 361
configuration 30, 38, 40
    files 31
configuring
    EJB 397
connection
    overhead 40, 108
connection pooling 39–40
connections 359
consulting 359, 367
container
    and CMR 46
    EJB 381, 391
    EJB and services 377
container-managed relation-
    ships *See CMR*
context 396
controller 69
controversy
    and EJB 5
Conversational Baggage
    antipattern 157
conversational state 128
CORBA 13, 23, 113, 350, 384
CORBA IIOP 84
Core J2EE 269
cost
    of complexity 252
    of EJB 22
    of EJB software vs.
        development 14
COUNT
    SQL 109
coupling 368
    and JDBC 265
criteria
    for EJB 23
CRM 227
cross-data-store relation 229
Crossing the Chasm 13
CruiseControl 341
custom DTO 73, 79
    and guesswork 74
    problems 74
    solution 75
    solution and traps 76
Custom DTO antipattern 73, 79
custom persistence
    framework 69

Customers in the Kitchen
    antipattern 66, 79
cycle time 357

D

Data Access Object (DAO)
    pattern 269, 282
data access service 76
data persistence 27
    EJB1.0 43
data store
    interfaces 268
    persistence 268
data transfer
    class 220
Data Transfer Object *See DTO*
Database Connection Hog
    antipattern 101, 124
database connection pool
    effect on response time 289
    effect on throughput 290
database design
    and antipatterns 215
database synchronization 67
databases
    and distribution 65
datasource 264
DB2 371
DCE 13, 350
Dead Message Queue
    (DMQ) 193
deadlock 88
Death March 23
declarative transactions 28, 32
decoupling
    EJB services 48
defensive copies 62
delete
    JDBC 266
dependent objects 59
deployment 40, 350
    EAR-based 338
    of entities 257
    and persistence 249
deployment descriptor 273,
    325–327, 398
    and EJB 1.1 7
    and JDO 274
    in logging example 36
    and remote interfaces 60

deployment strategy
    of EJB 354
deprecated methods 91
design patterns
    and antipatterns 359–360,
        366, 370
    defined 360
    in industry 367
    refactoring 364
designing
    bean interfaces 53
developing
    for EJB 378
directory structure 328
disabling re-entrancy 238
distributed 17
    applications 24
    component architecture 33
    domain 59
    domain model 64
    exceptions 62
    synchronization 88
    transactions 25, 27, 32, 84
distribution 256
    avoid 65
    and interfaces 63
    and logical tiers 65
    and transparency 54
domain objects
    and DTO 73
domain-driven
    design 57–58
domain-oriented design
    and entity beans 59
Dover Elevators 367
DriverManager 90
DTO 100, 104, 219, 253–254,
    256, 281
    and duplication 74
    with JDBC 281
    with many clients 73
    multiple variations 73
    with persistence
        frameworks 281
    and reuse 74
    sample 72
duplication
    EJB code 332
durable subscriptions 181
    cost of 181
    message expiration and 181

dynamic filter
    example 232
dynamic proxies 116
dynamic queries 231
dynamic query 231
dynamic relations 230–231

E

Eager Iterator antipattern 103, 124
EAI 178
EAR loader 332
Eavesdropping antipattern 195, 209
EJB
    and alternatives 350
    antipatterns 6
    basics 376
    in Bitter Java 371
    and economy 5
    evolution 6
    examples 366
    future enhancements 238
    history 23, 377
    next steps 351
    optional services 351
    overkill 30
    and re-entrancy 236
    release 6
    vs. JDO 273
EJB 1.0 7, 42
    persistence 12
EJB 1.1 7
EJB 2.0 8–9, 43, 387
    and CMP 223
    and CMR 45
    and local interfaces 59
EJB client 57
EJB Code Duplication
    antipattern 332, 344
EJB components
    fine-grained 60
EJB container 136, 378
    cache sizing 155
    and entity beans 260
    and interfaces 53
    managing stateful session
        beans 136
    memory thrashing 155
    and re-entrancy 238

and requests to session
    beans 84
and transactional integrity 28
EJB inheritance
    example 278
EJB interfaces
    optimizing remote 62
EJB invocations
    local vs. remote 55
EJB local interfaces
    problems with 59
EJB QL 8, 228, 231, 279
    bind time 279
EJBException 97
ejb-jar 326, 336, 339
    file 399
ejbLoad 67
ejbStore 67
EMACS 17
embedding transaction logic 68
enterprise application 24
enterprise development 14
Enterprise Java Beans. See EJB
entity bean
    antipatterns 214
    defined 379
    history 42
    implementing 393
    and location transparency 59
    problems 41
    transparency 41
    weaknesses 276
example
    bridge servlet mapping 114
    CMP 250
    deployment descriptor 328
    EJB inheritance 278
    JDO 270
    non-transactional update 217
    re-entrancy 236
    round- tripping 216
    servlet bridge 116, 118
    shuffled list 110
    stateless session bean 326
exception 94
    and remote interfaces 61
    throwing 396
    and transaction roll back 93
    wrapping 96
exception handling 95

exception type
    matrix 99
exclusive access
    and databases 68
exclusive caching 68
exporting results
    from iterators 108

F

façade See Session Façade
Face Off antipattern 215, 217, 240
failover 30, 42
    and stateless applications 71
Fast Lane Reader 282
Fat Messages antipattern 165
field granularity 67
findByPrimaryKey 227
finder method 386
fine-grained object models
    and persistence 45
Forrester 29

G

Gang of Four See GoF
Gartner 5, 22, 29
generated
    EJB code 252
generic interface
    vs. local and remote
        interfaces 60
generic servlet bridge 113
getConnection 90
Giga Information Group 22, 29
global unique identifier 235
GoF Singleton pattern 86, 331
golden hammer
    EJB 13
Golden Hammer
    antipattern 12, 20
Golden Hammers of Session
    State antipattern 143, 158
grouping
    by subclass 277
guaranteed messaging 179
GUI design 69
guidelines
    for primary key length 235

H

Ham Sandwich antipattern 222,
241
handling
exceptions within sessions 92
remote interfaces 62
hanging
transactions 68
hash table 364
heterogeneous
distribution 65
Hibernate 269
hierarchy
class loader 330
home interface 327
hot deployment 382
Hot Potato antipattern 191, 207
hot potato game 191
HSQL 340
HTTP 129, 140
HttpSession 140
clients 140
contents of 140
hodgepodge 153
invalidating 156
local cache example 150
memory requirements of 153
passivation/activation 142
scalability of 142
storing stateful EJB
references 147
volatility of 146, 150–151
hung threads 88
case study 89
hygiene
programming 369

I

IBM 6, 355, 362, 371
idempotent
methods 63
identity
and persistence 257
and session beans 85
IIOP 112, 384, 388
Immediate Reply Requested
mini-antipattern 182, 205
implementation class 326

IN keyword
SQL 225
index buffers 234
inheritance 278
and EJB 276
and exceptions 61
and JDO 279
insert
via JDBC 263
integrated development environment (IDE) 17, 337
integration 325
continuous 341
Integration Hell
antipattern 341, 347
interface
client 385
component 327
and consistency after
failure 63
designing 53
distributed 64
home 327
local vs. remote 387
and Session Façade 66
intermediate
programmers 369
Internet applications 369
interviews 369
InvocationHandler 116
invocations
local vs. remote and
performance 59
invoking
EJB from client 400
ISO 9000 367–368
iterating 99
shuffled data 110
iteration
major interface
boundaries 359
iterator
vendor-specific SQL 106

J

J2EE 371
and controversy 6
books 361
development skills 16
J2EE Connector Architecture

(JCA) 187, 248
J2EE guidelines
for loading 332
Jakarta Struts 69
JAR 332, 399
EJB 329
Java
passing parameters 55
Java Archive *See JAR*
Java Community Process 269
Java language
and EJB 1.1 7
and persistence 248
Java Message Service *See JMS*
Java Naming and Directory
Interface *See JDNI*
Java ServerPages *See JSP*
Java Specification Request 354
Java Virtual Machine 358
java.lang.Exception 92
Javadoc 325
JavaMail 187
JBoss 5
JDBC 28, 39, 101, 109, 246, 260
and criteria 267
evaluation 261
example 38
model 261
for object persistence 266
and persistence 260
and simplicity 274
suitability 261
vs. JDO 273
JDBCLogger 36
JDK 1.4 96
JDO 28, 69, 269, 280, 350
basics 269
example 270
JMeter 306
JMS 24, 91, 380
client 164
as compared to RPC 164
defined 163
loosely coupled communication and 164
provider 164
server 164
JMS and XML
advantages of 177
overused 177

JMS application
  defined 164
  example 171
JMS consumer 165
  access by synchronous
    clients 190
  delegating to modular
    components 189
  monolithic 188
JMS message models
  API 173
  point-to-point 173
  publish/subscribe 173
JMS messages
  designing 168
  fat 167
  headers and properties 165
  payload 165
  problems using
    references 170
  redelivery delay 194
  sizing 168
  skinny 170
  throttling delivery of 195
  use of references in 168
  use of state in 170
JMS performance 199
  factors 200
  testing 199
JMS producer 165
JMS queue 173
JMS topic 173
  wildcard topic names 198
JMX 87, 201
JNDI 35, 340, 381, 385
join
  buffers 234
  database 228
  and primary key length 234
JSP 10, 66
  versions 373
JTA 68, 248
JUnit 299, 307, 340
JUnitPerf 307
  as related to HttpUnit and
    Cactus 307
  as related to JUnit 307
  defined 307
  limitations of 309
justify
  EJB 50

K

Killer System Exceptions
  antipattern 97, 123

L

large datasets
  iterating 99
lazy loading 76
life cycle 38, 370
  entity bean 394
  management 381
  stateful session bean 392
  stateless sesson bean 391
litmus test
  for EJB 25
load
  JDBC 266
loader
  class 330
local and remote interfaces
  separating 61
Local and Remote Interfaces
  Simultaneously
  antipattern 60, 78
local interface 8, 44, 56, 220,
  252
  and EJB 1.1 7
local method invocations 54
location transparency
  and persistence 44
logging 30, 382
  example 31
  exceptions 94
Logic in Exception Implementations mini-antipattern 92
loop filters 232
loose coupling
  components 25
  and performance 10

M

Magic Servlet antipattern 358,
  362
managed resources
  as performance throttles 289
management
  server 382

managing connections
  database 103
managing files
  cost 36
MANIFEST.MF 330, 335
Manual Performance Testing
  mini-antipattern 305, 322
marshal
  method invocation 54
maximum effective
  throughput 290, 315
MDB 8, 26, 236, 380
  application exceptions 193
  bean-managed
    transactions 193
  as compared to standalone
    consumers 186
  container-managed
    transactions 192
  defined 184
  deployment descriptor 187
  onMessage() 185
  pool sizing 187
  pooling 185
  re-entrancy and 194
  system exceptions 193
memory
  leaks 368
mentoring 369
message driven beans 26
message eavesdropping 195
message selectors
  content-based routing 198
  defined 196
  example 196
  with MDBs 198
  performance of 197
  using XPath 198
  wildcard topic names and 198
message-driven beans *See MDB*
MessageDrivenContext.setRollb
  ackOnly() 193
MessageListener interface 185
message-oriented
  middleware 65, 164
method granularity 63
method invocations
  fine vs. coarse 55
methodology 358
Microsoft 6, 9, 11
Middleware Company 9–11

Mini 63
mini-antipattern
    Immediate Reply
        Requested 182, 205
    Logic in Exception
        Implementations 92
    Manual Performance
        Testing 305, 322
    Paging with a Scrollable
        ResultSet 106
    Passing DOM Objects 111
    Rotting Session Garbage 155,
        161
    Session Thrashing 155, 161
    Skinny Messages 169
    Stage Fright 317, 323
    Stateful Session Beans as
        Shared Data Caches 151
    Transparent Distribution 63
    Ubiquitous Distribution 63
mistakes
    EJB 349
modeling
    with entity beans 247
Model-View-Controller 69, 360
monitoring
    server 382
Monolithic Consumer
    antipattern 188, 206
multitier applications 17
Mythical Man Month 23

N

naming conventions 329
Narrow Servlet Bridges
    antipattern 113, 125
narrowing 112
.NET 6, 29
network
    latency 62
network traffic 65
non-persistent messages 180
nonrelational back-end 38
NotSupported
    and rollback 93

O

object persistence 43, 280
object relational mapping 223

Object type
    pass-by-reference vs. pass-by-
        value 56
Object.wait method 91
onMessage() 185
    optimizing 195
OODBMS 268
Open Source
    success 5
optimization 363
OR mapping 223, 268
Oracle 5–6, 268
OSS Java Initiative 26
OutOfMemoryError 108
overhead 217
    of coarse services and persis-
        tence frameworks 48
    of entity beans 46

P

Packages
    antipatterns 326
packaging 399
Packrat antipattern 179, 205
Page-by-Page Iterator 100, 102–
    103, 110
Paging with Scrollable ResultSet
    mini-antipattern 106
parameter passing
    and remote invocation 55
parameterize
    relations 231
pass-by-reference 56, 331
pass-by-referencer
    vs. pass-by-value 55
pass-by-value 54, 56
    and remote method
        invocation 57
Passing DOM Objects mini-
    antipattern 111
performance 28, 38
    application 369
    case study 66
    database 233, 358
    and EJB 1.0 7
    of entity beans 44
    JDBC vs EJB 39
    and local interfaces 222
    model 315
    and primary key length 234

process 358, 369
    round-tripping 216
    vs. transparency 59
Performance Afterthoughts
    antipattern 199, 210,
        296, 320
performance optimization
    and EJB 2.0 10
    local interfaces 62
    and PetStore 10
performance planning 297
performance tests 297
    advantages of 306
    as practice for
        production 317
    iterators 105
    methodology 304
performance tuning 294
    as related to Thrash-
        Tuning 303
    methodology 304
    well-factored code and 294
persistence 377
    coarse-grained 247
    container-bound 282
    with EJB 249
    EJB 1.0 7
    fixing EJB problems 353
    frameworks 246, 267, 275
    history 349
    landscape 267
persistence framework
    defined 267
    lightweight 60
persistence solutions
    comparing 274
persistent messages 179
    cost of 180
    with point-to-point
        messaging 181
persistent object model
    with EJB 233
Persistent Problems
    antipattern 275, 284
persistent state
    EJB vs. stateful session
        beans 41
persistent store
    and fine-grained access 59
    mapping 65

PetStore 9–11
    backlash 11
Poet 268
POJO 251, 260, 351
polymorphism 278
    and EJB 276
pooling
    session beans 87
portability 14
    and EJB 1.0 7
precise 9
preloading
    and DTOs 76
premature optimization 291
    with EJB applications 292
Premature Optimization
    antipattern 291, 319
primary key 233, 387
    defined 233
    length 233
procedural language 374
profiler 295
Progress 268
Publish 364

Q

Quality Circles 367
quality metrics 368
query
    language flexibility 279
query language
    object 280
queue specialization 196
QueueRequestor class 184

R

random access 364
randomized list
    with shuffled data 110
Rational 5
RDBMS 268
readability 363
recovery
    from hung threads 89
re-entrancy 29, 235
    checking 238
reentrant
    container configuration 238

Refactor
    custom DTO 75
refactor 374
    antipatterns process 364
refactoring
    and antipattern process 365
    exception logic 93
    re-entrant code 236–237
    targets 368
relation
    vs. filter 231
relational database 8
relationship
    database 7
    is null 76
    and JDBC 265
remote
    calls and performance 67
    interfaces 44
    invocation 54
    invocation performance 54
    invocations and session
        façades 70
    and local interfaces 60
    prefix 329
RemoteException 62, 97
Replication
    and state 64
Required
    transaction attribute 67
research consulting firms 29
resource
    management 31
resource competition
    and threads 86
resource loading 29
resources
    and iterators 103
response time
    defined 289
    example requirement 302
restrictions
    on threading 85
result set
    determining size 109
    iterating 99
ResultSet 101
    SQL 109
retry
    failed request 63
return trip 358

return value
    passing 54
Revolving Doors
    antipattern 235
RMI 381, 383
    over http 113
    sequence 384
roles 377
Rotting Session Garbage mini-
    antipattern 155, 161
round-tripping 216, 369
    and method invocation 55
Round-Tripping antipattern 369
ROWNUM
    keyword 104
Running with Scissors
    antipattern 339, 346
RuntimeExceptions 92, 97
Rusty Keys antipattern 233, 244

S

sample applications 12
scalability 23, 28, 42, 84
    defined 290
    example requirement 310
schema
    for logger 34
security 8, 17, 42, 84, 349, 383
sequence diagrams 362
server logs 94
server-side
    Java 361
    programming 371
service granularity 42
service methods 65
service request queuing 289
service-driven
    design 57
service-oriented
    design 58
services
    EJB 23
servlet 24, 140
    bridge 119
    on line 361
session beans 236
    defined 84, 378
    example 391
    in logger example 36
    stateful 378

stateful and stateless 84
stateless 378
Session Façade 31, 46, 65, 215,
  219, 253
  core services 247
  and domain logic 71
  with entity beans 247
  example with JDBC 265
  interface issues 70
  interfaces 70
  for JDO 272
  in logging example 38
  too many 70
  for transactional integrity 220
Session Hodgepodge
  antipattern 152, 160
session state 128
  best uses of 151
  defined 128
  locations for storing 143
  price of 130
  storing in database 148
  storing in HttpSession 145
  storing in stateful EJB 147
  storing on client 144
  tools for managing 134
Session Thrashing mini-
  antipattern 155, 161
session timeouts
  and iterators 102
session tracking 140
SessionSynchronization
  interface 151
setRollbackOnly 93, 99
shell sort 363
Single threaded transactions 16
skills 14, 16
  and EJB 2.0 9
Skinny Messages mini-
  antipattern 169
Sledgehammer for a Fly
  antipattern 30, 51
Slow Eater antipattern 194, 208
SOAP 25
Sonic 9
source files
  EJB 328
spawning
  new threads 86
specification
  EJB 377

SQL 39, 228, 260, 380
  and portability 280
  boolean qualifiers 231
  down side 265
  in iterators 104
Stage Fright mini-
  antipattern 317, 323
state 64
  and unchecked exceptions 98
  session 85
state diagrams 362
state management 377
stateful session bean 130
  activation/passivation 138–
    139
  and EJB 1.1 8
  clients 130
  defined 134
  life cycle 137
  memory requirements of 130
  removing 156
Stateful Session Beans as Shared
  Data Caches mini-
  antipattern 151
stateless
  applications and resources 71
stateless service 131
  advantages of 131
stateless session bean 132
  and session façades 71
  figure 132
  pooling 132
  scalability of 133
subclasses
  and EJB 277
Sun 6, 377
  economic woes 354
surrogate key 234
Swallowing Exceptions
  antipattern 94, 122
swing 24
synchronization 85
  and session beans 87
  session state 64
synchronization monitor 90
synchronization primitives 87
  and EJB 85
synchronized keyword 87
synchronous communication 84
synchronous request
  via JMS 91

synchronous request/reply
  messaging 183
system exceptions 97
System Loaded Application
  Classes antipattern 332,
  343

T

talent 28
Tangled Threads antipattern 86,
  121
telecommunications 26
test
  automated 339
TheServerSide.com 9, 350
thrash-tuning 303
  invoking the curse of 303
Thrash-tuning antipattern 303,
  321
thread dump 89
thread pool 92
  and databases 90
thread pools 91
Thread.stop 91
Threading 85
threads 29
throughput
  defined 290
TIMESTAMP 235
Tomcat 5, 371
tool vendors 28
tools
  for builds 326
  modeling 362
TopicRequestor class 184
TopicSubscriber.receive() 183
TopLink 5, 269
training
  costs 40
training requirements 357
transaction 378
  and database access 67
  granularity 68
  management 39
  timeouts 90
transactional
  awareness 256
  boundaries 28
  integrity 27, 217
    with a session façade 220

TransactionRolledBack-Exceptions 94
transactions 377, 382
  and consistency 88
  and JDBC 265
  and performance 67
  and threads 29
  defined 397
transparency
  and persistence 268
Transparent Distribution mini-antipattern 63

U

Ubiquitous Distribution mini-antipattern 63
UML
  books 361–362
  defined 362
unchecked exceptions 97
Unified Modeling Language. *See* UML
unique ID
  generator 86
unit testing 340
  and JSP 68
update
  JDBC 266
use case 362
  model design 58
UserTransaction 99, 220

V

value
  and EJB 14, 17
Value List Handler 100
Value List Iterator 100
Value Objects 100
VARCHAR 235
variable names 369
Versant 268
virtual machines
  multiple 87
VisualAge 5

W

WAR
  file 330
weaver
  and AOP 352
Web services
  and performance 55
WebGain 5
WebLogic 31, 36, 371
WebSphere 371, 373
WHERE clause
  SQL 230
WORA 23
wrapping exceptions 96
www.bitterjava.com 361, 366, 373

X

XDoclet 17, 39, 333–334, 339
XML 26
  and EJB 1.1 7
  descriptors 399
  on line 361
XML as the Silver Bullet antipattern 177, 204
XML messages 175
  as compared to MapMessage 177
  misuse of 177
  refactoring to MapMessage 178
XML parser 332
XPath 198

Y

Y2K bug 364

Z

Zero Defects 368